RENEWALS: 691-4574

Bonapartism and revolutionary tradition in France is a study of the personnel, organisation and activities of the *fédérés*, the massive para-military political associations that supported Napoleon during the Hundred Days. In tracing *fédéré* backgrounds, the author demonstrates that the federations were politically and socially heterogeneous – composed of old revolutionaries, Bonapartists and future liberals, and drawn from both the lower and middle classes. Analysis of *fédéré* literature and symbolism reveals the common ground of ideology and self-interest that enabled these diverse groups to unite in opposition to Bourbon rule, and thereby reverse the process of fragmentation that had beset the Revolutionary movement since 1789. Discussion of relations between the Imperial government and the *fédérés* explains why Bonaparte encouraged this development, despite his realisation that old Jacobins dominated the associations of 1815.

The *fédérés* played a prominent role in the suppression of royalist sedition during the Hundred Days, and thus became prime targets for subsequent repression. However, far from intimidating or isolating them, the White Terror made *fédérés* yet more intransigent in their hostility to the Bourbon monarchy. They remained at the forefront of opposition from 1815 to 1830, and were a consistent obstacle to reconciliation between the Crown and the interests spawned by the Revolution. The *fédérés* were thus central to the principal dilemma of the Restoration – the refusal to compromise between *ancien régime* and revolutionary France.

Bonapartism and revolutionary tradition in France

Bonapartism and revolutionary tradition in France

The fédérés of 1815

R. S. ALEXANDER
University of Victoria

The right of the
University of Cambridge
to print and sell
all manner of books
was granted by
Henry VIII in 1534.
The University has printed
and published continuously
since 1584.

CAMBRIDGE UNIVERSITY PRESS
Cambridge
New York   Port Chester
Melbourne   Sydney

Published by the Press Syndicate of the University of Cambridge
The Pitt Building, Trumpington Street, Cambridge CB2 1RP
40 West 20th Street, New York, NY 10011, USA
10 Stamford Road, Oakleigh, Melbourne 3166, Australia

First published 1991

Printed in Great Britain by J. W. Arrowsmith Ltd, Bristol

British Library cataloguing in publication data
Alexander, R. S.
Bonapartism and revolutionary tradition in France
1. France. Political events 1804–1848
I. Title
944.05

Library of Congress cataloguing in publication data
Alexander, R. S., 1954–
Bonapartism and revolutionary tradition in France: the *fédérés* of
1815 / R. S. Alexander.
p.   cm.
Includes bibliographical references.
Includes index.
ISBN 0 521 36112 5
1. France – History – Consulate and Empire, 1789–1815. 2. Napoleon I,
Emperor of the French, 1769–1821 – Elba and the Hundred Days,
1814–1815. I. Title. II. Title: *Fédérés* of 1815.
DC239.A44   1991
944.05 dc20 90–1856   CIP

ISBN 0 521 36112 5 hardback

Ramenés par l'étranger sur les cadavres de Waterloo, les Bourbons deviennent plus encore un object d'horreur pour l'armée, les fédérés, le peuple, les patriotes et les bonapartistes.

Etienne Cabet,
Révolution de 1830 et situation présente
(Paris, 1833)

Contents

Tables

Acknowledgments

Of the many people who have given me advice in the research and writing of this monograph, I would like particularly to thank Professor David Higgs of the University of Toronto who originally suggested the topic to me, Frédéric Bluche, *docteur d'Etat de l'Université de Paris II*, who helped me with my research in Paris, and Dr T. C. W. Blanning of Sidney Sussex College, Cambridge who gave all (and more) that one could ask of a supervisor. I would also like to thank Dr Robert Tombs of St John's College, Cambridge and Dr Geoffrey Ellis of Hertford College, Oxford for their trenchant and constructive criticism. Dr George Davison kindly devoted many hours to proof-reading the manuscript, and June Bull, Gloria Orr and Dinah Dickie patiently typed it. My wife Emma Alexander helped greatly with the preparation of the manuscript, and her constant encouragement enabled me to see the project through to its completion. To all of the above, I am truly grateful. Whatever errors or imperfections may remain are, of course, solely my own responsibility.

I could not have written this work without the generous financial aid of a St John's College Studentship, a doctoral fellowship from the Social Sciences and Humanities Research Council of Canada and a Henry Giles Fellowship. I would also like to thank Dr George Reid for helping me sort out the not so odd financial difficulty during my student days.

Finally, I would like to dedicate this book to my parents.

Abbreviations

The following abbreviations have been used in the notes.

AD, C-d	Archives Départementales de la Côte-d'Or
AD, H-G	Archives Départementales de la Haute-Garonne
AD, I-et-V	Archives Départementales d'Ille-et-Vilaine
AG	Archives de la Guerre
AM	Archives Municipales
AN	Archives Nationales
APP	Archives de la Préfecture de Police de Paris
BM	Bibliothèque Municipale
BN	Bibliothèque Nationale

Introduction

There has been nothing more dramatic in the history of France than the *vol d'aigle*. On 1 March 1815, having slipped free of captivity on the island of Elba, Napoleon landed on the shore of the Gulf of Juan and invaded France with a token force of some 1,200 men. When confronted at Laffrey by ostensibly hostile troops, Bonaparte stepped forward to offer himself as a target, forcing the soldiers to choose between himself and Louis XVIII. Past loyalties proved decisive; the troops refused to fire. Marshal Ney, having vowed to his Bourbon master to bring the Eagle back to Paris in an iron cage, proved no different. What had begun as a perilous forced march soon became a triumphal procession as peasants and workers flocked to the Emperor's side. First Grenoble and then Lyons gave Napoleon a rapturous reception. By 20 March he had flown from 'belfry to belfry', finally alighting in a Paris free of the hastily departed Bourbon king Louis XVIII. Although middle-class Parisians greeted Bonaparte with an indifference born of fear for the future, there could be no mistaking the satisfaction of lower-class Parisians with this extraordinary turn of events.[1]

The *vol d'aigle* was, however, more than simply the return of a beloved leader to his adoring public, for along the route the Emperor had donned new clothing – he now appeared in the curious guise of arch-defender of the Revolution. In a series of decrees issued at Lyons, Napoleon had dissolved the Chambers of Peers and Deputies (tainted by the membership of men who had fought against the Revolution), and abolished 'feudal titles', expelled the returned *émigrés* from France and ordered sequestration of their lands. A decree pregnant with Revolutionary associations had summoned the representatives of the people to assemble in May to pass their own laws at the Champ de Mars, scene of the federation of 1790. Perhaps even more remarkable was the rhetoric Bonaparte unleashed in subsequent

---

[1] There are many descriptions of the Flight of the Eagle; the best remains H. Houssaye's *1815 – Le Retour de l'Île d'Elbe* (Paris, 1901), pp. 200–365.

1

proclamations to French soldiers and citizens: 'I have come to save Frenchmen from the slavery in which priests and nobles wished to plunge them
... Let them [priests and nobles] take guard. I will string them up from the
lampposts.'[2]

Not unnaturally, historians have been inclined to view Napoleon's
Revolutionary conversion with scepticism, interpreting it largely as a
cynical device to rally support while the Emperor's position was weak, but
to be cast aside when his position strengthened. A less harsh interpretation
suggests that Bonaparte had simply been carried away by the fervour of
silkweavers of the La Guillotière quarter of Lyons who chanted 'Down
with the priests! Death to royalists!' in front of him. Whatever its cause, the
Emperor's conversion was soon to prove embarrassing. When subsequently confronted by similar manifestations in Paris, Napoleon commented: 'Nothing has surprised me more on returning to France than this
hatred of priests and the nobility which I find as universal and as violent as
it was at the beginning of the Revolution. The Bourbons have restored their
lost force to the ideas of the Revolution.'[3] The Emperor had tapped a source
much more powerful than he initially realised.

There was a fair measure of truth in Napoleon's assertion that the Bourbons had rejuvenated the 'lost force' of the 'ideas of the Revolution'. As the
Empire crumbled in 1813 and early 1814 Napoleon sought to employ tactics similar to those of the Hundred Days but, despite some signs of the
potential of appealing to memories of 1792, France generally refused to
rally. Although royalism was by no means a mass movement in 1814,
neither was there a great deal of opposition to the return of Louis XVIII
during the initial stages of the First Restoration. The primary reaction of
the French populace appears to have been one of indifference. Although the
association of Bourbon government with the triumph of the Allied Powers
was a grave liability, Louis XVIII could at least appeal for the support of
the many Frenchmen who desired peace above all else. In short, wounded
patriotic pride could have been counterbalanced by an almost universal
longing for stability and prosperity and a Bourbon Monarchy could have
been firmly established had the government been perceived to rule justly
and well. Although the fact that the King 'granted' the Charter was a calculated insult to the ideal of popular sovereignty, the Charter did at least
contain provisions indicating that past antagonisms would be forgotten

---

[2] Quoted in H. Houssaye, *1815 – Les Cent-Jours* (Paris, 1901), p. 3483. The Lyons decrees
were published in the *Moniteur Universel*, 21–2 March 1815.
[3] Quoted in J. Tulard, *Napoleon* (London, 1984), p. 333. For the argument that Napoleon
was momentarily carried away by revolutionary enthusiasm at Lyons, see G. Ribe,
*L'Opinion publique et la vie politique à Lyon lors des premières années de la Seconde
Restauration* (Paris, 1957), p. 38.

and that those who had gained by the Revolution could rest secure in their possessions and positions. Had this spirit of reconciliation been maintained by the Monarchy and its supporters, France in 1815 might not have mirrored Revolutionary France.[4]

Louis XVIII was not entirely the cause of renewed revolutionary *élan*. He could not justly be faulted for the aristocratic snobbery of returned *émigrés*, nor could he be expected to control the Catholic priests who refused sacraments to men who had purchased *biens nationaux* (lands sequestered by the State from the Church and *émigrés* and sold to private citizens during the Revolution). However, his government was responsible for a series of ill-considered measures which antagonised important sectors of the populace and, more importantly, gave credence to those who argued that the Bourbon Monarchy was bent upon removing liberties acquired during the Revolution. In one of his often quoted comments, Napoleon charged that the Bourbons had 'learned nothing and forgotten nothing' during their period of exile; it might also be noted that the mass of Frenchmen had not forgotten what life was like under the hierarchy of privilege known as the *ancien régime*, though they had learned a great deal since 1789.

It was inevitable that the Bourbon government should begin to dismantle the Imperial war machine; financial retrenchment and relations with the Allied Powers necessitated this, though it was bound to alienate officers put on half-pay. However, justification of such measures was undermined by the bestowal of high rank upon *émigrés* who previously had fought against France, if they had fought at all. Official ceremonies at Rennes honouring *chouans* who had waged civil war against the Revolution were perfectly calculated to raise questions about the prejudices of the government. Memorial services for the 'martyrs' of Quiberon angered the old 'blues' of Vannes.

Similar results were achieved throughout France by State ceremonies paying tribute to those who had died for their opposition to the Revolution; the uneasy reaction of men who had fought for, or profited by, the Revolution to these 'expiatory' fêtes can well be imagined. Clearly the past could not and would not entirely be forgotten, but how much expiation did the government deem necessary? Changes in government administrative personnel were not, by subsequent standards, drastic in the early stages of the First Restoration, but the process was gaining momentum. What were the career prospects of a man tainted by sinful association with

---

[4] For discussion of the mistakes of the First Restoration government, see A. Jardin and A. J. Tudesq, *La France des notables: l'évolution générale, 1815–1848* (Paris, 1973), pp. 24–5. On the conciliatory element in the new constitution, see Article 11 of the Charter in J. P. T. Bury, *France 1814–1940* (London, 1985), p. 294.

the Revolution? Could talent and ability be expected to overcome the claims of a rival blessed by the purity of long-term royalism or *ancien régime* nobility? The impression of being distinctly out of favour was reinforced by legislation in the Chambers to return unsold *biens nationaux* to the *émigres*, praising those who had refused to return to France until the King did. At least some members of the clergy were clamouring for the restoration of all *biens nationaux*; did not laws making mandatory the closure of shops on Sundays prove that the government favoured Church interests?

The dangerous impact of all such reminders of the past might have been diminished had Louis XVIII been perceived to be a strong ruler. Many Frenchmen who opposed Bourbon rule in 1815 did so not out of personal animosity to the King; they thought he was probably well-intentioned and committed to reconciliation, but they were also convinced that he was not sufficiently resolute to deny indefinitely the demands of retribution and favouritism of the ultra-royalist faction led by his brother Artois. Grotesquely fat and lazy, Louis XVIII made a poor contrast to his dynamic brother.

Artois played a leading role in undermining the Monarchy; at times he seemed the embodiment of all that was reactionary about the *émigrés*. There was little sign of reconciliation in his refusal to receive constitutional bishops in Dijon and Besançon. When he did bid for popularity by promising abolition of the hated *droits réunis* (an indirect tax, particularly on beer and wine), he only caused the Crown further harm because financial necessity obliged the government to maintain these taxes. Riots in Dijon were an immediate result; perhaps more significant was the obvious lesson to be drawn concerning the value of Bourbon promises.

It has often been noted that all of this played directly into Napoleon's opportunistic hands; after all, rumours of a return to feudal obligations and the *dîme* (an *ancien régime* Church tax) were rife among the peasants who greeted Napoleon so warmly in March 1815. Had not the Emperor responded by proclaiming that he had returned 'to banish forever memories of the feudal regime, serfdom and the glebe'? Napoleon can be blamed for exacerbating tensions in France by seeking to exploit this renewed revolutionary *élan*, but it is instructive to note that he certainly did not create it. Indeed, the Emperor was greatly troubled by the spirit of independence he found even amongst his old supporters. When asked by Napoleon whether he believed there was a republican party in France, Molé replied: 'Yes, Sire, and I even believe that party to be very powerful; it has been enlarged, for some time now, by all the discontent produced by the Bourbons, by that middle class which has become so powerful and which . . . the nobility has again antagonised.' This displeased

Napoleon, but revived republicanism was not something he could afford to ignore.[5]

Support for the Imperial government in 1815 was not, however simply a result of the Emperor's exploitation of renewed revolutionary vigour. Loyalty to Napoleon amongst the rank and file of the Army remained solid; his contention that he had been betrayed but not defeated in 1814 was generally accepted. Popular Bonapartism may well have accelerated after the defeat of Napoleon at Waterloo and the subsequent publication of his memoirs from Saint Helena, but there is a good deal of evidence to suggest that it was a significant force by the Hundred Days. Soldiers recently returned from the four corners of Europe had already begun their work of spreading the legend among peasants and the urban lower classes. More importantly, invasion of France in 1814, especially in the east, had made a strong impression upon those who suffered by it. In such areas, Bonapartism was not confined to the lower classes or old members of the Imperial Army. Napoleon had at least fought the *barbares du nord*, and Bonapartism had become linked with patriotism.

Popular Bonapartism has recently been analysed in B. Ménager's *Les Napoléon du peuple* (Paris, 1988). The first author to consider seriously this phenomenon during the Restoration, Ménager establishes the rhythm of manifestations of Bonapartism during this period and, implicitly, shows how extensive popular Bonapartism was. However, perhaps because his study commences after the Hundred Days, the author does not take much account of how the nature of Bonapartism, even at the popular level, had changed. After the *vol d'aigle*, Napoleon stood for many different, and often contradictory, beliefs and ideas. One does well to read Ménager's work in combination with the fifth chapter of F. Bluche's *Le Bonapartism* (Paris, 1980), which helps to explain how Bonapartism had evolved. Revolutionary Bonapartism was a curious legacy of the Hundred Days which blurred distinctions between liberals, republicans and traditional Bonapartists and ultimately gave all three groups a potential mass following. The latter aspect became especially apparent after Napoleon's death.

The extent of support for Napoleon during the Hundred Days is not easily measured and should not be overestimated. Vast areas of France, particularly in the old provinces of Flanders, Artois, Normandy, Brittany, Vendée, Languedoc and Provence, largely refused to ally. Moreover, loyalty to the government was by no means uniform in the other regions, wherein indifference and *attentisme* often appear to have been predomi-

---

[5] Napoleon's declarations at Grenoble are cited in Champollion-Figeac, *Fourier et Napoléon* (Paris, 1844), p. 224. Molé's comment on republicanism is cited in G. Weill, 'L'Idée républicaine en France pendant la Restauration', *Revue d'histoire moderne*, 2 (1927), p. 323.

nant. Open revolt broke out in Brittany and the Vendée and there could be
no mistaking the Bourbon sympathies of the majority of people in the Midi;
yet even here Napoleon retained significant support, and before concluding
that royalists were in the majority, we should recall that Napoleon fell in
1815 because of Waterloo – not because of domestic opposition to his
government.

In his authoritative biography of Louis XVIII, P. Mansel takes up the
knotty question of the relative strength of the two opposing sides. Recog-
nising the complexity of any such assessment, Mansel confines himself to
generalisations which, though probably impossible to prove in quanti-
tative terms, have the ring of truth to them. For example, many Frenchmen
continued to desire peace above all else and this was the Bourbons' long
suit. Similarly, it is probably true that most women with political opinions
preferred the domestic Louis XVIII to the martial Napoleon, although one
could cite many examples to the contrary. But where this study leads one to
take issue with Mansel's assessment is in the author's underestimation of
the extent of opposition to the Monarchy during and after the Hundred
Days. This opposition was not simply a matter of bellicose nationalism and
careerist opportunism; though vital, to these two elements must be added
the widespread revolutionary *élan* rekindled by the First Restoration. In
this respect it is important to note that whether or not Louis XVIII and his
ministers actually intended a return to the *ancien régime* was not very much
to the point; the fact was that many Frenchmen believed this to be the case.
In supporting Napoleon many believed they were taking the side of the
Revolution and this was a matter of self-interest and principle; honour was
by no means a royalist monopoly.[6]

Brave attempts to assess the extent of support for the Imperial government which go beyond the descriptive prove equally subject to qualification. For example, F. Bluche carefully analyses the results of the plebiscite
of the Hundred Days, but it should be noted that Frenchmen were voting
specifically for or against the *Acte Additionnel*: we should not jump to the
conclusion that negative votes or abstention necessarily indicated royalism
or opposition to Napoleonic government. Refusal to make a potentially
dangerous choice was not tantamount to opposition; more significantly,
descriptive accounts of the period indicate that the *Acte* often fared poorly
where support for the government was exceptionally strong. The latter
anomaly points to an important feature of the Hundred Days: not all those
Frenchmen who supported Napoleon's government were willing to accept
the *Acte* simply because it had Bonaparte's apparent approval. In short,
support for the government was based not just upon Bonapartism, but also

[6] P. Mansel, *Louis XVIII* (London, 1981), pp. 228–41, 254–5.

upon opposition to its alternative (Bourbon Monarchy) and patriotic determination to fight Allied invasion and intervention. Indeed, if there is one thing that study of plebiscites and elections during the Revolutionary and Imperial periods does teach us, it is that the majority of Frenchmen were either politically indifferent or too wisely cautious to manifest their opinions by voting. The logical conclusion to be drawn from this is that when we speak of committed Bonapartists, royalists, liberals or republicans, we must recognise that we are speaking of minority groups.[7]

To recognise that these groups were minorities is not to belittle their importance; after all, they monopolised political power and, during periods of crisis such as the Hundred Days, they could draw on significant support from men who otherwise remained uncommitted. The Hundred Days, therefore, is an exceptionally good period for testing the relative strength of these groups, but we should not forget that many Frenchmen simply refused to come down on any side whatsoever. When we find evidence of indifference to one political alternative, we should not conclude that it represents support for another.

Because Bonapartism and revolutionary tradition were linked in support of the government of the Hundred Days, it is simplest to interpret this period in terms of support for, and opposition to, the Bourbon Monarchy; such a perspective also sheds a great deal of light on the difficulties of government during the Second Restoration. Although Bonaparte departed France forever in 1815, opposition to the Monarchy remained.

Reaction to the government of the Hundred Days was extraordinarily complex and varied dramatically according to region. For this reason, an historian who focuses on the north will reach very different conclusions to those of an historian of the east. What the general reader requires is an overview which carefully weighs the strength of the claims of the competing political sides on a national level. Such an overview, if it is to be accurate, can only be gained after a great deal of preparatory analysis of how men acted and why they did so. The present study of a massive group which, above all else, opposed the Bourbon Monarchy, is a step in that direction.

One reason why studying the Hundred Days proves so fruitful is that this period provided men with an opportunity to voice their opinions to a degree significantly greater than in the periods which preceded and followed it. A reading of contemporary journals confirms to a surprising extent Charles Beslay's contention that 'France had unlimited liberty of

---

[7] For his analysis of voting for and against the *Acte Additionnel*, see F. Bluche, *Le Plébiscite des Cent-Jours* (Geneva, 1974). The point concerning abstentionism comes up repeatedly in D. M. G. Sutherland, *France 1789–1815* (London, 1985); see 'elections' in the index, p. 480.

the press; everything could be discussed; newspapers reproduced the manifestoes of enemy generals, even those that put Napoleon outside of civil and social relations.[8] In seeking to rally public opinion, Bonaparte relaxed the old Imperial press controls and allowed discussion of subjects which had been proscribed in the previous decade. This led to much heated debate not only over what the nature of government and society should be, but also over what the Revolution meant to France. As we shall see, the attitudes of Frenchmen to the Revolution, including the Terror, were much more complex than historians have recognised.

Perhaps more significantly, as the inevitability of renewed war with the Allied Powers grew increasingly apparent, Napoleon granted freedom of association to men who wished to rally to his government at least to the extent of putting down domestic subversion. In the six weeks prior to Waterloo a federative movement, modelled upon those of 1789–91, spread rapidly across France. This movement began spontaneously; it was not the result of government initiative and although the government could seek to direct and exploit the federations it could not entirely control them. The potential utility of the federative movement rapidly became apparent to Napoleon and his ministers and, for the most part, they sought to foster it. Nevertheless, Napoleon viewed these associations with some misgiving; he was fully aware of their revolutionary precedents and potential. He was not entirely wrong in his assessment and many *fédérés*, realising that the government had need of them, were willing to exploit this position by making demands upon the government and voicing their own opinions. Study of the federations, therefore, gives us the opportunity to discover what an important part of the French community wanted in 1815.

General histories usually place the federative movement in the context of the revolutionary *élan* apparent during the Hundred Days. In line with what appears to be a general consensus that revolutionary support for Napoleon declined shortly after the *vol d'aigle*, the federations are often discussed before the *Acte Additionnel* in order to contrast a manifestation of support with a disappointing vote which supposedly indicated Napoleon's waning popularity. The problem with this approach is that it all too conveniently overlooks the fact that the federative movement developed after publication of the *Acte*. Recognition of this anomaly immediately poses two questions. Were the federations part of the revolutionary resurgence? If so, what does the federative movement indicate concerning the nature, extent and duration of Napoleon's popularity?[9]

---

[8] C. Beslay, *Mes Souvenirs* (Paris, 1873), p. 50.
[9] The misleading juxtaposition of the federative movement and the *Acte Additionnel* has most recently appeared in J. Tulard's *Les Révolutions* (Paris, 1985), pp. 286–8.

The federations brought together an extraordinarily diverse collection of political and social groups into a single movement. Men who in the past had been enemies now found themselves working together for a common cause. As one would expect of the members of such a heterogeneous group, *fédérés* gave a multiplicity of reasons for backing Napoleon's government. No two federations were exactly alike in social or political composition, nor were they entirely alike in stated objectives or commitment, but one significant element bound all *fédérés* together: resolute opposition to restoration of the Bourbon Monarchy and any return to the days of the *ancien régime*.

At least two eminent historians have pointed to the potential utility of a monograph on the federative movement; this reflects the fact that enough is known about the associations to raise significant questions. To this point, articles have been published on federations in Paris, the Côte-d'Or, Saône-et-Loire and Tarn; additional information can be gleaned from a large number of articles which, though devoted to other subjects, occasionally mention the *fédérés* in passing. So, part of the task lies in piecing these fragmentary parts into a coherent whole. Moreover, one general account of the movement has been made, but it is now very dated.[10]

The first thing to be noted about E. Le Gallo's analysis of the federative movement is that it constituted a single chapter in a study of the Hundred Days published in 1924. Given this context, it was natural that the author did not concern himself directly with the *fédérés* outside this period, nor could he have said a great deal about the identity of *fédérés*, given the state of research at the time. Le Gallo's account was a preliminary sketch and, taken as such, is particularly useful for the questions that it asks and does not ask.

Le Gallo was especially impressed by the popular base of the movement and believed that the Hundred Days had galvanised the masses in a way similar to 1792. The masses were led by Jacobins who saw in Napoleon an instrument by which they could achieve their own ends. Bonaparte, fully

---

[10] Calls for study of the *fédérés* can be found in Tulard, *Napoleon*, p. 444, and D. Higgs, *Ultraroyalism in Toulouse* (Baltimore, 1973), pp. 54–5; Sutherland in *France*, p. 435, has noted that questions concerning the *fédérés* remain to be answered. The articles on federations are as follows: P. Guillaumot, 'Chalon pendant les Cent-Jours: souvenirs de la fédération bourguignonne', *La Bourgogne*, 2 (1869), pp. 165–80; K. D. Tönnesson, 'Les Fédérés de Paris pendant les Cent-Jours', *Annales historiques de la Révolution Française*, 54 (juillet-septembre 1982), pp. 393–415; J. Vanel, 'Le Mouvement fédératif dans le département du Tarn', *Gaillac et le pays tarnais, 31ᵉ congrès d'études de la fédération des sociétés académiques et savantes de Languedoc-Pyrénées-Gascogne* (Gaillac, 1977), pp. 387–95; P. Viard, 'Les fédérés de la Côte-d'Or en 1815', *Revue de Bourgogne*, 6 (1926), pp. 22–39, and R. S. Alexander, 'The fédérés of Dijon in 1815', *The Historical Journal*, 30, 2 (1987), pp. 367–90.

aware of this, sought to restrain the associations. Joseph Fouché (as always, the wild card in the Imperial pack) played his usual double game and encouraged the federations when he thought this would embarrass the Emperor. The ultimate result was that the *fédérés* were not allowed to do all they might have done – they became pawns in a high political power struggle and their willingness to save the *patrie* from foreign intervention and royalist intrigue was sacrificed.[11]

This bald summary of Le Gallo's account does not give sufficient recognition to his contribution in illustrating the vast extent of the federative movement, but it does enable us to isolate the main lines of investigation taken by the author. First of all, we shall want to consider further whether the associations did indeed have a popular base. Le Gallo derived his conclusion from readings of contemporary descriptions, but such sources often prove deceptive. To determine whether the associations truly did have a popular base we shall need to analyse their memberships. Moreover, as K. D. Tönnesson has correctly noted, Le Gallo did not pay sufficient heed to the role of Bonapartists in provincial federations.[12] Were the associations Bonapartist, revolutionary, or a mixture of both? Were there opposing factions within individual associations, or did the federations differ according to region? In sum, we need to know more about the social and political character of the associations and we can only learn this by identifying significant numbers of *fédérés*.

Fédérés were very active propagandists and we can use the large body of *fédéré* literature to scrutinise their opinions and ambitions. In analysing such material, however, we shall have to pay close attention to the circumstances under which they wrote. *Fédérés* clearly were exploiting the relative freedom of expression of the Hundred Days, but there were limits to how far they could go; they needed the consent and co-operation of the Imperial government and they could not afford to alienate the Emperor. This produced a certain ambivalence in *fédéré* writings and speeches, but it also led *fédérés* to search for a common ground between the Revolution and Empire which was to prove remarkably fertile.

When possible, it is best to judge men by their actions. As we shall see, *fédérés* did a great deal more than Le Gallo realised, and recognition of this in turn raises questions about the relationship between *fédérés* and the government; if the *fédérés* were active, the 'emasculation' argument will have to be either qualified or rejected. Moreover, by identifying *fédérés* we shall be able to judge them, not simply by their actions during the Hundred Days, but also in the broader context of the period from 1789 to 1830. This

---

[11] This summary is drawn from E. Le Gallo, *Les Cent-Jours* (Paris, 1924), pp. 287–328.
[12] See Tönnesson, 'Les Fédérés', p. 395.

will enable us to view more fully the *fédérés* as men, not just as faceless members of a short-term phenomenon.

The key to close analysis of an individual federation lies in the acquisition of a membership list. Few such lists remain of course; *fédérés* had good reason to destroy their registers after Waterloo, but we have been able to uncover extensive lists of the *fédérés* of Rennes, Dijon and Paris. This is all the more fortunate since the *fédérés* of each of these places were numerous and significantly active. In using them to build case-studies, we shall seek to understand better why and how associations differed by viewing them in the context of local history, but we shall also seek to establish what all federations had in common, in order to determine the essential characteristics of the movement as a whole. In other words, we shall pose national questions at the local level, without overlooking the way in which national movements are manifested in local terms.

Recently, historians of the period 1789–1815 have emphasised the fragmentation of the revolutionary movement from 1789 onwards. Such interpretations stress that the general *élan* apparent at the outset of the Revolution was destroyed by subsequent confiscation of Church lands, imposition of the civil constitution of the clergy, execution of Louis XVI, expulsion of Girondin deputies from the Convention, centralisation and more exacting administration of government under the Committee of Public Safety, and recourse to Terror during the reign of Robespierre. Even ardent *sans-culottes* lost heart as the Jacobin bourgeoisie wrested control from them and excluded them from power. The ranks of the counter-revolution steadily increased and republicanism was discredited. *Thermidor* saw the fall of the more radical exponents of the Revolution and, indeed, by the time of the Directory, a *coup d'état* had to be staged against resurgent monarchists. Intermittent attempts to resuscitate Jacobin clubs ultimately failed, despite a widening of membership which allowed the lower classes to participate. The road was well paved for Napoleon who, by *Brumaire* 1799, began the process of creating order from the chaos produced by the Revolution.

Napoleon, in his twin quests for national unity and personal hegemony, moved rapidly to consolidate his position against dissenting elements of both the Left and Right. The few remaining Jacobins and members of popular societies who dared criticise his government were harassed into silence by ruthless police persecution. Royalist resistance collapsed with the pacification of the west and the signing of the Concordat. Moreover, repeated military victories brought Napoleon unrivalled popularity amongst the masses and his provision of order and legal codes gained him the allegiance of the middle classes. He exploited this popularity by recourse to plebiscite, thus cynically using a democratic device to strangle political liberty. The political institutions he created, while allowed to be useful, were ultimately subservient. The Republic became an Empire with an hereditary monarchy, and rigid press censorship drove the Revolution further from the minds of Frenchmen. All that remained was vague obloquy, a fear of anarchy and terror.

Not one to rest on his laurels, Napoleon launched a series of measures and policies which would further reverse the work of the Revolution. Aristocratic *émigrés* were invited to return and retake their positions of local authority – provided they served, or at least did not overtly oppose, the new Charlemagne. Napoleon thought that men raised in the traditions of courtiership were the best of servants. A new social hierarchy was constructed which included the Legion of Honour and hereditary titles. But Napoleon took care not to alienate the middle classes, as entry into the new social élite would be based upon merit – service to the state, especially in the field of battle. Thus Napoleon created a new France in an image reflecting both the *ancien régime* and the Revolution, but better run than either. France was maleable; few complained so long as Bonaparte provided order and a prosperity based upon victory and plunder.

Ultimately Napoleon fell because of his incessant war-mongering. Bourgeois France began to wonder when he needlessly chose to engage French troops in a campaign to place a Bonaparte on the Spanish throne. An economic policy based upon the exigencies of war, the Continental System, proved unworkable and in combination with the English blockade furthered the devastation of maritime ports begun during the Revolution. Remorseless conscription and increasing tax demands decreased Bonaparte's popularity amongst the masses. His treatment of the Pope alienated a significant sector of the clergy. Napoleon's extraordinary good fortune with grain harvests came to an end in the second decade of his rule, necessitating recourse to a version of the Revolutionary price maximum. This exacerbated the growing discontent of the middle classes and when Imperial armies completed their disastrous retreat from Moscow, Napoleon found the support of Frenchmen, especially the governing classes, insufficient to repel invading Allied armies. Despite one of Bonaparte's greatest military campaigns, Paris rapidly fell to the Bourbons. France was exhausted.

This general interpretation is compelling and ultimately convincing because of its internal logic. But, as with all such broad interpretations, it must be rigorously scrutinised in the light of subsequent historical research. Study of the federations indicates that certain parts of it have been markedly overstated.

Creation of monarchical and hierarchical social institutions and rigorous enforcement of new laws perhaps could have altered public opinion over time, but it could not immediately erase memories of contrasting institutions and laws. Censorship and an increasingly competent police force could not entirely control a culture which was essentially oral. In 1813 the prefect of the Seine-Inférieure reported: 'the Jacobins speak in hushed tones, but songs which lead one to suppose that they dream of a revival are sung very loudly; I have seen children of twelve to fifteen years dance to the airs of the *Carmâgnole* and young people sing the hymn of the *Marseillaise*.'[13] When it suited him, Napoleon would maintain that he had successfully sapped 'the force of the ideas of the Revolution'; yet, as the Empire crumbled in 1814, it was to the revolutionary tradition that Bonaparte appealed in a last desperate attempt to rally support. Response to this 'crudely cynical move' was far from sufficient to ward off Allied victory, but it did give a portent of the future.[14] The point, of course, is that Napoleon knew well enough that the fires of the Revolution had not been entirely stamped out.

From the moment that Louis XVIII regained his throne (April–May 1814), Napoleon began to benefit by way of contrast. When confronted by the Bourbons' apparently full-blooded onslaught upon the Revolution, liberals and republicans became less disposed to distinguish clearly between the Empire and the Revolution. As early as July 1814 a revealing placard was posted on the door of the *hôtel-de-ville* of Auxerre; it read: 'Tremble, royalists, Napoleon is a republican; he does not want slaves and is about to stir himself to come crush you.'[15] The seeds sown in early 1814 had already begun to take root; revolutionary Bonapartism would spring to the surface shortly after Allied occupiers had left French soil.

Nowhere was this more clearly manifested than in the federative movement of 1815. Undoubtedly, the most striking feature of the associations was the pre-eminent role played by old champions of the Revolution. At least thirteen associations boasted regicide *conventionnels* as leading members. Alongside these figures of national notoriety stood a host of important local figures: men who had served as mayors during the Terror, sat on Revolutionary tribunals, and organised Jacobin and popular societies. In the west, *fédérés* were more apt to be of a less radical, Girondin, stamp; they had been committed republicans nonetheless. Moreover, these incarnations of revolutionary continuity consistently demonstrated that they had learnt the lessons of past factionalism; they were seeking to recall and

[13] Cited in J. Vidalenc, 'L'Opposition sous le Consulat et l'Empire', *Annales historiques de la Révolution Française*, no. 194 (Oct.–Dec. 1968), p. 478.
[14] The quote is from Sutherland, *France*, p. 423. For the response, see F. Rude, 'Le Réveil du patriotisme révolutionnaire dans la région Rhône-Alpes en 1814', *Cahiers d'histoire*, 16 (1971), pp. 433–55.
[15] Cited in Weill, 'L'Idée', pp. 322–3.

rebuild the *élan* of 1789. Joseph Cambon, who had been a member of the first Committee of Public Safety, but who had also striven to bridge the widening gulf between Montagnards and Girondins, founded the federation of the Hérault and made the first *fédéré* proclamation a clarion call for the old unity:

Patriots of 1789! Let us banish all of the nuances that divided us during the course of the Revolution. Have we no longer the same tendency, the same character? Have we not all wanted liberty? Let us form no more than a single and unique arm [*faisceau*]: it is a question now of avoiding slavery.[16]

To base the *fédéré* creed upon the principles of '89 was a shrewd tactic, for this was the phase of the Revolution that least divided opponents of the Bourbon Monarchy.

It was also a stratagem calculated to emphasise common ground between Revolution and Empire and it worked extraordinarily well throughout France. Darbois, a founder at Nancy, described the federation of Lorraine as 'a very bizarre union of old terrorists who had thumbed their noses at Napoleon and men who had pushed servility to the extreme under the Empire'.[17] Not all men of the Revolution had exited the political stage during the Empire; many had made the transition more or less comfortably and retained positions of local authority. Yet not all of these men were pleased by Napoleon's monarchical progress. Some were known by Imperial prefects to have retained their republican principles; such men were biding their time, waiting for an opportunity such as the Hundred Days momentarily presented them. Above all else, the twin threats of invasion and restoration called for compromise, a phenomenon not entirely alien to Jacobins in the past, but in measured tones these men put forward certain basic claims. Among these was the principle of popular sovereignty, the linchpin of republicanism. Broad as it was, the federative movement was able to accommodate the aspirations of such men; it also enabled notorious Terrorists to come out of the woodwork for the first time since the *coup d'état* of *Brumaire*. To find such men working hand-in-glove with traditional Bonapartists astonished monarchists during the Hundred Days. It was indeed an unnatural alliance in many ways, but it held – perhaps because Napoleon's government fell long before its own actions could have compromised revolutionary Bonapartism. The *Acte Additionnel* may well have disappointed the more revolutionary of Napoleon's supporters, but it did not prevent them from joining the federative movement.

Royalists were so impressed by this coalition that they took few pains to

[16] *Le Patriote de '89: journal du soir, politique et littéraire*, 3 June 1815.
[17] Cited in G. Richard, 'Les Cent-Jours à Nancy', *Pays Lorrain*, année 38 (1957), p. 89.

distinguish between old revolutionaries and Bonapartists when they unleashed White Terror after Bonaparte's second fall. This further consolidated what might have proved a fragile union. Primary victims of bloodshed and repression, *fédérés* of whatever hue shared the same experience and came to the same conclusion about their common interest. In an effort to destroy their influence, Bourbon officials purged *fédéré* leaders from positions of local authority. With few exceptions, this made such men inveterate enemies of the Monarchy. An extraordinary number of *fédérés* went on to help organise the various strands of opposition to the Second Restoration government. Their experience within the federations of 1815 taught them that they could work together and their participation within the opposition goes a long way towards explaining the subsequent co-operation of Bonapartists, republicans and liberals. Not only ultra-royalists were troubled by the republican and Bonapartist elements within the Liberal Opposition; genuine constitutional monarchists were also aware of the danger. Madame De Staël in 1818 issued the following warning in her *Considerations on the French Revolution*:

Whether Napoleon lives or perishes, whether he reappears on the continent of Europe or does not, a single motive leads me to speak yet again of him – the ardent desire that the friends of liberty in France entirely separate their cause from his, and that care is taken not to confound the principles of the Revolution with those of the Imperial regime.[18]

With the exception of the *doctrinaires*, De Staël's warning fell largely upon deaf ears and liberals, Bonapartists and republicans continued to work together throughout the Second Restoration; it was only the fall of the Bourbon Monarchy in 1830 that led these groups to look upon each other primarily as opponents.[19]

For our purposes, the standard division of the Second Restoration into four parts serves nicely. The first, August 1815 to September 1816, was marked by White Terror and ultra-royalist intransigence in the *Chambre Introuvable*. In its unofficial aspect, White Terror consisted of mob violence directed against all those compromised by their actions during the Hundred Days; in essence, it was anarchy which the central government struggled to control and end. Because important royalists, including the group surrounding the Duke of Angoulême, did very little to check murder and pillage in the south, the image of the Monarchy inevitably was

---

[18] See Madame G. De Staël, *Considérations sur la Révolution Française*, ed. J. Godeschot (Paris, 1983), p. 503.

[19] E. Cappadocia has pointed to the limited impact of De Staël's warning in 'The Liberals and Madame De Staël in 1818', in R. Herr and H. T. Parker, eds., *Ideas in History: Essays Presented to Louis Gottschalk* (Durham, N.C., 1965), pp. 183–95.

tarnished. The official aspect of White Terror comprised repressive laws (against sedition and facilitating the arrest of 'suspects'), trials of men held to have betrayed the Monarchy in 1815 (the most famous being Marshal Ney), and a systematic purging of disloyal government administrators.[20]

For *fédérés*, this was a traumatic period. Not only was the Monarchy they had opposed back in power, their support for Napoleon had been public. In consequence, they were the most obvious targets for reprisals. In Languedoc many were assassinated or arbitrarily imprisoned; elsewhere they were the victims of official harassment – house searches, arrests, trials, exile and the frequent companionship of police spies. None of this endeared them to the Bourbons.

Over time, however, it did teach them not to make public declarations of their political sentiments. In truth, there was little point in overtly expressing hostility; there was no possibility of successfully rising against a government backed by Allied troops. The Army had again been defeated and Napoleon, who had made himself the focal point and leader of opposition to the Bourbon Monarchy, was back in exile. The *fédérés* cultivated obscurity. Nevertheless, many could not resist the temptation to yell 'Vive l'Empereur!'; fortunately for those who were not immediately arrested, the police could not be everywhere and rumours of an impending return of the Eagle became the order of the day. More ominous still was the increasing volume of police reports on secret societies and conspiracies.

We can now see that these conspiracies were never a serious threat to the throne; they were poorly organised by amateurs probably encouraged by *agents provocateurs*. But royalists were not entirely wrong in viewing abortive uprisings in Paris, Lyons and Grenoble with alarm; men such as Jean-Paul Didier embarked upon their foolhardy schemes because they knew the Monarchy was deeply unpopular. The government had coercive weapons enough to deal with such plotters; perhaps its greatest asset was the lesson of the Hundred Days – overthrowing the Bourbons brought Allied invasion. To be assured of a secure future, however, the ruling family needed to make itself popular. Louis XVIII was king enough to realise this and, in September 1816, dissolved the ultra-royalist Chamber of Deputies in preparation for moderate government.

The period of 'liberal monarchy' lasted until February 1820. Under the ministries of Richelieu and Decazes, repressive laws were ended, the Army was reorganised in a manner to appease old soldiers, press censorship was relaxed, a new electoral law brought the franchise more closely in accordance with the provisions of the Charter, and France was freed of occu-

[20] For a standard interpretation of the Second Restoration, see Jardin and Tudesq, *France*, pp. 31–86.

pation. Despite the agricultural crisis of 1816–17, the government was easily able to overcome a series of minor rebellions. Yet, amidst apparent stability, problems lingered.

Royalists were especially perturbed by the rapid organisation and electoral success of a new Liberal Opposition. While these liberals repeatedly stressed their intention to work strictly within the confines of the Charter and, hence, respect constitutional monarchy, true royalists questioned the loyalty of these men to the throne. In certain cases such scepticism was entirely justified. Many *fédérés*, far from sympathetic to the King in 1815 and consequently purged from government positions, played an important role in organising Liberal Opposition. Had they changed their spots, or were they simply limiting the extent of their opposition while in public? Liberal electoral victories were especially striking in 1818 and 1819. The straw that broke the back of moderate government was the election of the Abbé Grégoire at Grenoble. Support for Grégoire, an old *conventionnel* 'regicide by intention', was largely a rejoinder to the repression that followed the Didier Affair. The republican Abbé had not even needed to make an appearance at Grenoble; his campaign was run by a secret society known as the Union – founded by Joseph Rey and Champollion *le jeune*, secretary of the federation of 1815. It was not only ultra-royalists who saw this startling result as a symbol of the revolutionary way things were going; moderates also began to fear for the throne. Such fears seemed confirmed by the assassination of the Duke of Berry in early 1820. Liberals in the Chamber were roundly condemned for guilt by association and reaction again became the keynote of government policy.

Individual liberty and freedom of the press were curtailed and the 'double vote' electoral law was passed to ensure that confirmed monarchists could look for better results. With the political deck thus stacked against them, opponents of the regime had immediate recourse to conspiracy. A rash of secret revolutionary societies, including the Union, *Chevaliers de la Liberté* and Carbonari, broke out. In each of these, *fédérés* played an integral part. Although none of the rebellions provoked by these groups proved any more effective than those of the immediate post-1815 period, such societies did demonstrate the rapidity with which supposed liberals could make the transition from constitutional to revolutionary opposition. This was to be expected of a group which included republicans and Bonapartists.

Napoleon died in May 1821. There was little immediate reaction in France; at most it seemed another sign of the strengthening Bourbon position. But the departure from the political scene of the man who had brought about revolutionary Bonapartism enabled those liberals who were not convinced of Napoleon's conversion to work in common cause with

Bonapartists, without the worrying concern that they might be re-establishing a dictator. The publication of Bonaparte's Saint Helena memoirs reinforced the image of Napoleon as a liberal and a revolutionary; the 'myth' was all the more attractive since it was now relatively safe to believe it. Perhaps more significantly, the death of Napoleon meant that the people of Paris had to find a new alternative to Bourbon Monarchy. Liberals became the heir apparent to these troops.

None of this was immediately apparent as the Richelieu Ministry gave way to that of Joseph Villèle. Indeed, in the aftermath of the rebellions of the early 1820s, royalists swept to a series of massive electoral victories. Attempts by liberals, including the old *fédéré* Cugnet de Montarlot, to disrupt a French military 'promenade' in Spain proved utterly futile, and by 1824 the liberals had been reduced to nineteen members in the Chamber of Deputies. Despite problems of detail raised by the Peers, Villèle was able to pass a law indemnifying *émigrés* for properties confiscated during the Revolution.

Still, there were warning signs enough to caution a wiser government. The million owners of *biens nationaux* worried about the security of their possessions; ultra-royalists continued to demand complete restitution of these lands. The medieval trappings of the coronation of Charles X in May 1825 provoked a good deal of irreverent comment – here was a king who all too evidently gloried in the ancient past. Worse yet, the King's fervent Catholicism was made manifest in laws which appeared to demonstrate undue clerical influence over the government. The most extreme of these, the law against sacrilege, was never acted on, but it provided fuel for an anti-clerical fire which raged in the opposition press. Perhaps because the throne seemed secure, royalists fell out among themselves and engaged in an internecine warfare which weakened the position of the government. Villèle again had recourse to doctoring electoral procedures and his prefects were not averse to fixing voter lists to ensure desirable results. In an effort to secure a reliable Upper House, Villèle had a large batch of 'ministerial' peers appointed. The latter manœuvre proved a major tactical error, for it left a large number of previously safe seats vacant in the Lower Chamber.

All of this enabled the opposition to recover ground lost in the early 1820s. Profiting from experience, liberals shunned the path of conspiracy and concentrated upon organising constitutional means of opposition. The *Aide-toi, le Ciel t'aidera* society set up a national machine for assuring that potential supporters were duly registered when eligible to vote. While on the stump, opposition candidates took pains to stress that they believed in constitutional monarchy as embodied in the Charter. Did they? They could hardly declare any republican or Bonapartist preferences; there were clear limits as to the extent of opposition the government would tolerate. More-over, they were appealing for the votes of a narrow electorate which had revealed its conservative tendencies when confronted by the apparent possibility of revolution in the early 1820s. Fervent avowals of allegiance to the Charter were taken by some royalists to be coded statements of oppo-sition to the throne. Perhaps it was simply a matter of degree, a question of whether one wished to emphasise allegiance to the constitution or the throne, while remaining loyal to both. After all, the Bourbon Monarchy was part of the Charter. But when the electoral tide suddenly reversed (there were some 170 liberal deputies in the Chamber by 1827), opposition hardened and liberals became more demanding. In 1829 Beslay, a founder of the Breton federation of 1815, launched an *Association Bretonne* with clear invocation of the federative past. The *Association* was based on the principle of refusal to pay taxes should Charles X revoke the Charter. Taken up by the *Aide-toi* society and given a national basis, the associations indicated that the lines of resistance were being drawn. In March 1830 Liberal Opposition deputies went a step further by presenting the King with an address stating that the Chamber could not work with the recently appointed ministry. This was tantamount to demanding ministerial responsibility for the Lower Chamber, which went well beyond the bounds of the Charter. Finally, when presented with the opportunity, liberals wasted little time in jettisoning the Bourbon Monarchy and altering the Charter which, apparently, was not so perfect after all. Perhaps there was more to Liberal Opposition than simple championing of the Charter.

These latter suspicions are reinforced by the leading role played by *fédérés* in the Liberal Opposition. Not only did old *fédérés* participate in the *Aide-toi* society, *Association* movement, Liberal Opposition press and electoral committees, they also entered the Chamber of Deputies in signifi-cant numbers prior to the Revolution of 1830. Such men had signalled themselves as enemies of the Monarchy in 1815 and were given little reason to change their opinions during the Second Restoration. They welcomed the fall of the Bourbons; they had been working for it all along.

Some of these men were old opponents of the Bourbons in 1815; some were new. Much has been made by historians of the generation that came of age in the period surrounding the Revolution of 1830.[21] What remains to be said is that many of the liberal members of the 'generation of 1820' cut their political teeth working alongside more experienced opponents of the Bourbons in the federations of 1815. The same link was forged in the revolutionary societies of the 1820s and the subsequent 'constitutional'

---

[21] For a recent example, see A. Spitzer, *The French Generation of 1820* (Princeton, N.J., 1987).

Liberal Opposition. Whatever the merit of investigating a generation as a collective unit, overemphasising its homogeneity can have the demerit of ignoring or undervaluing links with other generations. As a study of the *fédérés* reveals, there was a continuity in the personnel of opposition to the Bourbon Monarchy which was impervious to generational limits.

What follows, then, is a study of the men who were at the very heart of opposition to the Bourbon Monarchy. To learn why these men supported Napoleon's government during the Hundred Days we shall need to investigate their opinions, interests and actions from 1789 onwards. To comprehend why men of diverse social and political backgrounds united in a common movement in 1815 we shall have to look carefully at the historical context and see what they did under the most difficult of circumstances. This, in turn, will help to explain why they became the chief targets of White Terror and, more importantly, why there could be no accommodation between old *fédérés* and the Bourbon Monarchy. The Bourbon government was correct in mistrusting and seeking to isolate these men; the question was whether the Monarchy could be made sufficiently popular to check the constant efforts of *fédérés* to extend opposition and thereby undermine the throne.

Chapter 1

Origins and development of the federative movement

The news, brought by courier on 24 March 1815, that Napoleon had returned to Paris was received favourably by certain sections of the population of Rennes. On the following day a bust of Bonaparte was paraded through the streets of the city and placed at the *hôtel de ville* by a crowd of bourgeois and soldiers. A deputation was named by students of the law school to present an address of homage to the Emperor. It was no coincidence that the same groups had rioted three months previously when the Bourbon government had sought to establish a commission for the provision of indemnities to old *chouan* leaders.[1]

Other parts of the populace viewed Napoleon's return with a mixture of chagrin and anxiety. Indeed, at the very moment that the young bourgeois of Rennes were replacing a liberty tree uprooted by Russian soldiers in 1814, *chouan* leaders were engaged in preparing rural rebellion. The prospect of renewed civil war could not have left the citizens of Rennes indifferent. However, the very rapidity of Napoleon's *vol d'aigle* rendered attempts to defend the Bourbon throne futile, and a fragile peace was maintained in Rennes during the transition of power.[2]

Matters had deteriorated by 15 April. On that day Rouxel-Langotière, secretary of the *jeunes gens* of Rennes (an association of young shop-clerks, apprentices and students), wrote a long letter to Carnot, Minister of the Interior. Rouxel-Langotière warned that 'cette Caste trop privilégiée' continued to plot on behalf of the Bourbons, and explained that, due to the laxity of local government officials, aristocrats had neither been placed under police surveillance nor disarmed. They maintained important positions in civil and military administration, dominated the National

---

[1] *Le Moniteur Universel*, 30 March 1815; M. Lagrée, *Mentalités, religion et histoire en Haute-Bretagne au XIXe siècle: le diocèse de Rennes, 1815–1848* (Paris, 1977), pp. 416–20.

[2] Lagrée, *Mentalités*, pp. 416, 420.

Guard, and were seeking to foment civil war. To rectify this situation Rouxel-Langotière proposed that the *jeunes gens* be authorised to aid the garrison of Rennes in maintaining public order. Repeatedly he stressed that the *jeunes gens* were completely devoted to the Emperor and willing to sacrifice their lives in his service.[3]

Rouxel-Langotière had good cause for concern, and the timing of his letter was highly significant. When Napoleon realised that renewed war with the Allied Powers was unavoidable, he issued a conscription decree on 10 April. No sooner did news of this reach the west than the fragile tranquility of the region was shattered. Aided by priests who refused to take an oath of loyalty to the government, aristocratic leaders again set about organising bands of peasant *chouans*. Attacks on vulnerable towns, where most supporters of the government were concentrated, were the immediate result.[4]

At about the same time that Rouxel-Langotière sent his letter to Carnot, the *jeunes gens* of Rennes also contacted their counterparts in Nantes and stated their strong support of the 'cause nationale'.[5] Doubtless they also suggested that some sort of union of mutual aid would be highly advisable. Similar ideas had been circulating at Nantes and the *jeunes gens* of that troubled city responded with alacrity.[6] They drew up an address calling on all Bretons to gather round the 'grand homme qui fit si longtemps la gloire de la France, et qui nous promet son bonheur'. According to the *jeunes gens*, Napoleon had returned to save France from 'l'inquisition des moines et la tyrannie des nobles', and was in the process of preparing a constitution 'telle qu'a droit de l'attendre une nation puissante et éclairée'. While awaiting that 'constitution libérale qui doit rallier tous les Français redevenus égaux', measures must be taken to 'rendre inutile les efforts de la malveillance' of 'cette noblesse orgueilleuse et héréditaire' which had sought under the Bourbons to destroy all liberal ideas. The *jeunes gens* proposed that the *pacte fédératif* drafted in Pontivy in 1789 be renewed by the five departments of Brittany and delegated six deputies to travel to Rennes to help determine what their next step should be. They posted a similar address to Napoleon, avowing their intentions.[7]

The *jeunes gens* of Rennes began the series of assemblies that eventually was to produce a *pacte fédératif* on 29 April. The delegates from Nantes

---

[3] AN, F.[7] 9664, Rouxel-Langotière to the Minister of the Interior, 15 April 1815.
[4] F. Lebrun, editor, *L'Ille-et-Vilaine: des origines à nos jours* (Saint-Jean d'Angély, 1984), pp. 253–4; Lagrée, *Mentalités*, p. 420.
[5] *Moniteur*, 30 April 1815.
[6] M. A. Thiers, *Histoire du Consulat et de l'Empire* (Paris, 1861), XIX, p. 468.
[7] *Moniteur*, 29 April 1815; B. Constant, *Mémoires sur les Cent-Jours*, second edition (Paris, 1829), p. 179.

arrived on 22 April and were greeted by some 300 Rennais shouting 'vive l'Empereur, vivent les Nantais, vivent les Rennais, vivent les Bretons!' On the following day deputies from Vannes, Ploermel and Josselin also arrived. With the blessing of the prefect Méchin, the deputies then went about their business. The Nantais presented their address with the suggestion of simply adopting the old pact. It would appear that there was some dispute over this, and discussion began as to what should be said in the pact. At this point the delegates asked Joseph Blin, director of the post office of Rennes, to act as president of the federation 'afin de régulariser ses opérations'. Discussion of the wording of the pact went on well into the night and several proposals were voted on.[8]

The primary source for the events of that night is the *Notice rapide sur la fédération bretonne* that Benjamin Constant published in the second edition of his *Mémoires sur les Cent-Jours*. This is an interesting document, apparently written by a Nantais delegate, but it needs to be treated with caution. According to the anonymous author, several pacts were submitted for consideration before one was accepted in which 'le nom de Napoléon n'y figurait pas. C'était pour la patrie et pour le maintien de l'ordre que la jeunesse bretonne était appelée aux armes'. This version was about to be sent to the printers when 'un des principaux fonctionnaires publics de la ville de Rennes . . . nous donna le conseil de parler de l'empereur'. He warned that if silence concerning the Emperor were maintained, Napoleon would shatter the federation 'comme un verre'. He then rewrote the pre-amble to the pact and presented it the next day. Although the new preamble displeased many deputies because it gave the pact 'le couleur d'un parti', it was ultimately accepted due to fears that the government 'ne souffrirait pas une association qui paraîtrait s'isoler de Napoléon'.[9]

All of this gives the definite impression that the Breton federation was hardly a Bonapartist association, and it is not surprising when the author relates an anecdote in which the Emperor is portrayed as having been sorely irritated when first informed of the new association. Nor is it surprising to find that Le Gallo accepted much of this account, given his argument that the government was suspicious of the federative movement and inclined to constrain it.[10] But there are problems with the *Notice rapide* that need to be taken into consideration.

Although no date was assigned to it, the *Notice rapide* was certainly written during the Second Restoration. Given this context, it is not difficult

[8] *Moniteur*, 29 and 30 April 1815; Constant, *Mémoires*, pp. 179–80.
[9] Constant, *Mémoires*, pp. 179–80.
[10] *Ibid.*, pp. 180–1; E. Le Gallo, *Les Cent-Jours* (Paris, 1924), pp. 293–4.

to understand why the author wished to prove that the federation was not 'une faction révolutionnaire' and that the *fédérés* 'n'étaient point des esclaves dévoués à Napoléon'.[11] But Rouxel-Langotière, in his letter to Carnot on behalf of the *jeunes gens* of Rennes, had repeatedly cited their devotion to the Emperor, and the *jeunes gens* of Nantes had not fought shy of mentioning Napoleon in their address to the Rennais. None of which proves that the *fédérés* were 'slaves' of Napoleon; clearly there was some dispute over the wording of the pact, but we should be wary of concluding that the *fédérés* were reserved concerning the Emperor without further evidence. The address of the Nantais did indicate that the *jeunes gens* expected some sort of liberal constitution; it did not indicate indifference to Bonaparte.

On 24 April the new pact, which in fact had been written by the Rennais lawyer Gaillard de Kerbertin, was adopted and became the basis of the Breton federation. It was drawn up in one of the halls of the Palace of Justice and then published under the direction of four *commissaires*: Blin, Rouxel-Langotière, Gaillard de Kerbertin and Binet *aîné*.

The *Pacte Fédératif Proposé Aux Cinq Départements de la Bretagne* does indeed appear a work of compromise. The tradition of the Revolution is immediately apparent in it. The first line of the preamble sets the new pact in its historical context: 'Vingt-cinq ans se sont écoulés depuis que nos aînés se sont confédérés pour la conquête de la Liberté'. The *fédérés* declare that 'nous ferons prévaloir les saines doctrines et l'égalité des droits, première condition de la Liberté reconquise', and avow that 'le systême féodal dont les rameaux naguère prêts à se réunir' is forever destroyed. The second article reads: 'L'object de cette Confédération est de consacrer tous ses moyens à la propagation des principes libéraux, d'opposer la vérité à l'imposture, de répandre la lumière au milieux des hommes égarés.' But such revolutionary rhetoric is couched in very general terms. Indeed, the *fédérés* take care to avoid more particular statements; no suggestions are made concerning what the nature of the constitution should be or how liberty should be manifested in law.

Moreover, appeals to the tradition of the Revolution are carefully balanced with references to the Emperor. Napoleon is referred to as 'le guerrier que nous voulons pour Monarque', and his dynasty is declared to be 'consacrée par notre volonté'. Bonaparte is the leader of the Army, 'le Domaine des Héros', who will fight to preserve the rights of the Revolution now threatened by Allied invasion. To the Army the *fédérés* declare 'nous garantissions à nos intrépides guerriers, qu'en leur absence, leurs foyers seront préservés et qu'aucun attentat ne restera sans

[11] Constant, *Mémoires*, pp. 181–2.

vengeance et n'échappera à la sévérité des lois dont nous serons les défenseurs'.

The pact repeatedly emphasises that the association will act strictly within the bounds of law. That 'la Confédération n'a aucune autorité politique' is recognised. The federation is created as an auxiliary of the government: 'toutes les fois qu'ils auront à agir, ils devront être préablement munis des ordres, réquisitions ou consentement de l'autorité publique. Ils font partie nécessaire de la Garde Nationale, et n'en forment point un corps isolé.' Finally, the pact will last only until 'Sa Majesté daignera faire connaître que les dangers de la Patrie ont cessé.' Thus, the federation is to fulfil the function first suggested by Rouxel-Langotière in his letter to Carnot.

What ultimately emerges from an analysis of the pact is that it is a useful statement of what the *fédérés* intended to do for the government, but that it is not necessarily a precise indicator of the political opinions of the *fédérés* themselves. The pact was designed to unite all those who opposed restoration of the Bourbon Monarchy. For this reason, the *fédérés* had to confine themselves to general statements of principle; more specific statements would have risked divisions and reduced support. Moreover, the pact clearly was written with the intention of gaining the consent of the Emperor. Precise statements about the nature of government would have risked the loss of Napoleon's approval. In sum, then, we can use the pact to judge whether the *fédérés* succeeded in fulfilling their commitments, but we shall want to look elsewhere in our attempt to determine the political opinions of the *fédérés*.[12]

Of course, Baron Méchin informed Paris of these developments. On 22 April he reported to Carnot that the *jeunes gens*, full of enthusiasm and *bon esprit*, had asked for permission to form a mobile column which would march to communes where order was troubled or to the coast in case of invasion. Méchin had granted their request and allowed them to open recruitment registers at the prefecture and the *mairie*; already a sufficient number had signed to form a company. Carnot replied that he was satisfied with these measures and would inform the Emperor; however, he added that he did not think it necessary for the *jeunes gens* to form a 'corps particulier', suggesting that they be incorporated either into the National Guard or the free corps.

On 23 April Rebillard, a lawyer who appears to have played a key part in the foundation of the association, had undertaken to solicit Napoleon's approval. Rebillard was a native of Dijon and chose to approach Bonaparte through another Dijonnais, General Delaborde. He sent a letter describing

---

[12] The pact was published in the *Moniteur*, 29 April 1815.

the events that had taken place in Rennes to the General, who was residing in Paris. Delaborde received Rebillard's letter in the early evening of 25 April. He dined with the Emperor later that evening and picked a propitious moment to present Napoleon with the letter. Significantly, another Dijonnais, the Duke of Bassano, was also in attendance at the time. If Napoleon was initially irritated by the news, Delaborde made no mention of this in his return letter to Rebillard. He simply wrote that the Emperor had read the letter with close attention and 'a été satisfait de l'élan patriotique de la jeunesse Bretonne'.[13]

On the 25th, General Caffarelli arrived in Rennes as the government's *commissaire extraordinaire*. The following day he wrote favourable reports of the federation to the Ministers of the Interior and War. To Carnot he reported:

Cette association s'est faite librement et par un élan spontané, mais elle s'est placée elle-même sous la direction de l'autorité première de ce département. M. le Baron Méchin en a réglé et en réglera avec la sagesse nécessaire et le dévouement qui l'anime pour l'Empereur.[14]

Davout, in forwarding a copy of the pact sent to him by the *commissaire extraordinaire*, informed Napoleon that Caffarelli thought 'qu'il serait extrêmement utile et important d'adopter et exécuter sans delai cette utile réunion patriotique'.[15] Caffarelli then, on the 26th, attended the banquet by which the *fédérés* celebrated the foundation of their association. On the following day, deputies departed for Vannes, Nantes, Quimper, Saint-Brieuc, Saint-Malo, Fougères and Redon, to spread the movement.[16]

By 29 April, Napoleon had decided to make Delaborde the governor of the 12th, 13th, and 22nd military divisions, where he would exercise 'grands pouvoirs civils et militaires'. Delaborde was to make his general quarters at Angers, where he would give 'l'impulsion à cet élan qui existe à Rennes et Nantes où règne un excellent esprit'. By the 30th, Napoleon had decided to make Delaborde a Count and a Councillor of State. Carrying Rebillard's letter does not appear to have harmed the General's career![17]

Thus, there can be no doubt that the immediate cause of the Breton federation was the looming renewal of civil war. Rouxel-Langotière's letter makes clear that the *jeunes gens* of Rennes were primarily concerned with

---

[13] The correspondence between Méchin and Carnot can be found in AN, F⁹ 530, 22 April–3 May 1815. Delaborde's letter to Rebillard is in AD, I-et-V, IM96, dossier Rebillard.
[14] AN, F¹ᵃ 555, Caffarelli to the Minister of the Interior, 26 April 1815.
[15] *Ibid.*, AFIV 1937, Minister of War to the Emperor, 28 April 1815.
[16] *Moniteur*, 29 and 30 April 1815.
[17] AG, 1K1 46, Minister of War to the Emperor, 9 April 1815, and to the Minister of State, 30 April 1815.

stopping aristocratic attempts to pave the way for a return of the Bourbon Monarchy by organising marauding *chouan* bands. The *jeunes gens* wanted a government strong enough to secure public order and repress rebellion. Believing that the authorities were either too weak or unwilling to take the necessary measures, they contacted other *jeunes gens* in order to organise a mutual defence pact by which they might assure the safety of patriots.

The federative movement was, then, spontaneous in its origins; it certainly was not the work of an intriguing Fouché. But the *jeunes gens* were eager to gain government approval and Baron Méchin was closely involved with the association from its very inception. If the first version of the *pacte* made no mention of Napoleon, and this seems doubtful, the second version made sufficient reference to the Emperor. Certainly there is no evidence of the authorities showing any hesitation about supporting the movement, and much evidence to the contrary. Indeed, as we shall see, the government had great hopes for the movement. But the key point is that the Breton *fédérés* willingly put themselves under government direction. The Breton federation was organised in order to support the government, not to constrain it, and was not a vigilante group operating outside the bounds of the law.

Perhaps the presence of Maret, the Duke of Bassano, at Delaborde's meeting with Napoleon helps to explain why Dijon became the first French city to follow the Breton example and form a provincial federation. Certainly a circle of Maret's protégés played an important role in the Dijon association, and government officials of the Second Restoration long suspected the Duke of Bassano's influence. But there is no evidence of direct contact between Maret and the Dijon federation and, indeed, the men who first thought of forming a Burgundian federation chose to approach the government through another man.

On his first visit to Dijon as *commissaire extraordinaire*, Thibaudeau actually found himself being insulted by crowds for failing to respond positively to cries of 'Vive l'Empereur!' Indeed, Dijon had been the scene of repeated Bonapartist agitations well before the *vol d'aigle*, and the Emperor's return had given rise to a mixture of celebration and anti-Bourbon violence. However, Thibaudeau soon found himself in the more congenial company of a circle of Jacobin government officials who clearly were not smitten with popular Bonapartism. In one of his reports to the government, Thibaudeau wrote that 'à peine eut-on coinnaissance à Dijon de la fédération bretonne que quelques autorités me représentèrent qu'il pourrait être très utile de suivre cet exemple'. In their discussions with Thibaudeau, the circle of Jacobins first proposed the idea of following the

Breton example, though they also expressed strong reservations about supporting Napoleon.[18]

Perhaps due to their well-known ambivalent attitude towards Napoleon, the Jacobins proceeded cautiously. Escard, battalion commander of the 23rd line, made the initial appeal to form a federation to an assembly gathered in one of the halls of the prefecture on 2 May. Clearly, the approval of the prefect had already been gained.

Escard's address was primarily patriotic in tone, placing particular stress on the intention of the Allied Powers to impose their will upon the people of France. After applauding the address, the assembly elected a committee to prepare a *pacte fédératif* and then adjourned until 7 May, when the committee's report was to be given. On that day a slightly modified version of the Breton pact was presented and all good patriots of the Côte-d'Or, Haute-Marne and Saône-et-Loire were called upon to federate. The assembly, which now included several citizens from the surrounding countryside and deputies from Beaune, accepted the pact unanimously and chose *commissaires* to enroll members in the towns and communes of the old province and establish intermediary committees. The latter committees would then send deputies to Dijon where they would take a solemn oath of allegiance to the constitution of the Empire, and swear to fulfil the conditions imposed by the pact. A central committee, to be established in Dijon, was elected to handle correspondence with other branches of the association. A deputation was then sent to the prefect to gain official approval, which must have been a formality.[19]

On 10 May Prefect Bercagny sent a copy of the pact to Dumas, director general of the National Guard, and wrote to the prefects of the Haute-Marne and the Saône-et-Loire, asking them to aid in spreading the movement. The editor Carion published a shortened version of Escard's address in his *Petites Affiches de Dijon*, and reported that all local communes were joining the federation. By 13 May, Carion added, deputies from Chalon had enrolled 'au nom de leurs citoyens', the federation had spread to the Haute-Marne, and the prefect of the Saône-et-Loire had written that all his *administrés* would join the movement. Deputies from Dijon arrived in Chaumont and Mâcon on the 13th, and Langres two days later.[20]

Thus the origin of the federative movement was somewhat less spontaneous in Burgundy than in Brittany. Although the original suggestion had not come from Thibaudeau or Bercagny, both these officials had done their

[18] A.-C. Thibaudeau, *Mémoires 1799–1815* (Paris, 1913), p. 457; AN, F⁹ 476–7, *Département de la Côte-d'Or: Fédération*.

[19] AN, F⁹ 476–7, *Fédération Bourguignonne*.

[20] *Ibid.*, Prefect to Director General of the National Guard, 10 May 1815, F⁷ 3785, bulletins of 17 and 21 May 1815, and *Petites Affiches de Dijon*, 11 and 14 May 1815.

utmost to encourage and direct the movement. Although Dijon Jacobins had strong reservations concerning Napoleon, they were not at all shy about condemning the Bourbons, the nobility and certain elements of the clergy, as the original committee report made clear. But unlike the Bretons, who were particularly concerned with the imminent renewal of *chouannerie*, the Burgundian *fédérés* wished to serve notice to the 'barbares du nord' that a second invasion would be opposed by all means possible.

Like their Breton counterparts, Dijon *fédérés* were eager to work with the approval of the authorities. Indeed, the rapid organisation and growth of the movement can, at least in part, be attributed to the work of Bercagny. The association was by no means the work of Fouché. On the other hand, the federation was initiated by a group of Jacobins who were, as Thibaudeau happily noted, not necessarily the friends of Napoleon. The *fédérés* wished to unite behind the government to oppose invading Allied Armies and keep watch over any pro-Bourbon intrigues, but this did not make the association a Bonapartist tool.[21]

On 7 May, when the Dijon *commissaires* were presenting their report, a group of 'citoyens de tout âge et de toute condition' met at the *hôtel de ville* of Lyons to form a federation modelled on that of Brittany. Meeting under 'l'agrément de l'autorité', they adopted the Breton pact verbatim and on the same day gained the approbation of Count Maret, *commissaire extraordinaire*. A provisional bureau, composed entirely of local government officials, was set up at the *hôtel de ville*. Three days later, in the same setting, a general assembly was convened in order to select members of a central committee. No fewer than forty committee members were chosen, all of whom were government officials, *fonctionnaires*, or members of the National Guard. Jars, a bourgeois ex-military engineer and mayor of Lyons during the Hundred Days, was made president by acclamation.[22]

Jars, known for his devotion to the Emperor, appears to have been the driving force behind the Lyons federation and it is clear that he worked in close co-operation with Count Maret. Indeed, it is difficult not to suspect that the Lyons federation was conceived under the direction of the Imperial government. Certainly the preamble attached to the *fédéré* pact could have caused the central government no concern. It was strictly patriotic in character, calling upon all Frenchmen to unite behind the government to oppose invasion. No reference was made to aristocratic or clerical intrigue, and liberty was only given token mention. Moreover, there was no

[21] Thibaudeau, *Mémoires*, p. 467.
[22] The above details are culled from BN, LB[46] 319, *Fédération*, pp. 1–13; Le Gallo, *Les Cent-Jours*, p. 317.

mistaking the extraordinary popularity of Napoleon in France's second city. However, Lyonnais Bonapartism was stridently revolutionary in character; Baron Vouty-de-la-Tour, vice-president of the federation and First President of the Court of Lyons, had helped draw up the Lyons decrees of the *vol d'aigle*. In short, there was no need for the central government to give impulsion to the federative movement in Lyons; problems were more likely to occur as a result of the revolutionary nature of Lyonnais Bonapartism.[23]

In their *acte fédératif*, the Lyonnais invited all male citizens of the departments of the Rhône, Loire, Haute-Loire, Puy-de-Dôme, Cantal, Isère, Ain and Saône-et-Loire to join them in forming a single federation, to be named later.[24] As matters turned out, the citizens of the Saône-et-Loire chose to join the Burgundian federation, but the Lyonnais made up for that loss by gaining affiliations in other departments.

Most federations developed in the same manner. The original impetus was given by a group of patriots meeting in a departmental capital under the benign but watchful eye of the prefect. As soon as the *fédérés* had proclaimed their pact, they went about the business of selecting a central committee to handle correspondence and give direction, and chose deputies who would travel to the centres of neighbouring departments in order to spread the movement. There is little point in describing this process for all the federations, but it is useful to take the federation of Lyons as an example of how the movement was extended throughout the country.

The *fédérés* of Lyons went about their work with alacrity. No sooner was the pact prepared than it was published and copies posted to nearby departmental capitals. The deputies then carried proclamations, drawn up by the central committee, to the inhabitants of the departments to which they paid visit. Doubtless the local authorities had already been informed of the impending visit. One is inclined to doubt the royalist Audin's claim that the deputies travelled with police escorts, but his assertion that 'avant de partir, on eut soin de donner . . . une recette infaillible pour gagner les âmes au nouvel évangile' seems beyond dispute. There is no other way to explain the fact that deputies repeatedly found groups of like-minded citizens awaiting their arrival. In certain towns, such as Gap, local patriots had decided to send representatives to Lyons before the deputies of the Federation of Rhône actually arrived. When the deputies did arrive, a general assembly of all local officials and leading citizens was called. The deputies would

---

[23] Ibid., and G. Ribe, *L'Opinion publique et la vie politique à Lyon lors des premières années de la Seconde Restauration* (Paris, 1957), pp. 38–9. On the role of Vouty-de-la-Tour, see P. Gonnet, 'Les Cent-Jours à Lyon', *Revue d'histoire de Lyon*, 7 (1908), p. 56.

[24] BN, Lb⁴⁶ 319, *Fédération*, p. 4.

read an address to the assembly, calling upon them to join the federation and set up their own local bureau. After the latter had been put to the vote, local citizens would petition the prefect for permission to form an association. The prefect's approval was generally a matter of form.[25]

The *fédérés* of Lyons did not limit their travels to the departments cited in their original *acte*. Indeed, the association ultimately included ten departments. Within two weeks of the original general assembly of 10 May, deputies had arrived in Bourg-en-Bresse, Puy, Privas, Valence, Gap, Clermont-Ferrand, Grenoble and Montbrison. Later, they were to visit Chambéry.[26]

In Clermont-Ferrand, local patriots had already formed a departmental federation by the time the Lyons deputies appeared. The men of the smaller association readily joined that of the larger. A similar case arose in Grenoble, where, on 21 May, local patriots formed a *fédération dauphinoise*, which included the departments of the Isère, Hautes-Alpes and Mont-Blanc. Deputies from Grenoble departed for destinations such as Tullins, Saint-Marcellin and Valence where, indeed, they found a federative committee already established. It would appear that simple publication of the Breton pact in the *Moniteur* was sufficient to inspire emulation throughout France. Such certainly was the case at Montpellier and Besançon.[27]

After forming their own local chapter of the association, *fédérés* of towns such as Riom then sent deputies to nearby towns and communes. Within eight days of their original assembly, the *fédérés* of Riom had set up eleven bureaux in the towns and villages of their *arrondissement*. All but two of these bureaux were directed by the local mayor.[28]

However, not all visits produced the desired result. The citizens of Chambéry showed little interest in joining the movement. When three deputies from Lyons arrived at Aurillac on 25 May, the local officials and principal inhabitants decided to hold an assembly to deliberate upon the Lyonnais's proposal. The following day these men decided to form their own association, independent of that of the Rhône. According to the prefect of the Cantal, the deputies had irritated local officials by originally contacting men of poor repute. Nevertheless, the federation of the Rhône was a remarkable success. The conclusion of P. Gonnet in this regard cannot be

[25] J. M. Audin, *Tableau historique des événements qui se sont passés à Lyon depuis le retour de Bonaparte jusqu'au rétablissement de Louis XVIII* (Lyons, 1815), p. 111; AN, F⁷ 3785, bulletin of 25 May 1815; BN, Lb⁴⁶, 329, *Fédération*, pp. 1, 15–19.

[26] See the reports in AN, F⁷ 3785, bulletins of 15 May–5 June 1815.

[27] *L'Indépendant: chronique nationale, politique et littéraire*, 24 May 1815; *Moniteur*, 9 June 1815; A. Gras, *Grenoble en 1814 et 1815* (Grenoble, 1854), pp. 47–9; C. Weiss, *Journal 1815–22* (Paris, 1972), p. 55, and J. P. Thomas, *Précis historique des événements arrivés à Montpellier pendant les Cent-Jours de l'Interrègne* (Montpellier, 1976), pp. 32–3.

[28] BN, Lb⁴⁶, 319, *Fédération*, pp. 22–4.

improved: 'Le résultat de tous ces efforts fut la constitution, dans la région lyonnaise, d'une organisation formidable . . . les fédérés étaient les maîtres incontestés des vallées de la Saône, de l'Isère et du Rhône.'[29]

After the Dijonnais and Lyonnais had begun the process of making the movement truly national, federations sprang up throughout France. There is little point in narrating the origin of each federation, for the process was much the same wherever one occurred. Instead, the focus should now be on the extent to which the movement took root in the various regions of France and the general causes of federation.

In the west, the movement was a decidedly urban phenomenon, and the claim of the *fédérés* of Paimboeuf that a large number of inhabitants of the countryside were going to join their association must be regarded with a good deal of scepticism. Reports of public opinion made by Imperial and Restoration prefects alike emphasised that the countryside of Brittany remained largely pro-Bourbon. When columns of *fédérés* from such towns as Quimper, Brest, Landernau and Morlaix marched to the aid of smaller communities, the opposition they confronted was composed of 'cultivateurs'.[30] Nevertheless support was not restricted to large communities such as Nantes or Rennes; *fédérés* could be found in towns and villages as small as Thouars and Sérent.

Several towns in lower Normandy had joined the Breton federation by 29 April and, on 8 May, a *pacte fédératif* of the Maine-et-Loire was proclaimed in Angers. Patriots of other western departments joined the movement for much the same reasons as the Bretons. As the proclamation of the *fédérés* of Loches illustrated, behind their denunciations of 'factieux' and 'traîtres' loomed the shadow of civil war. This characteristic was also apparent in the preamble of the pact of Angers, in which specific reference to the horrors of civil war was made. At Niort, the federation of the Deux-Sèvres organised a fund to arm and equip an expanded National Guard which *fédérés* joined in large numbers. *Fédéré* centres in 1815 had been 'blue' strongholds during the Revolution.[31]

We have already seen that the federation of the Rhône spread as far south as the Drôme, and that the Burgundian federation reached as far north as

[29] AN, F[7] 3785, bulletins of 11 and 20 June 1815; Gonnet, 'Lyon', p. 121.
[30] *Moniteur*, 7 May 1815; R. Grand, *La Chouannerie de 1815* (Paris, 1942), pp. 39–40; C. Langlois, *Un Diocèse breton au début du XIXe siècle: le diocèse de Vannes, 1800–30* (Paris, 1974), p. 219; AN, F[7] 9650, prefectoral reports of 6 June and 7 August 1815, F[7] 9671, prefectoral report of 19 July 1815, F[7] 9656, *Rapport de l'expédition des fédérés de Quimper*.
[31] *Moniteur*, 16 May 1815; *Indépendant*, 8 June 1815; J. Richard, *Histoire du département des Deux-Sèvres sous le Consulat, l'Empire, et les Cent-Jours* (Saint-Maixent, 1848), pp. 286–7.

the Haute-Marne. This defensive band along the eastern frontier was further extended by a series of associations. A federation of the Moselle was proclaimed in Metz on 27 May; a federation of the Bas-Rhin was proclaimed in Strasbourg on 17 May; a federation of the Haut-Rhin was proclaimed in Colmar on 31 May, and a federation of the Doubs was proclaimed in Besançon on 26 May. There can be little doubt that fears of invasion produced in these regions a patriotic ardour which government authorities were more than willing to tap, but which required a minimum of encouragement. This was apparent in the *acte fédératif des Alsaciens*, which commenced: 'Considérant que la France, et particulièrement ses départements frontières, sont menacés une seconde fois d'une invasion aggressive . . . '. General Rapp commented that circumstances had produced an extreme patriotism in Alsace, the like of which had not been seen since the Revolution. According to the historian P. Leuilliot, the Bourbons were unloved in Alsace; their 'original sin' had been to return to France in the baggage train of the Allies.[32] In Nancy the federation was founded by eighty-eight citizens led by Azaiis, recently appointed rector of the university and a devout Bonapartist. Here again, territorial integrity and political independence were the central themes of the federative pact and response was strong. The *fédération lorraine* comprised the departments of the Meurthe, Vosges and Meuse. Under the auspices of *commissaires* from Nancy, a federative committee was formed at Saint-Dié and measures were taken to set up bureaux in the communes of the Vosges, where Napoleon enjoyed a great deal of popularity.[33]

Certainly there was nothing spontaneous about the movement in Alsace. Although the original federation of Strasbourg was formed by citizens, magistrates and *fonctionnaires* of that city, the provincial association was organised directly by the prefect Jean de Bry. In an *arrêté* of 22 May, he ordered that each mayor of the department of the Bas-Rhin convene his municipal council to prepare a local chapter of the association and recruit members. Each municipal council should choose two deputies who were to travel to Colmar, in the Haut-Rhin, to help form a *fédération alsacienne*. De Bry was ably abetted by Cunier, sub-prefect at Sélestat, and Golbéry, Imperial *procureur* at Colmar. Nevertheless, the movement was popular.

---

[32] *Indépendant*, 3 June 1815; *Moniteur*, 8 and 9 June 1815; AN, AFIV 1937, *Acte Fédératif des Alsaciens*; P. Leuilliot, 'L'Alsace en 1815', *Revue d'Alsace*, 75 (1928), p. 131, and by the same author, *La Première Restauration et les Cent-Jours en Alsace* (Paris, 1958), p. 232.

[33] *Le Patriote de '89: journal de soir, politique et littéraire*, 8 June 1815; Le Gallo, *Les Cent-Jours*, pp. 324–5; G. Baumont, 'Saint-Dié en 1815', *Le Pays Lorrain*, 16 (1924), pp. 226–34; G. Richard, 'Une conspiration policière à Nancy en 1816', *Annales de l'Est, année* 10, 3 (1959), p. 173, and by the same author, 'Les Cent-Jours à Nancy', *Pays Lorrain*, année 38 (1957), p. 89.

On 31 May the prefect of the Haut-Rhin reported to Davout that the citizens of his department 'se portent en foule à leurs mairies respectives pour se faire inscrire comme fédérés'.[34] A curious but not entirely unique situation arose at Besançon, capital of the Doubs. Several patriots, including the regicide Monnot, took it upon themselves to organise a federation, but found their efforts opposed by the prefect Derville-Maléchard. Fouché, Minister of Police, put an end to this anomaly by informing the prefect that, at least for the moment, federations were very much in the central government's scheme of things. The point to note, however, is that while the government was willing to make use of the federation in Besançon, it played no part in its origins.[35]

The associations considered until now generally developed rapidly and grew to fairly large proportions. To varying degrees, they were the product of both local patriotism and government direction. In these areas, the threats of civil and foreign war had done nothing but stimulate the movement. In other areas, however, where the movement often started late, federations were occasionally the direct product of government efforts to counterbalance opposition groups which could include the majority of citizens.

Hostility to Napoleon was particularly apparent in the south; yet even here, the Imperial government did find substantial support. In Provence, the department of the Bouches-du-Rhône appears to have been decidedly royalist terrain, whereas reaction in the Var was mixed. News of Bonaparte's return produced 'euphoria' at Draguignan, but at Toulon a *fédération provençale* was proclaimed on 22 May, ostensibly by 'une foule de citoyens de toutes les classes', but probably by the eleven government officials, *fonctionnaires*, soldiers and members of the National Guard who signed the pact. The pact called on patriots of the Var, Bouches-du-Rhône, Vaucluse and Basses-Alpes to join the Toulonnais, emphasised that 'ce n'est plus pour la cause d'un Roi que les Rois se liguent contre nous', and argued that the Allies were bent on nothing less than the complete destruction of France as a political entity. Bureaux were set up at Bandol, Beausset, Castellet, Saint-Nazaire, Six-Fours and Le Val and registered a significant number of recruits.[36] From the moment of his arrival in early June, the pre-

---

[34] AN, AFIV 1937, *Extrait des Registres de la Préfecture du Département du Haut-Rhin du 22 May 1815*, and Minister of War to the Emperor, 5 June 1815; Leuilliot, 'Alsace', pp. 257–8.

[35] Weiss, *Journal*, pp. 55–7.

[36] AN, F⁷ 3785, bulletins of 24 May and 2 June 1815, AFIV 1938, *Pacte Fédératif*; *Indépendant*, 10 June 1815; E. Baratier, editor, *Histoire de La Provence* (Toulouse, 1969), p. 444; C. Alleaume, 'La Terreur Blanche dans le Var', *Bulletin de la Société d'études scientifiques et archéologiques de Draguignan*, 45 (1944–5), pp. 5–17.

fect Didier set about organising the federation of the Basses-Alpes in order to combat royalists. A central committee was established at Digne and branches were founded in Mezel, Volonne, Châteaux Arnoux, Gréoux, Barcelonnette, Entrevaux and Forcalquier. This was the part of Provence in which Bonaparte probably enjoyed greatest support and, aided and advised by *fédérés*, Didier was able to strengthen the government's control of the department; when trouble did arise, it came from the western departments of the old province.[37]

On 3 June, Davout, acting upon instructions from Napoleon, ordered the Duke of Albufera to direct the *fédérés* of Lyons to federate with Marseilles. At the same time, he ordered Marshal Brune to 'pousser les patriotes de Marseille à se fédérer avec Toulon, Grenoble, Lyon, Tarascon, Arles et le Var'. Thus, in Provence the government, under direct instructions from the Emperor, did its utmost not just to encourage federations but actually to found them.[38]

In the Bouches-du-Rhône such efforts gained slim rewards. When the *fédérés* of Toulon duly arrived at Marseilles, the police lieutenant could only turn to the officers of the National Guard to gain signatures for the pact. Even then, approval was only apparent. According to the lieutenant, 'les officiers ont promis d'obéir à Sa Majesté sans préciser qu'il s'agit de l'Empereur'. He added 'il faut maintenant filer doux; la garnison est trop faible pour qu'on puisse faire tout ce qu'il faudrait'.[39]

Nevertheless, small groups of patriots in towns such as Salon, Arles, Tarascon and Avignon did manage to form federations. They found themselves sadly outnumbered by royalists and had to rely upon the authorities and local garrisons for protection. On 30 June the prefect of the Vaucluse reported that 'il se forme . . . des rassemblements dans les environs qui font croire que la ville d'Avignon ne pourra pas opposer une longue résistance'. Organised by men such as Jean-Baptiste Vinai, president of the association, Tissot, a lawyer, and the notorious Agricole Moreau, the *fédérés* of the Vaucluse did, however, put up enough of a fight to ensure a great deal of hardship in the months to follow.[40]

The situation in eastern Languedoc was similar. In the Gard, an especially truculent association was formed at Nîmes, and here *fédérés* could draw support from neighbouring Protestant communes in their efforts to dominate a population which otherwise was predominantly

[37] C. Cauvin, 'Le retour de l'Ile d'Elbe et les Cent-Jours dans les Basses-Alpes', *Bulletin de la société scientifique et littéraire des Basses-Alpes*, 21 (1926–7), pp. 126–7.
[38] AG, 1K1 47, Minister of War to the Duke of Albufera and to Marshal Brune, 3 June 1815.
[39] F. Tavernier, 'Les Cent-Jours à Marseille', *Provence historique*, 36 (1959), p. 181.
[40] AN, F⁷ 3785–6, bulletins of 30 June and 4 November 1815; APP, A A/331, reports 400–24.

Catholic, royalist and hostile. *Fédérés* in towns such as Uzès and Ners and villages such as Générac and Beauvoisin faced similarly long odds in their attempts to combat royalist sedition. Nevertheless, in predominantly Protestant areas such as the Gardonnenque, *fédérés* had the upper hand. Although P. M. Jones does not indicate in his study of the Massif Central whether there were federations in this region, we do know that there were associations in Le Puy, Saint-Hippolyte and Rodez, and the author's descriptions of the way in which 'Bonapartist nostalgia mingled with an older tradition of republicanism' suggest that Daniel Noyon, *négociant*, must have found Millau excellent recruiting ground for the federation of Aveyron.[41]

In a pessimistic account of public opinion at Montpellier, an Imperial *commissaire extraordinaire* reported that, whereas at Nîmes the government could count upon the loyalty of the one-third of the population that was Protestant and a minority of Catholics, at Montpellier there were few Protestants and all the social classes were royalist. He attributed the paucity of support to the economic decline of Montpellier during the Empire. Nevertheless, Joseph Cambon, apparently acting on his own initiative but co-ordinating his efforts with General Gilly, founded a federation of the Hérault in the third week of May which was nothing if not combative. Bureaux were established in neighbouring towns such as Saint-Pons, Lodève, Clermont-Lodève and Gignac and villages such as Lunel. In the first week of June, *fédérés* of Montpellier and Béziers joined forces with the Army to put down a seditious movement at Agde.[42]

Further to the west, the movement also confronted significant opposition, although *fédérés* appear to have been in a stronger position. Associations were founded at points as diverse as Perpignan, Salies-du-Salat, Condom and Pau. The federation of Foix was not organised until 1 June, but the prefect of the Ariège thought it useful to 'employer les fédérés à diriger l'esprit public, combattre les intrigues du parti royaliste, et les fausses nouvelles qu'ils ne cessent de répandre'. *Fédérés* were duly issued arms and munitions to enforce their 'patriotic' intentions. Six weeks later, it was the turn of royalist officials to proclaim against the seditious activities of *fédéré* agents at Pau. The ultra-royalist Villeneuve described the federation of the Basses-Pyrénées as an 'association monstrueuse, la plus monstrueuse qui ait jamais existé: celle des prolétaires armés contre des propriétaires désarmés'. Given that electors subsequently had to be warned

---

[41] E. Daudet, *La Terreur Blanche* (Paris, 1878), pp. 71–4, 96, 377–8, 384, 390–1; P. M. Jones, *Politics and Rural Society: The Southern Massif Central c. 1750–1880* (Cambridge, 1985), pp. 208–13; AN, F⁷ 3028, *Extrait des arrestations*, pp. 246 and 298.

[42] *Patriote de '89*, 12 June 1815; AN, F⁷ 9663, *Commissaire Extraordinaire* to the Minister of the Interior, 5 May 1815; *Moniteur*, 21 June 1815; Thomas, *Précis*, pp. 32–4.

not to submit to the pernicious influence of *fédérés*, one is disinclined to accept 'proletarian' as an accurate description of the social character of the association, though there probably was some truth in assertions that *fédérés* remained true to their 'affreuse mission: proscrire la maison royale de France'.[43]

Imperial authorities were less positive than the prefect of the Ariège in their assessments of the *fédérés* of Toulouse. Founded on 6 May, the federation of the Midi soon numbered 800 members. Although the *menu peuple* joined *en masse*, men of the 'première classe' remained aloof. Indeed, some lower-class *fédérés* showed so much enthusiasm that the police lieutenant concluded that action might have to be taken against them.[44] A *commission de direction* led by Baron Julien, *maréchal de camp*, and Major Maymat decided to suspend general assemblies while seeking a decision from Fouché whether to go forward with the association. Boyer-Fonfrède, an industrialist who had helped to organise the federation, wrote to Fouché as follows:

Le peuple se fédérera en masse, cela est sûr, mais c'est à vous à peser jusqu'à quel point cela doit aller, car sa tendance est de ressembler à '93. La résistance qu'il aperçoit dans la classe privilégiée le pousse à agir contre elle, et vous savez mieux que personne le danger qu'il pourrait y avoir à ne pas en être le maître.

By 3 June official sanction had been gained, however, and Boyer-Fonfrède had become president. In a letter to the prefect, Fouché gave unequivocal support for the federative movement:

Vous ne pouviez, Monsieur, faire rien de plus utile et qui soit plus à-propos que d'asseoir les bases d'une fédération nationale dans le département que vous administrez. Ne doutez pas de l'approbation du gouvernement.

The Minister of Police then added that precious time should not be wasted by seeking cautiously to select *fédérés*. Boyer-Fonfrède immediately requested the sub-prefect to provide him with a list of the mayors of nearby towns and villages who marched 'le mieux dans le sens du gouvernement'. By 18 June there were at least 1,200 *fédérés* in Toulouse and recruitment was progressing nicely in nearby towns. The prefect remained wary nonetheless:

Malgré l'utilité de ces réunions et la sagesse des statuts en réglement de la confédér-ation, je pense qu'il convient de rendre les assemblées peu fréquentes, de surveiller

---

[43] AN, F⁷ 3785, bulletin of 9 June 1815; Duc de Castries, *La Terreur Blanche* (Paris, 1981), pp. 153–4; P. Hourmat, 'Les élections des 14 et 22 Août 1815 dans les Basses-Pyrénées', *Société des sciences, lettres et arts de Bayonne, série no.* 166 (1965), pp. 45–6.
[44] AN, F⁷ 3785, bulletins of 10 and 18–19 June 1815; J. J. Hémardinquer, 'Un Libéral: F.-B. Boyer-Fonfrède (1767–1845)', *Annales du Midi*, 73 (1961), p. 174.

et d'en écarter même certains individus qui, par un zèle inconsidéré, ou par tout autre motif condemnable, ne se renfermeraient pas dans les bornes de l'institution à laquelle ils se sont soumis. J'emploierai à cet égard tous mes soins et l'influence de mon autorité si elle devenait nécessaire.

As we shall soon see, this reserved attitude on the part of the prefect was part of a national pattern: where federations were discouraged or simply not encouraged, this usually resulted from the scepticism of a prefect concerned by the revolutionary elements of Napoleon's new following. In the Haute-Garonne, as in several other departments, the federative movement was able to develop because of the firm backing of a minister of the central government. Ultimately, *fédérés* could be found in virtually all of the major towns, and most of the communes, of the department.[45]

A federation of the Tarn was declared on 5 June, and most towns of the department joined it. Led by Paul-Augustin Tridoulat, a retired colonel, and Jean-Eugène Fabre, mayor during the Terror and an officer of the National Guard, the *fédérés* of Albi concerned themselves strictly with maintaining public order. *Fédérés* at Rabastens, organised by Mayor Arquier 'sur les conseils' of the *conventionnel* Jean-Paul Gouzy, apparently did not have much impact on their community. At Roquecourbe, Enjalbert, 'ex-prêtre et notaire', carried his own hand- written appeal from door to door and enjoyed much success in enrolling local Protestants. At Gaillac the movement 'prit une certaine ampleur'. There the association was presided over by Gabriel Montaigne, president of the *tribunal de première instance*, and led by several *huissiers* and Serou, a Jacobin director of the post office. At Marssac 'l'élan d'adhésion à l'Empire fut spontané'. According to the royalist mayor, 'A peine l'usurpateur eut mis le pied sur le territoire français que la grande majorité des habitants de ma commune manifesta un dévouement sans réserve à cet ennemi du monde.' The only town of consequence in the department that resisted the movement was Castres, where the majority of citizens remained resolutely royalist. Indeed, on the day after Waterloo, before news of the débâcle had reached the Tarn, rumours circulated that the Bourbon flag had been hoisted at Castres. The *fédérés* of Albi, accompanied by troops of the line, therefore journeyed to Castres where they were met with cries of 'Vive le Roi! Mort au bonapartistes!' However, negotiations led to a peaceful resolution and the *fédérés* returned to Albi. Thus, although the movement was not entirely

---

[45] Hémardinquer, 'Boyer-Fonfrède', pp. 174–6; AN, F⁷ 9659, Prefect to Minister of Police, 22 June 1815; AD H.-G., 4M34, Minister of Police to Prefect, 3 June 1815, 4M35, *Etat pour faire suite.*

spontaneous in the Tarn, it was far-reaching and popular except in Castres.[46]

Such was not the case in Bordeaux and the Gironde. When Résigny arrived on 7 June, as *officier d'ordonnance de l'empereur* with the special mission of forming a federation, the prefect was surprised and suspicious. After having verified Résigny's credentials, the prefect informed him that such a project would be ill advised in Bordeaux. The prefect did, however, suggest that such an exercise might usefully be conducted in Libourne, where local Protestants had shown themselves to be willing. Résigny's attempts at Bordeaux appear to have met with a good deal of resistance. In a report to General Clausel, he advised that he would have to have money to purchase arms if the federation were to be successful. Without arms, royalists could not be disarmed and troops could not be freed to serve elsewhere. If troops of the line did leave, and *fédérés* were not sufficiently armed and organised, open rebellion would result. Although some recruits were ultimately gained in Libourne and Saint-Médard, the movement was hardly spontaneous in the Gironde, and, indeed, the chief organiser had to be recruited from elsewhere![47]

A much more promising association was formed at Périgueux in the Dordogne on 24 May, on the request of several owners of *biens nationaux*. Their pact was signed by 773 *fédérés*, many of whom hailed from diverse parts of the department, and called on all good citizens to rally round the *patrie*. Local bureaux were set up in the neighbouring towns of Forges, Robier, Nontron, Thiviers, Bergerac, Eymet, Monzié, Sarlat and Ribérac. It is instructive to note that none of the six members of the central committee were *fonctionnaires*, soldiers or government officials, although federative assemblies did take place under the watchful eyes of Lieutenant-General Lucotte and General Pinoteau. Apparently, demand for a federation did not need to be created by the government in Périgueux.[48]

However, an attempt to form a federation of the departments of the Dordogne, Lot, Haute-Vienne and Corrèze ran aground at Brive. V. de Seillac explained this by simply stating that Napoleon did not favour 'ce

---

[46] J. Vanel, 'Le Mouvement fédératif de 1815 dans le département du Tarn', *Gaillac et le pays tarnais, 31ᵉ congrès d'études de la fédération des sociétés académiques et savantes de Languedoc-Pyrénées-Gascogne* (Gaillac, 1977), pp. 390–3; J.-L. Biget, editor, *Histoire d'Albi* (Toulouse, 1983), pp. 246–7.

[47] AN, F⁷ 3785–6, bulletins of 15 June 1815, 20 and 22 February 1816; J. Cavaignac, 'Les Cent-Jours à Bordeaux', *Revue historique de Bordeaux et du département de la Gironde*, 4 (1966), p. 70.

[48] AN, AFIV 1937, bulletin of 28 May 1815 and *Pacte de la Confédération Périgourdine*, F⁷ 3735, bulletin of 24 December 1815; J. L'Homer, *Les Cent-Jours et la Terreur Blanche* (Paris, 1904), pp. 29–34; G. Rocal, *De Brumaire à Waterloo en Périgord* (Paris, 1942), I, pp. 253–5.

mouvement', but given what we have seen of governmental policy elsewhere, this seems unlikely. That Camille Périer subsequently lauded the
lack of a federation of the Corrèze, 'exemple bien peu commun et peut-être
unique dans ces temps de vertige et d'erreur', strongly suggests that the
movement foundered here because of a hostile prefect.[49]

In encouraging the federative movement in the south, the central government hoped to find a force capable of enforcing order amidst a population
which was often hostile, so that troops of the line might be free to serve elsewhere. Later we shall investigate to what extent these hopes were fulfilled,
but for the moment it can at least be noted that the federative movement in
the south was far from insignificant.

Response was relatively weak in the north. As was to be expected, the
enthusiasm of Brittany spread into the western parts of Normandy and
there were *fédérés* at Cherbourg, Avranches, Alençon and Argentan, but
the departments of the Calvados, Eure and Seine-Inférieure proved
resistant. Although federations were proclaimed at Evreux and Rouen,
these solely included members of the National Guard and had little
influence on the general populace. Indeed, when National Guardsmen
petitioned the prefect of the Eure for permission to federate with Guardsmen at Andelys, Bernay, Louviers and Pont-Audemer, Duval ignored the
request and thereby forfeited a potential means of rallying support for the
Emperor. Perhaps as a result of this failure of initiative, the Eure was one
department where Jacobins and Bonapartists failed to unite.[50] The same
appears true of the Seine-Inférieure; here also one must question the role of
the prefect. Though probably not a closet monarchist, de Girardin appears
to have done very little to rally support; he was constantly the target of
criticisms made by the *conventionnel* Le Pelletier, sub-prefect at Dieppe.
Despite repeated demands from old revolutionaries, de Girardin did little
to remove royalist mayors and administrators. The mayor of Rouen prohibited the singing of the *Marseillaise* at the theatre, thus blocking a standard manifestation of revolutionary Bonapartism, and here too federative
initiatives were ignored.

Le Pelletier argued that the masses were confused by seeing the agents of
counter-revolution left in administrative positions and, hence, no significant rallying could take place. Without taking the old *conventionnel*'s
argument too far (a town such as Le Havre apparently would not have

---

[49] V. de Seillac, 'Corrèze au Cent-Jours', *Bulletin de la société des lettres de la Corrèze*, 8
(1886), p. 480; P. Barral, *Les Périers dans l'Isère au XIXᵉ Siècle* (Paris, 1964), pp. 90–1.
[50] J. Vidalenc, *Le Département de l'Eure sous la monarchie constitutionnelle, 1814–1848*
(Paris, 1952), pp. 68–71; *Indépendant*, 2 June 1815.

rallied to Napoleon under any circumstances), it does seem logical to conclude that the failure of De Girardin to give support probably did prevent the movement from having any impact in the department. By the time de Girardin was transferred to another department, on 17 May, it was too late to reverse the situation. Where officials such as Le Pelletier and his fellow *conventionnel* Choudieu were more determined, a federation was organised at Dieppe. But the essence of the movement was to unite support throughout a region and the Dieppe *fédérés* must have felt decidedly lonely.[51]

Despite the efforts of both civil and military officials in Caen, who posted placards calling upon patriots to federate on 3 May, little of consequence was achieved. Although an association was ultimately organised, *fédérés* had little effect upon royalists, who enjoyed the backing of most of the population. At Lisieux, several *jeunes gens* expressed their desire to form a federation to the prefect of the Calvados, but he refused permission for an assembly. He had been warned that 'pendant que ces jeunes gens se fédéraient pour la cause de France, une contre fédération plus nombreusement se formait aussi', and had decided that the best policy lay in banning such associations altogether. As a result, he had to answer some searching questions from Davout, which made clear that he was not following general government policy.[52]

East of the Somme, at Laon on 23 May, a *confédération picarde* was formed, including the departments of the Somme, Aisne, Nord and Pas-de-Calais. Deputies were duly despatched to the three other departmental capitals. Although several members of the National Guard, including the commandant Oyon-Regnault, became members of the central committee, government officials do not appear to have played a leading part in drawing up the pact. Within two weeks the deputies had succeeded in rallying support in Amiens, Lille and Arras. Patriots at Château-Thierry, who had already set up their own federation, joined that of Picardy on 5 June. While it is difficult to assess how popular the movement was in Picardy, it does seem significant that Baron Merlin de Thionville thought the association sufficient to form a mobile force of 600 men.[53] The prefect of the Pas-de-Calais, André Dumont, an old Montagnard, terrorist and regicide, organ-

[51] W. A. Pruitt, 'Opposition to the Bourbon Restoration in Rouen and the Seine-Inférieure, 1815–20', Ph.D. dissertation, University of Virginia, 1981, pp. 56–74; J. Vidalenc, *Aspects de la Seine-Inférieure sous la Restauration* (Rouen, 1981), p. 49; AN, F⁷ 3784, bulletin of 20 June 1815.
[52] G. Lavalley, 'Le Duc D'Aumont et les Cent-Jours en Normandie', *Mémoires de l'Académie Nationale des sciences, belles lettres et arts de Caen* (1898), pp. 243–4, 256; AN, AFIV 1937, Minister of War to the Emperor, 23 May 1815.
[53] AN, AFIV 1935–6, *Confédération Picarde* and Thionville's letter of 9 June 1815; *Moniteur*, 8 and 9 June 1815.

ised a *fête de la Fédération* on 11 June, in imitation of that of 1793. Troops, members of the National Guard, firemen and government officials took part and recruitment was subsequently conducted in neighbouring towns. Nevertheless, the people of Arras remained unimpressed and when Imperial troops departed on 27 June, 300 *fédérés* from Amiens had to be imported to subdue royalists.[54]

As one would expect, the federations of west-central France were preoccupied by the royalist threat in the Vendée. There were strong federations at Le Mans, Angers, Niort, Loches and Poitiers, where Métirier, a professor at the law school, and L'Official, a judge, used the association to 'terrorise' royalists.[55] Less resounding echoes could be heard at Saintes, La Rochelle and Angoulême. But as one moves into the interior, it becomes more difficult to uncover information on the movement. There were, however, some notable exceptions. Mater, a lawyer and partisan of the Emperor, and several other lawyers, including Dumoustier, helped to form a *fédération berruyère* at Bourges on 27 May. As we shall see, these *fédérés* were to prove themselves a determined lot during the Second Restoration. Sauty, a judge, and Desbordes, a deputy of the Chamber of the Hundred Days, played the leading parts in setting up an association at Limoges.[56]

Given the extent of opposition to the Bourbon government in the early years of the Second Restoration, it is tempting to speculate that the Creuse must have been fertile terrain, but we know only that Bonapartists, Jacobins and liberals set up an association at La Souterraine. From the east, the tentacles of the federation of the Rhône reached far into central France. Lyonnais deputies helped found intermediary committees at Riom, Clermont-Ferrand, Montbrison, Saint-Etienne, Brioude and Le Puy; in general, response was greater in the Puy-de-Dôme than the Haute-Loire.[57]

Although the Nièvre had emerged unscathed by occupation in 1814, Allied armies had come close enough to leave inhabitants extremely worried by the possibility of a second invasion in 1815. Nevers was a prison centre where enemy soldiers had made a strong impression on local people. According to one citizen, Russian soldiers had to be kept isolated and manacled because at night they had 'l'habitude de pratiquer aux jambes des

[54] G. de Hautecloque, 'Les Cent-Jours dans le Pas-de-Calais', *Mémoires de l'Académie des sciences, lettres et arts d'Arras*, 36 (1905), pp. 137–40, 155.

[55] *Indépendant*, 8 June 1815; AN, F⁷ 6630, *Notes de police*, p. 456.

[56] *Indépendant*, 1 June 1815; AN, F⁷ 3737, bulletin of 3 April 1817.

[57] AN, F⁷ 3737, bulletin of 2 May 1816; R. Boudard, 'L'Agitation politique dans le département de la Creuse au début de la Seconde Restauration', *Cahiers d'histoire*, 13 (1968), pp. 303–6; D. Michel, 'Les "alliés" en Haute-Loire, l'occupation et ses problèmes (1814–1815), *Cahiers de la Haute-Loire* (1968), p. 45.

prisonniers endormis une incision au moyen d'un outil très tranchant, et ils suçaient le sang qui en coulait jusqu'au point que ces malhereux ne se réveillaient quelques fois que pour rendre le dernier soupir'. Blood did not run as freely at Nevers as in parts of the south during the Hundred Days, but political divisions were sharp enough, with the masses opting for revolutionary Bonapartism. During the *vol d'aigle*, when the prefect Fiévée had showed an inclination to muster resistance to Napoleon's advance, a crowd of some 4,000 had assembled in protest. Fiévée had been manhandled, stripped of his cross of the Legion of Honour for betraying Bonaparte, and forced to shout 'Vive l'Empereur!' Taking advantage of revolutionary fervour, Albon Lefiot, yet another old regicide retaining local influence, organised a federation whose radicalism worried Count Colchen, Napoleon's *commissaire extraordinaire*. According to the prefect Le Bergerie *fils* (Fiévée having discreetly disappeared), the association was more popular in the countryside than in the capital itself. Apparently not sharing Colchen's qualms, Le Bergerie threw himself fully behind the association, giving full publicity to the federative pact and, ultimately, providing *fédérés* with guns. In doing so he had the backing of the Minister of the Interior.[58]

On 6 May, four young men, animated 'du même patriotisme que les Bretons', drew up an appeal in which they called on the young men of Paris and the Ile de France to federate. Rather prudently, they sent their appeal to Fouché, so that he might make any necessary alterations and then send copies to the schools of Paris and centres of public administration. Instead, Fouché chose to forward it to Réal, who duly took measures to investigate the motives and character of the four students. Police officers subsequently gave favourable reports of the young men, but by then the matter of federating had passed into other hands.[59]

Although the government thus revealed itself to be wary, the possibility of some such mass organisation was being discussed in high government circles. Indeed, the Council of State had come to conclude that some sort of *levée en masse* might be useful, despite the inconvenience and difficulty of organising it. Although eager to make use of 'la classe des citoyens chez laquelle le sentiment de la liberté individuelle et l'indignation de joug de

[58] E. Duminy, 'Notes sur le passage des Alliés dans le département de la Nièvre' and 'Nevers pendant les Cent-Jours', *Bulletin de la Société Nivernaise des lettres, sciences et arts*, 11 (1906), pp. 249–50, 328–9; G. Thuillier, 'Le Corps Préfectoral en Nivernais de 1814 à 1830', *Actes du 96ᵉ Congrès National des Sociétés Savantes: Toulouse* (1971), vol. I, pp. 374–8; AN, Fⁱᶜ III, Nièvre 8, correspondence between prefect and the Minister of the Interior, 7 and 17 June 1815.

[59] APP, A A/330, 6 and 12 May 1815.

l'étranger se développent le plus fortement', the Council did not wish to create an institution capable of rivalling the Guard. This problem was overcome when General Dumas, commander of the National Guard, suggested that all men whose professions did not allow them to become members of that institution be organised into *bataillons de tirailleurs* of the National Guard.

Napoleon encountered just such a group of citizens when he visited the *faubourg* Saint-Antoine on 8 May. When workers complained of not having been armed to defend Paris in 1814, the Emperor replied that if such a situation were again to arise, he had 40,000 guns and 1,000 officers of the line 'pour armer et diriger la population'.[60] The good citizens took Bonaparte at his word, and on 10 May a *pacte fédératif* of the *faubourgs* Saint-Antoine and Saint-Marceau was proclaimed. The pact, signed by 3,000 inhabitants and workers, called upon the Emperor to give their association a military organisation and provide them with arms. The arms apparently were not to be used exclusively against the foreigner, however, for the *fédérés* cited the necessity to 'frapper de terreur les traîtres qui pourraient désirer encore une fois l'avilissement de leur patrie'. As well as their admiration of the Emperor, they also declared their devotion to 'la cause du peuple'.[61]

Their call was heard by the Emperor, and by 12 May instructions had been issued for a military review. Approximately 12,000 *fédérés*, many of whom revealed themselves to be old soldiers by their disciplined marching, attended the review on 13 May. After listening to an address read by an old soldier, but written by the *conventionnel* Thuriot, Napoleon officially promised to put the association on a military footing. Bonaparte, who was able to address some of the old soldiers by name, then marched several steps with the *fédérés*, and, according to some observers, thereby gained a devotion bordering on adoration. On 15 May, an Imperial decree announced the creation of twenty-four battalions of *fédérés-tirailleurs* which would be armed and organised as part of the National Guard.[62]

Also on the 15th, inhabitants of the *faubourgs* Saint-Martin and Saint-Lazare and the *côté du nord* met in 'la maison de Saint-Lazare' to prepare a second federation. Three days later they became affiliated to the original association.[63]

---

[60] AN, AFIV 1935, undated *Note sur la levée en masse.*

[61] *Moniteur*, 9 and 12 May 1815.

[62] *Patriote de '89* and *Indépendant*, 14 May 1815; *Journal de l'Empire*, 26 May 1815; J. Tulard, *Nouvelle Histoire de Paris: le Consulat et l'Empire* (Paris, 1970), pp. 400–1; *Correspondance de Napoléon I, publié par ordre de l'Empereur Napoléon III* (Paris, 1859), XXI, pp. 127–8.

[63] *Journal de l'Empire*, 18 and 26 May 1815; *Patriote de '89*, 19 May 1815.

Not to be outdone, on 17 May Parisian patriots launched an appeal to their fellow citizens to rally to the defence of the *patrie* and join them in federating. Significantly, no mention of 'terror' was made in this appeal, nor did the subject arise in the pact they proclaimed nine days later. Nevertheless, the Parisian *fédérés* did concur with Napoleon that France had fallen in 1814 due to the machinations of certain traitors, and saw the return of the 'Héros national' as a liberation of France. Carret, a *chevalier de la Légion d'honneur*, became president of the federation.[64]

Meanwhile, the federation of the *faubourgs* was growing rapidly; on 19 May, the entire corporation of the *ouvriers charbonniers* of Saint-Antoine had joined. By 20 May, recruiting for the *fédérés-tirailleurs* had begun, and on the following day the mayor of the eighth *arrondissement* informed the *fédérés* that their wish had been granted, and posted instructions of how they could become members of the *fédérés-tirailleurs*. Three days later, the mayor of the twelfth *arrondissement* followed the same procedure.[65]

Thus, after only three weeks, a powerful federative movement was well under way. Unlike other cities in France, there were three federative organisations in Paris. However, it is clear that the federation of the *faubourgs* formed the nucleus of the *fédérés-tirailleurs*, and, indeed, after the creation of the latter organisation, little was heard of the former. Could it be that the creation of the *fédérés-tirailleurs* removed the *raison d'être* of the original association? Whatever the answer, the revolutionary rhetoric of the *faubourgs* clearly indicated that this federation was not the result of government initiative. Whether Napoleon actually feared the revolutionary inclinations of these *fédérés* is a subject which will be developed later, but there can be no doubt that he, at least at first, seriously considered arming these men and knew of the influence he exercised over most of them.

The Parisian federation appears to have been a different kettle of fish. Certainly their pact, which has been attributed to Carret, gave the government little cause for concern over revolutionary tendencies.[66] Moreover, the Parisian federation did not affiliate to the association of the *faubourgs* and maintained a separate identity. Unlike the federation of the *faubourgs*, it was not reviewed by the Emperor, nor was it put on a military footing.

Finally, there is no evidence that Fouché had anything to do with the origins of the federations, and his treatment of the original request of the four young men indicated quite the opposite. The federation of the *faubourgs* had a spontaneous origin and the Parisian federation was

---

[64] *Patriote de '89*, 24 May 1815; AN, AFIV 1935, *Pacte Fédératif des Parisiens*.
[65] *Patriote de '89*, 20, 21, 24 May 1815.
[66] See Le Gallo, *Les Cent-Jours*, pp. 310–11.

probably more the product of a desire to follow the example of the
faubourgs than of government manipulation. Nevertheless, the government did show itself to be quite prepared and even eager to take advantage
of the patriotic *élan* of the populace of the capital. That *élan* was created by
the prospect of war and invasion.

By way of summary, then, the federative movement reveals itself as a very
complex phenomenon from its very origin. It cannot be defined simply as
the product of Fouché's intrigues, government manipulation, popular *élan*
or as a *levée en masse*.

The movement was massive. Although emulation of the Breton
precedent was by no means uniform over the many regions of France, the
movement spread with extraordinary rapidity throughout the country.
This in itself suggests that *fédérés* had previous experience of this sort of
endeavour, memories of which Imperial censorship had not quite erased.
The government clearly played an important part in facilitating the
expansion of the movement, but the arrival of the *Moniteur* reporting the
Breton pact was often sufficient to commence organisation. The latter
appeared six days after the edition announcing the *Acte Additionnel*.

Most federations resulted from a combination of spontaneous *élan* and
government support. In many associations, such as the Breton federation,
the first step had been taken by private citizens, but these individuals
inevitably approached Imperial authorities for encouragement as well as
approval. Elsewhere, as at Lyons, Strasbourg and Paris, government
officials were deeply involved from the very beginning, but little effort on
their part was required to produce massive support. Outside the west, the
capital, the eastern frontier and the Rhône Valley, a more energetic official
role appears to have been necessary. The prefects Didier (in the Basses-
Alpes) and Le Bergerie (in the Nièvre) played crucial parts in giving their
departmental federations significance.

The importance of the attitude of officials is underlined when one considers the areas where the movement was relatively weak. In the north, the
failure of at least three prefects to give direction was crucial. There are indications enough to suggest that the movement would have developed in
Normandy had prefects allowed Bonapartists and revolutionaries to rally
in support of the government. The example of Montpellier, where local
patriots stepped forward in the midst of a decidedly royalist populace, is
instructive in this regard. Nevertheless, in places such as Marseilles, determined efforts by the authorities bore no fruit. The conclusion to be drawn,
then, is that popular support and official encouragement had to be combined to produce significant federations.

Chapter 2

Organisation and official role
of the federations

Having discussed the process by which the federative movement was founded, our focus will now shift to what the *fédérés* did during the Hundred Days. In the first part of this chapter, the day-to-day routine by which *fédérés* organised themselves will be analysed. In the second part, what the *fédérés* did in an official capacity under the direction of the government will be investigated. Discussion of the actions that *fédérés* took on their own initiative will be reserved for the following chapter, for these actions tell us much of the political character of the associations.

At the heart of each association was a central committee. This body was selected by the *fédérés* themselves at their first assembly. In the cases of Grenoble and Chalon-sur-Saône, this was done by election and secret ballot; in the case of Rennes, at least one official, the president Blin, was petitioned by the *fédérés* and did not need to stand for election. If we are to believe the minutes of the first assembly of the federation of the Rhône, the entire central committee was elected by acclamation. The men who founded an association inevitably became members of the central committee. Lefiot became president at Nevers; Jars became president of the federation of the Rhône, and Dubois became president at Chalon.[1]

The central committee was composed of an executive and a body of members who might or might not be *commissaires*. The central committee of Lyons had forty members, that of Grenoble twenty-one and that of Périgueux six. The executives varied somewhat in composition, but generally included a president, vice-president, several secretaries and a treasurer. The Dijonnais proved quite innovative in this regard and added a

---

[1] A. Gras, *Grenoble en 1814 et 1815* (Grenoble, 1854), p. 48; B. Constant, *Mémoires sur les Cent-Jours*, second edition, (Paris, 1829), pp. 178–80; *Le Moniteur Universel*, 29 April 1815; P. Guillaumot, 'Chalon pendant les Cent-Jours', *La Bourgogne*, 2 (1869), pp. 170, 172; BN, Lb[46] 319, *Fédération*, pp. 10–13; G. Thuillier, 'Le Corps Préfectoral en Nivernais de 1814 à 1830', *Actes du 96ᵉ Congrès national des sociétés savantes: Toulouse* (1971), 1, pp. 376–7.

contrôleur des contributions and an *archiviste* to the usual list.[2] There is no evidence that these men were paid for performing their functions. Membership within the executive appears to have been fairly static, though in some instances noteworthy local personalities supplemented the original group.[3] No provision for change in the executive was made in the *fédéré* pacts and, with a possible exception at Angers (where the original executive was entirely changed after seventeen days), the associations did not have rotating presidencies.[4]

The central committees met daily and therefore required a permanent place of location. Often the necessary rooms were provided by the government, which doubtless served to reduce the independence of the associations. The central committees of the federations of Dijon and Laon met in a room of the prefecture, that of Périgueux at the sub-prefecture, that of Lyons at the *hôtel de ville*, and that of Rennes at the Palace of Justice. However, certain committees established themselves in more private settings. The Parisian *fédérés* met in a building they rented on the rue de Grenelle-Saint-Honoré, and the *fédérés* of Toulouse took the arresting step of meeting in a church. The two essential tasks of the central committee were to maintain a register of membership and to correspond with other points of the association, other federations and the government. In the exceptional case of Besançon, where the prefect attempted to oppose the association, *fédérés* had to travel from door to door, collecting signatures.[5]

To become a *fédéré*, a patriot had to travel to a nearby committee bureau in the leading town of the canton or *arrondissement*, swear an oath, and then sign the register. If the prospective *fédéré* was unable to write, the association secretary would make a note of the fact and sign for him. Each member was also required to cite his occupation and address. In the case of the federation of the Rhône, this information would then be forwarded, if it were taken at a 'commission intermédiare résidant dans les cantons', to the central committee at Lyons. The same procedure was employed in the Dordogne.[6]

---

[2] BN, Lb[46] 319, pp. 11–13; Gras, *Grenoble*, p. 48; AN, AFIV 1937, *Confédération Périgourdine*, F[9] 476–7, *Fédération Bourguignonne*.

[3] Compare, for instance, the executive cited in the original Breton pact in AN, AFIV 1935, with the executive cited in the *fédéré* circular in AD I-et-V, 1M96.

[4] Many Jacobin societies did, but then, they lasted longer! See M. Kennedy, *The Jacobin Clubs in the French Revolution, the first years* (Princeton, 1982), pp. 33–4. On the Angers executive, see Blordier-Langlois, *Angers et le Département de Maine-et-Loire* (Angers, 1837), II, pp. 196–7.

[5] AN, F[9] 476–7, *Fédération Bourguignonne*, AFIV 1935, *Fédération Picarde*, *Pacte Fédératif* (of the Bretons), F[7] 3785, bulletin of 18–19 June 1815; BN, Lb[46] 319, p. 13; C. Weiss, *Journal 1815–22* (Paris, 1972), pp. 57, 59.

[6] BM, Lb[46] 319, pp. 30–4; Guillaumot, 'Chalon', pp. 170–1; AN, AFIV 1937, *Confédération Périgourdine*.

Each association set daily hours for the signing of new members. Parisian patriots could register from 6.00 a.m. until 7.00 p.m.; those of Grenoble were expected to sign between the hours of 7.00 a.m. and 6.00 p.m. After joining, Parisian *fédérés* were given entry cards. At Chalon, entry cards were issued to assure that royalist spies could not attend general assemblies. At Angers, each member was given a copy of the pact.[7]

All of this required a good deal of expense, but we possess little information as to who paid for it. In the case of Rennes, we know that *fédérés* themselves bore the costs of the necessary paper, paraphernalia and furnishings of the central committee office. On the other hand, all such expenses incurred by the *fédérés* of Périgueux were paid by 'des autorités civiles et militaires'.[8] Whatever the case, prefects uniformly paid the costs of publishing and posting *affiches* proclaiming federation.[9] In Alsace the pact of Strasbourg was translated, under the direction of the prefect, into German; at Quimper the pact was translated into the local Breton dialect.[10] *Fédérés* could also use the local newspaper to pass on information, and frequently did.

Federations were not social circles. The offices of the central committees were designated for specific purposes. They did not provide a place where members could read newspapers at their leisure and informally discuss politics. There is no recorded instance of a federation subscribing to a national or local journal. In this regard, the federations bore little resemblance to Jacobin clubs. However, this perhaps may be ascribed to the short duration of the associations. The Parisian federation drew up plans for an official *fédéré* journal, and expected that provincial associations would subscribe to it. However, the fall of the government occurred long before such plans could be executed. At Grenoble, *fédérés* did manage to publish a journal and five editions appeared before it ended on 25 June.[11]

Unfortunately, we possess few substantial records of what *fédérés* said at their meetings. Though the Dijon archivist did keep minutes of Burgundian meetings, it may be safely assumed that he destroyed them after Waterloo. The extracts that we do possess of *fédéré* assemblies are in the form of published pamphlets which tell us little more than that *fédérés* were extremely

---

[7] *Moniteur*, 16 May and 3 June 1815; Gras, *Grenoble*, p. 48; *Le Patriote de '89*, 3 June 1815; Guillaumot, 'Chalon', p. 178.

[8] AD I-et-V, 1M96, *fédéré* circular; AN, AFIV 1937, *Confédération Périgourdine*.

[9] See, for example, the federation proclaimed at Loches as reported in the *Indépendant*, 8 June 1815.

[10] AN, AFIV 1937, *Acte Fédératif* (of Strasbourg); *Journal de Paris*, 26 March 1815.

[11] On the Jacobin societies, see Kennedy, *Jacobin Clubs*, pp. 53–5; on the proposed Parisian *fédéré* journal, see the *Patriote*, 31 May 1815; on the Grenoble journal, see Gras, *Grenoble*, pp. 49–50.

patriotic.[12] We must therefore content ourselves with second-hand accounts in newspapers and government reports – and these are few and far between.

Parisian *fédérés* appear to have concerned themselves particularly with military matters. At a general assembly held on 30 April, the vice-president gave a summary of a book on military fortification. Thinking that there must be many engineers with bright new ideas of improved defence, the *fédérés* opened a subscription for funds to encourage such men to put their plans into practice. The government could not have been displeased by such discussions. Nor could it have been troubled by the many addresses of support which *fédérés* sent to prefects, government ministers, and the Chamber of Representatives. However, authorities could not have been pleased when a Parisian *fédéré*, at a general assembly, denounced Marshal Ney for his poor showing at Waterloo and for the disastrous report which he subsequently gave to the Chamber of Peers.[13]

The *fédérés* of Albi assembled 'tous les jours du courrier' in order that newspapers could be publicly read. Nevertheless, they studiously avoided 'toute délibération'. At Lyons, Butignot, association secretary, read out addresses and proclamations to those assembled. Members were also treated to several fiery discourses by Teste, the *lieutenant-général de police*. Unlike their counterparts in Albi, *fédéré* leaders were not at all shy about discussing political matters. Teste took the lead in this regard, calling upon the 'people' to fix their attention upon royalist sedition in 'l'intérieur de l'empire'.[14]

The essential task of the central committee was to spread the movement to every community and add as many recruits as possible. The associations were open to men of all classes, at least in theory, and all *fédérés* were to be considered equals. The dictum that no 'espèce de marque distinctive' would be allowed among members was stipulated in every pact. However, only men over the age of eighteen were allowed to enter the association at Périgueux.[15] The *fédérés* did not charge an entrance fee, another indication that the associations were not designed to perform a social function.[16] General assemblies were held on a regular basis. The *fédérés* of Riom met

[12]   See, for example, BN, Lb[46] 319.
[13]   *Indépendant*, 1 June 1815, *Journal de l'Empire*, 27 June 1815.
[14]   J. Vanel, 'Le Mouvement fédératif de 1815 dans le département du Tarn', *Gaillac et le pays tarnais, 31ᵉ congrès de la fédération des sociétés académiques et savantes de Languedoc-Pyrénées-Gascogne* (Gaillac, 1977), p. 390; J. Audin, *Tableau historique des événements qui se sont passés à Lyon depuis le retour de Bonaparte jusqu'au rétablissement de Louis XVIII* (Lyons, 1815), pp. 117, 120; P. Gonnet, 'Les Cent-Jours à Lyon', *Revue d'histoire de Lyon*, 8 (1908), p. 118.
[15]   AN, AFIV 1935, *Pacte Fédératif* (of the Bretons), AFIV 1937, *Confédération Périgourdine*.
[16]   See Kennedy, *Jacobin Clubs*, p. 32.

every Saturday; Lyonnais *fédérés* met each Monday and Parisians appear to have met two or three times a week.[17] There were four means by which *fédérés* spread their movement. We have already noted the duties and activities of the peripatetic *commissaires*. The movement was further strengthened by alliances between separate associations. Deputies from Lyons, for instance, travelled to Dijon in order to unite the two federations. In turn, *commissaires* from Dijon travelled to the capital, where they attended a meeting of the Parisian *fédérés*.[18] All of the major associations sent representatives to the *Champ de Mai*.

The second means of spreading the movement was by simple correspondence. This could involve circulars sent to members of the local chapter, letters to and from affiliates, or petitions and addresses sent to government officials.[19] The *fédérés* of surrounding cantons sent a report to the *commission intermédiaire* at Riom once every eight days.[20]

The first task of the Breton federation, as stated in its pact, was the 'propagation des principes libéraux'.[21] Almost all *fédéré* writings constituted propaganda in that they were designed to elicit support for a certain cause. But *fédéré* writers devoted more energy to arguments in favour of supporting the government in order to buttress liberal principles, than to expounding what those liberal principles were. They simply assumed that patriots understood what those principles were and accepted their merits. The reasons cited by *fédérés* for supporting the government will concern us later when we investigate the political tendencies of the various associations.

Fédéré writings were couched in terms designed to appeal to both national and regional pride. The Bretons took obvious satisfaction in being the first to federate, both in 1789 and 1815. A *fédéré* of Quimper cited a glorious moment in the past when the forebears of contemporary patriots had sailed into the port of Plymouth and humbled the men of proud Albion. He further stated his opinion that Clisson, in the sixteenth century, had formed the first federation. In his original address, Escard appealed to the pride of Burgundians who 'dans les plaines de Champagne et sur mille champs de bataille illustrés par la victoire, ont scellé de leur sang la cause de la liberté'. The most striking example of such appeals to a glorious past can be found in the preamble to the *pacte provençale*:

17 BN, Lb⁴⁶ 319, p. 31; *Moniteur*, 20 May–2 June 1815; Gonnet, 'Lyon', pp. 120, 289.
18 B. M. of Dijon, *Fonds Delmasse*, no. 2218; *Indépendant*, 1 June 1815.
19 For an example of a circular, see AD I-et-V, 1M96; for a letter from an affiliate, see AD C-d, 3M18; for an address, see that of the *fédérés* of Chalon-sur-Saône to the Chamber of Representatives in the *Moniteur*, 2 July 1815.
20 BN, Lb⁴⁶ 319, p. 31.
21 AN, AFIV 1935, *Pacte Fédératif* (of the Bretons).

Habitans du Var, nous qui avons hérité du courage et du dévouement de nos pères, nous qui sommes fiers de nous rapeller qu'au commencement et vers le milieu du siècle dernier, sous les murs de Toulon, nos pères ont sauvé la patrie.

Thus, by referring to the past, *fédérés* sought to emphasise that their cause was that of independence from foreign domination in order to appeal to men of all parts of France.[22]

The fourth and final means by which *fédérés* sought to increase membership was through use of spectacle. Indeed, they seem to have been a festive lot. After a banquet of some 400 to 500 *couverts* held at Rennes at the foundation of the Breton association, happy *fédéré* deputies went on to enjoy three days of feasting at Brest, two days at Nantes and one day at Redon, where sixty tables were set. Deputies from all towns and communes of both the Haut- and Bas-Rhin converged upon Strasbourg in early June for a huge *fête nationale*. When the *commissaires* of the federation of the Rhône arrived in Dijon, they took part in a march which wound through the streets of the city and ended at the old palace of the Estates of Burgundy, where a banquet of more than 100 *couverts* was prepared. During the banquet, speeches were given by local civil and military officials, patriotic songs were sung and toasts were given. After prefectoral approval for the federation of Montpellier had been gained, patriots danced in the *salle des spectacles*.[23]

These festivities served several purposes. They were designed to bolster the courage of members who might otherwise have felt isolated, but now could experience a sense of fraternity and solidarity. They doubtless attracted the odd potential member and were a source of publicity. But more importantly, they served notice to opponents of the regime that the government possessed determined supporters.

Such techniques are familiar to those who have studied the Jacobin movement. But here it must be noted that while *fédérés* were quite willing to employ Jacobin methods, this did not necessarily indicate any desire to emulate them. *Fédérés* did not organise festivals of Reason, nor did they parade Goddesses of Liberty. When they did parade, it was usually with a bust of Napoleon.[24]

Le Gallo, in his account of the movement, was more struck by what the *fédérés* might have done than by what they actually did do:

---

[22] *Journal de Paris*, 18 May 1815; AN, F⁹ 476–7; *Fédération Bourguignonne*, AFIV 1938, *Pacte fédératif*.

[23] *Journal de Paris*, 29 May 1815; *Moniteur*, 30 April, 8 and 31 May 1815; *Indépendant*, 11 June 1815; B. M. of Dijon, *Fonds Delmasse*, no. 2218.

[24] For the Jacobin use of spectacle, see Kennedy, *Jacobin Clubs*, p. 45; for an example of a *fédéré* parade, see AN, F⁷ 3736, bulletin of 21 April 1816 for Périgeux.

Si Napoléon l'eût voulu ou l'eût compris, les fédérations eussent pu l'aider puissament moins par des prédications civiques que par l'organisation d'une levée en masse et par une offensive hardie contre les ennemis de l'Empereur, les complices de l'étranger, les autorités molles ou défaillantes.

From that perspective, Le Gallo logically concluded that the *fédérés* had done essentially nothing. Once again he blamed the government: 'On ne donna aux fédérations qu'un rôle vague, elles traduisirent principalement leur existence par des appels éloquents et des cérémonies oratoires.' There is doubtless a good deal of truth in Le Gallo's contention that the *fédérés* were not allowed to do all they might have done, but he overstates his case in asserting that they did nothing of consequence.[25]

In the pact that was to become the basis of most of the associations, Breton *fédérés* sought to define precisely their own role. Stressing that the association 'n'a aucune autorité politique', they vowed to act only with the 'consentement de l'Autorité publique'. They would not constitute 'un corps isolé', but would 'font partie nécessaire de la Garde Nationale'. When directed by the authorities, they would render 'un secours effectif et prompt ... partout où besoin sera'.[26]

We have seen that one of the first acts *fédérés* undertook after forming their associations was to put themselves under the direction of the authorities. While the government was quite willing to accept the support of these patriots, it took some time before officials could define precisely what they wanted of the *fédérés*.

This is not to say that officials did not have high expectations of the movement. At first, the government saw the movement essentially as a means to sway public opinion in its favour and to give warning to potential opponents of the regime. The government hoped that the movement would be broad in its appeal, and not be the exclusive concern of any one social class or political party. In a report to Carnot, the prefect of the Côtes-du-Nord expressed his initial satisfaction with the movement: 'en effet le mouvement était général et ... tout présentait l'aspect d'une union sincère d'un rapprochement d'opinions'.[27]

Newspaper reports repeatedly echoed this desire that the federations would represent a 'union sincère' of all classes, but in truth this seldom proved the case. Instead, the associations often confirmed old sociopolitical divisions, though they were not the cause of such divisions.

One finds traces of disappointment in the defensive tone that increasingly crept into *fédéré* writings. At first, *fédérés* wrote as if they could

[25] E. Le Gallo, *Les Cent-Jours* (Paris, 1924), pp. 289–90.
[26] All of these details are taken from AN, AFIV 1935, *Pacte Fédératif* (of the Bretons).
[27] *Ibid.*, F⁷ 9650, Prefect to Minister of the Interior, 10 May 1815.

hardly believe that anyone could be so misguided as not to join their cause. A *fédéré* of Riom stated: 'Des hommes faibles ou égarés peuvent un instant se laisser séduire; le bien public exige quelquefois des sacrifices pénibles auxquels tous les hommes ne se prêtent un égal courage.' Such a man needed only 'd'être rassuré ou éclairé pour remplir son devoir'. A rather disingenuous section of the *pacte provençale* commenced: 'S'il est vrai qu'il existe en France . . . des êtres dénaturés dont les vœux parricides appèlent les armées étrangères . . . '[28]

That the associations were immediately perceived as a divisive sectional interest, however, was made evident in an article written by one of the *fédérés* of Rennes: 'Qui croirait que la confédération bretonne . . . ait pu rencontrer des détracteurs, disons plus, des calomniateurs?' A *fédéré* of Quimper worked himself into a lather over an article published in the *Journal Général* in which the author had had the temerity to inquire against whom the Bretons federated and accused the *fédérés* of having 'des chefs particuliers'.[29]

Perhaps the sensitivity of such *fédéré* writers resulted from the fact that the movement had not lived up to early expectations in certain areas. Despite a visit of deputies from Rennes, the federation of Saint-Brieuc had gained no more than 250 to 300 members by the third week of May. In fact, it proved necessary for the prefect to take measures to expand the movement from a narrow base. He informed *fédéré* leaders: 'qu'il fallait envelopper dans cette généreuse association non seulement les habitans des villes dignes d'y être admis, mais encore ceux des campagnes sur lesquels l'on pouvait compter'. Despite the influence of local ex-nobles who led a crowd of inhabitants by an 'attrait irrésistible', the federation thereafter began to grow throughout the department. To assure progress, the prefect demanded that the central committee made certain that all its actions were conducted with probity and that it was free from corruption. He hoped that the association, by taking the high moral ground, would attract all honest citizens, and even some ex-nobles.[30]

Thus, direct governmental intervention had been necessary to make the federation modestly successful in the Côtes-du-Nord. Similar problems arose throughout the old province. On 21 May General Bigarré reported:

L'esprit public au lieu de se bonifier perd considérablement . . . On ne peut se dissimuler que c'est à deux ou trois articles de la constitution que ce changement est dû . . . La confédération bretonne se refroidit, et les nobles et les prêtres font des progrès.

---

[28] BN, Lb⁴⁶ 319, *Fédération*, p. 27; AN, AFIV 1938, *Pacte Fédératif*, p. 2.
[29] *Moniteur*, 17 May 1815; *Journal de Paris*, 18 May 1815.
[30] AN, F⁷ 9650, Prefect to Minister of the Interior, 6 June 1815.

In effect, Bigarré was repeating a warning made earlier by Cafarelli when the latter reported that the *Acte* was making a bad impression, particularly the articles which made the peerage hereditary.[31]

While the *Acte* may have proved an impediment, it did not stop the movement from expanding. It did disappoint certain old revolutionaries, but it did not cause them to drop out of the federations. We can see this in the example of two old republicans of Saint-Brieuc. Although both Le Gorrec and Aubrée signed a pamphlet highly critical of the *Acte*, they also organised the federation of that town. Moreover, deputies from Rennes did not reach the town of Brest until well after discussion of the *Acte* had begun, yet Brest became one of the strongest federative centres.[32] Finally, outside Brittany the movement did not commence until after the *Acte* had been published in the *Moniteur* and was well known. As we shall see shortly, men joined the federative movement for reasons which overrode reservations about the government.

The presence of a determined government authority could prove vitally important to the development of an association. Prefect de Bry was chief architect of the federation of Alsace and, with considerably less success, Prefect Dumont sought to build a similar structure in the Pas-de-Calais. If the association grew to a much greater extent at Angers than at Nantes, this could in large part be attributed to the presence of General Lamarque, who was also an instigator of the federation of the Deux-Sèvres at Niort. General Decaen played a similar role at Toulouse, as did General Gilly at Montpellier.[33]

On the other hand, a less than enthusiastic official, such as the prefect of the Calvados, could seriously hinder organisation or recruitment. Because the initiative to form an association in Besançon came from an old regicide, Prefect Derville-Maléchard attempted to restrict development of the federation. In both these cases, the prefects were acting on their own initiative, and both of them were subsequently reprimanded by government ministers. Fouché's criticism of Derville-Maléchard was especially revealing: 'Vous avez dû voir, Monsieur, par les fédérations qui ont eu lieu à Paris, en

---

[31] *Ibid*, AFIV 1937, Minister of War to the Emperor, 23 May 1815, Cafarelli to Minister of the Interior, 2 May 1815.

[32] *Ibid*., F⁷ 9656, 23 May 1815, F⁷ 9650, Minister of Police to Minister of the Interior, 6 June 1815.

[33] L. Pingaud, *Jean de Bry* (Paris, 1909), p. 362; Compte G. De Hauteclocque, 'Les Cent-Jours dans le Pas-de-Calais', *Mémoires de l'Académie des sciences, lettres et arts d'Arras, 2ᵉ série*, 36 (1905), pp. 137–40; AN, AFIV 1937, Prefect to Minister of War, 2 June 1815, Minister of War to the Emperor, 4 June 1815, General Delaborde to Minister of War, 16 May 1815; J. J. Hémardinquer, 'Un libéral: F.-B. Boyer-Fonfrède (1767–1845)', *Annales du Midi*, 73 (1961), p. 177, and J.-P. Thomas, *Précis historique des événements arrivés à Montpellier pendant les Cent-Jours de l'Interrègne* (Montpellier, 1976), pp. 32–3.

Bretagne, à Lyon, etc., que ces institutions momentanées concordent avec le système de défense adopté par le gouvernement.' Fouché's admonition contained an excellent summary of the Imperial government's attitude to the federative movement – under the circumstances it was valuable and should be encouraged. This position was definitely shared by Napoleon, Carnot, Davout and Maret; thus, Le Gallo's argument that the government restricted the federative movement is inaccurate. Certainly, the government did not envisage a political role for the federations other than supporting the Emperor. Fouché's use of the term 'momentané' accurately reflected the official view that the sole purpose of the associations was to help in national defence; if and when that purpose was fulfilled, there would no longer be a place for the federations in the Imperial scheme of things. Napoleon fell before the latter situation arose of course, and the supreme cause of defending the *patrie* during the Hundred Days assured that the government, while seeking to direct the movement, exercised very little constraint. The crucial factor was that Napoleon was in a poor position to be selective about who would fight for him. As a result, his government followed a consistent policy of encouraging the associations, although in the exceptional case of Paris, Bonaparte proved hesitant as to how far support should go.[34]

The growth of the movement, however, should not be attributed exclusively to official support. By and large, federations gathered momentum in direct relation to the growing threat of civil or foreign war. Impending battle led the government to give *fédérés* the official role for which they longed. In the second article of the Imperial decree of 19 May 1815, the 'garde des côtes des 12ème et 13ème divisions militaires' was entrusted to local *fédérés*. To this effect, *fédérés* were instructed to organise themselves into battalions and place themselves under the authority of departmental general commanders. The *fédérés* were granted the privilege of choosing their own officers. More significantly, on the day that the decree was published, Davout wrote to the prefects of Brittany and Anjou requesting that *fédérés* be organised into mobile columns and placed under the command of General Delaborde. The *fédérés* were to be used to supplement troops of the line and *gendarmes* in the pursuit of *chouan* bands.[35]

Once again, it would appear that the government initially harboured illusions about the contributions that *fédérés* could make. In a letter to the prefect of the Ille-et-Vilaine, the prefect of the Côtes-du-Nord reported that no regular service could be expected of the *fédérés* and that they would

---

[34] Le Gallo, *Cent-Jours*, p. 326; Weiss, *Journal*, pp. 57–8.
[35] AD I-et-V, 1M96, 19 May 1815; AG, 1K1 46, Minister of War to General Delaborde, 15 May 1815.

make themselves useful more 'par la force morale dont elle serait revêtue, que par le secours des armes'. *Fédérés* sent in pursuit of brigands were apt to become rapidly fatigued and disenchanted by any long absence from their homes.[36] Moreover, not every *fédéré* could be expected to serve, or should be looked upon as a new recruit. In a letter forwarded to Davout by General Lamarque, the prefect of the Loire-Inférieure explained that, although the federation of Nantes included more than a thousand members, many of these men had duties requiring them to remain permanently in the city. Furthermore, many were already seeing active service in the National Guard, the *chasseurs de la Vendée*, or the *garde des ponts*. A large number of *fédérés* had wives and children to support and were not eager to leave home when the enemy was at the gates of Nantes. In sum, only 300 of these *fédérés* could be sent into the countryside to aid 'les points menacés'. The prefect concluded:

Je crois qu'en général, on a trop compté sur les ressources qui présente la fédération … La fédération produit un excellent effet moral, elle a un grand but politique, mais ce serait se tromper que de calculer ses forces disponibles par le nombre de signatures et il importe que le Gouvernement soit bien convaincu de cette vérité.

On the margin of a similar report from the lieutenant-general of Nantes, Napoleon drew the obvious conclusion: 'Il faut dans l'Ouest quelques troops de ligne pour servir de points d'appui aux *fédérés*. Revoir à cet effet le ministre de la Guerre.'[37] General Bigarré sent similar tidings from Rennes to Davout:

Dans toute la Bretagne on réunirait à peine douze cents hommes armés de cette Confédération, encore si vous en excepter ceux de Rennes, les autres ne veulent point sortir de leurs villes, tant ils craignent d'être trompés par le Gouvernement.[38]

At least in the later regard, Bigarré was to be proven quite wrong in his assessment. Indeed, when local officials gave *fédérés* the opportunity to prove their zeal, the latter responded beyond expectations. This, in turn, appears to have given the movement a new impetus.

For the government, the essential decision was whether to give guns to the *fédérés*. Hesitation in this regard was not so much a matter of unwillingness to arm *fédérés* as a desire to conserve this precious resource. At first, larger associations such as those of Rennes, Nantes and Quimper were organised and armed. When these *fédérés* proved themselves useful, the government sought to acquire arms for others. After *fédérés* had taken part

[36] AN, F⁷ 9650, Prefect of the Côtes-du-Nord to Prefect of the Ille-et-Vilaine, 6 June 1815.
[37] For the two preceding quotes, see *ibid.*, AFIV 1940, Prefect to General Lamarque, 2 June 1815, and R. Grand, *La Chouannerie de 1815* (Paris, 1942), pp. 36–7.
[38] AN, AFIV 1937, General Bigarré to Minister of War, 2 June 1815.

in a successful battle at Redon which led to the capture of arms, Davout instructed authorities to give these guns to those *fédérés* who remained unarmed. When disillusioned peasants showed signs of forsaking the Bourbon cause, Davout sent instructions to authorities in Lorient, Saint-Malo, Brest and Rennes to offer ten francs to each insurgent who would give up his *fusil*. The guns in turn should be given to *fédérés*.[39] If early expectations had proven exaggerated, subsequent events convinced authorities of the efficacy of using the *fédérés* as a fighting force.

Chouan revolt had reached a critical stage in Brittany by the first week of June. To deal with this, civil and military officials co-ordinated assault forces to subdue rebellion. One theatre of operations included the departments of the Ille-et-Vilaine, Loire-Inférieure and Maine-et-Loire; a second included the departments of the Morbihan and Finistère. As the former theatre involved the *fédérés* of Rennes, it shall be considered in a subsequent chapter; at present operations in the latter theatre shall be considered.

Late in May, royalist peasant bands of the Morbihan had taken Auray, Le Faouët and Guiseriff, were besieging Napléonville, and had pushed into the Finistère and occupied Scaër. In the Côtes-du-Nord, insurgents were menacing Carhaix and Morlaix.[40]

On 25 May, a column of some 500 *fédérés* of Lorient, led by the lawyer Jossé, attacked a camp of *chouans* close to Auray, but the patriots were routed and forced to retreat to Vannes. Three days later, some 200 Vannetais *fédérés* clashed with another band of *chouans* at the bridge of Noyal-Muzillac; this time the *fédérés* fought their opposition to a draw. When *chouans* took control of Ploermel on 30 May, they found that a force of some 200 *fédérés* had already evacuated arms and the *caisses publiques*. On 4 June, when *chouans* overwhelmed Redon, a small battalion of *fédérés*, led by the sub-prefect Ropert, took refuge in a Church and the *mairie*. Lacking artillery, the *chouans* could do little more than exchange gunfire with their enemies and, although four *fédérés* were killed, the insurgents suffered greater losses and decided to depart Redon. This greatly boosted morale amongst government supporters.[41]

At Quimper, local *fédérés* offered their services to General Vabre, who accepted. On 31 May, 140 *fédérés* were put under the command of Captain Kermorial, and departed for Rosporden. There they were joined by a mobile column and sixty *fédéré* National Guardsmen from Quimperlé. At

---

[39] See AG, 1K1 47, Minister of War to General Lamarque, 3 June 1815, and general instructions from the Minister of War, 10 June 1815.
[40] AN, F⁷ 9656, prefectoral report of 8 June 1815.
[41] Grand, *Chouannerie*, pp. 106–18.

the same time, 400 *fédérés* of Brest, armed for the occasion by General Brenier, departed for Carhaix and Morlaix. Along the way they were joined by *douaniers, gendarmes, marins* and 300 *fédérés* of Landernau, Carhaix and Morlaix. In all, the two mobile columns comprised some 4,000 men, of whom 900 were *fédérés*. There would have been more, but military officials refused to send aid from Vannes, fearing that any reduction of forces might lead to the fall of that city.[42]

Nevertheless, the two expeditions proved entirely successful. Ill-equipped peasants took flight upon each occasion that a government force saw fit to open fire. Ninety-six *chouans* were forced to give up their arms at Gourin, and when *chouan* leaders announced their intention to submit, remaining peasants followed suit. By 6 June, Colonel Deseix, commander of the mobile column of Brest, could report that all *chouan* bands in the Finistère had been dispersed and that capitulation was complete. He foresaw no future difficulties.

Deseix reported that the conduct of the *fédérés* had been exemplary: 'toujours même activité, même zèle, même élan patriotique'. However, the chief contribution of the *fédérés* had been to bolster *l'esprit public* wherever they went: 'ils ne regrettent qu'une chose, c'est de n'avoir pas eu l'occasion d'en donner des preuves devant l'ennemi'. The *fédérés* had acted, therefore, chiefly in support of the troops of the line. At Rosporden they reassured citizens, some of whom had previously taken flight, that rumours of an impending attack were unfounded. In several communes, they helped to reinstal Imperial authorities and replaced the *drapeau blanc* with the *tricolore*. To Méchin, prefect of the Ille-et-Vilaine, such services were especially valuable because they bolstered the courage of government supporters otherwise constrained by their isolation.[43]

On 14 June, Chazal, prefect of the Finistère, ordered that 'nos braves fédérés jouiront de la faculté de se former à part en compagnies de volontaires et de se choisir leurs officiers'. He further added: 'les habitans des campagnes qui ne sont pas uniques soutiens de leurs familles resteront sur nos contrôles, mais ils ne seront levés qu'en cas de nécessité'. He felt certain that 'ils accouraient tous contre les Anglais'.

Chazal's optimism was based on what he perceived to be the beneficial effect that official organisation was producing upon the federative movement. He thought that the honour of such responsibility and the 'faculté qui leur est donné de choisir les officiers des compagnies . . . doit promouvoir

---

[42] These details have been culled from reports in AN, F^7 9656, 3–10 June 1815 and F^9 530, *dépêche télégraphique de Brest.*
[43] *Ibid.*, F^7 9656, Colonel Deseix to General Brenier, 6 June 1815, *Rapport de l'expédition des fédérés de Quimper*, F^9 530, Prefect to Minister of the Interior, 7 May 1815.

ces associations généreuses partout où elles n'existent pas et les étendre, les animer partout où elles existent'. Thus the assignment of an official role, and the confidence such a measure indicated, was expected to help the movement expand.[44]

Ultimately, Breton *fédérés* did play a vital role in fighting *chouannerie*. Although most of the actual combat was undertaken by troops of the line, *fédérés* did contribute in this regard. More important, however, was their role in defending towns and strategic points of the region. This was the essence of their service in the Loire-Inférieure, for example, where they served 'au gardiennage des localités, au renforcement des compagnies du train, à la surveillance de la Loire dans de petites embarcations armées'. They also helped build fortifications and acted as a passport control for ships travelling along the Loire.[45]

However, in the Vendée, where, according to General Lamarque, virtually the entire population was royalist, *fédérés* appear to have been less bold than their Breton counterparts. Here the *fédérés* 'ne voulaient pas sortir de chez eux . . . leur zèle avait besoin d'excitants . . . le risque se présentait d'organiser des unités rebelles'. Nevertheless, when Auguste de la Rochejacquelin and his Vendean rebels attacked Thouars, they found that the object of their efforts, some 1,200 guns, had already been spirited away to Parthenay by local *fédérés*. Thus, while not as numerous or as effective as the Bretons, Vendean *fédérés* did contribute to the Imperial cause.[46]

Fédérés in other regions also took up arms to combat either invasion or sedition. In certain instances they proved undisciplined, and some of their coercive activities took place not only after the fall of Bonaparte, but also after the return of Louis XVIII to Paris. Especially in the south, they were to pay dearly for this.

In order to prepare a suitably warm reception for invading Allied soldiers, with whom they were already too well acquainted, and realising that local authorities had no guns to give, the central committee at Chalon-sur-Saône levied a tax upon *fédérés*. Rich *fédérés* paid four francs each; less wealthy members paid one or two francs. By this means, and the aid of Carnot, brother of the Minister of the Interior, they were able to obtain some 800 guns. However, defeat of the French Army at Waterloo and Napoleon's abdication convinced Chalon *fédérés* that further measures would prove futile and, unlike in 1814, Allied soldiers did not have to lay

---

[44] *Ibid.*, F⁷ 9656, Prefect to Minister of the Interior, 14 June 1815, Prefect to General Dautry, 8 June 1815.
[45] R. Grand, *Chouannerie*, pp. 38–9; B. Lasserre, *Les Cent-Jours en Vendée d'après les papiers inédits du Général Lamarque* (Paris, 1906), pp. 120–4.
[46] Lasserre, *Lamarque*, p. 119; Grand, *Chouannerie*, p. 154.

siege to the town. At Nevers, a company of 100 *fédérés* was given arms and the uniforms of National Guardsmen. They declared their willingness to march to Paris to help defend 'la capitale de l'Empire' – indicating a measure of commitment which, although not unique, was not necessarily typical either. By and large, *fédérés* did not wish to stray beyond the bounds of their own region. The prefect also intended to use these men to search the houses of royalists for guns, but it is unclear whether they actually undertook this task.[47]

Matters at Paris and Lyons were somewhat different. At Paris, some 14,000 *fédérés* entered the National Guard as *tirailleurs*; approximately one-third of these men were given arms. Similar plans were made for Lyons, but sources do not indicate whether they were implemented. What is clear, however, is that *fédérés* in both Lyons and Paris had the opportunity to exchange fire with the enemy, and both groups were extremely disenchanted when local officials decided to capitulate rather than fight in earnest.[48]

Due to the forthcoming evacuation of troops from Arras on 27 June, Commandant-General Chamollet requested that *fédérés* from Amiens be sent to help maintain order. Described by a contemporary as 'vrais sans-culottes', 300 Amiens *fédérés* duly arrived, lodged themselves in the citadel, occupied the town outposts and patrolled the streets. Shortly thereafter, a small troop of royalists arrived and threatened to besiege the town, giving rise to manifestations of support for the Monarchy within Arras. Several skirmishes with local royalists occurred before the *fédérés* were convinced to retire to the citadel. When fired on there by a patrol of National Guardsmen, the *fédérés* replied with cannon fire and a sortie of fifty *fédérés* routed the Guardsmen. Comte du Bourg, emissary of the King and now in control of the town, decided to attack the citadel on 29 June, but his preparations were halted by a second sortie. After roaming the streets and exchanging gunfire with royalists, the *fédérés* then returned to the citadel. Royalists retired to the countryside to recruit a suitably massive body of support. Fortunately, on the following day, negotiations were commenced which ultimately led to *fédéré* capitulation. The 'vrais sans-culottes' did not however

---

[47] Guillaumot, 'Chalon', pp. 176, 179; Thuillier, 'Nevers', pp. 377–8; E. Duminy, 'Nevers pendant les Cent-Jours', *Bulletin de la Société nivernaise de lettres, sciences et arts*, 11 (1906), pp. 340–2.

[48] On the Lyonnais *fédérés*, see Gonnet, 'Lyon', pp. 111, 121, and H. Houssaye, *1815 – Waterloo* (Paris, 1909), pp. 442–3; subsequent incidents in Lyons will be related in the chapter on White Terror. On the Parisian *fédérés-tirailleurs*, see K. D. Tönnesson 'Les Fédérés de Paris pendant les Cent-Jours', *Annales historiques de la Révolution Française*, 54 (1982), pp. 406–7, 409–10; subsequent incidents in Paris will be related in the chapters on Paris.

evacuate the citadel until 11 July – well after the capitulation of Paris had signalled that the *fédéré* cause was truly lost.[49]

Although events at Montpellier were somewhat similar to those of Arras, clashes here proved much more bloody and tensions were exacerbated by the fact that Montpellier had its own indigenous federation. Montpellier was largely royalist; nevertheless, the regicide Cambon was able to establish a federation composed mostly of old Jacobins willing to work hand-in-glove with Imperial military officials. The Jacobins organised a committee of surveillance which dressed lists of royalist suspects and suggested appropriate punishments. Among such penalties was conscription into the mobile National Guard that was sent to Perpignan; *fédérés* were exempted from this service.

Violence did not flare up until 27 June, when news of Waterloo became known. The immediate result was royalist public rejoicing and harassment of *fédérés* who sought to defend the tricolour floating above the *hôtel de ville*. Soldiers intervened to save *fédérés* from the crowd, but the *fédérés* then went on a rampage of revenge, using suppression of sedition as a pretext for firing indiscriminately upon celebrating monarchist groups. Among the victims were several old men and women. Order was temporarily restored by General Gilly, but unfortunately on 2 July he then brought Protestant *fédérés* and National Guardsmen from the Gardonnenque and Vaunage into Montpellier. The disastrous consequence was pillaging and violence until Gilly departed on 5 July. The grim determination of Montpellier *fédérés* to carry on could be measured by the fact that, as late as the second week of July, they were still making plans for a grand public banquet to commemorate Bastille Day. Such schemes were scuttled by news of the occupation of Lyons and, on 15 July, tidings of the return of Louis XVIII led to the hoisting of the *drapeau blanc*. Local officials and National Guardsmen enabled some 300 *fédérés* and soldiers lodged in the citadel to make good their escape without further clashes with the populace, but the day of royalist reprisal had dawned.[50]

Events at Nîmes were to provoke similar retribution and here also General Gilly's influence was to prove unfortunate. While the *fédérés* of Nîmes may have rested 'à peu près inertes' under the early direction of Blanc Pascal, 'un personnage très catholique et très conservateur', they did not long remain so. During the critical days following Waterloo, the central committee at Nîmes, now presided over by Etienne Paris, worked in close co-operation with General Gilly and conscripted men from nearby Protestant towns and villages to defend Nîmes from royalist insurgents. The resultant urban guard of some 900 men was mostly comprised of *fédérés*;

[49] Hautecloque, 'Arras', pp. 155–77.   [50] Thomas, *Précis*, pp. 33–62.

moreover, the central committee also provided 600 *fédérés* who helped Gilly take control of Montpellier in early July. In Nîmes, *fédérés* showed marked signs of indiscipline and persecuted royalists. Antagonism was exacerbated by the fact that Gilly, after his return from Montpellier, refused to recognise the Bourbon government until 15 July. When the Imperial prefect, Ruggieri, did recognise the restoration of Monarchy, *fédérés* arrested police officers who sought to raise the Bourbon standard, firing upon several royalists. When Gilly and Imperial troops subsequently stole away from Nîmes, *fédérés* foolish enough to remain paid the price of such actions.[51]

From the standpoint of the Imperial government, the most desirable result of the federative movement would be a show of force sufficient to make potential opponents think twice about agitating. In departments such as the Haute-Garonne, however, the government assigned *fédérés* a more specific role:

Vous avez des malveillans à désarmer, des volontaires dits royaux à rendre au devoir et à l'honneur, en les faisant conduire et incorporer dans les rangs de l'armée: pour cela une fédération bien unie, bien cimentée et qui ne connaisse point d'obstacles, est le moyen le plus direct et le plus sur.

Moreover, *fédérés* could protect owners of *biens nationaux*, 'et générale-ment toutes les personnes dont l'existence civile est intimement liée à la révolution', from royalist attacks. Often the mere organisation of a federation proved useful:

La fédération du midi a produit d'excellents effets. Elle a neutralisé en peu de temps les efforts des ci-devant nobles et détruit leurs espérances. Le nombre des fédérés est déjà considérable; il s'accroit journellement et plusieurs villes du département s'empressent d'imiter l'exemple du chef lieu. Un nouveau locale est devenu nécess-aire au fédérés. Je le leur ai accordé et leur translation a été pour la ville de Toulouse un espèce de solemnité. Le buste de SMI a été porté en triomphe par les *fédérés* réunis au nombre d'environ 1200 qui précédés d'une musique guerrière ont par-couru une partie de la ville pour le rendre à leur nouveau locale.

But a display of strength did not always suffice and, especially after Water-loo, *fédérés* often found themselves taking on the role normally performed by the police or the National Guard. From Toulouse, an officer of the line wrote to Davout suggesting that if the *fédérés* were organised on a military basis they would soon number 4,000 and could be used to police deserters.

---

[51] AN, F⁷ 3786, bulletin of 30 June 1815; Le Gallo, *Cent-Jours*, pp. 327–8; F. Ponteil, *La Monarchie parlementaire, 1815–48* (Paris, 1949), p. 18; Duc de Castries, *La Terreur Blanche* (Paris, 1981), p. 187; H. Houssaye, *1815 – La Terreur Blanche* (Paris, 1909), pp. 463–73; G. Lewis, *The Second Vendée* (Oxford, 1978), pp. 180–6.

General Decaen, however, decided to form a single *fédéré* battalion, which was defined as an auxiliary of the National Guard and placed under the command of Boyer-Fonfrède. The battalion comprised six companies, each composed of thirty-two fusiliers and thirty-two *lanciers* armed with pikes. The value of this force soon manifested itself to royalists and Imperial officials alike. Due to the perhaps treasonous complacency of Imperial officials (including Romiguières, who was later to be arrested for having been a *fédéré chef*) in May, royalists in the countryside surrounding Toulouse had been able to make preparations to overthrow the government. A certain number of guns were procured and perhaps some 800 Toulousains were recruited to the cause. After news of the defeat of the Imperial Army had arrived, rebellion was attempted on the morning of 26 June; *fédérés* and soldiers responded immediately, and within several hours all monarchist manifestations had been brought to a halt. Thereafter *fédérés* patrolled the streets; as late as 14 July they were still demanding cries of 'Vive l'Empereur' from all whom they met. In consequence, royalist forces were not mobilised until 17 July – after Decaen had directed the *fédérés* to disband in an order full of praise, and departed for Narbonne with his troops.[52]

Although less dramatic, another official contribution of the *fédérés* lay in building fortifications.[53] This gave *fédérés* in many parts of France something constructive to do, and also provided an opportunity to display patriotism. The example of the federation of Paris is instructive in this regard. On 13 June, 600 Parisian *fédérés* travelled to the *barrière d'Italie* to commence the defence works that had been assigned to them by the *commandant du génie*. They left their headquarters at the rue de Grenelle at 6.00 a.m., marching to the martial beat of drums and carrying a bust of the Emperor adorned with laurels and violets. While at the barrier, they listened to a speech given by their president, Carret, and proceeded to burn 'un drapeau blanc, . . . une cocarde blanche et la proclamation de Louis XVIII aux français'. They worked well into the evening.[54]

The *fédérés* returned to their redoubt each day. On 18 June, they received a visit from a deputation of the ninth regiment of the *fédérés-tirailleurs*, who were working nearby. The latter deputies requested permission to pay homage to the bust of Napoleon that the Parisian *fédérés* carried each day to their redoubt. Their request was granted and the *fédérés-tirailleurs* duly

---

[52] Hémardinquer, 'Boyer-Fonfrède', p. 177; AN, F⁷ 9659, Prefect to Minister of Police, 22 June 1815; J. Loubet, 'Le gouvernement toulousain du Duc d'Angoulême après les Cent-Jours', *La Révolution Française*, 64 (1913), pp. 149–55; AD, H-G, 4M34, Minister of Police to Prefect, 3 and 7 June 1815.
[53] See, for example, Houssaye, *1815 – Les Cent-Jours*, p. 629, and Gonnet, 'Lyon', pp. 203–4.
[54] AN, F⁷ 3785, bulletin of 13 June 1815.

arrived in order to 'fraterniser en masse' with the Parisian *fédérés*. Carret gave another patriotic address and then all the *fédérés* swore to 'vaincre ou mourir pour l'indépendance nationale, la liberté et l'Empereur'. After parading before the bust, the two groups then returned to work.[55]

The pact of the Parisian *fédérés* called upon members to contribute by whatever means possible to the defence of the *patrie*. The fourth article read: 'Ils se promettent de seconder le gouvernement par des dons voluntaires, chacun selon ses moyens.' A register was begun and the *offrandes* were published in the *Patriote de '89*. Donations ranged from 716 francs to five francs, with several contributors offering to pay on a monthly basis.[56]

Judging by the carefully defined and limited objectives set forth in *fédéré* pacts, the federative movement was successful. *Fédérés* had set themselves the task of aiding the government in the suppression of royalist agitation and the maintenance of civil order; this was largely attained and *fédérés* contributed significantly to its achievement. *Chouan* revolt was well on the road to defeat prior to Waterloo, and in the south royalist forces did not launch their offensive until the Napoleonic cause was well and truly lost. Napoleon and his supporters were defeated by the Allied forces, not by French royalists.

To a large extent, mere organisation of the federations checked royalist inclinations to manifest their opposition to the Imperial government. That the federative movement took on such proportions so rapidly attests to a large measure of support for Napoleon, but it was also the result of a combination of official encouragement and experience of organisation gained during the Revolution. *Fédérés* employed the methods pioneered by the Jacobin clubs, although analogies to the Jacobins should not be pushed too far. Federations did not exist long enough to 'educate' the public, nor did they duplicate the social functions of the Jacobin clubs. They did, however, at least to some extent, manifest similar political tendencies, but as this can hardly be considered an official function, discussion of it has been reserved for subsequent chapters.

In opposing royalism, *fédérés* in many places resorted to force. This and the public nature of their support for Bonaparte assured that they would be subjected to a measure of revenge when their opponents regained the upper hand. The nature of retribution was not uniform however. In the west, *fédérés* had conducted themselves in a relatively disciplined fashion and civil war had not been as bitter or as brutal as in the past. Matters had been otherwise in parts of the south however, and there a very different fate awaited *fédérés*.

[55] *Patriote*, 21 June 1815.   [56] *Ibid.*, 3 June 1815; *Indépendant*, 28 May 1815.

Chapter 3

The federative movement in general: social and political characteristics

After seeing what *fédérés* did in an official capacity, we can now turn to what they did and said of their own account. First, *fédéré* writings will be considered to determine what *fédérés* wanted. Then, the political tendencies of the federations will be discussed, paying particular attention to whether individual associations were Jacobin, Bonapartist, or a mixture of both. Finally, the extent of the movement and the social basis of the associations will be assessed.

Fédéré *writings*

Fédéré writings give us the common denominator of *fédéré* aspirations. Any movement which wished to emphasise unity had to be built on certain common principles and objectives. Significantly, most of these were closely associated with the early years of the Revolution. Historians have recently placed great stress on how, through the passage of time, more and more Frenchmen were alienated by the evolution of the Revolution, and how opposition to it slowly mounted and gained force.[1] Internecine battles between groups of men who initially had supported the Revolution eventually fragmented the movement and weakened it to the point that Napoleon was able to impose dictatorship.

Observers in 1815 repeatedly pointed out that the federative movement had drawn on men from all epochs of the Revolution. This amalgamation was brought about by the experience of 1814. Invasion, occupation, return of intransigent *émigrés* and Bourbon government had combined to remind patriots of what they had fought to achieve during the early years of the Revolution. This can be seen in the following declaration published by Cunier, organiser of the federation at Sélestat:

---

[1] For a recent example, see D. M. G. Sutherland, *France 1789–1815, Revolution and Counter-revolution* (London, 1985).

Lorsque des siècles d'humiliation; lorsque la marche progressive des lumières eurent amené la grande révolution de 89, ils saluèrent avec transport ces premiers jours; ces jours si purs, entourés de si douces espérances, et au bruit des chaînes d'une honteuse féodalité qui se brisaient, ils firent sur l'autel de la Patrie le serment solennel que, désormais unis de cœur avec tous les Français, affranchis des dixmes, des impots arbitraires et soumis seulement à la Loi, ils réuniraient leurs forces et leurs moyens pour asseoir leur bonheur commun sur un pacte qui consacrerait leurs droits et qui fixerait leurs devoirs.

The attempt to focus attention on this stage of the Revolution, which least divided Frenchmen, was part of a conscious effort to rebuild the *élan* and unity of '89.[2]

Fédérés were joined by an intricate web of political, social and patriotic ideology and self-interest. Each of these strands will be considered separately, although they were so closely bound that such a process is exceedingly difficult.

In the decrees of the *vol d'aigle*, Napoleon had presented himself as the saviour of the Revolution. He had declared himself 'moins le souverain de la France que le premier de ses citoyens'. Many *fédérés* took Bonaparte at his word; they accepted that 'Napoléon vient nous réintégrer dans nos droits'. In their pacts, *fédérés* repeatedly referred to Bonaparte as the freely chosen leader of the nation. The *fédérés* of Tours described him as 'ce héros qui s'honore de régner par notre choix'. Moreover, Napoleon was the choice of the people because he recognised the fundamental principle of national sovereignty; he was 'pénétré de cette vérité philanthropique que les trônes sont faits pour les peuples'. The *fédérés* of Foix wrote: 'Napoléon, puisque tu ne veux régner que pour soutenir les droits du peuple français qui t'a salué du nom de grand, il jure de vaincre ou de mourir avec toi.' The *fédérés* of Montpellier announced that they were at war with despotism, and the *fédérés* of Dijon flatly stated that the nation was sovereign. A *fédéré* of Riom saw the Emperor as guarantor of the liberties won during the Revolution: 'une funeste expérience nous a trop appris que la conservation de notre liberté est attachée au règne de Napoléon et de sa dynastie'.[3]

The reverse side of this was resounding rejection of the Bourbon monarchy. The same *fédéré* of Riom referred to it as a 'dynastie dès longtemps réprouvée, rejetée par la volonté nationale'. The *fédérés* of Toulon said of the restored Bourbon monarchy that 'les premiers actes ont signalés

[2] Quoted in P. Leuilliot, 'L'Alsace en 1815', *Revue d'Alsace*, 75 (1928), p. 38; *L'Indépendant*, 8 June 1815.

[3] H. Houssaye, *1815 – Les Cent-Jours* (Paris, 1901), p. 483; R. Grand, *La Chouannerie de 1815* (Paris, 1942), p. 38; *L'Indépendant*, 8 June 1815; *Le Moniteur Universel*, 28 June 1815; *Le Patriote de '89*, 3 June 1815; AN, AFIV 1935, *Pacte Fédératif* (of the Bretons), AFIV 1937, *Confédération Périgourdine* and *Acte Fédératif des Alsaciens*, F^9 476–7, *Fédération Bourguignonne*; BN, Lb^{46} 319, *Fédération*, p. 26.

l'ineptie, la faiblesse et le despotisme'. Pichois, a deputy of the federation of Lyons, stated:

Les restes oubliés de cette vieille dynastie n'ont annoncé leur existence qu'en méconnaissant la souveraineté nationale. Ils ont prétendu régner par leur propre droit, sans avoir besoin du consentement du peuple.

Fédérés were convinced that the government of Louis XVIII unjustly favoured the Catholic Church and the old nobility. Referring to the First Restoration, the *fédérés* of Lyons wrote: 'Des fléaux dévastateurs, la féodalité, la dîme, la noblesse privilégiée, la renaissance des préjugés menaçaient notre existence nationale.' In their call for a federative pact, the *jeunes gens* of Nantes wrote: 'Le gouvernement des Bourbons marchait à l'anéantissement de toutes les idées libérales. Encore une génération, et les plébéiens retombaient sous l'inquisition des moines et la tyrannie des nobles.' The rhetoric of the Lyons decrees had fallen on fertile ground.[4]

There could be no mistaking the hatred of social privilege felt by *fédérés*. In Loches, *fédérés* railed against nobles who pretended to have the right to dictate laws to their fellow countrymen. The future fédérés of Nantes referred to the nobility as 'la honte de la civilisation'. The *fédérés* of Riom spoke of the flight of Louis XVIII with pleasure because, 'La chute de cette puissance odieuse a anéanti des prétentions plus odieuses encore: le noble, qui croyait avoir réconquis des vassaux, parlait déjà avec orgueil de ses privilèges.'[5]

Closely tied to this antipathy towards the nobility was suspicion of the Catholic Church, though it was not expressed as often or as virulently. Doubtless certain *fédéré* orators expressed a desire for the proscription of all priests, but in their pacts *fédérés* limited themselves to opposing any reinstitution of the *dîme* and religious intolerance. At Strasbourg, *fédérés* distributed a circular signalling priests as especially worthy of surveillance. However, given the necessity of obtaining official approval, it is not surprising that few *fédérés* went beyond those of Foix who warned against the re-establishment of 'les horreurs de toutes les inquisitions'.[6]

It would be unwise to assume that all men who rallied to the cause of the government in 1815 were either Bonapartists or old revolutionaries. For many Frenchmen, the issue at stake was that of national independence. The

---

[4] BN, Lb⁴⁶ 319, *Fédération*, pp. 13–14, 25; AN, AFIV 1938, *Pacte Fédératif*, p. 1; Grand, *Chouannerie*, p. 38; J. Audin, *Tableau historique des événements qui se sont passés à Lyon depuis le retour de Bonaparte jusqu'au rétablissement de Louis XVIII* (Lyons, 1815), p. 115.

[5] *Indépendant*, 8 June 1815; Grand, *Chouannerie*, p. 15; BN, Lb⁴⁶ 319, *Fédération*, p. 25.

[6] Audin, *Tableau*, pp. 109–10; BN, Lb⁴⁶ 319, *Fédération*, p. 25; AN, F⁹ 476–7, *Fédération Bourguignonne*; P. Leuilliot, *La Première Restauration et les Cent-Jours en Alsace* (Paris, 1958), p. 232; *Moniteur*, 16 May 1815.

pride of many patriots was stung by the fact that the Bourbon government had been imposed on them by foreign rulers. The *fédérés* of Périgueux called on the Allied 'potentats' to 'renoncez à la prétention extravagante de vouloir nous imposer des souverains de votre choix, et de régler les formes de notre gouvernement'. The *fédérés* of Angers believed that the true purpose of the Allied monarchs was 'l'humiliation de la France ... peut être son anéantissement'. The Allies intended to trample the 'droits sacrés des peuples', as they had done already in Poland, Saxony, Italy and Belgium. In order to end French independence they planned 'l'entière destruction de l'armée'.[7]

Destruction of this buttress of national independence was a work begun by the Treaty of Paris, and continued by the Bourbon government. The *fédérés* of Rennes raged at the fate of:

ces Guerriers qui virent tout-à-la-fois ... cinquante forteresses rendues à l'ennemi sans combats: nos canons, nos vaisseaux, nos plus riches chantiers livrés sans compensation; le Domaine des Héros ... abandonnés sans qu'on ait daigné consacrer une seule ligne diplomatique; 30,000 officiers éprouvés dans tant de batailles, chassés pour faire place à des hommes, qui, pour états de services offraient vingt-cinq ans de nullité.[8]

Fulsome praise of the army occurs frequently in *fédéré* writings; experience of invasion had dramatically increased the stature of the army and its leaders.

The federation of Nancy devoted itself to 'la résistance très-prononcée à toutes les hostilités locales qui menaceraient l'indépendance de l'Etat et du peuple'. Memories of invasion and occupation were particularly evident in the pact of the Picards:

Fédérons-nous donc, et si vous pouviez hésiter un seul instant, venez dans nos contrées: vous y verrez dans quel abîme de maux nos ennemis nous ont plongés ... parcourez nos campagnes: les traces sanglantes qu'ils ont laissés sur leur passage vous feront frémir d'horreur.

Such sentiments, widespread in the east, help explain why the Bourbon Monarchy was so unpopular in the region.[9]

Warnings about destruction of property indicated concerns tied at least as closely to self-interest as ideology. *Fédérés* throughout the country cited their desire for the preservation of law, order and property. The *fédérés* of Angers described their association as 'une pacte sainte pour le maintien, dans ce département, des lois qui sont la sûreté des personnes et la garantie

---

[7] AN, AFIV 1937, *Confédération Périgourdine*; *Moniteur*, 16 May 1815.
[8] AN, AFIV 1935, *Pacte Fédératif* (of the Bretons).
[9] *Moniteur*, 8 June 1815; AN, AFIV 1935, *Confédération Picarde*.

des propriétés'. The *fédérés* of Riom swore to maintain 'respect sans bornes pour les personnes et les propriétés'. In this they were echoing the sentiments of their *confrères* of Puy who spoke of the necessity of consecrating 'tous nos moyens au maintien de bon ordre'. Behind all of this we can see the concern of purchasers of *biens nationaux* for their properties. In their initial address, the *fédérés* of Montpellier called upon local 'acquéreurs de domaines nationaux' to join their association. They cited 'les avantages personnels qui en résulteront' and avowed that the federation 'auront pour objet la sûreté des individus et le respect de propriétés'. At Toulouse, Boyer-Fonfrède issued circulars informing holders of *biens nationaux* that their interests would best be served by joining the federation of the Midi.[10]

In the hands of a practised rhetorician such as Cambon, all the basic components of the federative movement – revolutionary tradition, Bonapartism, patriotism and material self-interest – could be crafted into a single appeal:

Le moment est favorable, y disait-on; faisons éclater cette énergie que nous concentrions naguère dans le fond de nos cœurs, apprenons à l'étranger que nous ne voulons pas plus que le reste de la France d'un Chef qui serait d'un choix de nos ennemis, parce qu'il est impossible que nous veuillons le retour des Dîmes, de la morgue féodale et de toutes les distinctions odieuses et serviles dont le souvenir soulèvera toujours les hommes de 1789 et leurs dignes enfans . . . Fédérons-nous! La patrie le réclame, le héros de l'Europe nous y invite, notre propre sûreté le commande.

No other statement better illustrates the fusion that was the federative movement.[11]

Political tendencies

Any attempt to use federative literature to prove that the movement was influenced more by revolutionary tradition than by Bonapartism would prove largely futile; *fédéré* writers were adroit at balancing references to the glories of the Revolution with praise of Napoleon. However, after long perusal of *fédéré* writings, one cannot help but remark that *fédérés* were lauding the Revolution in a way which they could not have done at the apogee of the Empire, nor escape the conclusion that the Bonapartism

---

[10] *Moniteur*, 16 May 1815; BN, Lb⁴⁶ 319, *Fédération*, pp. 17, 27; *Patriote*, 3 June 1815; J. Hémardinquer, 'Un libéral: F.-B. Boyer-Fonfrède (1767–1845)', *Annales du Midi*, 73 (1961), p. 176.

[11] J. Thomas, *Précis historique des événements arrivés à Montpellier pendant les Cent-Jours de l'Interrègne* (Montpellier, 1976), pp. 32–3.

championed by *fédérés* was very much the new, revolutionary variety described by F. Bluche.[12] Whether *fédérés* truly believed that Napoleon himself was an adherent of revolutionary Bonapartism can, at least regarding certain individuals, be questioned, but it is of crucial importance, in examining this literature, to remember that Napoleon fell before he had a chance to prove the *fédérés* wrong in championing him as a proponent of the Revolution.

In the previous chapter, we noted that Breton *fédérés* in formulating the original pact, took care to define clearly their role in relation to the Imperial government – they recognised that they had no political authority and stated they would work in co-operation with, and accept the direction of, the central government. In part this reflected a realistic appraisal of contemporary circumstances; without Napoleon's approval there would have been no federative movement in the first place. But it also reflected a genuine desire to aid the government. *Fédérés* were acting on their own initiative; they were not forced to form associations.

Yet, there was a certain ambivalence in the original pact; *fédérés* declared they would 'propagate liberal principles' and 'oppose truth to imposture'. This was tantamount to declaring war upon those who sought a return to the *ancien régime*, yet it was also a declaration which would not have been published with official approval earlier in the Empire. After all, Napoleon had renewed social hierarchy in the early years of the nineteenth century and liberties such as freedom of the press and association had not fared well under Imperial rule, nor had representative government prospered, despite the sops thrown to national sovereignty by Napoleonic plebiscites. Herein lay an essential paradox of the federative movement: championing of Liberty combined with support for a man who had been no worshipper of the Goddess. Were *fédérés* convinced by Napoleon's revolutionary conversion? Undoubtedly, some of them were not entirely convinced, but given the alternative to Bonaparte, they could only hope for the best and watch to see how Bonaparte acted in the future. Many were convinced, however, and it should be noted that Napoleon's claim to represent the Revolution was stronger than historians have generally recognised. The *Acte Additionnel* certainly was disappointing, but it granted a franchise marginally larger than that of the Charter. Liberty of expression flourished during the Hundred Days, except for royalists. Federations bore testimony to reviving freedom of association. Last, but not least, Napoleonic government was certainly not the puppet of the *ancien régime* privileged élite. In 1814, no one had more directly criticised Bourbon pandering to the

---

[12] See F. Bluche, *Le Bonapartisme* (Paris, 1980), pp. 99–122.

aristocracy and Catholic Church than Carnot, the organiser of the victory in 1792 and government minister during the Hundred Days.

There is a good deal of evidence that *fédérés* wanted desperately to believe in the new revolutionary Bonapartism; undoubtedly they were convinced that, even at his worst, Napoleon was the lesser of two evils. Military defeat in 1814 had produced a certain trauma in France; it was humiliating and an affront to the centre of civilisation. The seductive power of Napoleonic *gloire* grew in consequence. Provided there was no second betrayal, would not the combination of Bonaparte and Carnot prove invincible? *Fédérés* had a multitude of reasons for believing, not the least of which was calm appraisal of self-interest. Napoleon was not the only gambler in 1815.

The will to believe was especially apparent in the pact of the federation of the Nièvre drawn up by Albon Lefiot, an old regicide who, according to the prefect, continued to enjoy 'l'estime générale' of the people of Nevers. As befitted a man of great experience, passages in Lefiot's pact were highly original:

Un ami du pouvoir illimité aurait tenté de conserver seul les rênes du gouvernement, avec l'influence du nombreux bataillons qu'il a réunis et qui sont accoutumés à vaincre sous son commandement, tandis que Napoléon, à qui sont familières toutes les conceptions de la véritable grandeur, a pris pour premier soin celui de poser volontairement des bornes à sa propre puissance. Il a fait aux français la proposition d'un contrat social dont le perfectionnement doit faire luire pour nous les beaux jours de la liberté sagement modifiée par les lois. Et il s'est empressé d'appeler autour du trône les électeurs représentants immédiates de la volonté nationale, et les deux Chambres des Pairs et des Députés qui doivent se contre-balancer l'une et l'autre, en même temps qu'elles serviront de digue contre l'extension du pouvoir ministériel.

After giving the Emperor and the *Acte Additionnel* this ringing endorsement, Lefiot proceeded to warn the Allied Powers against attempting to replace 'le chef reconnu des français' by 'les instruments du despotisme, de l'intolérance et de la féodalité'. He even went so far as to state that the Allies would have to be punished if the Empress and her son were not returned 'à notre amour'.

These were not the words of a political innocent or of a man of the traditional Bonapartist variety; praising Napoleon for limiting his own powers by offering to enter into a 'social contract' was a means of defining a basis of support. Napoleon was not being given *carte blanche*, but he was being taken at his word. The reason for Lefiot's belief in the new revolutionary Bonapartism was also apparent in the pact; like other *fédérés*, the old regicide hated those who wished 'd'opprimer le peuple et de faire ramper des vassaux à leurs pieds'. At worst Napoleon was the lesser of two evils, but in his present form he was quite acceptable.[13]

The ambivalence of the *fédérés*' position was apparent in their references to liberty. Clearly, certain *fédérés* had expectations in this respect. The *jeunes gens* of Nantes wrote of Napoleon:

> ce héros législateur convoque les Français à l'assemblée patriotique du Champ de Mai; il prépare les élémens d'une constitution telle qu'a droit de l'attendre de lui une nation puissante et éclairée; il nous l'a promise, nous lui devons ce bienfait. Sa parole et son intérêt même en seront les garans infaillibles.[14]

Here we find more fruit born of the Lyons decrees and, noting that this was written before the publication of the *Acte Additionnel*, it is logical to conclude that such men were disappointed by the ultimate changes to the constitution. The *Acte* was given a stormy reception and the towns of Brittany were particularly notable for voting against it. *Fédérés* were not so disillusioned as to give up the good fight however; moreover, as can be seen in the above quotation, they were very careful not to make explicit demands regarding political liberty. It was one thing to champion a vague abstraction; it was another to make concrete proposals which might have roused the Emperor's ire. Napoleon still commanded the Army and there was no denying his coercive power. Furthermore, even if some *fédérés* were not entirely satisfied with the backtracking Eagle, the truth was that they needed him at least as much as he needed them. Without the Emperor and his Army, there could be no prospect of warding off the Allied Powers and the King in their baggage train. *Fédérés* knew that at most they could play only a supporting role and that, in consequence, there were significant limits to the rewards they could claim.

At their most bathetic, *fédéré* evocations of Liberty could be utterly meaningless. This can be seen in the second article of the pact of the *Confédération Artésienne et Boulonnaise* drawn up by Dumont, an old regicide reborn as Imperial prefect:

> L'objet de cette fédération est le maintien des principes libéraux, savoir: dévouement à la patrie, garantie de la sécurité publique intérieure, opposition à tout projet d'invasion étrangère, de discordes civiles, à tout esprit de désordre, à tous complots contre la liberté, nos constitutions et l'empereur.[15]

This curious definition of liberty was proclaimed at Arras; one wonders what The Incorruptible would have thought of it. Then again, Robespierre

---

[13] The federative pact of the Nièvre can be found in AN, F^{ic} III, Nièvre 8.
[14] Grand, *Chouannerie*, p. 38.
[15] G. de Hauteclocque, 'Les Cent-Jours dans le Pas-de-Calais', *Mémoires de l'Académie des sciences, lettres et arts d'Arras*, 2e série, 36 (1905), p. 139.

was not a man to shy away from circumscribing liberty when the *patrie* was in danger.

One must search long and hard to find *fédéré* references to specific liberties. Pichois, of the Lyons federation, did castigate the Bourbon government for failing to secure 'la liberté de la presse, ce droit qui est le sauve-garde de tous les droits'. But against this, one can place the following sycophantic address made by Lyonnais *fédérés* to Madame Mère: 'Nous contemplons, avec la plus haute vénération, celle qui a mis au monde l'enfant chéri de la victoire, l'illustre soutien du nom Français et l'ornement futur de l'histoire des Grands Hommes.'[16]

The necessity of flattering the Great Man who was again about to lead France into war did not stop *fédérés* from speaking with conviction about their favourite subject – the Revolution. *Fédérés* were on solid ground when they denounced *ancien régime* privileges which had been abolished during the Revolution and, equally important, had not been renewed during the Empire. Pichois condemned the Bourbon Monarchy for re-establishing 'cette noblesse féodale, qui, se transmettant à tous les membres d'une famille divisait la nation en deux castes'. The key word, of course, was 'féodale' – making a crucial distinction between *ancien régime* nobility and an Imperial nobility supposedly based on merit. Such nice distinctions were not simply a means to avoid offending the Emperor; they represented a constant, conscious attempt to find common ground between revolutionary tradition and Bonapartism. Historians have long emphasised that Napoleon sought to woo men of the Revolution during the Hundred Days, but this was a blade which sliced both ways and, with an eye towards the Second Restoration, it is instructive to note that old revolutionaries were also wooing followers of Napoleon. Many rank-and-file *fédérés*, described fairly accurately by Le Gallo as being led by old Jacobins, were clearly affected by popular Bonapartism.[17]

Among a legion of examples of the search for common ground, we can point to the pact of the *fédérés* of Périgueux. Their preamble commences, 'Il y a 25 ans la France était courbée sous le poids des abus'; by the third paragraph of their potted history we find, 'Napoléon est devenu à notre tête le plus grand des mortels: il a remplis l'Univers du bruit de nos exploits, et porté en tous lieux la gloire du nom Français.' Thus, laudatory references to the Revolution and the Empire are combined. Moreover, elsewhere we discover: 'L'amour de la liberté nous égara quelques instans: bientôt, revenant à nous-mêmes, nous confiâmes ce dépôt sacré, et surtout notre haine implacable contre les anciens privilégiés, au premier de nos guerriers:

[16]　Audin, *Tableau*, pp. 115–16.
[17]　*Ibid*.; E. Le Gallo, *Les Cent-Jours* (Paris, 1924), pp. 288–91.

nous saluâmes Napoléon du titre d'Empereur.' This would have provided excellent grist for de Tocqueville's mill, but as well as the inclination to place social equality above political liberty, we should note the tendency to hearken back to '89 and not the subsequent divisive periods when 'la liberté nous égara quelques instans'.[18]

Fédérés repeatedly stressed continuity by linking the Revolution and the Empire. Jean de Bry, in one of several fiery discourses, accomplished this most adroitly:

Il y a vingt-cinq ans, la liberté était le but, aujourd'hui elle est le moyen; et ce moyen remplira son objet: le peuple français et son Empereur sortiront vainqueurs de cette dernière lutte, de cette lutte des privilégiés contre l'égalité naturelle, de la super-stition contre la religion éclairée et la liberté de tous les cultes, de la tyrannie contre le système représentatif.

Le monstre féodal à l'agonie pourra bien, sans doute, dans ses convulsions hideuses, agiter pour un moment notre patrie: mais, c'en est fait, il n'en ébranlera plus les fondemens. Les changemens opérés depuis vingt-cinq ans sont dans nos cœurs et dans nos habitudes, plus encore que dans nos lois; ils n'en sortiront plus: il faudrait, pour les extirper, anéantir jusqu'au dernier Français.

By overlooking the matter of Napoleonic dictatorship and stressing con-tinuity, de Bry and *fédérés* like him were forging a revolutionary Bona-partism which would outlast the Emperor himself.[19]

There were limits, of course, to viewing 1789–1815 as a lineal pro-gression. Thuriot, an old regicide and member of the Committee of Public Safety, who had the intriguing distinction of having denounced Robes-pierre for moderation, clearly overstepped the mark in authoring an address of the federations of the *faubourgs* Saint-Antoine and Saint-Marceau which called for resumption of Terror. This caused a great deal of perturbation, and led to official apologies in the press. By and large, how-ever, *fédérés* were shrewd enough to avoid references to the more divisive aspects of the Revolution; it was not simply the history of the Empire that posed potential problems for unity in 1815.[20]

Ploughing common ground did not prevent *fédérés* from reminding the Emperor of recent promises; the rhetoric of the *vol d'aigle* was crucial to the federative movement. The *fédérés* of Dijon, for instance, drew attention to the fact that Bonaparte had avowed his intention to refrain from wars of aggrandisement. The *fédérés* of Foix flatly stated that they would fight for Napoleon because he had recognised the principle of national

[18] AN, AFIV 1937, *Confédération Périgourdine*.
[19] BN, Lb[46] 396, *Relation des Journées des 5 et 6 Juin 1815*, pp. 12–13.
[20] On Thuriot, see A. Robert, E. Bourloton and G. Cougny, *Dictionnaire des Parlementaires Français* (Paris, 1891). On the address, see chapter 8.

sovereignty.[21] But to infer from such statements that *fédérés* were seeking to place constraints on Napoleon is to assume that they envisaged the possibility of the Emperor breaking his promises. To make the latter assumption, and the former inference, we must have evidence that *fédéré* writings do not provide.

How much should be made of the fact that the *fédérés* of Chalon-sur-Saône and Clermont-Ferrand were quick to change their allegiance from Bonaparte to the Chamber of Representatives after Napoleon's second abdication? After all, this occurred at the same time as the Chamber was declaring its support of the rule of Napoleon II. Perhaps the best indication of the sentiment of the *fédérés* of Chalon-sur-Saône lies in their address to the Chamber: 'Nous interdit à tous la faculté de rappeler et de penser même au rétablissement des Bourbons sur la trône.' Such strong words could have left little doubt of what the *fédérés* thought of the Bourbons. Nor did they indicate blind faith in the intentions of the Chamber of Representatives.[22]

Much *fédéré* writing certainly has a revolutionary flavour to it. After news of Waterloo and the 'noble sacrifice de Napoléon Premier' had reached Clermont-Ferrand, *fédérés* advised the Chamber of Representatives that they had 'juré de répandre jusqu'à la dernière goutte de notre sang pour la défense commune' and advised that 'nous sommes debout pour nous porter par-tout où les ordres du gouvernement nous appeleront'. Jean de Bry did not fight shy of the revolutionary resonance of the expression 'La France est debout!' He well knew the implications, but, then again, Napoleon himself had given the lead in this regard. Nevertheless, it is difficult to conceive of any association during the height of the Empire using 'tu' to address Napoleon, as did the federation of Foix in 1815.[23]

Although we do not possess adequate sources to describe a *fédéré* 'mentalité', there is something sufficiently humourless in the following to suggest what Professor Cobb has cited as characteristic of the 'mentalité révolutionnaire':

Qu'ils s'agitent en tous les sens; qu'ils s'attachent à répandre, tantôt les alarmes et la défiance, tantôt le ridicule et l'ironie; nous leur opposerons avec orgueil la sagesse des status qui nous régissent, le mérite, la considération, les vertus des citoyens qui président à nos délibérations.

Moral rectitude was to be expected of men who were waging 'la guerre de la raison, de la liberté et de l'indépendance, contre l'erreur, l'oppression et

---

[21] AN, F⁹ 476–7, *Fédération Bourguignonne*; *Moniteur*, 28 June 1815.
[22] *Moniteur*, 2–3 July 1815.
[23] *Ibid.*, 28 June and 3 July 1815; BN, Lb⁴⁶ 396, *Relation*, p. 9.

la tyrannie'. For an association to be truly useful to its country, its members must have 'de bonnes mœurs et une conduite sans reproche'.[24]

Classical allusions were standard to revolutionary rhetoric. Jean-Baptiste Teste, a master of this art, referred to the attitude of the French people as being that of the 'Janus des Romains, d'un côté regardant l'ennemi et de l'autre fixant ses regards sur l'intérieur de l'Empire.'[25] Napoleon and his followers, however, were by no means foreign to the classical verbal tradition.

If one were so inclined, one could tabulate the number of allusions to the Revolution in *fédéré* literature and establish that these clearly were in the ascendent over allusions to the Empire. It is difficult, however, to believe that this would prove a great deal – there were references enough to Napoleonic *gloire*, and it is not possible to quantify the emotive impact of individual references to past epochs. Moreover, such an approach would be essentially anachronistic; as should now be clear, the Bonapartism of *fédéré* literature was the new revolutionary version. *Fédérés* did not wish, nor did they feel a need, to distinguish between revolutionary tradition and Bonapartism. Waterloo assured that they were not forced to do so.

In their writings and pronouncements, *fédérés* had to forego critical appraisal of the past, and they could not put forward specific, concrete demands as to the nature of government. *Fédéré* literature was full of vague statements of principle because this was necessary; the aim of these writings was to foster unity and avoid the divisions of the past. Consequently, liberty, patriotism and Napoleon were linked in a way which now seems disingenuous. One clear point does, however, emerge from analysis of *fédéré* literature – determined opposition to the Bourbon Monarchy and all it was held to represent. The fundamentally negative characteristic of opposition proved sufficient for *fédéré* unity during the Hundred Days; to a surprising extent, it would continue to do so until 1830.

Fédéré opposition of 'la verité à l'imposture' all too often took the form of denunciation of suspected royalists to the authorities. Indeed, the *fédérés* of Riom cited public denunciation as a necessary virtue:

si des actes précurseurs des désordres se laissent apercevoir; si l'on osait exciter le peuple à la révolte, détourner la jeunesse du service militaire, provoquer ou favoriser la désertion, ayons le courage de faire connaître ces odieuses manœuvres.

---

[24] BN, Lb[46] 319, *Fédération*, pp. 17, 18, 30. For Professor Cobb's comments, see R. Cobb, 'Quelques aspects de la mentalité révolutionnaire (avril 1793–Thermidor An II)', *Revue d'histoire moderne et contemporaine*, 6 (1959), pp. 84–5.

[25] Quoted in G. Ribe, *L'Opinion publique et la vie politique à Lyon lors des premières années de la Seconde Restauration* (Paris, 1957), p. 40.

At Lyons, secretary Butignot gave the same message 'étouffons par notre vigilance le dernier espoir des traîtres, déjouons leurs perfides complots'. While it is difficult to believe that Roederer heard 1,200 denunciations in Lyons over just two days, there is no doubt that *fédérés* did conduct these exercises in Lyons and Nancy. At Colmar, *fédérés* suggested surveillance of civil servants. It is difficult to say whether Charles Weiss was exaggerating when he termed the federative central committee of Besançon a 'comité de surveillance', but certainly these *fédérés* did not hesitate to denounce leading civil and military officials. Arrest of suspects did take place at Nîmes, and it is highly likely that *fédérés* elsewhere also took part in these activities reminiscent of the Terror. Such actions were not, of course, simply the result of ideological differences; as often as not they were the product of ongoing struggles between rival factions bent on securing their own material interests and desires for personal vengeance. Especially where a prefect was newly arrived and unfamiliar with his department, and inclined to tap the advice of *fédérés* while conducting administrative purges, *fédérés* were in an excellent position to further their own interests and those of their friends and allies. Such appears to have been the case in the Basses-Alpes, where Prefect Didier relied on information supplied by *fédérés* to determine new appointments.[26]

Denunciations were part of a general plan to keep royalist agitators in check. Where the movement was strong, *fédérés* appear to have succeeded in this. Verbal intimidation and gestures were sufficient to drive nobles out of Dinan and reduce monarchist manifestations to a minimum at Lyons, Nancy and Périgueux. *Fédérés* achieved similar results at Arles, Nîmes, Albi, Auch, Carcassonne and Draguignan. The *fédéré* at Lyons who shouted 'Nous savons où sont les royalistes. Nous avons des baïonnettes, sachons nous en servir' probably contributed to this end. Threats of violence were not always necessary, of course; the *fédérés* of Grenoble acted as the town police and assured that there was not 'le moindre excès durant toute cette période'.[27]

Encouraged by General Decaen to terrorise royalists, several Toulouse

[26] AN, AFIV 1935, *Pacte Fédératif* (of the Bretons), second article; BN, Lb[46] 319, *Fédération*, p. 29; Audin, *Tableau*, pp. 108, 120, 121, 123, 170; P. Gonnet, 'Les Cent-Jours à Lyon', *Revue d'histoire de Lyon*, 7 (1908), pp. 114, 116, 118; G. Richard, 'Les Cent-Jours à Nancy', *Pays Lorrain* (Nancy, 1957), pp. 89–90; Leuilliot, *Alsace*, p. 233; C. Weiss, *Journal 1815–22* (Paris, 1972), p. 55; R. Huard *et al.*, *Histoire de Nîmes* (Aix-en-Provence, 1982), p. 261; C. Cauvin, 'Le retour de l'Ile d'Elbe et les Cent-Jours dans les Basses-Alpes', *Bulletin de la société scientifique et littéraire des Basses-Alpes*, 21 (1926–7), p. 127.

[27] AN, AFIV 1937, General Lucotte to Minister of War, 28 May 1815; Audin, *Tableau*, pp. 108–9; Richard, 'Nancy', p. 89; Houssaye, *1815 – Les Cent-Jours*, p. 484; H. Dumolard, 'Grenoble au début de la Restauration', *Annales de l'Université de Grenoble* *(Lettres)*, 3 (1926), p. 132.

fédérés went beyond threats and killed two monarchists on 4 May, after catching them tearing down proclamations. In June *fédérés* acted as a police force, arresting royalists and forcing them to serve in the Imperial army. When a royalist planted the *drapeau blanc* on 26 June, street fighting erupted. Six royalists were killed, but it would appear that soldiers accounted for this. Boyer-Fonfrède the *fédéré* president, counselled his charges to act with prudence. Nevertheless, as late as 14 July, *fédérés* were still rampaging through the streets of the city and forcing suspected royalists to cry 'Vive l'Empereur!' Although the number of casualties in Toulouse was relatively small, *fédérés* such as the retired officer Louis Savés, who constantly threatened murder and revenge, did cause panic and hardship amongst royalists. Thus, while *fédérés* did manage to constrain royalists during the Hundred Days, they also made enemies who would seek their own revenge during the White Terror.[28]

Some of these activities were probably more than most order-loving Bonapartist officials could condone, but there can be little doubt that the authorities at least tacitly approved some of the less violent acts of intimidation. Teste, lieutenant-general of police, must have realised the possible consequences when he directed Lyonnais *fédérés* to keep a close watch over royalist traitors. He, however, was only following the line previously established by Mayor Jars. The complaisance of public officials at Nancy allowed *fédérés* such as the haberdasher Ajot, Brulfer, a joiner, Gaurrot, a *demi-solde*, and the bailiff Girardon to persecute royalists. One week after Waterloo, Ajot took it upon himself to order Demontzey, a National Guardsman, to surrender his arms. When Demontzey, a royalist, refused, Ajot recruited several companions and resorted to force, striking Demontzey with a sabre. Fortunately, Matton, a retired officer, intervened before Gaurrot could execute his intention to shoot the National Guardsman. Apparent official sanction could prove embarrassing later. General Brenier, who had armed the expedition of Brest *fédérés*, found himself forced to shout 'Vive l'Empereur!' by angry *fédérés* when he wished to recognise that Napoleon's regime no longer existed.[29]

If we look for political tendencies in the actions of *fédérés*, we find the same mixture of Bonapartism and revolutionary tradition apparent in *fédéré* literature. Here the common ground was the tricolour, a symbol of

---

[28] E. Newman, 'Republicanism during the Bourbon Restoration in France, 1814–1830', Ph.D. dissertation (University of Chicago, 1969), p. 69; H. Ramet, *Histoire de Toulouse* (Toulouse, 1935), p. 850; Hémardinquer, 'Boyer-Fonfrède', p. 176; D. Higgs, *Ultraroyalism in Toulouse* (Baltimore, 1973), pp. 54–7.

[29] Gonnet, 'Lyon', pp. 114–18; G. Richard, 'L'Esprit public en Lorraine au début de la Restauration', *Annales de l'Est, série 5, année 4*, no. 2 (1953), p. 204; AN, F⁷ 3786, bulletin of 4 July 1815.

both the Revolution and the Empire. After royalist crowds had pelted the tricolour with stones, Montpellier *fédérés* went on the rampage. The parade of Paris *fédérés* behind the bust of Napoleon gave clear evidence of devotion to the Emperor, and *fédérés* at Toulouse, Lyons, Montpellier and Dijon performed similar rituals. Perhaps more significantly, the *fédéré* banquet at Strasbourg took place in front of portraits of Napoleon and Marie-Louise, but it should be noted that this was very much an official ceremony, presided over by civil and military authorities. On the other hand, several *fédérés* planted liberty trees and at Albi, J.-B. Pecheloche donned a *bonnet rouge*. The *Fête de la Fédération* held at Arras in 1815 was in conscious imitation of the ceremony held in June 1790, and the second abdication of Napoleon did not so grievously afflict Montpellier *fédérés* as to prevent them from planning a 14 July banquet. Committees of surveillance and the tactic of denunciation were closely associated with the men of the Revolution, but revolutionaries did not have a monopoly on them. At the review of the federation of the *faubourgs* of Paris, several *fédérés* shouted 'Vive la liberté! A bas la calotte! A bas les riches!' However, they also mixed their singing of the *Marseillaise* and *Ca Ira* with cries of 'Vive l'Empereur!' Similarly, their Lyonnais counterparts sang the *Marseillaise* and *Chant du départ* while bellowing 'Vive l'Empereur!' Apparently the aged regicide Monnot was not the only *fédéré* who knew the words of the old revolutionary songs in 1815.[30]

Such actions at most inform us that the federations had Jacobin and Bonapartist elements. The best sources for determining which of these elements was dominant are to be found in local archives. For this reason, our best recourse is to turn to local studies. Failing these, we can turn to contemporary assessments, taking care to determine the objectivity of the source of information.

There certainly was a strong element of republicanism in the associations of the west, especially in Brittany. Count Floriac reported that the *fédérés* of Saint-Brieuc had 'manifesté des sentiments très républicains'; as we shall see shortly, the information he provided was accurate. J. Thiry has drawn attention to the patriots of Morlaix who planted liberty trees. Perhaps our

---

[30] Thomas, *Montpellier*, pp. 36–7, 40, 59; Newman, 'Republicanism', p. 69; Audin, *Tableau*, p. 110; B. M. of Dijon, *Fonds Delmasse*, no. 2218; Leuilliot, 'L'Alsace', p. 257; AN, F⁷ 9650, Prefect to Minister of the Interior, 23 August 1815; J. Vanel, 'Le Mouvement fédératif de 1815 dans le département du Tarn', *Gaillac et le pays Tarnais, 31ᵉ congrès de la fédération des sociétés académiques et savantes de Languedoc-Pyrénées-Gascogne* (Gaillac, 1977), p. 391; Cobb, 'Quelques Aspects', pp. 95–7; A. Roserat, ed., *Mémoires de Madame de Chastenay* (Paris, 1896), p. 529; Houssaye, *1815 – Les Cent-Jours*, p. 625; Gonnet, 'Lyon', p. 294; Weiss, *Journal*, p. 95.

best evidence of the ascendancy of republicanism in the Ille-et-Vilaine comes from the following report made in June 1817: 'Il y a dans ce département plus de républicains que de Bonapartistes. Les premiers se composent à Rennes d'un certain nombre de jeunes légistes; les autres ne se composent guère que d'officiers à demi solde.' On the other hand, the royalist prefect of the Loire-Inférieure estimated that Bonapartists and Jacobins were about equal in number in his department.[31]

Another indication of republicanism in the west can be found in the response of *fédérés* to the *Acte Additionnel*. As F. Bluche has shown, opposition to the *Acte* was nowhere greater than in Brittany, especially in the Côtes-du-Nord and Finistère. With a good deal of insight, Bluche has speculated that many a 'jacobin rallié à l'Empire' may well have voted against the *Acte*, due to his opposition to hereditary nobility, without necessarily disapproving of Napoleon.[32]

Bluche's speculation is confirmed by several prefectoral reports of the Hundred Days. The prefect of the Ille-et-Vilaine reported a pamphlet that rejected the *Acte* but vowed support for the Emperor and requested a constitution capable of gaining support from the general public. The prefect of the Finistère warned that opinion at Brest had been greatly damaged by discussions of the *Acte* in local journals. Two days after founding the federation at Saint-Brieuc with a banquet of 300 tables, Le Gorrec, Aubrée and Ropartz published a brochure comparing the *Acte* with the promises of the *vol d'aigle* in the following unflattering terms:

Nous avions compris, en effect, qu'une représentation nationale allait coopérer avec des commissaires de Votre Majesté à la formation d'une charte qui présenterait la code politique complet destiné d'une part, à garantir la liberté publique par des institutions appropriées aux mesures et aux sentiments délicates des Français. Au lieu de ce travail que voyons nous, Sire? Un fragment d'acte qu'on doit agréger à des actes précédents adoptés dans des situations politiques différentes de celles où nous sommes, les uns accompagnés de quelque solennité pour leur adoption, les autres donnés avec des formes inusitées chez les peuples qui possédent une représentation nationale.

. . . il nous a semblé qu'en général on s'est trop attaché dans cet acte à restreindre l'action des Corps qui tiennent les pouvoirs immédiats du peuple, sans faire attention que le Trône n'est jamais plus menacé que par le sombre mécontentement qui résulte de la privation des droits d'une sage liberté.

---

[31] AN, F^7 9682, Count Floriac to Minister of the Interior, 13 July 1815, F^7 3740, bulletin of 12 June 1817, F^7 9671, Prefect to Minister of the Interior, 19 July 1817; J. Thiry, *Les Cent-Jours* (Paris, 1943), p. 256.
[32] F. Bluche, *Le Plébiscite des Cent-Jours* (Geneva, 1974), pp. 89, 95.

Nevertheless, after stating their rejection of the *Acte*, and calling on Napoleon to return to the promises of March, the three *fédérés* added: 'mais nous vous demeurons toujours unis, Sire, par les liens de l'amour et de la reconnaissance. Nous vous supplions de n'écouter que votre propre penchant dans vos rapports avec le peuple qui s'honore de vous avoir pour Empereur et veut garantir sa liberté par la conservation de votre personne auguste et le maintien de votre dynastie.' This was about as far as *fédérés* could go in calling Napoleon back to his promises. Republican tendencies were apparent in references to 'le peuple', and the oblique references to the Empire were hardly favourable. But clearly this did not constitute rejection of, or opposition to, Bonaparte himself. The ties that bound lay in the *fédéré* conviction that Napoleon was the guarantor of liberties which would be destroyed by a restored Bourbon Monarchy.[33]

Judging by the account of J. Mouchet, it would appear that 'révolutionnaires forcenés' predominated in the Morbihan. At Lorient, La Touche, a lawyer, was an 'homme dangereux connu par ses principes révolutionnaires'. Le Guével, *avoué*, was the author of a 'motion pour mettre hors de la loi des ascendants et descendants des défenseurs de la cause royale' made in the Hundred Days Chamber of Representatives, and Corbel de Squirio, law student, was the son of the *conventionnel* Corbel. Nevertheless, Bunel, guard, Duplessis, wigmaker, and Lemerle, master cobbler, were all 'chauds bonapartistes'.[34]

Outside Brittany, in the Sarthe, the *fédérés* were organised by Le Rebours, 'ancien complice de Robespierre', and were 'plus républicains que bonapartistes'. Le Rebours, who wrote the *fédéré* pact at Le Mans, had been responsible for the reports made by the ministry of *Secours Publics* to the Committee of Public Safety in 1794. On 9 *Thermidor*, he had been part of a Robespierrist assembly at the *hôtel de ville* of Paris, but was fortunate enough to escape and went into exile at Hamburg. Nevertheless, he had returned to Le Mans during the Empire, serving as a tax collector and the 'fédéré jacobin' of the Sarthe was of an 'inspiration impériale'. Other important *fédérés* at Le Mans included René Levasseur, regicide and friend of Philippe Buonarotti, and Goyet, the Second Restoration 'grand elector' of liberal deputies, whose republican convictions were well known.[35]

[33] AN, F⁷ 3785, bulletin of 10 May 1815, F⁷ 9656, Prefect to Minister of the Interior, 23 May 1815, F⁷ 9650, Minister of Police to Minister of the Interior, 6 June 1815; R. Durand, *Le Département des Côtes-du-Nord* (Paris, 1925), II, pp. 443–5.

[34] J. Mouchet, 'L'Esprit public dans le Morbihan sous la Restauration', *Annales de Bretagne*, 45 (1938), p. 129.

[35] A. Bouton, *Le Maine, histoire économique et sociale au XIXᵉ siècle* (Le Mans, 1974), pp. 210–11, 214; A. Bouton, *Les Francs-Maçons Manceaux et La Révolution Française (1741–1815)* (Le Mans, 1958), pp. 289–90, 293; A. Bouton, *Les Luttes Ardentes des*

At Angers, in the Mayenne-et-Loire, the federation was led by Mamert-Couillon, a man who in certain regards typified *fédérés* of the west. Despite having led republican troops who captured Angers from the *Armée Catholique et Royale* in July 1793, thereby setting the Terror in motion, Couillon was actually a Girondin and had taken part in the federalist revolt. As a result, he had been arrested and imprisoned until freed during *Thermidor*. Couillon then was elected to the Council of Five Hundred, indicating a fair measure of influence. During the Empire he was secretary-general of the prefecture and played a useful role in consolidating the Bonapartist regime. This Girondin background was shared by Jean-Pierre Guilhem, a deputy for Brest at the original federative meeting at Rennes in 1815. In 1793, Guilhem had been appointed municipal councillor by a *représentant en mission*, but had refused the post. Instead, he had concentrated on helping Girondins hide from their Montagnard persecutors. He had no qualms about joining the municipal council in 1808 however, and in 1815 he was elected to the Chamber of Representatives. As we shall see in our study of Rennes, this Girondin background was not untypical of western *fédérés*, although Beaugéard at Vitré was a notable exception. Having begun his political career by organising the Jacobin club of Vitré in 1792, Beaugéard had gone on to sit with the Mountain in the Convention and had voted for the death of Louis XVI.[36] Thus, we find both Girondins and Montagnards within the federative movement. Some of these men had served Bonaparte also, but, republican tendencies predominated in this region.

In southern and central France, leadership was often given by men of the Revolution, and here again there was a mix of old Girondins and Montagnards. At Toulouse, Boyer-Fonfrède, brother of a Girondin *conventionnel*, 'se vante d'avoir toujours été fidèle aux principes libéraux'. Jean-Dominique Romiguière's moderate patriotism had gained him the enmity of both Montagnards and royalists in the past. Scion of a Toulousain *robe* family, Romiguières had volunteered in 1792 for service in the Army and served as a captain in the artillery; however he had been imprisoned by the *représentant en mission* during the Terror. Released in 1795, he had published the *Anti-Terroriste*, 'organe du parti modéré'. Placed on a deportation list after *Fructidor An 5*, he had then gone into hiding and had not returned to Toulouse until after Napoleon's *coup d'état*. During the

Francs-Maçons Manceaux pour l'établissement de la République, 1815–1914 (Le Mans, 1966), pp. 33–40.

[36] F. Lebrun, ed., *Histoire d'Angers* (Toulouse, 1975), pp. 168, 189, 195; for Mamert-Couillon, Guilhem and Beaugéard, see A. Robert *et al.*, *Dictionnaire des Parlementaires*.

Empire he had taken up legal practice with some *éclat*, and in 1814 had re-entered military service to contribute to the defence of France. Again obliged to go into hiding during the First Restoration, Romiguières had returned to Toulouse during the Hundred Days as *lieutenant-extraordinaire de police*. Elected to the Chamber of Representatives, he attended the Champ de Mai and authored the famous declaration of 3 July, in which the Chamber informed enemy Monarchs of the necessity of 'l'égalité des droits civils et politiques, la liberté de la presse, la liberté des cultes, et le système représentatif comme forme de gouvernement'.

Although apparently not on the federative central committee, the presence of the regicide Marc-Guillaume-Alexis Vadier in the association must have frightened royalists and moderate Bonapartists alike. Vadier had been a member of the Jacobins of Toulouse and president of the mother society at Paris. He became the *'enfant terrible'* of the Convention, supporting Marat against the Girondins, denouncing Danton while a member of the Committee of Public Safety, and ultimately turning against Robespierre too (which he subsequently regretted). Under the Consulate he had been put under surveillance; thereafter he retired from the political arena until the Hundred Days. A fourth Toulousain *fédéré*, the actor Desbarreaux, had also been a leading Jacobin and Terrorist, and was known for his demagoguery.[37]

A list of 'the most dangerous individuals of the Dordogne', drawn up by the royalist prefect Montureux in March 1816, indicated that the *fédération périgourdine* had a decidedly Jacobin character. Although Giry, a member of the founding committee, was described simply as 'the leader of the revolutionary party', five other *fédérés* were identified specifically as Jacobins. Only one *fédéré* earned the epithet 'partisan outré de Bonaparte'. At Brive, in the Corrèze, a federation was founded by Rome, Laland, Eschapasse, Dalmay, Ledon and Bessat. According to V. de Seillac, 'ces derniers noms rappellent des souvenirs de la Révolution et la fin tragique d'un Girondin'. The *fédérés* of the Aveyron were led by Fualdès, criminal prosecutor at Rodez and an 'ancien juré du tribunal révolutionnaire'. Despite his revolutionary background, however, Fualdès was a convinced Bonapartist and in Rodez 'le prestige de Napoléon était intact dans les milieux populaires et . . . parmi les notables, il avait beaucoup de partisans'.[38]

[37] Le Gallo, *Les Cent-Jours*, p. 325; Ramet, *Toulouse*, pp. 655–7; Robert *et al.*, *Dictionnaire des Parlementaires*; J.-P. Giboury, *Dictionnaire des Régicides* (Paris, 1989), pp. 387–8; P. Wolff, ed., *Histoire de Toulouse* (Toulouse, 1988), pp. 400, 413.
[38] Le Gallo, *Les Cent-Jours*, p. 327; E. Enjalbert, *Histoire de Rodez* (Toulouse, 1981), p. 210; V. de Seillac, *Histoire politique du département de la Corrèze* (Tulle, 1888), p. 213; J. L'Homer, *Les Cent-Jours et la Terreur Blanche* (Paris, 1904), pp. 29–34.

No one could have questioned the republican credentials of Pierre-Joseph Cambon when he founded the federation of the Hérault, reputedly to cries of 'Vivent les sans-culottes!' Though ultimately crucial in bringing about the fall of Robespierre, and sympathetic to the Girondins, Cambon had also voted for the death of Louis XVI, presided over the Convention, and been a member of the first Committee of Public Safety. In May 1795, during the reaction of *Thermidor*, he had taken flight from Paris to cultivate an obscurity which lasted until the Hundred Days. After initiating the federation at Montpellier, Cambon departed for Paris to take his place in the Chamber of Representatives, but he left direction of the association in the hands of Valantin, mayor of Lunel and a Director of his district in the Year II, and Subleyras, a lawyer who had been a member of the Parisian Revolutionary Tribunal that condemned Marie-Antoinette. The revolutionary aspect should not be overstated however; other committee members such as Larmand, Avignon, Roussac and Demoulin had served as Imperial officials.[39]

At Avignon, the *fédéré* Agricole Moreau had been a Jacobin champion of Terror and friend of Robespierre. Etienne Paris, president of the federation of Nîmes, had commanded a battalion of National Guardsmen who, in 1790, had commenced the infamous *bagarre de Nîmes* that led to the slaughter of hundreds of royalist Catholics. Indeed, the bells ringing in the Protestant areas of the Gard did have a distinctly Montagnard air. In the words of G. Lewis, 'Federalism as it emerged in the summer of 1815, appears to have had more in common with the federation of popular societies led by Antoine Teste during the summer of 1793 than with the "girondin" movement of the previous summer.' Etienne Paris called on the mayor of Milhaud 'de venir au secours des patriotes et de sauver encore une fois la patrie en danger'. Again according to Lewis, 'a host of village Robespierres were ready to respond to this powerful evocation of the times of the Red Terror'. The *fédérés* of the commune of Saint-Paulet-de-Caisson proclaimed that they were citizens 'who from the first act of the Revolution had identified themselves entirely with the cause of the people'. They appear to have shared the sentiments of over a hundred citizens of Générac who signed a petition stating 'One of the gravest errors contributing to the collapse of the Imperialist regime was to place in public office sworn enemies of our Revolution against whom we have had to struggle, at home and abroad, for twenty-five years.' This was plain speaking and it reached the ears of General Gilly. Yet, despite their reservations about the past, Protestants lined up with Bonaparte virtually to a man, such was their hatred of

[39] AN, F⁷ 3735, bulletin of 8 December 1815; Thomas, *Montpellier*, pp. 32, 75–8; Robert et al., *Dictionnaire des Parlementaires*.

the Bourbons. *Fédérés* worked in perfect harmony with Gilly and J.-B. Teste (son of Antoine), Napoleon's lieutenant of police for ten southern departments.[40]

However, we should not jump to the conclusion that the participation of leading revolutionaries necessarily determined the overall political orientation of a federation, or that it caused problems for Bonapartists. For example, it would be unwise to conclude that the association at Albi was predominantly revolutionary in character simply because Jean-Eugène Fabre was its secretary. Fabre, who had become mayor in 1792, was a Girondin who had signed a protest against the expulsion of Girondin deputies in 1793. Nevertheless, neither he nor Albi in general had supported the federalist revolt, which perhaps accounts for his having retained his post and Albi not having suffered grievously during the Terror. Revolutionary ideals remained deep-rooted in Albi, but the Empire was a period of general prosperity for the town and revolutionaries who supported Napoleon's government in 1815 were joined by Bonapartist notables of the traditional stamp. In his study of the *fédérés* of the Tarn, J. Vanel states:

Les noms des chefs et des adhérents qui nous sont connus indiquent bien que l'élément révolutionnaire ne fut pas en majorité. Il y eut certes toute l'évocation des principes de 1789 dans le seul mot de Fédération … mais il y eut surtout l'occasion de manifester une opposition au gouvernement royal.

Thus, Vanel is careful not to conclude that the federation of the Tarn was either Bonapartist or revolutionary, emphasising the common opposition to the Bourbon Monarchy binding the two elements together.[41]

It is important that we do not overlook this aspect of the federations. The fact that the old regicide Lefiot, for instance, organised the federation of the Nièvre, did not necessarily indicate that the association was Jacobin and not Bonapartist; after all, the prefect felt no qualms about arming these men in order to conduct house searches. Moreover, alongside Lefiot on the central committee were Meunier, secretary at the prefecture, and the *Maréchal de camp*, d'Argens – men who had made their careers under the Empire. A fourth member of the committee, Armand de la Moinière, was well known for his devotion to Napoleon. Conversely, a federation which appears to have been Bonapartist, may well have contained republican elements. Prefect Didier, who organised and relied on the federation of the Basses-Alpes, was aided by a central committee composed of 'les bonapartistes les plus actifs du département'. Yet, when he was forced by

---

[40] APP, A A/331, 424; G. Lewis, *The Second Vendée* (Oxford, 1978), pp. 71–2, 147, 179–86.
[41] Vanel, 'Le Mouvement', p. 394; J. Biget, editor, *Histoire d'Albi* (Toulouse, 1983), pp. 235–7, 246–9.

royalist armies to retreat from Digne to Sisteron, Didier was joined by both Bonapartists and republicans.[42]

It is also important that we do not forget that other factors may have transcended normal political allegiance. This appears to have been the case in many parts of north-eastern France. In these regions, the essential motivating factor was determination to organise opposition to the Allied armies massing on the frontier.

The following, taken from a speech given by Jean de Bry to the *fédérés* of Strasbourg, gives a good indication of why the federative movement was so popular along the eastern frontier:

Que l'ennemi se présente; nous l'attendons: qu'ils arrivent surtout ces Prussiens, fameux ... par l'affreux mérite d'avoir surpassé naguères les barbares eux-mêmes en cruautés, contre des femmes, des vieillards et des enfants sans défense; ceux que le sort des combats et la trahison ont fait tomber entre leurs mains, ne les ont pas oubliés.[43]

Above all else, *fédérés* in the east rallied to the cause of Napoleon because of their fear of a second occupation. But there are signs that they were also satisfied with the government he gave them. Unlike in the west, the *Acte Additionnel* was given significant support in eastern France, particularly in the Côte-d'Or, Haute-Marne, and Meurthe. Moreover, the *Acte* did not encounter republican opposition comparable to that in Brittany. This indicated a strong measure of support for what has been termed the 'Liberal Empire'.[44]

Accounts of the east indicate that liberals, Bonapartists and revolutionaries alike joined in the movement. The central committee of the *fédération dauphinoise* provided a striking example of the fusion of Bonapartism and revolutionary tradition. Joseph-Marie de Barral, vice-president of the association, had become a premier president of the *Parlement* of Dauphiny in 1770, but when the Revolution came, he warmly advocated the 'new ideas', hastened to renounce his title of nobility, and helped organise the Jacobin *Société patriotique des amis de la Constitution*. In 1790 he became mayor of Grenoble and retained this post until the decree of 16 April 1794 prohibited all *ci-devants* from holding public office. Barral had to retire from Grenoble to La Tranche, but the *Conseil Général* took up his cause and in a petition to the Committee of Public Safety wrote: 'considérant que

[42] G. Thuillier, 'Le Corps préfectoral en Nivernais de 1814 à 1830', *Actes du 96ᵉ Congrès National des Sociétés Savantes: Toulouse* (1971), 1, p. 152; Cauvin, 'Le retour', 21 (1926–7), pp. 126–7, 22 (1928–9), pp. 72–3.

[43] BN, Lb⁴⁶ 396, *Relation*, p. 14.

[44] Bluche, *Plébiscite*, p. 112; Bluche, *Bonapartisme*, pp. 99–100, 105–6.

le citoyen Barral avait merité par sa conduite la haine glorieuse de la caste privilégiée dont il était lui-même, ce qui prouvait mieux que tout qu'il était encore digne du nom de sans-culotte'. By the end of 1794 he had been restored to full citizenship and made president of the military criminal tribunal of Grenoble. Thereafter he went on to hold a host of official positions and became mayor again in 1800. In 1804 he became a deputy in the Legislative Chamber and in 1811 the *ci-devant* became a former *sans-culotte*, honoured by the titles of Baron, Count of the Empire and Officer of the Legion of Honour.

Joseph Chanrion also prospered throughout the two epochs. A *marchand-peigneur*, he rose to prominence in 1791 by organising and leading the 'Association dite des Cardinaux ou Bonnets Rouges' – Grenoble's popular society. Although a Montagnard instrumental in the defeat of federalism at Grenoble, Chanrion's eloquence had a moderating effect upon the *Cardinaux*. When word arrived that the Committee of Public Safety was planning to establish a *commission révolutionnaire* at Grenoble, Chanrion travelled to Paris and convinced Robespierre that Grenoble was already sufficiently patriotic. A member of the *corps municipal* and administrator of the Isère in 1792, Chanrion held the post of *juge de paix* from 1792 to 1795. In the Year VII, he and Barral were leaders of a neo-Jacobin society and organised an *Association des propriétaires de biens nationaux du département*. The influence of these two patriots appears to have been a moderating one, which perhaps explains why Chanrion was again made a *juge de paix* in 1808.

Jean-Claude Michaud made a similarly comfortable transition between Revolution and Empire. A merchant in 1789, he was elected *juge de paix*, mayor of Brangues and administrator of the Isère in 1790. In the following year he was elected to the Legislative Assembly, where he appears to have had little impact. In 1808, he was made *conseiller auditeur* of the Imperial court of Grenoble.

Nostalgia perhaps accounted for Jacques Berriat Saint-Prix's willingness to act as vice-president of the federation in 1815. He had warmly embraced the principles of '89 and had been elected a deputy of the National Guard of the Isère at the federation of 1790. Berriat Saint-Prix was not, however, a political figure; he was first and foremost a scholar – a trait which he shared with the first secretary of the *fédération dauphinoise*. Although the name of Champollion immediately conjures up visions of Egypt, and although Champollion *le jeune* certainly was on friendly terms with the Emperor, in 1816 he was a co-founder of *l'Union*, a secret, republican society. Thus, even when we discover a name closely linked with the Empire, we do not necessarily find traditional Bonapartism. In similar fashion, when we uncover names associated with the Revolution in

Grenoble, we also find men who had not disdained the Empire. The conclusion to be drawn is that the federation was pre-eminently revolutionary–Bonapartist.[45]

The royalist Audin, in his description of Lyons during the Hundred Days, argued that, although certain *fédéré* orators recalled frightful memories of the Terror with their bloodthirsty speeches, the association actually conducted itself with an unexpected degree of moderation. He gave credit to liberal leaders of the association for achieving this moderation. However, what is most significant about the following passage is that it indicates that the mass of *fédérés* had both revolutionary and Bonapartist tendencies:

Dirons-nous ici ces motions féroces où l'on proposait, pour sauver la France, de rappeler la loi du tribun Merlin, ces harangues révolutionnaires où l'on assurait que le salut de la patrie était dans la proscription des prêtres et des nobles? . . . Dirons-nous ces orgies scandaleuses où le buste de l'assassin de d'Enghien, le front couronné des lauriers, était promené en triomphe dans les rues de la ville, précédé d'une populace qui faisait retentir les cris de 'vive l'Empereur! à mort les Royalistes! mort aux Bourbons!'[46]

Similar characteristics were apparent amongst *fédéré* leaders.

Three members of the central committee of the federation of the Rhône subsequently became Liberal Opposition deputies. Antoine-Gabriel Jars, a merchant, was a Bonapartist; in 1815 he was made mayor of Lyons as a reward for handing the keys of the city to Napoleon at the time of the *vol d'aigle*. Jean Couderc, also a merchant, was the son of a member of the Constituent Assembly of 1789. The most interesting of the three, Claude Tircuy de Corcelles, had a background which was probably unique among *fédérés*. In 1792 he had been a member of Condé's *émigré* army, but had subsequently retired to England before returning to France in 1799. Perhaps his experience in Condé's army had not been a pleasant one; in 1813 he helped defend Lyons against the Allies as lieutenant-general of the National Guard of the Rhône. He repeated this role during the Hundred Days and consequently had to take flight after the Second Restoration. As we shall see in subsequent chapters, de Corcelles had little love for the Bourbons and was to prove a dangerous opponent. Perhaps the most notorious of Lyonnais *fédérés*, J. B. Teste, had a long revolutionary career. At the tender age of twelve he had addressed an assembly of seventy-one popular societies, held at Valence in 1793, a grand total of six times. He was undoubtedly allowed to do so because his father was the leading Terrorist of Bagnols (in the Gard). This experience must have sharpened the

---

[45] For the background of the members of the central committee of the *fédération dauphinoise*, see A. Rochas, *Biographie du Dauphiné* (Paris, 1856, 1860).
[46] Audin, *Tableau*, pp. 108–10.

oratorical skills which were to mesmerise *fédérés* in 1815. However, despite this background and the violent nature of his speeches, Teste was Napoleon's lieutenant of police for ten departments and, at crucial moments, had a calming influence upon *fédérés* bent on destruction. Teste shared this characteristic with the prefect Pons, ex-director of mines on the island of Elba. Because their opposition to the Bourbons could not be questioned, these men could restrain *fédérés* when necessary. Nor, for that matter, could the loyalty to Napoleon of central committee members Vouty-de-la-Tour and Count Maret, brother of the Duke of Bassano, seriously be doubted.[47]

In his study of the federation of the Côte-d'Or, P. Viard concluded that the *fédérés* were both Bonapartist and republican. On the other hand, the federation of the Saône-et-Loire appears to have been composed mostly of liberals and republicans. Bigonnet, a former deputy of the *Cinq-Cents* and member of the association at Mâcon, wrote a pamphlet entitled 'La Restauration de la liberté, profession de foi d'un républicain sur le retour de Napoléon' in which he advised fellow republicans to rally to the Emperor. This was all the more impressive in that, under the Directory, Bigonnet had repeatedly argued on behalf of freedom of the press and political associations; when Napoleon had entered the assembly hall of the *Conseil des Cinq-Cents* during the *coup d'état* of 18 *Brumaire*, Bigonnet had fallen upon him shouting 'Que faites-vous? Téméraire! Vous violez le sanctuaire des lois, sortez!' Unlike in Lyons, Napoleon had never been popular in Mâcon. It was all the more significant, then, when Mâconnais republicans rallied to his government. Two members of the founding committee of the federation of the Saône-et-Loire, Moyne and Coste, went on to become leaders of the Chalonnais Liberal Opposition during the Second Restoration. Moyne, who became a member of the Chamber of Deputies, was a son-in-law of the *constituant* J.-B. Petiot. A third founding member, Emiland Menand, became one of the leading republicans of his department during the July Monarchy.[48]

At Nancy, Jacobins and Bonapartists shared the leadership of the federation of Lorraine. The leaders of the *fédération alsacienne* inclined towards 'libéralisme impérial'; according to Jean de Bry, regicide, a member of

[47] Robert *et al.*, *Dictionnaire des Parlementaires*; Lewis, *Second Vendée*, pp. 66, 118, 145–51, 180; Gonnet, 'Lyon', p. 118; A. Kleinclausz, *Histoire de Lyon* (Lyons, 1952), III, pp. 18–19.

[48] P. Viard, 'Les Fédérés de la Côte-d'Or en 1815', *Revue de Bourgogne*, 16 (1926), pp. 23–39; Le Gallo, *Les Cent-Jours*, pp. 322–3; Robert *et al.*, *Dictionnaire des Parlementaires*; M. Vitté, 'L'Opinion publique Mâconnaise à la fin du Premier Empire', *Annales de l'Académie de Mâcon*, 43 (1956–7), pp. 14–21; P. Guillaumot, 'Chalon pendant les Cent-Jours', *La Bourgogne*, 2 (1869), pp. 165–80; P. Lévêque, *Une Société Provinciale: La Bourgogne sous la Monarchie de Juillet* (Paris, 1983), p. 481.

the Council of Five Hundred, Imperial prefect and Baron, Napoleon was 'le protecteur de l'œuvre révolutionnaire'. At Saint-Dié, organisation of national defence was the main concern and Napoleon was remarkably popular amongst the urban lower classes and the peasantry. The same appears true of the Moselle, though here the ties of the federation to the Revolution were more pronounced. At Metz, the association was a 'manifestation symbolique d'union patriotique qui rappelait, comme beaucoup de mesures de cette époque, les jours héroiques et si oubliées de la Révolution'. According to de Serre, the *fédérés* were Jacobins renewing the patriotic ardour of 1793. Such men would have responded warmly to the arrival of a battalion from the Meurthe carrying a black flag with a death-skull and the inscription 'La Terreur nous devance, la mort nous suit; Vaincre ou mourir.' The federation at Besançon also had a revolutionary flavour. Jacques Monnot, president, had voted for the death of Louis XVI in the Convention and had been a member of the Council of Five Hundred. However, under the Empire he had served as receiver general of the Doubs and in 1815 was appointed mayor by Napoleon's government. Despite being led by the mayor, *fédérés* had a great deal of trouble gaining official recognition from the prefect. Perhaps this was due to their proclivity for denouncing Imperial civil and military authorities, and demanding retribution against the members of the previous Bourbon municipal government. Ultimately, Marshal Jourdan had one of the founding members, Gaiffe, 'connu par ses opinions anarchiques', arrested. Other founding *fédérés* acted in a more respectable fashion however; Clerc was elected to the Chamber of Representatives and Dugallier directed a free corps of partisans.[49]

Our picture of the federations of the north is regrettably poor. We do know that Napoleon could rely on the loyalty of some 200 to 300 *jeunes gens* at Caen, who ran the streets of the city shouting 'Vive l'Empereur!' and ultimately founded a federation, despite the reluctance of the prefect to give approval. At Amiens, Bonapartists sang patriotic couplets in a theatre and the federation was able to send 300 men to impose order on an Arras which remained stubbornly royalist despite the efforts of the regicide prefect Dumont. When General Duhem called on retired soldiers of the Pas-de-Calais to form federations to defend strategic military positions, he based his appeal strictly on patriotism – suggesting that neither Bonapartism nor revolutionary tradition had much currency in the department. The fact that

[49] Richard, 'Nancy', p. 89; Leuilliot, *Alsace*, pp. 232–4; Robert *et al.*, *Dictionnaire des Parlementaires*; G. Baumont, 'Saint-Dié en 1815', *Le Pays Lorrain*, 16 (1924), pp. 228–30, 234; H. Contamine, *Metz et la Moselle de 1814 à 1870* (Nancy, 1932), I, pp. 302–10; Weiss, *Journal*, pp. 55–62, 172.

the motto of the *fédérés* of the Somme was 'La Patrie et l'Empereur' perhaps indicates that the Bonapartist element was predominant. One of the *fédérés* of Dunkirk, the regicide Choudieu, certainly had not given up his republican sentiments, nor his suspicion of the Emperor's ambition, but there is little evidence that he exercised great influence over local *fédérés*. At Evreux the federation appears to have been dominated by liberals and old republicans.[50]

Of the *fédérés* of the capital, we know most about those of the federation of the *faubourgs*. Here too there were mixed political tendencies. Although there were 'quelques anciens cordeliers, jacobins, hébertistes ou autres' at the military review of 14 May, there were undoubtedly more old soldiers and confirmed Bonapartists. There is general agreement amongst historians that the people of the *faubourgs* were devoted to Napoleon, and the behaviour of *fédérés* at their review indicated as much. Of the leaders of the association, we know only that Thuriot wrote the address to the Emperor. 'Conqueror of the Bastille', regicide and fierce opponent of the Girondins, Jacques-Alexis Thuriot de la Rozière had also been instrumental in the fall of Robespierre. Forced to take flight during *Thermidor*, Thuriot's friendship with Sièyes had enabled him to return under the Directory. Advocate General of the Imperial Court of Cassation, Thuriot was another revolutionary who had continued to prosper under the Empire, albeit in a less illustrious role.[51]

The Parisian federation also appears to have drawn on old revolutionaries and Bonapartists. Carret, president of the association, had been a deputy of the *Cinq-Cents* and member of the *Tribunate*, and had been granted the cross of the Legion of Honour. In 1815 he was a confirmed Bonapartist. On the other hand, General Parein, one of the leading members of the federation, had an especially striking revolutionary pedigree. A determined republican, Parein had taken part in the capture of the Bastille, served in the Vendée, and presided over the infamous military commission that executed so many Lyonnais after the federalist revolt. Disgraced at the time of *Thermidor*, and further compromised by the Babeuf conspiracy, he

[50] Le Gallo, *Les Cent-Jours*, pp. 325–7; *Moniteur*, 3 June 1815; Hauteclocque, 'Pas-de-Calais', pp. 114–25, 137–8; V. Barrucand, ed., *Mémoires et notes de Choudieu* (Paris, 1897), pp. 340–53; J. Vidalenc, *Le département de l'Eure sous la monarchie constitutionnelle, 1814–1848* (Paris, 1952), pp. 69–71.

[51] Roserat, *Mémoires*, p. 520; J. Tulard, *Nouvelle histoire de Paris. Le Consulat et l'Empire* (Paris, 1970), pp. 401–2; R. Monnier, *Le faubourg Saint-Antoine (1789–1815)* (Paris, 1981), pp. 288–9; K. Tönnesson, 'Les fédérés de Paris pendant les Cent-Jours', *Annales historiques de la Révolution Française*, 54 (1982), pp. 397–401; Le Gallo, *Les Cent-Jours*, pp. 302–6; *Journal de l'Empire*, 21 May 1815; Robert *et al.*, *Dictionnaire des Parlementaires*.

had opposed the *coup d'état* of *Brumaire*. As late as February 1813, he was still under surveillance of the Imperial police at Caen.[52]

When all is said and done concerning the political character of the federative movement, the outstanding feature remains the willingness of old revolutionary gladiators to do battle for Napoleon. The participation of at least thirteen regicides (Thibaudeau at Dijon, de Bry at Strasbourg, Cambon at Montpellier, Corbel de Squirio at Lorient, Thuriot at Paris, Choudieu at Dieppe, Beaugéard at Vitré, Lefiot at Nevers, Dumont at Arras, Monnot at Besançon, Levasseur at Le Mans, Vadier at Toulouse and Jean-Paul Gouzy at Rabastens) speaks legions. At least two other regicides (Pons de Verdun and Goupilleau de Montaigu) were linked in police reports to federations, but it is unclear whether they actually were members.[53] Yet even here, we must take care not to overstate the matter; of these men only Vadier, Levasseur, Beaugéard, Cambon, Gouzy and Lefiot had not served Napoleon in one administrative capacity or another during the Empire. This is not to say that all Imperial officials were necessarily enamoured by Napoleon's illiberal progress; clearly Thibaudeau had his reservations. Yet, the rallying of men such as Cambon and Vadier was more dramatic. Equally significant was the support of men such as Choudieu, Bigonnet, Blin and Levasseur – republicans in the full sense of the term and opponents of Bonaparte under other circumstances. But alongside these men we find old revolutionaries such as de Bry, Chanrion, Dumont and Carret, apparently reconciled to Bonapartism long before the Hundred Days.

If we descend from the national plateau to the local level we find similar complexity. Fualdès, de Barral, Le Rebours, Michaud and Mamert Couillon had all accepted positions in Imperial administration. The reappearance of men such as Teste, Moreau, Etienne Paris, Fabre and Subleyras pays more striking testimony to renewed revolutionary *élan*. Le Gorrec, Aubrée and Ropartz were clearly inclined to hold Napoleon to the promises of the *vol d'aigle*; in the case of Ropartz, this was all the more interesting in that he was an Imperial noble. On the other hand, Vouty-de-la-Tour, who helped draw up the Lyons decrees, was a convinced Napoleonist. He shared the latter characteristic with men such as Jars and Azaiis.

The task of determining whether the federative movement as a whole

---

[52] Le Gallo, *Les Cent-Jours*, p. 310; E. Forgues, 'Le dossier secrèt de Fouché', *Revue historique*, 90 (mars–avril 1906), p. 276; J. Dautry, 'La police impériale et les révolutionnaires', *Annales historiques de la Révolution Française*, no. 194 (Oct.–Dec. 1968), p. 558.
[53] See AN, F[7] 3735, bulletin of 13 October 1815, and F[7] 6630, note 262.

was revolutionary or Bonapartist thus reveals itself to be largely futile. Moreover, such a perspective very much risks throwing the baby out with the bathwater. Fusion was the central aspect of the federative movement and its character was revolutionary–Bonapartist. That this fusion seems paradoxical to the historian inclined to stress differences between Revolution and Empire means little; it was born of circumstance and shared opposition to the Bourbon Monarchy. Unless we find evidence that Bonapartists and revolutionaries were rivals within the federations, or acting in uneasy co-operation and remaining distinct political groups, we must stress the elements of co-operation and fusion. The way to go about this lies in close examination of individual federations, a process which will start in the next chapter.

Extent of the movement and social background

Before turning to the social characteristics of the federations, it is useful to consider first just how many *fédérés* there were. The best sources for this are the registers kept by the central committees, but few of these have survived. Even when such records do exist, certain problems remain. The registers indicate only those *fédérés* who signed a pact, and thus officially became members. But, as we shall see in our case-study of Rennes, several men who thought of themselves as *fédérés*, and were so considered by their fellow citizens, did not actually manage to sign the registers. It is hardly feasible to include all the men who were cited as *fédérés* in our count, nor can we accept avowals that came well after the date, especially in July 1830, when past participation suddenly became an asset. When referring to the number of *fédérés* in Dijon, Rennes and Vitré, only those who signed the registers will be included.

We can state definitively that there were 749 men in the federation of Dijon, 490 in Rennes and 72 in Vitré.[54] At first glance, these do not appear to be large numbers. Nevertheless, as we shall see in our case-studies, these figures do take on some significance when compared with the number of men who joined the revolutionary societies of these towns.

In the absence of registers, we must turn to contemporary accounts. Although less accurate, the estimations in these accounts do give a rough idea of the significance of individual federations. However, when the figure cited appears unduly large, we shall express our reservations.

The estimation of Choudieu that Dieppe's federation eventually would number 2,000 must be viewed with scepticism. Normandy was generally

---

[54] For Dijon, see the list of *fédérés* in *ibid*, F⁷ 9649; for Rennes and Vitré, see the lists in AD I-et-V, 1M96.

royalist and local histories give little indication that Dieppe was a hotbed of revolutionary-Bonapartism, despite the presence of Choudieu and Le Pelletier. However, 1,064 men signed the registers of the federation of Cherbourg, and the association at Amiens was large enough to send 300 men to Arras, suggesting a significant federation.[55]

Thiers estimated that there were some 20,000 members of the Breton federation. If we include the affiliated associations of the Maine and Maine-et-Loire, this appears to be a fairly accurate figure. The federation at Saint-Brieuc numbered slightly more than 300 men before the prefect directed *fédéré* leaders to be less selective in recruitment. According to the prefect of the Loire-Inférieure, there were a thousand registered *fédérés* at Nantes in late May. A Bourbon official, Count Floriac, accurately estimated that there were 500 to 600 *fédérés* in Rennes, and confirmed that there were roughly a thousand in Nantes. For the military expedition previously discussed, Brest produced 400 *fédérés*, Quimper 140, Quimperlé 60, and Landernau, Carhaix and Morlaix another 300. For similar purposes, Lorient, Vannes and Ploermel produced 900 *fédérés* at one point or another. Given the repeated reports of local officials that most *fédérés* could not be expected to go on such operations, it seems reasonable to conclude that these figures represent significantly less than half the actual associations; this certainly was the case concerning Rennes and its expedition. When we add that virtually every town of even minor consequence (such as Redon, Pontivy, Fougères, Châteaubriand, Thouars and Vitré) had its group of *fédérés*, and that Dinan, Saint-Malo, Laval and Ancenis provided large federations, the figure of 20,000 begins to look reasonable. Moreover, it should be noted that battle against *chouannerie* increased recruitment. According to General Lamarque, there were some 1,200 *fédérés* at Angers by 2 June, but recently an historian has increased the total figure to at least 1,500, suggesting that the association continued to grow throughout the month. In contrast to the vast hordes of *chouans*, the figure of 20,000 may not appear especially large, but in a region where recruitment in the countryside was often futile, it marked a welcome complement to the Imperial Army.[56]

There can be little doubt that the movement reached its greatest proportions in the east. A government estimate that there were some 4,000 *fédérés* in Lyons appears reasonable, given the popularity of Napoleon

[55] AN, F[7] 3785, bulletin of 20 June 1815; Le Gallo, *Les Cent-Jours*, pp. 325, 327; L. Lemaire, *Histoire de Dunkerque* (Dunkirk, 1927), p. 400; Hauteclocque, 'Pas-de-Calais', p. 155.
[56] M. Thiers, *Histoire du Consulat et de l'Empire* (Paris, 1861), XIX, p. 471; AN, F[7] 9650, Prefect to Minister of the Interior, 6 June 1815, AFIV 1937, General Lamarque to Minister of War, 2 June 1815, F[7] 9682, Count Floriac to Minister of the Interior, 13 July 1815; Lebrun, *Angers*, p. 195; Grand, *Chouannerie*, pp. 106–7, 116–17.

amongst the people and the fact that the association 'recevait tout, et ne renvoyait personne'. Audin was probably correct in stating 'il est peu de villes où cette association ait été plus nombreuse qu'à Lyon'. Response to the federative appeal was sufficient for military and civil officials to plan the organisation of fifteen battalions of *fédérés-tirailleurs* drawn from citizens ineligible for the National Guard. Unfortunately, sources in local archives do not indicate whether matters proceeded beyond the planning stage. Nor do we know the size of the association at Grenoble, although the size and composition of the central committee and historical accounts of public opinion suggest that it must have been large.[57]

The federative movement was probably nowhere more popular than in the Saône-et-Loire. Close to 2,000 *fédérés* of Chalon and *environs* attended a ceremony honouring deputies of the federation of the Rhône. Half of these men were from Chalon itself. Moreover, 2,462 men signed the registers of the federation at Verdun-sur-Doubs (canton of Verdun). These figures outstrip Dijon's membership of 749 and give substance to de Tocqueville's claim that the Burgundian federation was more powerful than any other. Reports indicate that this was a region where the movement took root throughout the countryside, and the figures for Verdun-sur-Doubs certainly back up this claim. This would seem to be indicated also by the fact that support for the *Acte Additionnel* was much greater in the rural areas of the Côte-d'Or than in Dijon itself.[58]

Following the lead of civil and military officials, more than 4,000 Strasbourgeois signed the registers of their association. The pact of the *fédération franc-comtoise* was signed by 3,000 men at Nancy; doubtless many of these *fédérés* came from the surrounding region. We have noted previously in regard to the north that the role of the prefect in fostering the movement could prove vital; this factor could also prove important in terrain which was essentially favourable. Due to the opposition of the prefect, *fédérés* at Besançon could not simply establish an office and register at the prefecture, and had to resort to going from door to door. By 23 June this procedure had netted some seventy signatures and was apparently gaining momentum, despite the fact that the National Guard had produced its own *pacte fédératif* as a rival to that 'des gens turbulents et mal intentionés'.[59]

[57] AN, F⁷ 3735, bulletin of 1 November 1815; Audin, *Tableau*, p. 110; Ribe, *Lyon*, p. 40; Gonnet, 'Lyon', pp. 193–4; A. Gras, *Grenoble en 1814 et 1815* (Grenoble, 1854), pp. 47–9; Dumolard, 'Grenoble', pp. 132–3.

[58] Guillaumot, 'Chalon', pp. 174, 177; Lévêque, *Société*, p. 481; Bluche, *Plébiscite*, pp. 112, 119.

[59] BN, Lb⁴⁶ 396, *Relation*, p. 6; *Patriote*, 19 July 1815; G. Richard, 'Une conspiration policière à Nancy en 1816', *Annales de l'Est, année* 10, no. 3 (1959), p. 173; Weiss, *Journal*, pp. 59–62.

It is particularly difficult to find precise figures for the south. At Toulouse, where royalist estimates rose as high as 4,000, it would appear that numbers did not greatly exceed 1,800. To the latter figure could be added another 300 *fédérés* in the *arrondissement* of Villefranche. Given that the movement swept into most of the communes of the Haute-Garonne, the federation of the Midi must have numbered well into the thousands. At Périgueux the association commenced with 773 members, although many of these men resided elsewhere in the department. With the exception of the town of Bergerac, the Dordogne appears to have uniformly rallied to the Imperial government, suggesting that this was an exceptionally large association.[60]

Elsewhere we have clues, but little of substance. Toulon appears to have been receptive. In early August, *fédérés*, *demi-soldes* and retired soldiers marched in front of a crowd of some 500 Toulonnais shouting 'Vive Napoléon! Mort aux Bourbons!' At Montpellier, the association gained a certain amplitude, aided by the fact that *fédérés* were exempt from the mobile National Guard. This, of course, did not indicate that they were unwilling to fight; there were some 300 *fédérés* and soldiers still holding the citadel on 15 July. They must have felt extremely lonely; two weeks previously, they had enjoyed the company of some 600 *fédérés* of the Gardonnenque. There can be little doubt that *fédéré* recruitment in the Protestant regions of the Cevennes and Gard was massive. Although no general figure can be put forward, the fact that the small town of Saint-Hyppolite provided 240 *fédérés* for the central committee at Nîmes is instructive.[61]

Estimates of the number of *fédérés* in Paris have varied a good deal. Houssaye put the figure at 25,000, but Tönnesson has called his deductions into question. What is clear is that 12,000 and perhaps 14,000 *fédérés* of the *faubourgs* Saint-Antoine and Saint-Marceau marched before Napoleon. Given that the city of Paris and several other *faubourgs* federated later, Houssaye's estimate does not seem wildly improbable. Unfortunately, we know little of the Paris federation, other than that some 600 of them marched to the *barrière d'Italie* in a single parade; nothing is known of the other *faubourgs*. Tönnesson has estimated the number of *fédérés-tirailleurs* at approximately 13,000. The *contrôles* of the *fédérés-tirailleurs* of 20 June indicate that there were 13,725 men enlisted. As will be seen in

[60] Hémardinquer, 'Boyer-Fonfrède', pp. 176–7; AN, AFIV 1937, *Confédération Périgourdine*; AD, H-G, 4M35, *Commissaire-Générale de Police* to Prefect, 9 August 1815 and *Etat pour faire suite.*
[61] Thomas, *Montpellier*, pp. 51–61; Lewis, *Gard*, pp. 180–6.

our case-study of Paris, there is reason to believe that the final figure was higher still.[62]

In sum, then, despite the general absence of precise figures, it does seem reasonable to conclude that the federative movement numbered in the hundreds of thousands. The bottom line, of course, is that an enormous amount of research would have to be conducted at the local level before we could arrive at anything like an accurate estimation. Moreover, such an investigation would probably prove largely futile; most federations were shrewd enough to destroy their registers and few records have been left for the historian.

Given this state of affairs, it is best to keep conclusions general. The movement was massive and, at the time of Waterloo, growing. In the west and north, it was largely urban; in the east, it spread into the countryside. In the south, the situation varied dramatically from region to region. In certain departments, such as the Dordogne, Haute-Garonne, Tarn and Var, the movement spread into small towns as well as large. In the Protestant regions of the Cevennes and Gard, it swept into villages and the countryside. But in most southern departments, such as the Bouches-du-Rhône, Vaucluse and Hérault, its impact was largely restricted to urban centres.

If we are to believe certain newspaper reports, we must conclude that the federations were composed of nothing but the best and the brightest. The *Moniteur*, for instance, reported that 'les plus aisés et les mieux famés' had formed the nucleus of the association of Besançon. President Monnot certainly was 'famé', in that being a regicide always gave one a bit of notoriety, but this description of the association rests uneasily with the account in the *Journal* of Weiss, and the prefect of the Doubs certainly viewed the federation with a less admiring eye. An account in the *Indépendant* stated that at Redon the Breton pact 'a été couvert des signatures de tous les citoyens les plus distingués'. Similarly, the *fédérés* of Montpellier were described as 'citoyens recommandables et estimés'.[63]

On the other hand, the federation at Rennes was said to be composed of 'citoyens de tout âge et de toutes conditions'. We shall have more to say about this later, but let us simply note for the present that Cafarelli thought that the *fédérés*, because they were recruited exclusively from the middle class, would serve to counterbalance the nobility and the people.[64]

---

[62] Tönnesson, 'Les Fédérés', pp. 393–4, 404; *Patriote*, 15 June 1815; AN, F⁹ 661–2, *rapport du 20 juin 1815*.

[63] *Moniteur*, 31 May and 9 June 1815; *Indépendant*, 27 May 1815; Weiss, *Journal*, pp. 59–61.

[64] *Moniteur*, 30 April 1815; Le Gallo, *Les Cent-Jours*, p. 297.

Table 1. *Occupational groups of Vitré* fédérés

Category	Number	% of the federation
1 Liberal professions	17	27.9
2 Merchants	5	8.2
3 Clergy	—	0
4 Proprietors and *rentiers*	14	23.0
5 *Fonctionnaires*	2	3.3
6 Shopkeepers	3	4.9
7 Food and lodging trades	3	4.9
8 Artisans	11	18.0
9 Personal service trades	—	0
10 Manual labour	2	3.3
11 Military	4	6.6

Cafarelli's description appears to fit most of the *fédérés* of the west. A royalist in the Finistère, after noting the loyalty of the nobility and the people, described the chief opponents of the Bourbon Monarchy as being 'riches propriétaires . . . beaucoup d'hommes en place, d'avocats et d'avoués'. The royalist prefect of the Côtes-du-Nord reported that many of the *fédérés* of his department 'appartient à des familles honnêtes et aisées'. At Ancenis, the prefect of the Loire-Inférieure spoke of the hatred that existed between *fédérés* and local peasants.[65]

We can see something of these trends if we look at the occupations of the *fédérés* of Vitré. Of the seventy-two men on the *liste de fédérés*, the occupation of sixty-one can be established. They fall into the eleven categories shown in Table 1.

Among the members of the liberal professions, we find twelve involved in one form or another of legal practice. All of the men in the fourth category listed themselves as *propriétaires*, the most notable of these being Beaugéard, the *conventionnel* regicide. Of the eleven artisans, four were tanners and two were locksmiths. All four soldiers were retired officers.

Without pushing matters too far (we do not know, for instance, whether the artisans actually owned and sold the produce or whether they simply worked on it), we can point to certain apparent tendencies. If we combine the first five categories, we find that thirty-eight of these men (62.3%) were

---

[65] AN, F⁷ 9671, Prefect to Minister of the Interior, 19 July 1815, F⁷ 9656, *Situation politique du département du Finistère*, 31 July 1815, F⁷ 9650, Prefect to Minister of the Interior, 8 November 1815.

of the middle class. Several men from the other categories were probably also of this social status. Not surprisingly, we find no nobles, priests or peasants in this group.[66]

It would appear that elsewhere in France the federations drew their membership from both the lower and the middle classes. The *haute bourgeoisie* appears to have played an active role in certain federations, but participated very little in others.

Although Boyer-Fonfrède, the president of the association at Toulouse, was a leading industrialist, he reported that 'les citoyens d'une classe un peu élevée' did not join the federation. The lower classes appear to have been divided in their political sympathies. While *fédéré* recruitment was particularly noteworthy in the impoverished area around the Place Saint-Michel, the populace in the area of the old *parlement* was decidedly royalist. A list of men signalled for official attention in August 1815, and probably extracted from the federation registers that had been seized from Boyer-Fonfrède at the time of his arrest, offers a small sample of the association. Of 206 Toulousains of whom the occupation is cited, 98 (47.6 per cent) fall into middle-class categories, while only 85 (41.6 per cent) are lower class. The nature of this document, however, almost certainly prejudices the count in favour of men considered to be of significant social standing, and these figures should not be taken as representative of total membership. The list does, nevertheless, demonstrate that the federation was not entirely lower class, and that it contained an important element of government officials and *fonctionnaires*, men in the liberal professions, and merchants. Another noteworthy group was military men, most of whom were retired officers.[67]

There was an ardent band of *fédérés* at Nevers drawn from 'l'élément populaire et révolutionnaire'. One hundred of these men were given guns and uniforms requisitioned from National Guardsmen. Indeed, members of the National Guard were unsympathetic to the Imperial government and had uneasy relations with the *fédérés* throughout the Hundred Days. This appears to have been the case in many parts of France and we shall have occasion to comment upon this apparent social clash in our case-studies. National Guardsmen were, of course, drawn largely from the upper ranks of the middle class and, in general, this group maintained a reserved attitude towards Napoleon. In many towns and cities of France, these reser-

---

[66] AD I-et-V, 1M96, *liste de fédérés* (of Vitré).
[67] Hémardinquer, 'Boyer-Fonfrède', p. 174; Higgs, *Ultraroyalism*, p. 75; AD H-G, 4M35, *Etat pour faire suite* and Boyer-Fonfrède to Prefect, 14 August 1815. I would like to thank Professor Higgs for informing me of the sample.

vations were not shared by their 'social inferiors', and officials were concerned by the possibility of social conflict.[68]

On the other hand, while most Lyonnais *fédérés* were lower class, leadership was given by 'des hommes enrichis, des négociants, des avocats, des professeurs'. In the Côte-d'Or, where the movement was especially broad, the Burgundian federation was joined by 'bien de paysans, des ouvriers, des fonctionnaires'. Although several 'industriels, maîtres de forges ou tisseurs' also became *fédérés*, men of these occupations did not join in large numbers. In Lorraine, where 'parmi les classes inférieures, Napoléon bénéficie d'une extraordinaire popularité', the liberal bourgeoisie also joined due to their 'haine des Bourbons'.[69]

The federation of the *faubourgs* of Paris was composed, without doubt, largely of workers. Brucker's description of the *fédérés* was representative of the more sympathetic contemporary accounts: 'Ce carnaval de guenilles, ces physionomies dures et basanées, ces mains que le travail de la forge avait rendues noires et calleuses, tout ce peuple inconnu qui reassemblait en faisceau ses misères et son courage.' It is interesting to note, however, that during their review the *fédérés* were accompanied by the 'principaux fabricants' of their *quartiers*, and that afterwards they were treated to banquets by these manufacturers. Tönnesson has asserted that the Parisian federation was bourgeois, without proving the point. Due to lack of information, we will probably never be entirely certain of the social composition of the association, but as will be seen later, there is some evidence that supports Tönnesson's claim.[70]

Although several Restoration prefects, particularly in the eastern departments, stated that the federative movement had had significant impact in the countryside, it is very difficult to get hard evidence in this regard. We do know that in the Gard many of the *fédérés* who joined Gilly's troops long enough to pillage Montpellier were Protestant peasants. It was perhaps significant that the prefect of the Nièvre predicted that the association founded at Nevers 'aura beaucoup plus de succès dans les campagnes que dans cette ville où les prêtres, les vieux nobles et les femmes exercent une influence considérable'. Of twenty *fédérés* arrested at Le Beausset (in the

[68] Thuillier, 'Nivernais', p. 376; E. Duminy, 'Notes sur le passage des Alliées dans le département de la Nièvre', *Bulletin de la Société nivernaise des lettres, sciences et arts*, 11 (1906), pp. 252–3, and by the same author in the same volume, 'Nevers pendant les Cent-Jours', pp. 340–2.

[69] Gonnet, 'Lyon', pp. 119–20; Viard, 'Les Fédérés', p. 29; M. Parisse, ed., *Histoire de la Lorraine* (Toulouse, 1978), p. 367; R. Taveneaux, ed., *Histoire de Nancy* (Toulouse, 1978), pp. 341–2.

[70] Tulard, *Paris*, p. 394; Tönnesson, 'Les Fédérés', pp. 396–7. R. Brucker, 'Le Champ de Mai', *Paris Révolutionnaire* (Paris 1838), 4, pp. 173–4.

Table 2. Occupational groups of central committee men

Category	Number	% of the federation
1 Liberal professions	64	40
2 Merchants	19	12
3 Propriétaires	9	6
4 Government officials	12	7.5
5 Fonctionnaires	27	17
6 Military officers	18	11
7 National Guard officers	11	6.5

Var) by the Second Restoration government, nine were cited as propriétaires and eight as cultivateurs.[71]

Obviously, much work remains to be done before we can generalise about the social composition of the federations with any certainty. Part of this work will be undertaken in the next six chapters. One step which can be taken immediately, however, is to consider the social composition of the central committees. To gain a representative sample, we can combine the central committees of Périgueux, Montpellier, Toulon, Grenoble, Lyons, Nevers, Dijon, Besançon, Laon, Rennes, Angers and Niort. The 160 committeemen whose occupations we know fall into the categories shown in Table 2. It is apparent that the entire leadership of these associations was drawn from above the lower classes. Of the eighteen military officers, half were retired and most were in the federation of the Rhône. The merchants were mostly négociants. Of the sixty-four men in the liberal professions, forty-two were involved in legal practice (seventeen lawyers, thirteen public prosecutors, six judges and six notaries), five were doctors, two were pharmacists, three were editors, six were university professors, two were engineers and two were architects. Government officials included prefects, sub-prefects and, especially, mayors; most of the fonctionnaires were tax collectors, employees at the mairie, councillors at the prefecture or court clerks. There may well have been pressure on such men to demonstrate support for the government they represented, but it should be noted that they knew they were taking a potentially momentous step in publicly avowing their allegiance as members of the central committees. Moreover, as we shall see in our case-studies, by no means all officials or civil servants felt

[71] Lewis, Gard, pp. 178–81; Thuillier, 'Nivernais', p. 376; Duminy, 'Notes', pp. 252–3 and 'Nevers', pp. 340–2; C. Alleaume, 'La Terreur Blanche dans le Var', Bulletin de la Société d'études scientifiques et archéologiques de Draguignan, 45 (1944–5), p. 12.

Table 3. *Occupational groups of intermediary committee men*

Category	Number	% of the 22
1 Liberal professions	15	68
2 *Propriétaires*	1	4
3 *Fonctionnaires*	6	27

obliged to join the federations; those who joined out of 'weakness' were not apt to be members of central committees.

While the predominantly middle-class nature of *fédéré* leadership was obvious, there were also traces of nobility. Eleven men in the sample were of the Imperial nobility and two (de Corcelles and de Barral) had also been of the *ancien régime* nobility. At least three others had the suggestive particule 'de' in their names. At least three *fédéré chevaliers* gained their status as *federation* representatives at the Champ de Mai, something of a curious irony, given *fédéré* opposition to social privilege. One *chevalier*, Ropartz, had written against the *Acte Additionnel* because of its provision of hereditary peerage. All in all, however, the nobility was not a natural recruiting ground for the federative movement, and de Corcelles and de Barral certainly were exceptions to the general rule.

With regard to the *comités intermédiares* set up in smaller centres, we can point to the examples of the *arrondissements* of Riom, where eleven such local chapters were organised, and Chalon-sur-Saône, where nine were formed. Each of the intermediary committees of the *arrondissement* of Riom had either three or four members. Of the twenty-two *fédérés* whose occupation is known, see Table 3. To this total can be added ten *fédérés* identified simply as the mayors of their commune. Seven men of the first category were judges. At Chalon, each intermediary committee had either two or three members. Five of these men were mayors, three were notaries, two were judges and two were civil servants. One man listed himself as a member of the *garde génerale*, another as a proprietor. Thus, the committees of both *arrondissements* were dominated by men of the liberal professions, particularly the legal trades, and *fonctionnaires*.[72]

The prominent role of government officials, *fonctionnaires* and men of the legal professions was noted repeatedly in contemporary descriptions of the associations. At Lorient, almost all lawyers were said to have been *fédérés*. A similar report cited 'l'ordre judiciare en générale' of the Finistère

---

[72] BN, Lb⁴⁶ 319, *Fédération*, pp. 22–4; Guillaumot, 'Chalon', pp. 172–3.

as having taken the lead, and magistrates were signalled for their activities at Angers. Lawyers also founded the federations of Bourges and Limoges. The leadership of government *fonctionnaires* was noted in points as diverse as Saint-Brieuc, Perpignan and Chagny (Saône-et-Loire). The central committee of the Basses-Alpes was dominated by tax collectors.[73]

Students formed another group which joined in large numbers. The prefect of the Côtes-du-Nord reported that student *fédérés* at Dinan had formed a company of *canonniers*. Veterinary students joined the federation in Lyons, following the example of their professors. Teachers also often played notable roles within the movement; perhaps like Métirier, professor of the law school of Poitiers, they could not resist the temptation to draw up a pact. Proudhon and Jacotot at Dijon, Carré at the *école Charlemagne* in Paris, Berriat Saint-Prix, Champollion *le jeune* and Bilan at Grenoble, Guillemet and Pelletier at Lyons, and a handful of professors at Rennes all took the fateful step of publicly supporting Napoleon. While students and professors often played an important founding role, this did not mean that they dominated the movement. Although the federation of the Mayenne-et-Loire was founded by *jeunes gens* at Angers, a report in the *Indépendant* claimed that 'ici, ce ne sont pas seulement les jeunes gens, ce sont tous les habitans, les jûges, les avocats, les négocians, les artisans'; given that membership rose to 1,500, this must have been the case.[74]

Protestants joined the movement throughout France. They formed the bulk of the federations in the Cevennes and Gard and thus patriotism in towns such as Nîmes and Millau became sadly mixed with religious strife. At Nîmes, the *collets jaunes*, a paramilitary force of young Protestant textile workers, met regularly at the café Isle d'Elbe and doubtless joined the association, for this was the federation centre. Protestants in the Tarn joined federations at Albi and Roquecourbe, but this department did not experience violence similar to that of the Gard and the Lozère. Nor does there appear to have been much conflict between Catholics and the Protestant *fédérés* of Libourne (Gironde). In Alsace, despite minor incidents between Protestants and Catholics, men of both denominations appear to

[73] AN, F[7] 3735, bulletins of 11 and 26 November 1815, F[7] 9656, *Situation politique du département du Finistère*, 31 July 1815, F[7] 3736, bulletins of 4 February, 1 March and 8 April 1816, F[7] 3737, bulletin of 2 May 1816, F[7] 9650, Prefect to Minister of the Interior, 22 August 1815, F[7] 9698, undated letter from Minister of Justice to Minister of the Interior; Cauvin, 'Le retour', 21, pp. 126–7.

[74] AN, F[7] 9650, Prefect to Minister of the Interior, 23 August 1815; *Moniteur*, 24 May 1815; *Indépendant*, 13 May 1815.

[75] Lewis, *Second Vendée*, pp. 178–81; E. Daudet, *La Terreur Blanche* (Paris, 1878), p. 366; Vanel, 'Le Mouvement', pp. 391–3; AN, F[7] 3737, bulletin of 15 October 1816, F[7] 3785, bulletin of 15 June 1815; Leuilliot, *Alsace*, pp. 215, 219, 232–4.

have forgotten their differences in order to prepare to repulse Allied invaders.[75]

Thus, it can be established that *fédéré* leadership was overwhelmingly middle-class, with a preponderance of government officials, civil servants and men in the liberal professions. For the rank-and-file, pointers can be gained from general descriptions, but more solid evidence is needed. Such evidence can only be gained by close analysis of individual associations. We shall take the latter consideration up as part of the following case-studies, and then return to our general description of the movement.

In general terms, the federative movement can best be described as heterogeneous in social and political character. Given the numbers involved, this is perhaps not surprising. Moreover, to a certain extent the diversity of the movement reflected Napoleon's ability to offer something to virtually everyone, and this was in line with the traditional Bonapartist credo of national unity. The threats of invasion and restoration led patriots of widely different backgrounds to rally to the Imperial standard, but what that standard actually stood for was as unclear in 1815 as it is today. There were many ways of interpreting the meaning of Bonapartist government.

From the material assessed to this point, we can conclude with certainty that *fédéré* leadership was largely middle-class, though in certain areas the Imperial nobility also played an important part. Within this leadership we find the fusion of revolutionary tradition and Bonapartism that was the hallmark of the Hundred Days and was to influence greatly subsequent Restoration politics. That Bonapartists and old revolutionaries could find substantial common ground in their opposition to the Bourbon Monarchy and the Allied Powers was amply demonstrated in *fédéré* literature. Moreover, the bond of opposition was strong enough to unite old Montagnards and Girondins in an association which consciously sought a return to the general *élan* of the early Revolution.

We can also point to certain apparent characteristics of rank-and-file membership. It would appear from broad descriptions that social character varied dramatically according to region. In the west, the movement was largely middle-class; elsewhere, especially in the east, middle-class leaders enjoyed substantial popular support. Moreover, numerous reports of clashes between *fédérés* and National Guardsmen suggest that participation of the upper middle classes was often marginal. As was to be expected, *ancien régime* nobles seldom entered a movement violently hostile to social privilege, though even in this regard there were noteworthy individual exceptions.

We can speak with certainty about national *fédéré* leadership because identification of *fédéré* leaders is relatively simple. However, general descriptions of the broad social and political character of large groups can occasionally be inaccurate due to the biases of the reporter. For this reason, we shall now look closely at the federations of three different cities.

Chapter 4

The fédérés of Rennes during the Hundred Days

When they founded the Breton federation, the *jeunes gens* of Rennes were deliberately following important historical precedents. R. Dupuy, in his study of the Breton National Guard during the first three years of the Revolution, has drawn attention to the 'rôle déterminant d'une minorité d'étudiants et de jeunes gens', and has termed this group a 'force para-militaire'. Indeed, when aristocratic members of the Bastion sought to influence the Breton *parlement* of 1789 in favour of vote by Estate rather than head, *jeunes gens* led by the future General Moreau confronted the nobility with force. During the ensuing battles in the streets of Rennes, the *jeunes gens* called on young men of the other Breton towns and cities to come to their aid. The appeal was heard by large numbers of these men (as many as 600 from Nantes alone), and the aristocratic faction was forced to retire from the city. In order to take advantage of the resultant *élan*, and assure future defence, the *jeunes gens* drew up a pact and formed a federation. In 1790 the pact was renewed at Pontivy.[1]

As Dupuy has shown, more moderate proponents of the Revolution in Rennes soon took measures to consolidate the gains made by the *jeunes gens* and to bring the latter under control by incorporating them, in a subordinate role, into the National Guard. This is particularly noteworthy because similar tactics were employed by government authorities whenever the *jeunes gens* showed signs of taking law enforcement into their own hands. Such was the case in 1815; young Rennais had already demonstrated their continuing propensity for violence with a series of attacks on a Catholic seminary in early April.[2]

Although the *jeunes gens* had originated the idea of forming a new

---

[1] R. Dupuy, *La Garde Nationale et les débuts de la Révolution en Ille-et-Vilaine (1789–mars 1793)* (Rennes, 1972), pp. 55–9, 261; E. Corne, *Pontivy et son district pendant la Révolution* (Rennes, 1938), pp. 55–9.

[2] Dupuy, *Garde Nationale*, pp. 79–89; R. Gildea, *Education in Provincial France* (Oxford, 1983), p. 86.

federation in 1815, the Breton pact indicates that they willingly accepted the leadership of their elders:

Nous, jeunes Bretons, fils de pères qui nous ont legué un précieux héritage à défendre et dont les frères ainés mûris par vingt-cinq ans de vicissitudes sont encôre là pour nous guider et marcher à notre tête, nous avons . . . des devoirs à remplir, des engagements à contracter.[3]

As will be seen when the social composition of the association is analysed, government *fonctionnaires* entered the federation in droves. More importantly, leadership of the association passed from students to government officials and wealthy merchants. Thus, control of the federation was taken from the more radical proponents of the Revolution by local moderates who were more apt to act in concert with the Imperial government. This did not, however, make the federation simply a Bonapartist political association, an observation which becomes apparent if we consider what the *fédérés* actually did during the Hundred Days.

The primary object of association, according to the second article of the *pacte fédératif*, was the propagation of liberal principles. However, there is little evidence that the *fédérés* acted as a political pressure group, and if they did, it certainly was not on behalf of the Emperor. As F. Bluche has shown, political support for Napoleon actually declined in Rennes during the Hundred Days. On 6 May, the prefect Méchin reported the circulation of a pamphlet vowing support for the government but rejecting the *Acte Additionnel* and demanding a constitution capable of gaining popular approval. Méchin noted that the pamphlet was making a bad impression and would have to be combatted. Whatever measures he may have taken came to no avail, however, for while monarchists contented themselves with abstention, many republicans actually voted against the *Acte*. Among the latter group was Bernard de Rennes, a *fédéré* who subsequently became a charter member of the Second Restoration Liberal Opposition.[4]

Instead, the *fédérés* concentrated on organising themselves into a paramilitary force to maintain public order and offer aid to patriots threatened by rebel bands. When deputies from the intermediate committee of Vitré travelled to the commune of Châteaubourg, they presented local patriots with a letter from the central committee of Rennes. In the letter, the citizens of Châteaubourg were informed that the sole *raison d'être* of the federation was to provide defence for any community threatened by the enemies of

[3] See the Breton pact in AN, AFIV 1935.
[4] F. Bluche, *Le Plébiscite des Cent-Jours* (Geneva, 1974), pp. 70–2; AN, F⁷ 3785, Prefect to Minister of the Interior, 6 May 1815; A. Robert, E. Bourloton and G. Cougny, *Dictionnaire des Parlementaires Français* (Paris, 1891).

peace. Thus, the *fédérés* of Rennes took care to state that they were not a political organisation.[5]

With *chouan* bands already menacing towns throughout Brittany, the *fédérés* had to act quickly. As early as 26 April, deputies from Rennes travelled to Vitré to aid troops of the line about to pursue a band of rebels. In his report to the Minister of Police, Méchin drew attention to the fact that the *fédérés* intended to fight the *chouans* at home, and did not wish to be sent to the frontier. On 9 May, he developed this point in a letter to the Commander of the National Guard, emphasising that the government's initial view of the federation as a substitute for the Army was misguided:

Nos confédérés dont le zèle est au niveau des engagements qu'ils ont prié, sont bien loin de suffire aux obligations qui leur sont imposées, parce qu'un grand nombre d'entr'eux se compose d'hommes voués à des travaux utiles, indispensables pour le soutien de leurs familles. S'il faut aller secourir un point du département menacé, s'il faut aller se mesurer avec l'ennemi, au moment d'un débarquement, ou secourir un point de la confédération en péril, ils sont tout prêts, mais il serait impossible qu'ils se formeront des bataillons destinés à tenir, plusieurs mois, garnison loin de leur pays.

If they were not a political pressure group, neither were the *fédérés* a simple *levée en masse* to be used for any purpose that the government chose.[6]

By 9 May, two *fédéré* battalions had already been formed at Rennes. They did not have to wait long before seeing action. On 6 May, a band of *chouans* had attacked the small town of Saint-Brice. When news of the attack reached Rennes, fifty *fédérés* joined the troops of the line that marched to Saint-Brice. Chausseblanche, editor of the departmental newspaper, commented: 'nous avons grand besoin d'activité de nos braves fédérés pour le maintien de la liberté et de la tranquilité, car nous avons en présence un parti ennemi'. He praised the association for being as sage as it was patriotic. More significantly, he added that 'nos jeunes gens ne sont pas moins épris de la liberté que dévoués à l'Empereur qui est pour eux l'homme de la nation et de la liberté publique'. At least in the opinion of Chausseblanche, the *fédérés* were willing to fight for Napoleon because of what he represented; their loyalty was not a matter of simple personal devotion.[7]

Organisation of the federation naturally incurred significant expense. In a circular addressed to members of the association, the central committee-

---

[5] AD I-et-V, 1M96, 7 May 1815.
[6] AN, F[7] 3785, Prefect to Minister of Police, 26 April 1815, and Prefect to Commander of the National Guard, 9 May 1815.
[7] *Ibid.*, F[7] 3785, 13 May 1815; *Le Patriote de '89*, 13 May 1815; *L'Indépendant*, 19 May 1815.

men stated that they 'ont fait diverses avances pour les impressions, timbres, affiches, fournitures de bureaux, etc.', and advised that they relied on 'Mm. les Fédérés' for reimbursement. They warned that without the necessary 'moyens pécuniaires' the federation would not be able to continue its functions. The central committee also opened a register to take subscriptions for purchase of military equipment. One *fédéré*, an *aubergiste* named Roussel, reputedly contributed 5,500 francs. The federation thus remained independent of the government for its funding and, indeed, the relation between the association and the government remained undefined during the first four weeks of the federation's existence. However, *fédéré* intentions were made clear in the final paragraph of the circular, wherein each member was requested to provision himself with a rifle and be prepared to 'se rendre à la première invitation'.[8]

The official role of the association was clarified by the Imperial decree of 19 May, which assigned it the guard of the coasts of Brittany. To this effect, the *fédérés* were instructed to organise themselves into battalions and place themselves under the authority of departmental general commanders. In essence, this regularised what had already been done by giving it official sanction.[9]

On the day of the decree, the Minister of War wrote to Méchin requesting that the *fédérés* be organised as part of a mobile column and placed under the command of General Lamarque, who had replaced the ailing Delaborde. On 24 May, General Bigarré wrote to Méchin advising him of Lamarque's request that a battalion of the *fédérés* be prepared to march under Bigarré to the embattled city of Nantes. Méchin immediately took measures to provision the *fédérés*, who needed horses to transport a piece of artillery to Nantes. The *fédérés* were instructed to march alongside soldiers of the garrison of Rennes. By 26 May, two companies of *fédérés*, with flags provided by the prefect, had departed. According to Méchin, the *fédéré* expedition included 'des chefs de famille' and 'les plus riches capitalistes'.[10]

Only in the absence of departed soldiers and *fédérés* did the government take measures to reorganise and arm the National Guard. Indeed, only 200 Guardsmen who were thought to be loyal and willing to defend the town were to be issued rifles. Clearly, not all Rennais bourgeois were thought to

[8] AD I-et-V, undated *fédéré* circular in 1M96; C. Laurent, *Histoire de la Bretagne* (Paris, 1875), p. 276.
[9] AD I-et-V, 1M96, *Extrait des minutes de la Secrétaire d'Etat*, 19 May 1815.
[10] *Ibid.*, Minister of War to Prefect, 19 May 1815, General Bigarré to Prefect, 24 May 1815, Prefect to Mayor of the commune of Bain, 24 May 1815, Mayor of Rennes to Prefect, 25 May 1815; AN, AFIV 1937, report of 29 May 1815.

be reliable, and those who were, were apt to have joined the federation already.[11]

On 21 May, Bigarré had issued a proclamation designed to mobilise support for the government. In it he rhetorically asked whether Bretons could be indifferent to the cause to which all other good Frenchmen were rallying. More ominously, he warned that if Bretons failed to rally to the government, under pretext that the organisation of the Guard was 'vicieux', the military would be forced to take rigorous measures. Evidently, the fédérés 'dont les noms iront à la postérité', were a small minority.[12]

In a report to Davout, Bigarré stated that it would be unwise to rely on the National Guard because its members were 'sans bons principes'. He added:

A Rennes, si vous exceptez 400 jeunes gens de la Confédération, le reste de la population est dans une apathie décontenançante. Il est vrai qu'on manque d'armes partout et que c'est là ce que refroidit les habitants qui ont le désir de se montrer.

Indeed, Bigarré was so keenly convinced of the bad impression produced by the paucity of arms that he falsely announced that 10,000 guns had arrived at Saumur and that they were to be distributed to the fédérés of the thirteenth and fourteenth military divisions![13]

In Rennes the prefect sorely felt the absence of the fédérés and expressed fear that they would be attacked during their return from Nantes. He warned of the potential effect on public morale throughout the department should Rennes be invaded and vengeance inflicted on 'cette cité, berceau de la confédération'. By 7 June the fédérés had returned home, however, and Chausseblanche could wax eloquent over them: 'Nos fédérés arrivent de Nantes à l'instant. On les eût pris pour une vieille troupe de ligne. Il n'est point difficile de se peindre la joie que leur retour a caussé.' They were treated to a banquet and publicly complimented by the prefect outside the hôtel de ville. Chausseblanche then drew the following contrasting pictures:

Que l'on compare cette brave élite, sacrifiant tout à l'honneur, et toujours prête à voler au secours de leurs concitoyens, à ces bandes de malheureux cultivateurs arrachés à leurs foyers, et traînés au combat par des hommes qui les égarent et les immolent à leurs prétentions ou à leurs ressentiments. Un plebëien se dévouant à la mort pour la cause des privilégiés, n'offre-t-il pas un spectacle aussi digne de pitié que de mépris?

[11] AD I-et-V, 1M96, General Bigarré to Prefect, and Prefect to Mayor of Rennes, 30 May 1815; AM of Rennes, 2D1/6/, 16 June 1815.
[12] AN F⁹ 530, proclamation of 21 May 1815.
[13] Ibid., AFIV 1937, General Bigarré to Minister of War, 31 May 1815.

This was, of course, very much the perspective of an old 'blue', but in this statement we can discern several attitudes basic to the federative movement. The main enemies were the members of the nobility and the clergy who wished to regain their *ancien régime* social and political privileges. Any government which appeared to support such pretentions would be the target of *fédéré* enmity. Peasant *chouans* were dupes, tricked into acting against their own interests by aristocrats and priests – such men were to be treated with a mixture of mistrust and pity; perhaps this sort of attitude helps to explain why the brief civil war of 1815 was much less bloodthirsty than those that had preceded it.[14]

Under Bigarré's command, the *fédérés* of Rennes and Pontivy subsequently fought at Redon and at the battle of Auray (21 June), where the *chouans* were defeated. At Auray, the student *fédérés* of Rennes defeated the royalist *écoliers* of Vannes. During the action, one *fédéré*, Guichard, lost his life and several others were seriously wounded. One of the latter was Bachelot, a law student. News of victory at Auray filled Méchin with joy: 'La conduite des fédérés est digne d'éloges et elle est une bien belle réponse aux calomnies. Combien j'ai a me féliciter d'avoir imprimé et secondé ce mouvement patriotique.'[15]

Nevertheless, the situation in Rennes remained critical. Méchin warned that there remained 'un parti de royalistes nombreux' which the *fédérés* would not be able to contain if the town were attacked. No such attack took place, however, and the *fédérés* were able to maintain order. During the difficult days following Bonaparte's second abdication, *fédérés* insisted that the Emperor's bust be kept in its place at the *hôtel de ville* and stood guard over it. On 2 July, the prefect reported that the *fédérés* remained resolved 'de maintenir les choses en état' while they awaited news of the nation's destiny. However, Méchin also noted that they had begun to spread false rumours in order to maintain morale.[16]

In sum, then, during the Hundred Days the *fédérés* of Rennes did precisely what their pact stated they would do. They did not act as a political party. They certainly did not act as a pressure group on behalf of the *Acte Additionnel*, nor did they place any political demands on the government. Although they were in favour of constitutional government, they did

[14] *Ibid.*, F⁷ 9664, Prefect to Minister of the Interior, 2 June 1815, and extract from the *Journal du département d'Ille-et-Vilaine et de la Confédération Bretonne*, 8 June 1815; D. Maillet, *Histoire de Rennes* (Rennes, 1845), p. 516.

[15] Laurent, *Bretagne*, pp. 277–8; AM of Rennes, 2D1/6/, 30 June 1815; AD I-et-V, 1M97, police report of 3 February 1816; R. Grand, *La Chouannerie de 1815* (Paris, 1942), pp. 183–200; AN, F⁷ 9664, Prefect to Minister of the Interior, 29 June 1815.

[16] AN, F⁷ 3785, bulletins of 19, 26 and 30 June 1815, F⁷ 9664, Prefect to Minister of the Interior, 2 July 1815.

not concern themselves directly with political matters, even at the local level.

Instead, they devoted themselves to helping the government maintain order. Due to the dubious loyalty of the National Guard, such support was more than welcome. Without the *fédérés*, Rennes might have become the scene of open counter-revolution. Moreover, the *fédérés* contributed significantly to the suppression of *chouannerie* and provided a good, disciplined example for patriots throughout the west. As their pact indicated, they were willing to fight in support of any town or city within the confines of their association. If royalist bands rose again after the Emperor's second abdication, this was due to the defeat of French armies at the frontier, and not to any inadequacy on the part of the *fédérés*.[17]

Before proceeding to what became of the *fédérés* during the Second Restoration, it is useful to examine who they were and why they acted as they did: a list of persons persecuted proves largely meaningless without some knowledge of the individuals involved, and knowledge of the collective groups within the federation helps to explain why the Restoration government acted as it did. To this end, the social composition of the federation will be analysed, then the individual histories of some of the *fédéré* leaders will be considered, and, finally, the reasons why men joined the association will be discussed.

There is a good deal of unanimity among historians as to the social background of the Breton *fédérés*. Le Gallo described the *fédérés* as being of 'la classe aisée . . . riches propriétaires ou possédant des emplois et une bonne éducation'. M. Lagrée has drawn attention to the narrow social base of the association, stating that it was composed of 'jeunes gens des écoles, bourgeoisie libérale du barreau ou de petit commerce, fonctionnaires, militaires, quelques artisans'. Contemporary sources confirm these descriptions. Chausseblanche wrote that the federation included some of the richest capitalists of the city of Rennes. The royalist replacement of the prefect Méchin, Louis D'Allonville, described the *fédérés* as mostly from good bourgeois families. In a subsequent appraisal, however, he stated that the association was composed of 'artisans, légistes, marchands, militaires licenciés et hommes de bas peuple'. D'Allonville based the latter description on a list of the *fédérés* in his possession.[18]

---

[17] See E. Gabory, 'La Révolte des Cent-Jours en Loire-Inférieure', *Annales de Bretagne: Mélanges offerts à M. J. Loth* (Paris, 1927), pp. 206–19 and Grand, *Chouannerie*, pp. 205–11.

[18] E. Le Gallo, *Les Cent-Jours* (Paris, 1924), p. 292; M. Lagrée, *Mentalités, religion, et histoire en Haut-Bretagne au XIXe siècle: le diocèse de Rennes 1815–1848* (Paris, 1977), p. 423; *Indépendant*, 26 May 1815; AN, F[7] 3785, bulletin of 13 December 1815; F[7] 3735, bulletin of 16 April 1816.

Table 4. Occupational groups (Rennes federation)

Category	Number	% of the 454 fédérés
1 Liberal professions	64	14.1
2 Merchants	46	10.1
3 Clergymen	0	0
4 Proprietors and rentiers	25	5.5
5 Fonctionnaires	93	20.5
6 Shopkeepers	13	2.9
7 Food and lodging trades	1	0.2
8 Artisans	40	8.8
9 Personal service trades	2	0.4
10 Manual labour	29	6.4
11 Military	49	10.8
12 Students	92	20.3

How accurate was the latter appraisal? In a letter to the Minister of the Interior, D'Allonville explained that the list was absolutely authentic, though somewhat incomplete. It had been copied from the registers of the federation during the Hundred Days by Courteille, who subsequently became a commissaire de police. D'Allonville also possessed lists for the surrounding towns of the Ille-et-Vilaine, but, as he was not absolutely certain of their authenticity, he chose not to rely on them. In a subsequent letter, the prefect estimated that there must have been some 600 fédérés in Rennes.[19]

D'Allonville's list enables us to analyse the social composition of the association.[20] Of the 480 individuals who signed the pact, 454 cited their occupations. In Table 4, individual occupations have been grouped into general categories. The selection of such categories is difficult, and it cannot be denied that there are good arguments for placing certain occupations in any number of categories. However, the broader characteristics of the socio-economic background of the fédérés emerge so clearly from such a procedure that such minor imprecisions cannot greatly affect the conclusions.[21]

[19] AN, F⁷ 9664, Prefect to Minister of the Interior, 21 December 1815, F⁷ 3735, bulletin of 16 April 1816.
[20] The following is based on the list of the fédérés of Rennes in AD I-et-V, 1M96.
[21] Several of the categories perhaps require explanation. In the 'liberal professions', category I have placed lawyers, notaries, doctors, judges and men with similar educational backgrounds. In the 'merchant' category I have grouped men who listed themselves as either négociants or marchands and were involved in trade or commerce on a large scale. Boutiquiers and small-scale merchants make up the 'shopkeeper' category. I have placed

The first thing to be noted from this table is that it demonstrates that students did not dominate the federation. The *jeunes gens*, who were mostly students, had been joined by many older Rennais. Indeed, the large number of men in the 'liberal professions', 'merchants' and *'fonctionnaires'* categories illustrates the extent to which the nature of the federation had changed. This is a point to which we shall return when discussing the leadership of the association, but for the moment it should be noted that some of these men, particularly the forty-one *fédérés* practising law or medicine, may have been associated with the *jeunes gens* in the past.

Many of the *fédérés* were wealthy. In 1817 the Lainé law entitled all French males over thirty years of age who paid 300 or more francs annually in taxes to vote in elections for the Chamber of Deputies. Thus, by collating our list of *fédérés* with Second Restoration voter lists, we can identify *fédérés* who, by the standards of the time, were well-to-do. While some of these men may have acquired part of their fortune after 1815, it is reasonable to assume that most of them were relatively prosperous during the Hundred Days.

Voter lists inform us that fifty-seven *fédérés* were entitled to vote at one time or another during the Second Restoration. However, *fédéré* voters were not particularly well off in comparison with other voters. In the election of 1817, 44 residents of Rennes who had been *fédérés* paid an average of 447.34 francs in taxes, whereas the 369 voting residents who had not been *fédérés* paid an average of 538.27 in taxes.[22] Thus we can see that, although the federation did include many comparatively rich Rennais, most wealthy citizens chose not to join the association. Indeed, of the twenty-eight notables who paid 1,000 francs or more in taxes in 1817, only Thomas Rouessart had been a *fédéré*. It is instructive to note that of these twenty-eight, twenty were of noble origin. The federation held no appeal for local aristocrats.

Voter lists also enable us to make the original table somewhat more precise. The first five categories are composed of essentially middle-class occupations; the sixth to the tenth are essentially lower-class. However, a man wealthy enough to vote was more apt to be middle than lower-class. By removing *fédéré* voters from the sixth to the tenth categories, we can

---

butchers, bakers and grocers in this group. On the other hand, I have placed men who owned cafés, restaurants, hotels and the like in the 'food and lodging' category. In the 'personal service' category I have grouped men involved in wigmaking, gardening and domestic work. In the 'manual labourers' category will be found men who worked by their hands but did not produce finished articles. Men in the building trades or involved in textile production have been placed in this category.

[22] These figures have been derived by collating the list of *fédérés* of Rennes with Restoration voter lists in AD I-et-V, 3M32–3M37. The electoral list of 1817 is in 3M32

Table 5. Occupational groups revised (Rennes federation)

Category	Number	Removed	% of the 454
1 Liberal professions	64	—	14.1
2 Merchants	46	—	10.1
3 Clergymen	0	—	0
4 Proprietors and rentiers	25	—	5.5
5 Fonctionnaires	93	—	20.5
6 Shopkeepers	11	2	2.4
7 Food and lodging trades	1	0	0.2
8 Artisans	36	4	7.9
9 Personal service trades	2	0	0.4
10 Manual labour	28	1	6.2
11 Military	49	—	10.8
12 Students	92	—	20.3
13 Voters removed	7	—	1.5

identify these categories with the lower classes more accurately. This alters the initial table, but only marginally.

The Rennes federation was essentially middle-class. The first five categories alone account for 228 of the 454 fédérés of whom occupations are known. To this number, the seven voters removed from the sixth to the tenth categories can be added, for a total of 235, or 51.8 per cent of the 454. Moreover, forty-seven of the ninety-two students identified themselves as law or medical students, strongly suggesting a middle-class background. However, this cannot be proved, nor can we identify the social background of the other forty-five students. It is wise, therefore, to leave the students out of our calculations. The same holds true of the forty-nine militaires. Even when the rank of these individuals is known, their social status cannot be identified with sufficient accuracy to bring them into the analysis. If these two uncertain categories are removed from our calculations, 313 fédérés remain, of whom 235, or 75.0 per cent, were middle-class.

On the other hand, the sixth to the tenth categories provide only seventy-eight lower-class fédérés. This figure amounts to 25.0 per cent of the 313 fédérés of whom the social background is relatively certain. Thus, both royalists and their opponents were correct in drawing attention to the middle-class nature of the Rennes federation. The presence of seventy-eight lower-class fédérés suggests that such men were welcome within the association, but that most of the 'people' of Rennes chose not to join.

D'Allonville was undoubtedly correct in reporting that men of the lower classes were for the most part devoted to the King.[23] That men in the personal service trades, such as domestics and gardeners, ignored the *fédéré* appeal is perhaps explained by the close ties of such men to noble patrons and employers. But the small number of artisans, shopkeepers and manual workers requires a fuller explanation which only consideration of the Revolution in Rennes can give.

The population of Rennes in 1789 has been estimated at between 35,000 and 36,000. By 1798 it had fallen to 24,950. In the early years of the Consulate and the Empire, the city appears to have recovered somewhat and the population rose to 29,000, at which figure it hovered until the 1830s. This drastic decline in numbers did not lead to improved economic circumstances for those who remained. In 1813, there were 3,000 indigents in Rennes, comprising more than ten per cent of the total population. As we shall see, many of the Rennais who had profited from the Revolution joined the federation, but many Rennais had not and did not.[24]

There were several important causes of massive unemployment in Rennes during the Revolution and the Empire. When the province of Brittany became five departments, much legal and administrative work was transferred elsewhere. Similarly, when aristocrats emigrated their dependents were left unemployed. As early as 1790, the municipal council wrote to the National Assembly demanding funds for the city 'de relancer son activité économique en partie paralysé depuis la clôture des organismes d'Ancien Régime et la départ de beaucoup de ci-devant privilégiés'. This, and numerous other requests for the creation of institutions that might combat unemployment, went unheeded.[25]

More devastating for the commerce and industry of Rennes were the foreign and civil wars of the Revolution. Loss of markets in America, Spain and the Levant led to a dramatic decline in the textile industries. Manufacture of sailcloth, which employed some 1,250 workers, declined by ninety per cent during the Revolution, leaving most of these men unemployed. Because the Revolutionary government could not spare money for the upkeep of roads and canals, transportation of goods into and out of Rennes became much more difficult. Civil war exacerbated economic disruption.

[23] *Ibid*, 1M91–2, Prefect to Minister of the Interior, 21 October 1815.

[24] M. Denis, 'Rennes au XIXe siècle: ville parasitaire?', *Annales de Bretagne*, 80 (1973), p. 405; AD I-et-V, *Indicateur historique: contribution des archives à l'histoire du département d'Ille-et-Vilaine de 1789 à 1980*, p. 152; F. Lebrun, ed., *L'Ille-et-Vilaine: des origines à nos jours* (Saint-Jean d'Angély, 1984), p. 260.

[25] L. Benaerts, *Le Régime Consulaire en Bretagne* (Paris, 1914), p. 15; H. Sée, 'L'Etat Economique de la Haute-Bretagne sous le Consulat', *Annales de Bretagne*, 2 (1925), p. 162; J. Bricaud, *L'Administration du département d'Ille-et-Vilaine au début de la Révolution, 1790–1791* (Rennes, 1965), p. 326.

How could trade be conducted when most post relay stations had to be abandoned due to repeated *chouan* attacks?[26]

Although he put an end to civil war, economic decline continued under Napoleon. The Emperor's Continental System put much of the west at a distinct trading disadvantage, which the British blockade exacerbated. Despite massive military expenditure under Napoleon, the municipal government of Rennes found begging such a problem in 1810 that it had to open new charity institutions. Economic crises provoked by poor harvests in the Year IX and 1811 were particularly harsh. In January 1812 Rennes was the scene of grain riots. By 1813 the large military presence had become a burden, and discontent with conscription and requisitions had become general. Throughout the Empire textile industries continued to decline.[27]

From 1788 onwards, the Breton nobility sought to use this economic distress to divide the Third Estate. The first battle between aristocrats and the *jeunes gens* of Rennes occurred in January 1789 after some 600 domestic servants had gathered outside the *parlement* to hear an address that demanded both the lowering of bread prices and maintenance of the old constitution.[28] In December 1789 the master saddlers, coach-builders and wigmakers of Rennes presented a petition to the intermediary commission of the Breton Estates which Dupuy has described as 'un véritable programme contre-révolutionnaire'. A subsequent inquiry determined that the petition had been written by the Abbé Delaunay. In the summer of 1792 agents of La Rouërie recruited unemployed wage earners and artisans for an aristocratic conspiracy known as the *Association Bretonne*. Among twenty-five men arrested in the affair were seven joiners, four weavers, four gardeners and three workers in the tailoring trade. In March 1793 workers

[26] Sée, 'L'Etat', pp. 158–60; F. Crouzet, 'Les Conséquences économiques de la Révolution Française. A propos d'un inédit de Sir Francis d'Ivernois', *Annales historiques de la Révolution Française*, 34 (1962), pp. 202–4, 314; Benaerts, *Le Régime*, p. 63; on *chouannerie* in the Ille-et-Vilaine, see D. Sutherland, *The Chouans: the social origins of popular counter-revolution in Upper Brittany, 1770–1796* (Oxford, 1982), pp. 258–303.

[27] Benaerts, *Le Régime*, pp. 68–70, 329; Denis, 'Rennes', pp. 412–14, 419; J. Meyer, ed., *Histoire de Rennes* (Toulouse, 1972), pp. 328–9; P. Viard, 'Les subsistances en Ille-et-Vilaine sous le Consulat et le Premier Empire', *Annales de Bretagne*, 32 (1917), pp. 479–82 and 33, pp. 146–51. On the Continental System and how it favoured eastern regions such as Alsace, see G. Ellis, *Napoleon's Continental Blockade* (Oxford, 1981), particularly pp. 16–22, 116, 149, 250, 264–6. On the effect of foreign war upon maritime commerce in general, see F. Crouzet, 'Wars, blockade and economic change in Europe', *Journal of Economic History*, 27 (1964), pp. 567–88; J. Tulard, *Napoleon* (London, 1985), pp. 153–9, 203–5; L. Bergeron, *L'Episode Napoléonien: Aspects intérieurs* (Paris, 1972), pp. 188–94.

[28] Dupuy, *Garde Nationale*, p. 54; Meyer, *Rennes*, pp. 304–5; R. Dupuy, 'Aux origines de "fédéralisme" breton: le cas de Rennes (1789–mai 1793)', *Annales de Bretagne*, 82 (1975), p. 346.

Table 6. *Jacobin occupational groups (Rennes)*

Category	Number	% of the 186
1 Liberal professions	67	36.0
2 Merchants	21	11.3
3 Clergymen	16	8.6
4 Proprietors and *rentiers*	0	0
5 *Fonctionnaires*	40	21.5
6 Shopkeepers	3	1.6
7 Food and lodging trades	0	0
8 Artisans	3	1.6
9 Personal service trades	1	0.5
10 Manual labourers	1	0.5
11 Soldiers	34	18.3

joined peasants in manifestations against conscription; their leaders declared the need to 'abattre le bonnet de la Liberté'.

Although one of the objectives of the original federation was to combat the influence of the nobility over the lower orders, there is little evidence that patriots succeeded in this. Indeed, the Revolution in Rennes became the exclusive concern of the bourgeoisie, particularly of the lawyers who seized power at the local and departmental levels and made it their private preserve. This becomes apparent if we analyse the occupations of the members of the *Société des Amis de la Constitution* of Rennes. Table 6 uses a membership list drawn up in 1791; although we do not know the occupation of 46 of the 232 members of the Society, the above table does indicate that the Society had an even narrower social base than the federation of 1815. Indeed, the fact that only eight members of the Society were drawn from the sixth to the tenth categories leads one to suspect that members of the lower social orders were not particularly welcome in it.[29]

The presence of sixteen clergymen in the Society is particularly eye-catching, and serves to remind us that the Catholic Church was not entirely opposed to the Revolution at its outset. However, the policies of the National Assembly, and most particularly the sequestration of Church lands, soon made priests radical opponents of the government. In the district of Rennes, 110 out of 123 priests refused to take the oath of the civil constitution of the clergy. Rennes became a haven for the refractory clergy

---

[29] The table is based on the membership list of the *Société des Amis de la Constitution* in AD I-et-V, L. 1557. On the domination of public office by the bourgeoisie, and lawyers in particular, see Sutherland, *Chouans*, pp. 12–13, 47, 154, 159–62.

and the attempts of patriots to combat the influence of priests on the populace produced few positive results. Although a division within the *Société des Amis de la Constitution* in December 1791 did produce a small popular society with a *sans-culotte* personnel, these men did not have much influence and the 'faction démocratique' was neither particularly active nor effective. Perhaps they were intimidated; on 25 May 1793 a band of *jeunes gens* demanded the expulsion of 'anarchistes' from the popular society and on 1 June this demand was met by the purging of 'exagérés'.[30]

When the *représentant en mission*, Carrier, brought his personal version of Terror to Rennes, he rapidly concluded that the bourgeois who dominated local government and the Society were counter-revolutionary. They were, in so much as they supported local Girondin deputies to the Convention and opposed Montagnard solutions to the Revolutionary crisis. The *Conseil Général* of the department of the Ille-et-Vilaine, meeting at Rennes, had even gone so far as to organise an armed force for the federalist revolt. But although they were opposed to the Jacobins led by Robespierre, the Rennais bourgeois were not truly counter-revolutionary. Even during their brief period of insurrection (from 31 May to 13 July 1793), they continued to take measures against the *chouans*, who were a much more serious threat to the government. Despite his efforts to recruit support from local *sans-culottes*, Carrier found that he had to rely on a military commission for the execution of Terrorist government. In a report to Paris, Carrier stated: 'J'ai fait quelques destitutions et de très bons remplacements sont très difficiles; tous les ouvriers étaient ici en pleine contre-révolution.' In short, there simply was no substitute for the moderate Breton patriots.[31]

After the fall of Robespierre and the Mountain, the *jeunes gens* of Rennes made their position clear in a petition to the Chamber of Representatives. Having claimed that they themselves had started the Revolution and referred to the Mountain as 'ce volcan qui avait vomi ensemble tous les crimes et tous les malheurs sur notre patrie', the *jeunes gens* went on to request permission 'de nous réunir pour surveiller sans cesse les ennemis de l'humanité, du repos public, et porter la confiance dans l'âme de nos citoyens'. In essence, the *jeunes gens* were once again offering their services to protect the revolution of the bourgeois patriots of Rennes. Such services were not deemed necessary, however, and the Representatives replied with a proclamation lauding the sentiments of the *jeunes gens* but urging them to offer their services within the National Guard and directing them

---

[30] Meyer, *Rennes*, p. 305; Bricaud, *L'Administration*, p. 524; Dupuy, 'Aux origines', pp. 344–5.

[31] R. Kerviler, *La Bretagne pendant la Révolution* (Rennes, 1912), p. 235; D. Stone, 'La Révolte fédéraliste à Rennes', *Annales historiques de la Révolution Française*, 43 (1971), pp. 368–87.

'd'exercer aucun police'. The position of the *jeunes gens* remained the same: they could be used as a paramilitary wing of the bourgeois patriots, but only in times of extreme necessity. Such occasion did not arise again until 1815.[32]

Napoleon, by bringing an end to civil war in Brittany and negotiating the Concordat, had gained at least passive support for his government. During the Consulate and the Empire, local government remained the preserve of the upper middle classes and few nobles rallied to the government. The few nobles who did rally revealed their true convictions in 1814. As we have seen, the economic situation of Rennes did not improve and most of the populace joyously received news of the First Restoration.[33]

When civil war began anew in April 1815, the clergy refused to endorse Napoleon's government. Not a single priest joined the federation in Rennes and there were no former *constitutionnel* clergymen who might have been favourable to Bonaparte during the Hundred Days. Moreover, at least some student *fédérés* were hostile to the clergy. By donning the guise of a revolutionary, Napoleon had gained the support of the old patriots of Rennes, but this did not carry the approval of the general populace. We can see further evidence of this by turning our attention to the leaders of the federation.[34]

That many *fédérés* were old patriots is suggested by the fact that at least thirty-two and perhaps as many as forty-six of them had purchased *biens nationaux* during the Revolution. Unfortunately, it has not proved possible to collect sufficient data to give a statistical account of the age of the *fédérés*. Although the list of *fédérés* informs us that 231 members were married, and that 228 were not, this tells us little of how many actually had been adults during the Revolution. Nevertheless, information concerning the leaders of the federation does enable us to draw several conclusions about their participation in the Revolution.[35]

Joseph Blin, president of the federation, had a long revolutionary pedigree. At the beginning of the Revolution he had been a member of the *jeunes gens* and was a deputy of Rennes at the federation of Pontivy in 1791. He was twice wounded while fighting in revolutionary armies.

[32] L. de la Sicotière, 'L'Association des étudiants en droit de Rennes avant 1799', *Mélanges historiques, littéraires, bibliographiques*, published by La Société des bibliophiles Bretons (Geneva, 1972), II, pp. 72–4.
[33] Lebrun, *L'Ille-et-Vilaine*, p. 233; J. Meyer, *Rennes*, pp. 323–30.
[34] Benaerts, *Le Régime*, pp. 357–60; Lagrée, *Mentalités*, p. 423.
[35] These figures have been reached by collating the list of the *fédérés* of Rennes with A. Guillau, ed., *Biens Nationaux: Index Alphabétique des acquéreurs et des soumission-aires* (Rennes, 1910), pp. 667–762.

During the Terror he bravely opposed Carrier and was thrown into prison for his efforts; only the intervention of his fellow patriots saved his life. He was released during *Thermidor* and in 1798 became a deputy of the department of the Ille-et-Vilaine in the Council of Five Hundred. The *coup d'état* of *Brumaire*, to which he was opposed, appears to have brought an end to his political career, but he held the office of director of the post throughout the Empire. During the Hundred Days, Blin was awarded the cross of the Legion of Honour for his part in founding the federation. He had a moderating influence within the association, opposing vigorous measures which other members wished to take against local royalists. When the Second Restoration mayor, Desvallons, wished to insure that the *fédérés* would disband, he turned to Blin, who responded by directing the *fédérés* to lay down their arms.[36]

Perhaps the most distinguished of the *fédérés* was Leperdit, who had been mayor of Rennes during the Terror and was a member of the *Société des Amis de la Constitution*. Leperdit, a master tailor, appears to have greatly prospered during the Revolution. In 1791 he had purchased two houses formerly belonging to the Jacobins and valued at 7,241 francs; by the Year I he was one of the *plus imposés* of Rennes. Like Blin, Leperdit had staunchly opposed the stern measures proposed by Carrier, refusing to provide the latter with a proscription list. He lost his position during *Thermidor*, but remained a municipal councillor until 1815. During the Empire, several requests by the municipal council that Leperdit be awarded the cross of the Legion of Honour went unheeded, perhaps because Leperdit's republicanism led him to clash with Napoleon during a stormy interview in 1807.[37]

Leperdit was one of the first to sign the *pacte fédératif*, and with the respect that he commanded amongst both the lower and middle classes, played an important role. As a member of the central committee, he was placed in charge of procuring military greatcoats for the *fédérés*. Despite his sixty-four years, he and Rebillard marched at the head of the *fédérés* who went to Nantes. Leperdit's prestige remained so high after the Hundred Days that he was asked to join the Second Restoration municipal council, but refused.[38]

[36] A. Cochin, *Les Sociétés de pensée et la Révolution en Bretagne (1788–1789)* (Paris, 1925), II, p. 260; R. Kerviler, *Répertoire général de bio-bibliographie bretonne* (Rennes, 1888); Le Gallo, *Les Cent-Jours*, p. 293; *Indépendant*, 27 May 1815; AN, F⁷ 9664, *Employés de l'état fédérés*; AM of Rennes, 2D1/6/, 17 July 1815.

[37] See the list of the members of the *Société* in AD I-et-V, L 1557; Meyer, *Rennes*, pp. 315–16; Maillet, *Histoire*, p. 518.

[38] See his letter to Couannier in *Mémoires sociales archéologiques d'Ille-et-Vilaine*, 42 (1913), pp. 222–3; AM of Rennes, 2D1/6/, 26 May 1815; AN, F⁷ 3785, bulletin of 3 June 1815; Maillet, *Histoire*, p. 518.

Of the three original members of the central committee other than Blin, we have already seen the role of the secretary Rouxel-Langotière. The other secretary, Binet *ainé*, was the city architect and a freemason. His father had been a deputy at the federation of Pontivy, and the son had served in the *garde d'honneur de Napoléon* in 1807 and the cavalry formed by the *jeunesse d'écoles à Rennes* in 1808. He was reputed to be very influential amongst the *jeunes gens* and was closely involved in the preparations of the *fédéré* expedition to Nantes. After the return of Louis XVIII, Binet was ordered to replace the *tricolore* with the *drapeau blanc* and to lead in the demolition of fortifications built during the Hundred Days. He complied in both cases, but during the Second Restoration was thought to be an ardent republican whose revolutionary principles led him to hate royalists. That Gaillard de Kerbertin was a lawyer and wrote the ultimate federative pact suggests that he was also influential amongst the *jeunes gens*. As we shall see, Gaillard was at the very heart of continued opposition to the Bourbon Monarchy. Having authored the Breton pact does not appear to have diminished Gaillard's standing with the Imperial government: in June 1815 he was first installed as an *avocat à la cour impériale*.[39]

By 9 May, Alexandre Brenet, Antoine Chabot and Presvot had joined the central committee. Brenet and Chabot were both *négociants*, and the latter was also a freemason. Of Presvot we know only that he did not sign the registers of the association. Sometime after 9 May, Julien-François Couannier also joined the committee. Couannier was a *négociant* and an *adjoint* at the *mairie*. On 6 May he was made a member of the Legion of Honour and later headed a delegation of the Breton *fédérés* presented to the Emperor. He had been a member of the association of law students and, hence, one of the *jeunes gens* during the Revolution, which suggests that he may have remained influential with the *jeunes gens* in 1815.[40]

The man who appears to have played the key role in bringing about the federation was not a famous personality in Rennes. Rebillard, an actor turned lawyer, was a native of Dijon who, as we have seen, happened to have valuable contacts with other Dijonnais. But his most important connections were with Rennais law students, over whom he exercised a good deal of influence. If the pact was not his original idea, he was at least

[39] G. de la Vieuxville, 'La loge de Rennes en 1815', *Revue des études historiques* (1924), p. 191; Kerviler, *Répertoire*; AN, F⁷ 9664, *L'état des employés fédérés*, F⁷ 9665, Prefect to Minister of the Interior, 7 May 1818; AD I-et-V, 1M96, *Activités de la fédération Bretonne*, 25 May 1815; AM of Rennes, 2D1/6/, 14 July and 4 October 1815; A. Maulion, *Le Tribunal d'appel et la Cour de Rennes* (Rennes, 1904), pp. 17–19.

[40] AD I-et-V, *Activités de la fédération Bretonne*, 9 May 1815; Vieuxville, 'La loge', p. 191; Leperdit's letter in *Mémoires sociales archéologiques d'Ille-et-Vilaine*, 47 (1913), pp. 222–3; *Journal de l'Empire* and *Le Moniteur Universel*, 12 June 1815; de la Sicotière, 'L'Association', p. 7.

involved in the first initiative taken by the *jeunes gens*. Rebillard was not a member of the central committee, but he did march at the head of the expedition to Nantes and spoke there on behalf of the *fédérés*. Although he led the *jeunes gens* to seek official approval during the Hundred Days, he appears by his actions subsequent to the second abdication to have been one of the more radical *fédérés*, being reluctant to give up his overt opposition to the Bourbon Monarchy. Rebillard was also a close friend of Colonel Millet, another native of Dijon, who commanded the *fédérés* on their march to Nantes.[41]

Personal influence acquired during the Revolution accounted for the leading role played by certain *fédérés*. Thomas Jollivet, a wealthy *entreposeur*, was thought by Bourbon officials to have held great influence over government *fonctionnaires*. Thomas Rouessart, vice-president of the federation and an extremely wealthy landowner, was presumed to exercise similar influence; his friend Chevallier acted as *commissaire* to the *fédérés* of Vitré. Both Rouessart and Jollivet had been members of the *Société des Amis de la Constitution*; Jollivet had also been a member of the *jeunes gens* in 1790.[42]

Although the editor Chausseblanche threw his full support behind the association and renamed his newspaper the *Journal Politique du Département d'Ille-et-Vilaine et de la Confédération Bretonne*, he was by no means a devoted follower of the Emperor. He had been the 'imprimeur révolutionnaire de Rennes' and during the Empire found himself opposed to the government. Indeed, in the year XII, the republican Chausseblanche was imprisoned by Napoleon's government for his political views.[43]

Several important points emerge from this collective biography of the leaders of the Rennes federation. A significant number of these men, particularly Blin, Leperdit, Rouessart and Jollivet, were old revolutionary leaders. Their experience taught them to moderate and direct the enthusiasm of the *jeunes gens*. The circumstances of 1815 brought them back into a local power struggle which had begun during the Revolution, and they acted much as they had done as Girondin patriots. Alongside such veterans there were also younger men such as Binet, Gaillard de Kerbertin, Rouxel-Langotière and Rebillard, who would gradually take the lead in opposition to the Monarchy during the Second Restoration.

There were no notorious Bonapartists in this group and at least three

---

[41] AD I-et-V, 1M97, dossier Rebillard, report to the Minister of Police, 29 October 1815; AN, F⁷ 9664, *l'état des employés fédérés*.

[42] AD I-et-V, 1M96, *Commissaire de Police* to Prefect, 2 February 1816 and L 1557, *liste des Amis de la Constitution*; AN, F⁷ 9664, *l'état des employés fédérés*; Dupuy, *Garde Nationale*, p. 63.

[43] Kerviler, *Répertoire*; see also the dossier on Chausseblanche in AD I-et-V, 1M97.

fédéré leaders, Blin, Leperdit and Chausseblanche, had been hostile to the Emperor in the past. This helps to explain why *fédéré* support for Napoleon in 1815 was muted. The *fédérés* were willing to fight *chouannerie*, oppose royalist intrigue and defend the coast from the British, but they were unwilling to act as a political pressure group in favour of the Emperor. The leaders of the association were all drawn from the ranks of the middle classes. Indeed, in their own descriptions of the association, *fédérés* often stressed this point. But the *fédérés* did have members reputed to have close ties with the people. Leperdit, Jollivet and Meunier, *orfèvre*, were all thought by the authorities to exercise a good deal of influence amongst *ouvriers*. Meunier certainly had close relations with numerous soldiers, and was suspected of having distributed money to *fédérés* through Jean Mary, a 'malveillant de plus bas étage'.[44] However, it is wise to see in such official suspicions indications, but not necessarily confirmation, of connections between the social classes. Police spies and even *commissaires*, after all, had a vested interest in providing evidence that could be construed by officials as signs of danger that necessitated vigilance.[45]

Evidence of popular Bonapartism amongst the ranks of the *fédérés* is relatively rare. We have seen that some of them insisted on keeping vigil over the bust of the Emperor at the *hôtel de ville* after the second abdication. This may well be interpreted simply as an act of defiance to local royalists, but the fact that the bust was soon covered with garlands indicates a certain devotion to the Emperor. House searches conducted by Second Restoration police officers on several occasions uncovered signs of lingering affection for Napoleon. The glazier Chevet was found to possess an engraving of Bonaparte; Loyer, a clerk, kept buttons with Napoleon's image on them, and Thierry made pieces of pottery with the Emperor's image on them. Such signs of popular Bonapartism are few, however, and most evidence points to the conclusion that a majority of *fédérés* harboured republican rather than Bonapartist political preferences.[46]

The republican character of the association can be seen clearly in a circular drawn up by the central committee and distributed solely amongst members. Given that it was written only for the perusal of *fédérés*, it is undoubtedly a better example of the political attitudes of the *fédérés* than other writings, which were intended for public and official consumption. In it devotion to *la patrie* is continually cited, but not a single reference is

---

44 For *fédéré* self-description, see the *Notice Rapide* in B. Constant, *Mémoires sur les Cent-Jours*, second edition (Paris, 1829), p. 184; on *fédéré* influence upon workers, see the reports in AD I-et-V, 1M99, 13 October 1815–9 January 1816.
45 See the comments of R. Cobb in *The Police and the People* (Oxford, 1970), pp. 5–8, 14–45.
46 See the police reports in AD I-et-V, 4M90, 9 January and 8 July 1816, and 4M91, 21 May 1816.

made to the Emperor. The object of federation is stated to be the maintenance of public order and opposition to those who wish to rekindle civil and foreign war. In an arresting passage, reference is made to the original federation and true patriots are said to want only 'une constitution libérale, adaptée aux mœurs et à l'esprit d'une nation grande et éclairée, qui pût garantir à tous les citoyens l'égalite des droits, et assurer la prospérité nationale'. This emphasis on equality of rights explains not only *fédéré* opposition to the Bourbon dynasty, but also indicates why Constant's *Acte Additionnel*, with its provisions for an hereditary peerage, received little support in Rennes. It is also significant that the *fédérés* chose to recall the early, moderate stage of the Revolution, and made no mention of the tumultuous later phases. The *fédérés* of Rennes were middle-class, moderate republicans. They were willing to aid Bonaparte's government in securing public order and opposing the Bourbon Monarchy, but they had little taste for either Jacobin or Bonapartist-style dictatorship.[47]

[47]   The undated *fédéré* circular can be found in *ibid.*, 1M96.

Chapter 5

The fédérés of Rennes during the Second Restoration

After Waterloo, the *fédérés* remained a potentially dangerous source of opposition to the government of Louis XVIII, but Prefect D'Allonville was able to assure that the transition from Imperial to Bourbon government was free of violence. Thereafter D'Allonville established a policy designed to reduce the influence of *fédéré* leaders by removing them from positions of authority, while simultaneously encouraging supposedly less intransigent *fédérés* to reconcile themselves to the Monarchy. This policy failed, however, and D'Allonville's successors found themselves obliged to grapple with an intractable opposition led by *fédérés* throughout the Second Restoration.

When Louis D'Allonville arrived at Rennes as prefect of the Ille-et-Vilaine on 26 July 1815, he found the department divided by two warring parties. While *fédérés* dominated most urban centres, royalists controlled the countryside. In the towns, the lower classes and nobility were solidly royalist, the *haute* bourgeoisie hated the aristocracy but accepted the Charter, and the middle bourgeoisie was decidedly opposed to the Monarchy. *Fédérés* in the larger towns were especially troublesome because they feared reprisals from royalist leaders who continued to enroll peasants into their armies and threatened to march on Rennes. To avoid such an eventuality, D'Allonville concluded that *chouan* chiefs must be offered financial recompense, *fédérés* must be disarmed, and the National Guard immediately reorganised. The latter step must be taken first, so that *fédérés* would be kept in check after the royal armies were disbanded. While outlining his plans to the Minister of Police, he emphasised that either of the two parties would be quick to profit by any false moves made by the government.[1]

---

[1] AN, F[7] 3786, Prefect to Minister of Police, 1 August 1815, F[7] 9664, Prefect to Minister of the Interior, 27 July 1815.

On 14 July, a prefectoral *arrêté* had incorporated the *fédérés* into the National Guard. Although the prefect thanked the *fédérés* for their role in maintaining order during the Hundred Days, this measure was undoubtedly a first step towards bringing the *fédérés* under control. On 15 July, the major-general of the National Guard ordered the *fédérés* to disband and directed them to return their arms. In fact they had already returned the guns issued to them by the Imperial government a week before this, at which time a large number of them had also 'jureront et signeront haine et mort au Roi'. Although Courteille's copy of the register indicated that some sixty *fédérés* had taken this oath, the prefect was inclined to doubt the authenticity of some twenty of the signatures. Among the sixty noted in the register copy were Brice, Chausseblanche, Gaillard de Kerbertin, Thomas Jollivet *père*, Leperdit, Rebillard, Rouxel-Langotière, Meunier, Bodin, Blin and Millet. It would appear that some attempt was made to verify the authenticity of the signatures; this process confirmed that the first eight *fédérés* noted had definitely sworn and signed the oath. This, of course, meant that they were marked men, which in turn made them all the more obstinate in their opposition. On 17 July, the mayor of Rennes wrote to Blin requesting that he ensure that the *fédérés* no longer held meetings. By 19 July, reorganisation of the Guard had begun, the first step of which was the return of all firearms; the next step was the removal of all *fédérés* from the Guard. On 31 July the mayor advised the prefect that the Guard should be rearmed, and on 3 August permission was given for the distribution of some 400 guns.[2]

Simultaneously, measures were taken to bring royalist bands under control. On 25 July the Minister of Police wrote to D'Allonville instructing him to order all 'chefs de corps irreguliers' to disband their troops. On 27 July a prefectoral *arrêté* ordered the cessation of all such organisations, and on 3 August D'Allonville directed the sub-prefect of Rennes to put an end to all disorders caused by the *corps royales*.[3]

The task of regaining the 1,300 guns distributed among the *fédérés* of the department was begun on 14 August when the prefect ordered all *fédérés* to return their arms to the *hôtel de ville* within two weeks. Those who had not returned their arms at the end of this period would be prosecuted. By 21 August 138 guns had been returned. On 23 August D'Allonville

[2] *Ibid.*, F[7] 9664, prefectoral order of 15 July 1815, F[7] 9665, Prefect to Minister of the Interior, 9 May 1818; AD I-et-V, prefectoral order of 14 July 1815; AM of Rennes, 2D1/6/, 17 and 19 July and 3 August 1815.
[3] AD I-et-V, 1M91, Minister of Police to Prefect, 25 July 1815, Prefect to Sub-Prefect of Rennes, 3 August 1815, 1M89, prefectoral order of 27 July 1815.

reported that disarmament was being vigorously pursued, so that the government would get the arms before the Prussian army did.[4]

The Prussians presented significant problems for the prefect. In early September antagonism between Prussian soldiers and Rennais led to the posting of a placard calling upon all *fédérés* and National Guardsmen to take up arms against the foreigners. On 18 September the Rennais *fédéré* Bellonard was arrested at Antrain by Prussians for urging locals to rise against the Allies. D'Allonville did not doubt that the *fédérés* 'cherchent à inviter le peuple contre le Roi, profitant par cela de l'occupation de ce pays par les prussiens' and had reports from Fougères, Redon, Rennes and other towns to confirm his suspicions. On 21 September the Prussian commander used rumours of a *fédéré* march on Paris as a pretext to order a general disarmament of all citizens who were not members of the National Guard. Although house searches ordered by von Tauentzien produced another seventy guns, the prefect had to admit on 24 October that these measures had not produced the expected results. However, he attributed this to the fact that royalist volunteers had previously conducted their own unofficial disarmament.[5]

Nevertheless, by 21 October the prefect could report that the National Guard included four companies of a hundred men, each well armed and uniformed. He added that he expected soon to have 1,000 reliable armed men and stated his intention to draw a large contingent from lower-class men who were devoted to the King. He also stated his opinion that public order should be maintained solely by the National Guard and that there should be no recourse to former royalist volunteer groups whom he thought undisciplined and troublesome. On 24 October the mayor of Rennes confirmed that the National Guard was devoted to the Bourbon cause. Indeed, on 11 October the Guard had been used to disperse a gathering of *fédérés*. This had been all the more necessary since the imminent departure of Prussian forces had emboldened *fédérés* to spread rumours similar to those of the Great Fear of 1789 and post placards recalling Bonaparte. On 14 November the *fédérés* were reported to be intimidated by the Guard, and circumspect in their behaviour. By 31 December the prefect felt his position strong enough to allow twenty or so *fédérés*

---

[4] AN, F⁷ 9664, prefectoral order of 14 August, Prefect to Minister of the Interior, 6 October 1815, F⁷ 3785, bulletin of 26 August 1815.
[5] *Ibid.*, F⁷ 3785, bulletin of 9 September 1815, F⁷ 9664, Prefect to Minister of the Interior, 19 September 1815; AD I-et-V, 1M98, Prefect to Minister of the Police, 24 October 1815.

back into the Guard. D'Allonville continued this policy of reintegration in the early months of 1816.[6]

By a thorough purge which was to see the positions of no fewer than 600 *fonctionnaires* changed throughout the department, D'Allonville ensured that government was in the hands of men he thought loyal. Such a massive transition could not be conducted overnight, however, and the prefect proceeded with as much deliberation as circumstances allowed. Although he used his list of *fédérés* in making his decisions, he did not remove all *fédérés* from their positions and took pains to discern to what degree individuals were compromised by their actions during the Hundred Days.[7]

On 12 July, Lorin, mayor of Rennes during the Hundred Days and a *fédéré*, wrote to Trublet, Delavillebrune and Desvallons to inform them that a royal order had removed him from office and reinstalled all officials of the First Restoration. Desvallons again became mayor and the other two *adjoints*. Interestingly, four of the fifteen returning members of the municipal council had been *fédérés*, but of these, Leperdit alone refused to serve. Not until 16 March 1816 were the other three removed.[8]

In a letter to the Minister of the Interior, dated 3 January 1816, D'Allonville described the sweeping changes he had made in the department since 16 July. More importantly, he also included a list of *fonctionnaires* who had been *fédérés*. Alongside the names of each of the *fédérés* cited, an account was given of their influence within the association and the measures taken concerning them. From this source we learn that thirty had already lost their positions, that the fate of sixteen remained under consideration, that nine had been retained and that the whereabouts of six was unknown. Not surprisingly, we find *fédéré* leaders Blin, Binet and Jollivet all removed from their offices. We also find that comments on influence range from 'fort actif' and 'dangereux' to 'peu influent' and 'homme âgé, tranquille, qui paraît avoir craint de perdre sa place'. In an instance in which the sub-prefect and mayor of Rennes gave conflicting reports, D'Allonville supported the more generous report of the mayor. In two instances the prefect showed leniency when assured that a *fédéré* would take an oath of loyalty to the King. In several instances the wealth of a *fédéré* was referred to, with the clear implication that a

---

[6] AD I-et-V, 1M91, Prefect to Minister of the Interior, 21 October 1815; AM of Rennes, 2D1/6/, 24 October 1815; AN, F⁷ 3736, bulletins of 16 October, 14 November, 31 December 1815 and 16 January 1816.

[7] AN, F⁷ 3736, bulletin of 27 March 1816.

[8] AM of Rennes, 2D1/6/, 12 July 1815, 1D1/6/, 12 July 1815; AD I-et-V, 1M89, 8 August, 1815.

rich *fédéré* was thought to be influential and therefore less worthy of clemency.[9]

The administrative purge was conducted slowly and in piecemeal fashion while D'Allonville collected reports and consulted with ministers. One such report, drawn up by a crown prosecutor, specified whether lawyers and law students were *fédérés*. Ultimately the prefect concluded that wholesale changes would have to be made in the judiciary, *gendarmerie* and tax administration.[10]

The police department appears to have been the first to undergo major change, with Courteille being placed in command. Tax collectors and receivers were particularly hard hit, with eleven removed in December 1815 and another two in February 1816. Two *fédérés* were transferred to other parts of the department, and a third was transferred to Nantes. Not unnaturally, *fédérés* such as Gaillard de Kerbertin and Louis Bernard, who had been appointed to the *cour impériale* in place of royalists during the Hundred Days, immediately lost their positions with the advent of the Second Restoration. Members of longer standing, such as Couannier and Duval de la Villebogard, were dismissed in January 1816. On 21 October 1815 the *Journal du Département d'Ille-et-Vilaine* was taken from Chausseblanche and given to the royalist, Frout. According to the prefect, Chausseblanche continued to be 'dans le fond de l'âme, un fédéré très fougueux'. The one member of the *conseil général* who had been a member of the federation, Richelot *jeune*, was replaced in May 1816.[11]

Removal of *fédérés* from office was a means by which the government sought to assure loyalty among civil servants, but it was also a punishment. The prefect, however, lacked such a simple means for chastening *fédérés* who were not employed by the government. To have been a *fédéré* was not sufficient reason to bring legal action against an individual, especially given that the government had more or less recognised the legitimacy of the association by officially incorporating it into the National Guard. In certain instances, however, *fédérés* themselves provided the authorities with the necessary pretext.

[9] AN, F⁷ 9664, Prefect to Minister of the Interior and *état des employés fédérés*, 3 January 1815.
[10] AD I-et-V, 1M96, prefectoral order of 6 January 1815; AN, F⁷ 9664, prefectoral reports of 29 September and 21 October 1815.
[11] AN, F⁷ 9664, Prefect to Minister of the Interior, 29 September 1815 and 3 January 1816; AM of Rennes, 2D1/6/, 11 December 1815 and 17 February 1816; AD I-et-V, 1M96, Councillor of the *Etat Domaines Général* and Director General of the *Contributions Indirects* to Prefect, 6 and 9 February 1816, 1M91, Minister of Police to Prefect, 21 October 1815, 2M50, *Conseil Général*, 9 May 1816; A. Maulion, *Le Tribunal d'appel et la Cour de Rennes* (Rennes, 1904), pp. 30–40.

D'Allonville soon learned that it was difficult to harass *fédérés* in courts of law, a lesson which became evident during the Gaudin Affair. On 7 July 1815, Gaudin, an officer of the National Guard, stabbed the royalist bookseller Frout to death. Because he was a member of the Guard, Gaudin was sent before a military tribunal at Brest. This caused difficulties for the authorities. Many witnesses were unwilling to travel to Brest to give testimony without financial recompense, which the government could not give. Nor could the trial be transferred back to Rennes. When witnesses did arrive at Brest, they were intimidated by large groups of local *fédérés* outside the courtroom and fifteen inside who continually interrupted proceedings. The witnesses failed to confirm their original depositions and Gaudin was acquitted. Royalists in Rennes were naturally outraged and, in order to prevent any further violence, D'Allonville ordered Gaudin to take himself off to Perpignan where he would be kept under surveillance.[12]

D'Allonville drew certain conclusions from this. Trials of individuals, even for murder, could rapidly take on a political character and further polarise the community. Moreover, courts, even civil, could not be considered reliable because many judges and lawyers had been *fédérés*. The affair was an embarrassment which D'Allonville did not wish to see repeated, and the Minister of Police advised the prefect to take action himself if the courts proved weak or powerless. This was the course that the prefect chose to take.[13]

On 28 December 1815, Courteille was informed that an 'incendiary' note was circulating at the law school. Courteille therefore interrogated several students and learned that a paper requesting royalists not to wear *cocardes blanches* had been circulated among the students. Courteille then visited the law school and found the writing in a wastepaper bin. A student named Magrez confessed to having written the note, and five other students were inculpated by having distributed it. All six were placed in the *maison d'arrêt*.[14]

On 5 January 1816, Mayor Desvallons wrote a report of the affair in which he advised that certain *fédérés* who continued to exercise influence over the students be punished. On the following day the *procureur du roi* sent a similar report in which he drew particular attention to the disruptive role played by Rebillard.[15]

---

[12] AN, F⁷ 9664, bulletin of 21 October 1815; AD I-et-V, 1M96, *Affaire Gaudin*, 17, 20, 30, and 31 October 1815.

[13] AD I-et-V, 1M96, *Affaire Gaudin*, 29 October 1815, 1M98, Minister of Police to Prefect, 14 October 1815.

[14] *Ibid*, 1M96, *Affaire du 28 décembre 1815: Ecole de Droit*, reports of 29 December 1815–8 January 1816.

[15] *Ibid.*, 5 and 6 January 1816.

D'Allonville took action on 9 January 1816. In the preamble of a prefectoral order, he cited examples of sedition at the law school which included the letter, seditious inscriptions on writing tablets, and classroom behaviour indicating sympathy for Bonaparte. In the first article of the order, the six students involved in the writing or distribution of the letter were ordered to be detained in the *maison d'arrêt*. Among them was Thomas Jollivet *fils*, *fédéré*, future Liberal Opposition leader, and son of Jollivet *père*, *fédéré* central committee member. In the second article, ten members of the 'ci-devant confédération bretonne' were banished from Rennes for their alleged influence over the students. In a third article, nine students who were not connected with the letter, but who were thought to set a bad example because they had been members or partisans of the federation, were also banished. In this group could be found Corbel de Squirio, son of the regicide, and Le Gorrec, son of a *fédéré* leader at Saint-Brieuc.[16]

Although D'Allonville possessed police reports of meetings between law students and *fédéré* leaders, he had little evidence that could be used in court, and therefore had chosen to act by prefectoral *arrêté*, as the sedition laws of October 1815 enabled him to do. The choice of the ten *fédéré* leaders was significant in that it included certain individuals, such as Rebillard, Millet, Rouessart, Jollivet and Meunier, but did not include other important leaders such as Blin and Leperdit. This distinction was probably made because the latter two had made their peace with the government and no longer posed a threat. On the other hand, the ten exiled *fédérés* had continued to spread false rumours and hold meetings with other *fédérés*.[17]

All of this reflected D'Allonville's general policy of simultaneously punishing recalcitrants while encouraging those willing to reconcile themselves to the regime. In a letter to the Minister of the Interior, dated 8 February 1816, the prefect noted that the measures taken against the 'principaux fauteurs de la fédération' had produced a salutary effect. However, rumours that many more *fédérés* would be banished had begun to circulate. In order to reassure the other *fédérés*, D'Allonville had the *arrêté* published in the *Journal du Département d'Ille-et-Vilaine*, and the royalist editor Frout, brother of the murder victim, commented that if the prefect had thought it necessary to banish other *fédérés*, he would already have done so.[18]

---

[16] *Ibid.*, prefectoral order of 9 January 1816.
[17] *Ibid.*, 1M97, dossier Rebillard, 22 January 1816.
[18] D'Allonville's letter and the article in the *Journal* can be found in AN, F^7 9664, 8 February 1816.

While these measures may well have produced the desired effect on the general populace, they failed to alter the political opinions of the law students. Almost exactly a year after Courteille's investigations had been begun, his counterpart, Le Villain, received reports that seditious writings were still being circulated at the law school. Although searches of the homes of several students produced no evidence, Le Villain did find more seditious inscriptions on the writing tablets of several students. Although this was not sufficient to warrant action against individual students, D'Allonville decided that basic changes had to be made in the law school itself. He believed it necessary to attack the problem at its root in order to produce judges and lawyers who would be devoted to the king. It is instructive to note that only students had been involved in this second affair, and perhaps it was this that led D'Allonville to conclude that the students were themselves a cause of sedition, and not simply the tools of others. In order to bring about the changes proposed, certain measures were taken. A government inspector arrived from Paris to evaluate both students and teachers, from whom certificates of political loyalty were required. Toullier, *doyen* of the faculty, was replaced and a new commission was set up to evaluate the 'morality' of prospective students.[19]

Despite his desire to assure other members that he did not intend to banish all *fédérés*, D'Allonville found it necessary to take further measures. Thus we find that two more leaders, General Bigarré and Binet *ainé*, were exiled in 1816. Certain lesser figures, such as Lecoq, Briand and Dufourneau, continued to be troublesome and met with the same fate. All those banished were put under the surveillance of local authorities. This entailed regular visits to the mayor, who in turn sent conduct reports to the prefect. In time, good behaviour ensured a return to Rennes, generally within nine months. Surveillance would then be continued by Rennais police officers for another year.[20]

Fédérés who avoided banishment by remaining circumspect were also watched by the authorities. A group of tanners, including Brizou, Leroux and Gosse, were given special attention. Gosse's correspondence with a brother in Paris was perused by the royalist postmaster. *Fédérés* who requested passports were interrogated, and in several instances their requests were denied. When the army officer Meret was banished, attempts were made to turn him into an informer so that action could be taken against certain *fédérés*.[21]

---

[19] AD I-et-V, 1M98, Prefect to Minister of Police, 26 December 1816 and 23 January 1817.
[20] *Ibid.*, 1M96, prefectoral order of 10 October 1816, 1M94, *état des individus détenus*, 31 January 1816.
[21] *Ibid.*, *dossiers individuels*, Gosse, 6 August 1816, Burnel, 31 October 1815, Meret, 24 July 1816.

Authorities were particularly concerned about contacts between *fédérés* and other groups suspected of disloyalty. Efforts were made to stop returning soldiers from meeting local *fédérés*. The prefect informed the Minister of Police whenever a *fédéré* was granted permission to travel to Paris so that the suspect's activities could be closely observed. The local masonic lodge naturally attracted the prefect's attention: eleven of the twenty-three members, including Binet *ainé* and Chausseblanche, were *fédérés*. The president of the lodge proved obliging and surreptitiously sent the prefect a membership list and the minutes from previous meetings.[22]

Any gathering of *fédérés*, no matter how small, interested the authorities. *Fédéré* leaders increased the attentiveness of royalist officials by working on behalf of liberal candidates during the national elections of August 1815. Cafés patronised by *fédérés* also enjoyed a brisk trade with police spies. The authorities were aided in their information-gathering by an unidentified *fédéré* who turned police informant. The prefect paid this agent one hundred *francs* per month and appears to have had his money's worth. It was this spy who reported on the activities of the 'chefs de la basse classe des fédérés', a report which led to the exile of Meunier and Thomas Jollivet. In March 1816, the same spy uncovered information that led to the arrest of Gauthier *fils* for sending a copy of the *Nain Tricolore* to *fédérés* in Rennes. Although Chausseblanche was suspected of having been involved in the circulation of the *Nain*, no legal action was brought against him.[23]

Other means could be used to harass *fédérés*. Searches of the homes of Binet *ainé*, Martineau, Loyer and Fleury led to the discovery of arms and subsequent arrest. A visit to the residence of André de la Verdrie produced no fewer than five guns and twelve packets of cartridges.[24]

Some *fédérés* abetted the authorities by rash actions. Grandpré attacked a royalist and had to take flight. While in a state of sublime drunkenness Cochard and Biomenay insulted a police officer and bragged of having been *fédérés*. They were imprisoned for their troubles. Renault *fils* was arrested for having insulted a National Guardsman in public. Hamelin was arrested for literally vomiting 'Vive le Roi.' However, after an interview with the

[22] *Ibid.*, 1M91, Prefect to Minister of Police, 21 October 1815; AN, F⁷ 9664, Prefect to Minister of the Interior, 11 October 1815; G. de la Vieuxville, 'La Loge de Rennes en 1815', *Revue des études historiques* (1924), pp. 189–96.

[23] AN, F⁷ 3736, bulletin of 27 November 1815, F⁷ 3786, bulletin of 12 August 1815, F⁷ 9664, Prefect to Minister of Police, 1 December 1815; AD I-et-V, 1M99 *bis*, Mayor of Rennes to Prefect, 10 November 1815, Prefect to Minister of Police, 9 January 1816 and reports of 12 March to 10 May 1816.

[24] AD I-et-V, 1M94, *état des individus détenus*, 1M97, *dossiers individuels*, Martineau, 18 May 1816, 4M90, *Sous-Lieutenant de la gendarmerie* to Prefect, 8 July 1816, 1M99 *bis*, Prefect to Minister of Police, 15 January 1816.

prefect in which he promised to conduct himself in a more respectful manner, he was allowed to go free.[25]

The stern measures taken against *fédérés* were partly a result of their penchant for spreading false rumours. Although these rumours were often ludicrous, they had the effect of rekindling hopes amongst enemies of the regime. D'Allonville took this matter seriously, for he believed that when these false hopes were put to rest opponents of the Monarchy would see the folly of their ways and rally to the Bourbons. For this reason, on 29 January 1816 he had a pamphlet printed and distributed in which various rumours were cited and proved false. The two opposing sides in Rennes engaged in a war of placards, with the *hôtel de ville* as the chosen field of battle. This had the unhappy effect of exacerbating the antagonism of the two sides and endangering the peace. D'Allonville had the placards removed as quickly as possible, but police investigations of authorship produced few results. D'Allonville also took action against anti-*fédéré* writings circulating amongst royalists. One such pamphlet argued that only men who had supported Bonaparte should be forced to pay the war indemnity.[26]

Duels between royalists and *fédérés* also gave the authorities cause for concern. The first in a series of such encounters had taken place in mid-June 1815 when a royalist, Durocher de Saint Riveul, shot and killed Malherbe, a *fédéré* of less than seventeen years of age and son of the deputy of the Chamber of Representatives. In a subsequent duel another *fédéré* was lightly wounded by a royalist. Although he had not learned of it in time to intervene, D'Allonville immediately took measures to ensure that the matter did not go any further. On 12 February 1816 Binet *aîné* was insulted by an archivist of the prefecture. In this instance the prefect was able to intervene before a duel resulted. Although the prefect was not always able to prevent such private battles, and several more duels involving law students were fought, calm was eventually established as the authorities gained control of the situation.[27]

D'Allonville's initial approach to the troubled situation of Rennes had been moderation in his treatment of *fédérés* willing to accept the authority of the

[25] *Ibid.*, 1M97, *dossiers individuels*, Grandpré, 15 December 1815, Hamelin, 18 January 1817, 1M91, Minister of Police to Prefect, 30 December 1816, 1M99 *bis*, Mayor of Rennes to Prefect, 2 May 1816.

[26] *Ibid.*, 1M91, Minister of the Interior to Prefect, 29 January 1816, 1M96, Prefect to Minister of Police, 27 August 1815; AN, F[7] 9664, Prefect to Minister of the Interior, 16 and 23 December 1815, F[7] 3736, bulletin of 7 January 1816.

[27] AN, F[7] 9664, Prefect to Minister of the Interior, 18 June 1815, F[7] 3786, bulletins of 13 September 1815 and 19 February 1816; J. Meyer, ed., *Histoire de Rennes* (Toulouse, 1972), p. 335; F. Lebrun, ed., *L'Ille-et-Vilaine: des origines à nos jours* (Saint-Jean d'Angély, 1984), p. 266.

Bourbon government. This could be seen in his treatment of Blin who, because he complied with requests to end *fédéré* meetings, was retired with full pay from his government position and not banished from the city. Other leaders such as Rouessart and Rebillard did not prove accommodating, however, and the affair of the law school forced the prefect to take stern measures against them. Nevertheless, the prefect continued to keep an eye peeled for sheep that might be led back into the fold. On 21 February 1816 he stated that if proscriptions of the *fédérés* were lifted, they would become attached to the government. Later he reported that most young *fédérés* wished to have their past errors forgotten. He was confirmed in this opinion by a Bourbon *représentant en mission* who, in April 1816, reported that few *fédérés* remained in opposition to the King, though they were sorely vexed by local officials.[28]

The prefect continued to file such reports as the year progressed. News of the uprising in Grenoble produced no similar manifestations in Rennes. Indeed, the prefect reported that at that time local *fédérés* were openly renouncing their former culpable ambitions. On the other hand, local ultra-royalists were increasingly becoming a source of alarm. On 21 February 1816, D'Allonville had reported that *fédérés* only caused problems when royalists treated them in an especially disdainful or vengeful manner. In July, rumours of an assembly of *fédérés* actually turned out to be a gathering of ultra-royalists hoping to make the government more reactionary.[29]

In several instances the prefect clashed with civil and military officials who wished to pursue vigorous measures against *fédérés*. Although the most significant of these battles took place in Vitré, the prefect's opposition to, and criticism of, a house search of the *fédérés* of that town showed clearly that he wished to continue a moderate policy. In August, several overly zealous officers of the Rennes *gendarmerie* took it upon themselves to attempt to catch several young *fédérés* thought to possess a seditious placard. In doing so, they ruined the prefect's carefully laid plans. He had wanted the *fédérés* arrested after they had posted the placard, but did not want the police to act on suspicion alone.[30]

By October 1816, D'Allonville had become so exasperated with ultra-royalists that he wrote a secret report of their activities to the Minister of the Interior. He complained that he and the mayor were being impugned by a dangerous circle of *ancien régime* nobles and ecclesiastics as Jacobins,

---

[28] AD I-et-V, 1M96, prefectoral order of 9 January 1816; AN, F⁷ 9664, *état des employés fédérés*, F⁷ 3736, bulletins of 22 February, 25 March, 16 and 28 April 1816.
[29] AN, F⁷ 3736, bulletins of 26 February, 26 June, and 8 July 1816.
[30] *Ibid.*, reports of 25 May, 30 June, 22 and 31 August 1816.

fédérés and enemies of God, the State and the nobility. More ominously, these men were seeking to win over the lower classes by distributing free bread and seeking to undermine the government. Clearly, the focus of the prefect's attention was shifting to the ultra-royalists of Rennes as potential troublemakers.[31]

On the other hand, D'Allonville felt confident enough to recommend that surveillance of most *fédérés* be lifted. Reports from his *fédéré* spy had long indicated that old *fédérés* had grown sympathetic to the cause of Louis XVIII, though they continued to hold doubts about D'Artois and his ultra-royalist circle. One such report stated that certain *fédérés* had gone so far as to declare their willingness to march to Paris if the King required their services. The *fédérés* apparently had ceased to be a source of opposition.[32]

D'Allonville was overly optimistic in his assessments. While the *fédérés* may have ceased their overt opposition to the government, they did not change their political convictions. Repressive government measures did bring about a temporary period of public tranquility in Rennes, but, in the long term, D'Allonville's policies did not produce the reconciliation he desired.

The primary result of official harassment was to make *fédérés* more circumspect. As early as December 1815, D'Allonville noted that they had learned to make their communications verbal only. This made him all the more suspicious of the wealthier 'fédérés voyageurs' who frequently travelled throughout Brittany. But while *fédérés* remained cautious in public, they were inclined to drop their defences while in company they presumed select. Thus D'Allonville was able to learn from his spy that *fédérés* were advising loyal members of the National Guard to detach themselves quickly because the regime was about to fall. According to certain *fédérés*, Orleans was about to be placed on the throne, with the consent of the English, and was sending arms for a *fédéré* rebellion. Although immediately aware of this latest example of *fédéré* rumour-mongering, D'Allonville could not take action without compromising his informer and decided to wait for more significant information. He also warned against the appointment of *chouan* military officers, knowing that this played into *fédéré* hands.[33]

Judging by a song entitled *Confession d'un Etudiant en Droit*, written in 1817, measures taken to alter the opinions of law students were a manifest

---

[31] *Ibid.*, F⁷ 9664, Prefect to Minister of the Interior, 15 October 1816.
[32] *Ibid.*, report of 15 October 1816, F⁷ 3786, bulletin of 5 November 1816; AD I-et-V, 1M96, *arrêtés du préfet*, Minister of Police to Prefect, 6 November 1816.
[33] AN, F⁷ 9664, Prefect to Minister of the Interior, 14 December 1815.

failure. In the song, the student confesses to 'crimes' such as having fought for the honour of France under Bonaparte, despising the nobility, liking wine and women, and holding little respect for 'les missionaires'. The priest readily forgives all of these sins, but when the student admits to having been a *fédéré* at the battle of Auray, his confessor calls him a brigand and wishes him to the devil.

Although they could not prove it, local authorities thought the author was Massey, a young *demi-solde* turned law student. They became all the more convinced when Massey took part in three successive demonstrations of *jeunes gens* in late January and early February 1817, at the time of a Jesuit mission at Rennes. A large number of *jeunes gens* interrupted services held at the *église* Saint-Germain, and put on a show of their own in the company of several *filles publiques* – including mock executions, obscene songs, rude gesticulations and threatening gestures. Among three *fédérés* (two of whom were not students) in the performance was Jollivet *fils*, recently returned from an engagement (exile) in the provinces. Brevelet, another *fédéré*, also got himself into trouble for using the expression 'calotin' in an offensive manner. As a result of this episode, another disciplinary order concerning the law school was put into effect and it was at about this time that Alexandre Bertrand, future Carbonaro, was removed from the school. The students responded by sending a petition to the Chamber of Deputies demanding revocation of the order.[34]

A favoured zone of student opposition was the theatre, where Taillandier, another of the *fédéré* law students exiled in 1816, insulted a royalist officer in March 1817. In July 1817, some twenty-five to thirty old *fédérés* seized on a performance of *Othello* to reveal their feelings. They stared 'insolently' at officers of the garrison of Rennes occupying the box seats, and repeatedly applauded lines in the play making unflattering allusions to the nobility or referring to the Republic. Apparently the applause doubled 'à cet hémistiche du 4ᵉ acte "J'aimai la république"'. The prefect commented: 'cette fièvre de la république et de la haine contre la noblesse qui tourmente plus ou moins un certain nombre d'individus, manque rarement une occasion de se manifester'. Although military officials were all for strict reprisals, such disturbances were not repeated the following night during a performance of *Hamlet*, and nothing came of this incident.[35]

D'Allonville had the good fortune to be replaced as prefect by Louis de

---

[34] *Ibid.*, prefectoral reports of 15 February and 1 March 1817; AD E-et-V, 1M97, *affaire d'école de droit*; A. Spitzer, *The French Generation of 1820* (Princeton, N.J., 1987), p. 247.
[35] AN, F⁷ 9664, Prefect to Minister of the Interior, 6 March 1817 and 29 September 1817, F⁷ 3740, bulletin of 3 July 1817.

la Villegontier in 1817. Unfortunately for the latter, one of the first tasks assigned to him by the Minister of Police was a reorganisation of the National Guard; this opened a Pandora's box which was never quite closed until 1830. In order to assure that the Guard was loyal to the Monarchy, D'Allonville had admitted many lower-class Rennais after the Hundred Days and excluded most of the leading middle-class *fédérés*. This made the Guard of Rennes something of an anomaly in France – generally such bodies were the preserve of the bourgeoisie. Service within the Guard required a serious sacrifice on the part of men who were not wealthy, since they had to give up a day's wages once a week to be Guardsmen. Moreover, such men could not provide their own uniforms and guns. In order to regularise the Guard along lines similar to those of other towns, and increase the number serving, the prefect set about a complete reorganisation. In order not to snub the loyal lower-class members who had previously served, he gave them the option of continuing to serve or of retiring. To increase membership in accordance with the Minister's directives, he set up a committee which, in selecting Guardsmen, would only exclude those whose political opinions were not just 'pronounced', but actually 'culpable'. In other words, only the most recalcitrant *fédérés* would not be welcomed back into the Guard. The committee appears to have interpreted the prefect's instructions in a liberal manner and only eight Rennais were excluded, but among these were Gaillard de Kerbertin, Binet, Rebillard and Bodin. Exclusion of the latter two does not appear to have caused much trouble, but refusal to admit Gaillard and Binet, both members of the federative central committee, brought a storm of protest from their old comrades. Complaints were made by a host of *fédérés*, including Couannier and Jollivet *père*, who sent letters to the Minister of Police. Among letters sent to the prefect by the *fédérés* La Gallonais, Ristorini, Lancelot Duplessis, Roussel and Brenet, passages written by the latter are particularly worth citing:

J'ai été exclus comme mes amis. Si l'on crut alors (en 1815) que vu mes opinions on ne pourait me confier des armes, les mêmes raisons existent encore. J'étois alors honnête homme, je puis affirmer l'être encore, mais ma manière de penser n'a pas changé . . . ainsi que plusieurs de mes amis qui ont été rayés, j'étois *fédéré* et même Commissaire de la fédération en 1815. La raison qui paroit avoir commandé leur radiation existant pour moi comme pour eux, j'ai l'espoir que vous ordonnerez que je partage leur exclusion.

According to the prefect, Brenet's attitude was typical of the *fédérés*: 'ils soutiennent pour la plupart qu'ils fîrent très bien de s'enroler dans la fédération. Enfin ils se tiennent presque tous et font corps. Dans ce moment plusieurs se déclarent solidaires de ceux qui n'ont pas admis.' D'Allonville's attempts at conciliation had not borne fruit; the *fédérés* were still acting as a collective unit and they had not changed their opinions.

In a further attempt at accommodation, de la Villegontier decided to allow the excluded eight to enter the Guard provided they put in writing 'leur dévouement au Roi'. They refused, and worse yet, some 200 other Rennais joined in refusing to acknowledge allegiance to the King. The prefect drew the obvious conclusion about the continuing existence of the federation: 'cette association plus ou moins étendue conserve à peu près les mêmes habitudes et . . . plusieurs de ceux qui en font partie ne dissimulent point leur opposition'. De la Villegontier ultimately decided to give up reorganisation of the Guard and allow matters to remain as before, but this was also to prove a poor solution to the problem.[36]

More serious difficulties arose in May 1818 when a Monsieur Béchu of Rennes brought charges of libel against the journalist Dunoyer for an article published in the *Censeur Européen*. Because Dunoyer was a liberal seen to be persecuted by the authorities, the trial at Rennes soon became a *cause célèbre*. Mérilhou, who defended Dunoyer, used the standard liberal tactic of attacking the government during court proceedings. The president of the tribunal had to threaten several times to empty the courtroom due to the interruptions of Dunoyer's supporters. Worse still for the authorities, large numbers of *jeunes gens* from Nantes, Fougères, Vitré, Saint-Malo and Montfort descended on Rennes to attend the proceedings. Gazon, an old *fédéré*, managed to rent an apartment directly across from where Dunoyer was held, and some sixty *jeunes gens* joined Gazon to serenade the defendant. Soon a crowd of some 600 had assembled. Fearing the consequences, de la Villegontier decided against repressive measures and violence was thus avoided. He did, however, decide to have Bodin, who had been inciting the *jeunes gens*, sent to Châteauneuf and detained long enough to calm down. On subsequent occasions, when Dunoyer was being transferred to the courtroom, the *jeunes gens* formed a cortège, which Dunoyer strode through, saluting as he advanced.

Although Dunoyer was ultimately found guilty, fined and then released, the main consequence of the trial was the publicity given to opponents of the regime. Large banquets were organised in honour of both Mérilhou and Dunoyer, after which bread was distributed to the poor. Even Bodin was treated to serenades when he was allowed to return to Rennes.

Perhaps more significant than the events of the trial were the subsequent activities of Mérilhou and Dunoyer. When Mérilhou left Rennes in mid-June, he went straight to Vitré: conducted by fourteen *jeunes gens*, he was

---

[36] *Ibid.*, F⁷ 9665, Prefect to Minister of the Interior, 7 and 9 May 1818.

led to the home of Aubrée, one of the founders of the federation of 1815 at Saint-Brieuc. After taking refreshments with some twenty-five others, Mérilhou then continued on his journey to Paris. Two weeks later Dunoyer also stopped at Vitré and was accompanied by twelve *jeunes gens* to the home of Losne-Rochelle, a leading local *fédéré*. After a dinner of thirty *couverts*, at which musicians played the air of 'où peut-on être mieux', Dunoyer and Losne-Rochelle then paid their respects to Aubrée. Without jumping to hasty conclusions, one may at least suspect from these meetings that Aubrée and Losne-Rochelle had already advanced significantly in their project of forming a secret association which eventually would emerge as the *Chevaliers de la Liberté*.

Tempers continued to flare in the immediate aftermath of the trial. Massey, already in trouble for his actions at the time of the Jesuit mission and suspected author of the 'Confession of a Law Student', provoked a duel with the royalist officer Le Cargne, which left the latter wounded. An anonymous letter was sent to the prefect expressing exasperation at the exile of Bodin and trial of Dunoyer. It warned that the *jeunes gens* of the department had renewed their pact and concluded in the following ominous terms: 'Les amis de la liberté feront toujours cause commune. Si dans la lutte qui va s'élever nous périssons, nous aurons la jouissance de mourir en purgéant Rennes de ses Tyrans, en commençant par vous M. Le Préfet.' Despite such threats, the prefect kept his head and Rennes gradually returned to tranquility.[37]

Taking advantage of relaxed press censorship under the Decazes Ministry, Michel Chausseblanche re-entered the journalistic fray in early 1819 with a succession of Liberal Opposition newspapers which demonstrated that his opinions had not greatly changed. While paying lip service to King and Charter, the old revolutionary lampooned Jesuit missionaries as 'artisans de trouble' participating in 'pieuses farces'. With regard to elections to the Chamber of Deputies held in the Loire-Inférieure in 1819 he wrote the following facetious recommendation: 'Electeurs . . . si vous applaudissez aux prétentions de la noblesse, si vos vœux hâtent le retour des moines, si vous vous trouvez assez riche pour dôter le clergé, pour renoncer à vos propriétés nationales, nommez M. Desesmaisons.' His *Organe du Peuple* undertook to remind the government that 'les intérêts révolutionnaires sont en France dans une immense majorité, qu'ils sont soupçonneux, surtout depuis 1814'. The *Organe* was distributed throughout the major towns of Brittany for several months, but then perished due to problems concerning caution money. Undaunted, Chausseblanche soon

---

[37] *Ibid.*, prefectoral reports of 30 May to 17 July 1818.

returned with the *Echo de l'Ouest*, which was to prove equally offensive to the authorities.[38]

During 1819, fierce debates raged in the Chamber of Deputies over proposed legislation to make press censorship more rigorous, and to amend voting laws by giving the wealthiest quarter of the electorate a second vote. In reaction to the debates, liberals in Rennes drew up petitions opposing these changes and sent them to the Chamber. Rouxel-Langotière and Bodin carried a petition to maintain the current electoral law to the mayor of Rennes, who duly reported to the prefect that fifteen large pages of signatures had already been collected. While the debates in the Chamber continued, Rennes remained calm, but passage of the 'law of the double vote' in the following year soon provoked a storm of discontent which tested local government agents to the utmost.[39]

At a public flag-raising ceremony in late March 1820, General Coutard addressed the troops and finished by shouting 'Vive le Roi!', to which approximately 150 *jeunes gens* in a crowd of spectators responded with calls of 'Vive la Charte! Vive la Constitution! Vive l'armée nationale! Points des lois d'exception!' After some ten minutes of this, General Coutard addressed the *jeunes gens*, stating that 'Vive le Roi!' and 'Vive la Charte!' were one and the same, given that Louis XVIII was the 'father' of the Charter. Far from calming matters, this provoked a general tumult, but fortunately for the authorities, the soldiers refused to take the side of the *jeunes gens*.

In a report on the incident, the mayor of Rennes, Desvallons, informed the prefect that because the ceremony had taken place three days before originally planned, most of the *jeunes gens* from outlying points of the department had missed the occasion, and that there had been plans to amass 500 to 600 of them. He added:

Ces messieurs s'entendent donc toujours dans tout ce qu'il entreprent. Ils se correspondent, ils sont organisés; le nom seul de fédération manque aujourd'hui à leur permanente association. J'ai dit que dans leur intention, dans leur pensée, le mouvement d'hier était séditieux. Je suis bien loin de ne pas approuver, en lui-même, le cri de Vive la Charte. Mais n'est-ce pas le profaner que de l'employer à couvrir, à étouffer avec une sorte de fureur, les cris sacrés de vive le Roi, vivent les Bourbons?

---

[38] C. A. Cardot, 'Les débuts de la presse libérale à Rennes (mars–octobre 1819)', *Actes du Quatre-Vingt-Onzième Congrès National des Sociétés Savantes: Rennes* (1966), vol. III, pp. 23–32.

[39] AN, F⁷ 6740, Prefect to Minister of the Interior, 10 March 1819, and Prefect to Minister of Police, 6 December 1819.

Desvallon's comments contain three valuable insights which help to explain the agitation that constantly troubled government officials throughout this period. First, for all intents and purposes, the federation was still in operation. Second, *fédéré* leaders were still directing the *jeunes gens* in an attempt to destabilise and ultimately overthrow the regime. Third, by their actions, opponents of the government were walking a fine line between constitutional and unconstitutional opposition; this was the reason why royalists came to view ostensibly legal manifestations, such as cries of 'Vive la Charte!', as signs of seditious intent. Were they wrong in doing so?

The prefect believed that Chausseblanche, who wrote a misleading account of the incident in his *Echo de l'Ouest*, was purposefully encouraging the *jeunes gens* to brave the authorities without going so far as to justify arrest. His suspicions in this regard were strengthened by the fact that Taillandier, another old *fédéré* and an editor of the *Echo*, had been seen leading the *jeunes gens*. Taillandier was one of several well-known individuals who were sufficiently clever to direct the *jeunes gens*, without placing themselves directly in the line of battle. The apparent objective of the incident had been to encourage the troops to rebel in the hope of creating 'un bouleversement général' which perhaps might lead to a seizure of power. Moreover, de la Villegontier was convinced that such manifestations were directed by secret societies and suspected that Chappey, an old *fédéré commissaire*, was acting as a liaison between the *jeunes gens* and a *comité directeur* in Paris. In other words, the *jeunes gens*, who were not, the prefect stressed, simply law students (who had played a small part in the incident), were acting as the shock troops of the federation once again, and the *fédérés* were in contact with enemies of the regime in Paris.[40]

Pressure on the authorities was maintained the following month. In mid-April approximately fifty men, including several students, gathered in a public place to sing the *Marseillaise*, and placards reading 'Vive l'Empereur!' were posted. De la Villegontier further described the source of trouble as 'une affiliation entre ceux qui ne veulent pas de l'ordre actuel et ceux qui ne veulent aucune espèce d'ordre, entre les prétendus républicains ou ultras libéraux et les partisans du gouvernement tombé ou même de tout gouvernement qui ne seroit pas celui des Bourbons. Ils ont entre'eux des correspondances et se nourissent sans doute de projets sinistres.' It would be difficult to find a better description of the *Chevaliers de la Liberté*, or,

---

[40] Information concerning the flag-raising incident has been culled from *ibid.*, F⁷ 9665, Prefect to Minister of the Interior, 21 March 1820, Mayor to Prefect, 31 March 1820, and reports of Prefect to Minister of Police of 31 March 1820 and to Minister of Police, 31 March and 2, 9 and 16 April 1820.

for that matter, the *fédérés*. The prefect did not think, however, that these men commanded enough support to threaten the government seriously and was determined not to be drawn into repressive measures which might, as at the time of the trial of Dunoyer, swell opposition numbers. It was not only the opposition that had to walk a fine line.[41]

Later in the month the prefect reported that the discussions of a newly appointed Academic Council concerning surveillance of law students had given rise to a series of minor disturbances. 'Vive la Charte!' was chanted by groups of individuals standing facing the *hôtel de ville*; among the crowd the presence of Taillandier and Jollivet *fils* was duly noted. More ominously, crowds of 100 to 150 students began to cluster in the centre of the town before dispersing into groups of four in order to wander the streets of Rennes shouting 'Vive la Constitution! A bas les nobles!' and beat the streets with walking canes. A large number took to standing in front of the bookstore of Madame Frout, where various portraits of the royal family were displayed. One depicted the assassination of the Duke of Berry, and apparently elicited comments such as 'belle chose . . . c'est bon pour des chouans'. The proprietress and her daughters were subjected to various rude comments. According to the prefect, the young men 'ne pardonnent pas à son fils de les avoir abandonnés, car il étoit leur camarade de fédération avant le massacre de son père'. Frout, of course, had been killed by the *fédéré* Gaudin; memories in Rennes were long and unforgiving. Among these *jeunes gens* were law and medical students who exercised an 'empire de crainte' over other students and forced them to participate in activities they would otherwise shun. Behind these students were 'des meneurs habiles qui ne les laissent pas s'avancer jusqu'au délit mais qui en deça les poussent à tout ce qui peut tourmenter l'autorité, fatiguer la surveillance et alarmer les gens paisibles'. In this war of nerves, the prefect was determined to wait and watch for an opportunity which would fully justify repressive measures and not provoke sympathy for opponents of the regime. In the meantime, he strongly advised that laws against sedition be tightened.[42]

Hostilities continued in May, with clashes between *jeunes gens* and royalist private citizens. Rumours of imminent revolution abounded, copies of a song entitled 'Le vieux drapeau' were circulated, and soldiers found no need to pay for their drinks in certain cabarets, although warnings that further commotions would bring expulsions seemed to bring law and medical students into line. The prefect continued to keep an eye on the travels of the emissaries of 'les affiliations'.[43]

[41] *Ibid.*, Prefect to Minister of Police, 18 and 21 April 1820.
[42] *Ibid.*, 23, 27 and 30 April 1820.
[43] *Ibid.*, 3, 5, 7, 10, 14 and 17 May 1820.

After this brief respite, troubles again erupted in late June when Corbières, a royalist deputy and professor at the law faculty, was treated to two nights of charivari. The legion of the Charente had to be called in, due to the hesitations of the *gendarmerie*, and nine arrests resulted. Four law students were apprehended and one was found to possess a seditious 'Chant Breton' written to the air of the *Marseillaise*. The refrain gave a fairly typical example of the attitude of the opposition to Louis XVIII:

Marchons, Marchons
Le Roi, La Charte . . . La Charte, ou sinon . . . non.

Among the others arrested was Cauchard, an old *fédéré* and *entrepreneur des routes*, suspected of being one of the *commissaires* of the new secret society. The nine were defended by Thomas Jollivet *fils*, who used the trial to attack government ministers in a fashion which provoked applause from the usual crowd attending the proceedings and gained several warnings from the presiding judge. Worse still, Jollivet succeeded in his defence and the accused were declared innocent due to insufficient evidence. At this point the general prosecutor intervened to reverse the decision. According to the prefect, it was essential that several salutary examples be made of the accused because the latter were emboldened by failure to bring successful action against them. Moreover, royalists were becoming afraid to act as witnesses when they saw the authorities reduced to impotence. Even the worthy Courteille was beginning to lose heart and regret the day he had decided to leave Amiens for Rennes![44]

In a reply to an enquiry from the Minister of Police as to whether the *fédération bretonne* had been reformed, the prefect stated that he had no doubt of it and opined that the *fédérés* were taking directions from Paris as to when to act. In a subsequent letter, de la Villegontier further elaborated that this association continued to agitate against religion, order and aristocracy, and seized every opportunity, such as debates in the Chambers, press censorship and events abroad, to create trouble. Rennes was the centre of this association: 'C'est de cette ville que partent les émissaires pour prévenir les affidés ou faire des prosélytes.' He estimated the number of the 'parti' at '250 à 300 individus auxquels il faut ajoindre peut-être 150 à 180 étudiants'. Neither trials nor favours could be used to separate these men from an opposition engendered by thirty years of revolutions and failed ambitions. The strategy of the government must be to isolate them from the mass of individuals 'disposée à se porter vers la force et dont les Libéraux profitent aujourd'hui', and the best means of doing so was to assure that

---

[44] *Ibid.*, extract of report from Prefect to Minister of War, 23 June 1820, Prefect to Minister of Police, 24, 25, 28 June, 6 and 16 July 1820.

government positions were restricted to men known for their loyalty. This was very much the language of 1815; matters had not changed in Rennes, Vitré, Fougères, Saint-Malo and eight or ten communes where opposition remained intractable. To this list could be added Dol, where the *jeunes gens* were thought to be 'en esprit de fédéralisme'.[45]

In August, Desvallons, ex-mayor, was subjected to numerous provocations by several *jeunes gens*. Pressed to cry 'Vive la Charte!', Desvallons replied that good citizens cried 'Vive le Roi!' and 'Vive la Charte!' in a single breath. This was not sufficient to appease the *jeunes gens* who demanded 'Vive la Charte!' pure and simple. Desvallons was then accused of yelling 'A bas les libéraux!' He hotly denied this but allowed himself to be provoked into agreeing to a duel, which fortunately never took place. All of this further illustrated the way in which 'Vive la Charte!' had come to serve as a rallying cry of men who wished to exclude the Bourbon Monarchy from the constitution.[46]

Seditious comments and rumours of rebellion continued in the autumn, but Rennes remained superficially tranquil as the authorities and the opposition settled into a cat-and-mouse game which tested the resolve of both. A notice of the birth of the Duke of Bordeaux was received with whistles and general disapprobation; the prefect concluded that it was best to avoid publishing any information which might fuel the discontent of the 300 to 400 middle-class trouble-makers. In September, the following note was discovered by the authorities: 'Les jeunes gens sont partis de Paris pour le Bretagne afin d'y organiser des mouvements semblables à ceux de Grenoble en 1816 et dans le même but.' Nothing came of this, however, perhaps because the opposition realised that the authorities were aware of their activities. De la Villegontier ruefully noted the following warning published by Chausseblanche in the *Echo*:

Des avis sont arrivés de Paris à Rennes portant que des agens provocateurs militaires et bourgeoises avoient été dirigés sur notre département, pour y porter à des mouvements semblables à ceux de Grenoble en 1816. Déjà ces avis se sont vérifiés en quelques points et nous engageons nos compatriotes à tenir sur leurs gardes.

The war of nerves continued.[47]

In late October, the mayor of Rennes was presented with a petition demanding, yet again, reorganisation of the National Guard. Because the earlier attempt to reconstitute the Guard had proven problematic, the

---

[45] *Ibid.*, Prefect to Minister of Police, 8 August 1820, Sub-Prefect of Saint-Malo to Minister of Police, 2 September 1820.
[46] *Ibid.*, Prefect to Minister of Police, 31 August 1820.
[47] *Ibid.*, 3 October, 6 and 15 November 1820.

prefect had decided to drop the matter. The number of serving Guardsmen had dropped precipitously and the Guard was reduced to performing ceremonial functions; public order was maintained by the police and the army. Not content to let matters rest, Joualt, an editor of the *Echo*, Rebillard and Jollivet (it would appear that Couannier was also involved, though he subsequently disavowed certain passages) drew up a petition claiming that the Guard in Rennes was invalid due to royal ordinances regulating composition of the Guard for all of France. As de la Villegontier noted, however, behind complaints of Rennes being 'insulted' by a Guard composed of 'prolétaires' lay the fact that lower-class Rennais had been loyal to the Bourbon government in 1815, unlike many signatories of the petition. There was indeed a good deal of audacity in the demand of men such as Chappey and Férail to be given permission to carry arms as Guardsmen, when they were already members of revolutionary societies. Quite understandably, the prefect ignored the demand of reorganisation and the Guard was allowed to continue to ossify. Some 112 of the 360 names on the petition belonged to old *fédérés*, and it is tempting to see in this evidence of expanding *fédéré* influence. But before jumping to this conclusion we should heed the comment of the prefect that many of those who signed the petition had simply been asked whether they favoured the National Guard.[48]

By 1821 the tide had turned fully against the Bourbon experiment with moderate government, and reaction had again become the order of the day. Rennes, stronghold of the opposition, remained a source of trouble. In a long report, the prefect described the nature of this opposition. He began with an outline of the bitter antagonism between ultra-royalists and liberals, describing the latter as 'beaucoup d'acquéreurs de propriétés d'une médiocre fortune, hommes de loi et militaires en non activité ou retraite'. Of the Liberal Opposition, he stated:

Ceux-ci plus agissant et moins soumis que les Royalistes, frondent souvent l'autorité, échappent à la rigueur des lois par adresse et par ruse en moquant la charte dont ils affectent d'isoler le nom de celui de son auguste auteur. Liés par l'horrible serment qu'ils prêtèrent à l'acte fédératif des Cent-Jours et que quelques cents d'entre eux ne craignerent pas de renouveller à Rennes dans la grande salle du Palais de Justice, le 8 Juillet 1815, au moment de poser les armes qu'ils avaient portaient jusqu'alors contre le Gouvernement légitime, leurs chefs font, depuis ce tems, tous leurs efforts pour que le parti se soutienne et qu'ils se trouve prêt à tout événement. Leurs moyens consistent à se réunir le plus souvent possible sous différents prétextes, à mal interpreter les actes du gouvernement, à faire circuler de fausses

---

[48] *Ibid.*, 21 and 25 November 1820.

nouvelles, à répandre des gravures, des chansons, des libelles et des signes séditieux. Si les entreprises du Comité Directeur de Paris échouent, ils ne manquent jamais d'en être prévenus à temps pour ne pas se commettre inutilement, si au contraire elles réussissent en tout ou en partie, leurs visages décèlent le sinistre espoir de plus grandes catastrophes.

One could not ask for a better summary of the situation. The *fédérés* continued to act as a single corps, organised local opposition, disseminated propaganda, played hide-and-seek behind the guise of constitutional opposition and co-ordinated their actions with the secret societies of Paris. Although the 'parti' had lost most of its spokesmen in the Chamber of Deputies, it continued to work at the local level. Chausseblanche, for example, was having free copies of a 'prospectus' distributed in the major centres of Brittany. The prospectus, handed out in Rennes by the old *fédéré* Cormier, contained *apologiae* for the tricolour made by several deputies in the past. Despite his recognition of attendant dangers, de la Villegontier had come to the conclusion that toleration was insufficient for dealing with these 'remorseless' opponents; firm authority and repression were the only tactics to be relied on in an effort to prevent these men from increasing their influence on 'l'esprit crédule et facile du peuple des villes et des campagnes'.[49]

Nevertheless, the prefect was determined to bide his time and wait for the correct opportunity; in April 1821 he rapidly dismissed a report from General Coutard that the old *fédérés* Desnoyers, Brice, Meret and Cauchard were planning an assassination attempt on the King and the royal family. In truth, the failure of recent attempts at revolt had intimidated the opposition. News of Napoleon's death, received in July, produced no threatening manifestations, although his followers attended a banquet with ribbons of black crêpe attached to their hats. Although they affected to disbelieve the news, their demeanour spoke eloquently of defeated hopes and aspirations. By December, the prefect believed that the government had emerged victorious from the concerted assault; although the opposition had not changed its opinions, it was now more isolated than previously and the less committed 'se rattachent au Gouvernement au moins d'une manière temporaire'.[50]

The year 1822 brought further progress for the government. As a measure of safety, the prefect secretly had 400 *fusils*, stored in the *hôtel de ville*, partially dismantled in March. Although he did not consider an assault by 'factieux' likely, he thought such precautions necessary under present circumstances. De la Villegontier continued to watch Chausse-

---

[49] *Ibid.*, 15 February 1821.
[50] *Ibid.*, 21 April, 17 July and 5 December 1821.

blanche and the *Echo*, noting allegations made against himself and the Ministry, but refrained from taking legal action, believing that this would give opposition lawyers yet another platform and increase the readership of a journal in decline. One Chausseblanche article gave an especially good indication of the opposition's declining fortunes:

Le gouvernement, s'appuyant sur une majorité composée en grande partie des mêmes éléments que celle de 1815, doit employer, envers la nation, les mêmes moyens d'administration qu'en 1815. Les visites domiciliaires, les arrestations sur les vains prétextes, les emprisonnements, les mises au secret, les interrogatoires inquisitionnels, bientôt les exils et les proscriptions doivent signaler un ministre qui cherche sa force hors de la majorité nationale . . .

Depuis hier des fouilles ont été faite chez plusieurs citoyens des plus recommandables de notre ville. Un de nos concitoyens, M. Férail, charron, a été arrêté, emprisonné . . . On l'arrête, autant qu'il peut le supposer, sous le prétexte qu'il a traversé cette ville [Saumur] à l'époque de la tentative faite par le général Berton.

As Chausseblanche went on to note, Chappey and Bodin had also been detained; all three were old *fédérés* and at least Chappey and Férail were *Chevaliers de la Liberté* (it is difficult to believe that Bodin, Berton's old *aide de camp*, was not). The attempts of the *Chevaliers* and Carbonari to provoke revolution had, of course, run aground by this point.

The Rennes chapter of the *Chevaliers de la Liberté* was composed of perhaps some 300 old *fédérés* and *jeunes gens* who had been too young to join the association of 1815. At an assembly of delegates from towns and cities throughout the west, Rennes was represented by Férail and Chappey; the latter was accustomed to the role – in 1815 he had travelled to Brest as *commissaire* of the federative central committee. In 1820 he was the *Chevaliers'* treasurer. For their involvement in the uprising at Saumur (February 1822), Férail was sentenced to five years of imprisonment and Chappey was incarcerated until released as part of the general amnesty at the time of the coronation of Charles X (1825). The *Chevaliers* were part of a broader network of conspirators called the Carbonari. In an article on the Carbonari written in the 1830s, Ulysse Trélat lamented that older men, especially at Rennes, had taken over direction of the secret societies from younger men like himself. What he overlooked, although he must have known it, was that conspirators at Rennes, *jeunes gens* or otherwise, hearkened back to a tradition of opposition to the Monarchy that dawned with the Revolution and continued unabated from 1815 onwards.[51]

---

[51] *Ibid.*, F⁷ 6769, Prefect to Minister of the Interior, 7 March 1822, F⁷ 9665, excerpt from *L'Echo de l'Ouest* dated 4 April 1822, Prefect to Minister of the Interior, 27 March and 4 April 1822. On the participation of Rennes *fédérés* in the *Chevaliers de la Liberté*, see C. Laurent, *Histoire de la Bretagne* (Paris, 1875), p. 289; A. Calmette, 'Les carbonari en

Although in February 1823 opponents of the government at Rennes were still hopeful that war with Spain would bring about the fall of the Bourbon Monarchy, attempts to subvert the Army once again failed and revolutionary agitation gradually petered out. Resorting to violent and unconstitutional opposition did, however, produce two important results in the early 1820s. First, it isolated the opposition and drove the majority of electors into the arms of royalist and ultra-royalist candidates for the Chamber of Deputies. Second, it accelerated the political reaction which began under Louis XVIII in 1891 and reached its peak under Charles X. Liberals ultimately reaped the benefits of this, although the likelihood of such a result was far from apparent in 1823. Liberals learned from the mistakes of the period of revolutionary opposition, returned to overtly constitutional opposition, and portrayed themselves as champions of a Charter under siege from government ministers. This was a tactic more likely to gain sympathy from wealthy electors, and by the late 1820s it had begun to bear fruit; Rennes was no exception to the national pattern in this regard.[52]

Although duels, street demonstrations and serenades in honour of liberal deputies such as Le Graverand and Tréhu de Monthierry continued throughout the 1820s, the way forward for the opposition now lay in electoral organisation. A chapter of the *Aide-toi, le Ciel t'aidera* society had been set up at Rennes by October 1827. It concentrated on assuring that voters with liberal tendencies were registered on jury lists and cast their votes on polling day. With a solid block of the middle class in constant opposition, this was a potentially successful tactic, provided that liberals did not compromise their chances with the wealthier elements of the middle class by associating themselves directly with revolution. It should be noted that while liberal domination of the middle class became increasingly more marked during this period, it was the more conservative upper sectors of the middle class that had to be won over to achieve electoral success. As time passed, this task was facilitated by the increasing association of the government of Charles X with undue clerical and aristocratic influence. As D'Allonville had remarked, the bourgeoisie, though 'constitutional', was decidedly antagonistic towards the nobility. By 1827, the Villèle government's bill indemnifying *émigrés* stripped of their lands during the Revolution had alienated many voters. The indemnity was financed by a

France sous la Restauration', *La Révolution de 1848*, 10 (1913–14), pp. 69, 120, 136; U. Trélat, 'La Charbonnerie', *Paris Révolutionnaire*, 2 (1838), pp. 330–1. On the conspiracy at Saumur, see A. Spitzer, *Old Hatreds and Young Hopes* (Cambridge, Mass., 1971), pp. 104–19, 175–84. On Chappey as *commissaire*, see AD I-et-V, 1M96, letter from the federative central committee to Chappey, 9 May 1815.
[52] AN, F⁷ 9665, Prefect to Minister of the Interior, 2 February 1823.

reduction in the rates of government *rentes*, which were held by many electors who had formerly voted for royalist candidates to the Chamber. As the prefect anxiously noted in March and July 1827, divisions in the ranks of royalists were strengthening the opposition.[53]

Yet the opposition continued to be led by old *fédérés*. At the head of the *Aide-toi* in Rennes was Louis Bernard, known as Bernard de Rennes. Removed from the *cour d'appel* by D'Allonville as part of the post-Hundred Days purge, Bernard gained 'une grande célébrité parmi les patriotes sous la Restauration . . . il a défendu comme avocat une grande foule d'accusés politiques'. A close friend of Odilon Barrot, Bernard actually practised at Paris, but maintained close contact with Rennais liberals. He was president of the local *Comité Directeur* of the Liberal Opposition – a group of seven which included five old *fédérés*. Among the latter was Jollivet *fils*, who made frequent visits to the prefecture, verifying voter registration lists. According to the General Secretary of the Prefecture, Jollivet did not disguise the fact that he was working to overthrow the Monarchy. When asked in December 1828 how, as a lawyer, he could have sworn loyalty to the King, Jollivet replied that the oath was a necessary formality to allow him to earn his living, but that he had forgotten nothing of his old principles. He still believed that Liberty and Bourbon rule were incompatible. In the autumn of 1829, Bernard and Jollivet helped organise the Rennais chapter of the *Association Bretonne*, an organisation based on the principle of withholding taxes should the government 'violate' the Charter. Although the Association apparently had little impact in Rennes, setting himself up as a defender of the Constitution did Bernard no harm: in June 1830 he was elected to the Chamber of Deputies – a clear sign of dangerous discontent with the government of Charles X.[54]

The bar was at the very centre of Liberal Opposition in Rennes. This had been made particularly apparent when, after the trial of Dunoyer, virtually the entire *barreau* had attended a banquet in the journalist's honour. It was natural, therefore, for the prefect to view with suspicion an attempt of twelve Rennais lawyers to turn the local *Journal d'annonces* into a political newspaper. His doubts were only confirmed by rumours that the old *fédéré*, Joualt, who had written for Chausseblanche's *Echo*, would be a leading contributor to the new journal. Although the identity of the twelve lawyers was not cited by the prefect in his correspondence with the Minister of the Interior, it is difficult to believe that Jollivet and Gaillard de Kerbertin

[53] *Ibid.*, 27 March 1822, F⁷ 6769, Prefect to Minister of the Interior, 4 March and 6 July 1827, F⁷ 9664, Prefect to Minister of the Interior, 27 July 1815; Meyer, *Rennes*, pp. 335–7.

[54] J. Pascal, *Les Députés Bretons de 1789 à 1983* (Paris, 1983), p. 172; Vieuxville, 'La Loge', p. 189; C.-H. Pouthas, *Guizot pendant la Restauration* (Paris, 1923), p. 427; AN, F⁷ 6769, Prefect to Minister of the Interior, 6 October 1827, 8 December 1828, 5 January 1829.

were not involved in the initiative. That the latter two were the leaders of local opposition became fully apparent in October 1830, when they were both elected to the Chamber of Deputies.[55]

At the end of the Dunoyer banquet, free bread had been distributed to the poor. Gradually such wooing of the lower classes began to bear fruit and by 1830 previously solid lower-class support for the Monarchy had largely turned to indifference. As early as August 1820, de la Villegontier noted that the opposition included several hundred *ouvriers*; this represented a significant increase from the small number of lower-class Rennais who had participated in the federation of 1815. Perhaps more ominously, by the summer of 1829 Bonapartist propaganda had again become a source of official alarm. During a period when grain prices were high, the popularity of busts and engravings of Napoleon and his son indicated that the number of enemies of the ruling dynasty was growing. Given that Restoration prefects had had to rely on the lower classes to form a loyal National Guard, the tenuous position of local Bourbon officials becomes apparent. As we have seen, the hold of old *fédérés* such as Gaillard and Jollivet over middle-class Rennais, who under normal circumstances would have composed the bulk of the Guard, remained strong. This helps to explain why, when news of an uprising in Paris first reached Rennes in July 1830, students and middle-class liberals joined to form a new National Guard to oppose the royalist authorities. Attempts by the military commander to resist these movements proved futile because the troops refused to follow his orders. By 29 July the Bourbon authorities had been overthrown; the long-awaited opportunity had been swiftly grasped. Though the impetus may have come from the capital, all of the groundwork enabling such a rapid seizure of power had been prepared by a determined opposition led by old *fédérés*. Thus, Rennes had completed her own version of the Revolution of 1830 by the time that news of the flight of Charles X finally arrived. At the head of the provisional administration organised at Rennes during the revolution was Thomas Jollivet *fils*.[56]

Not unnaturally, *fédérés* led the charge into the vacuum of power they had helped create. In August 1830, Dubois du Sauzelay entered the prefecture as secretary-general. On 14 September a royal ordinance completely changed the municipal council: eight of the twenty-three new members were old *fédérés*. In 1831, Gaillard de Kerbertin and Porteu entered the *Conseil Général*; one year later, Gaillard became its president. In 1832,

[55] Pascal, *Les Députés*, pp. 174, 176; AN, F⁷ 9664, Prefect to Minister of the Interior, 28 June 1818, F⁷ 6776, 12 December 1829.
[56] AN, F⁷ 6769, Prefect to Minister of the Interior, 9 August 1829, F⁷ 9665, Prefect to Minister of Police, 8 August 1820, A. Robert, E. Bourloton and G. Cougny, *Dictionnaire des Parlementaires Français* (Paris, 1891); Lebrun, *L'Ille-et-Vilaine*, p. 266; Meyer, *Rennes*, p. 337.

Pontgérard became the mayor of Rennes. Among the magistrates 'retired' in 1816 (for their actions during the Hundred Days), Gaillard, Couannier and Duval de la Villebogard were either reintegrated or made honorary councillors in 1830.[57]

The extent to which having been a *fédéré* in 1815 suddenly became an asset is perhaps best revealed by a list of 'demandes d'emplois en juillet 1830' made at the prefecture. In their applications, candidates repeatedly cited their past affiliation and, in several instances, added that they had lost their positions in 1815 due to their 'sentiments politiques'. If one could claim to have been imprisoned for political opinions, so much the better. Several petitions were supported by Jollivet, who could make both claims. Six *fédérés* were successful in their applications. Thus, some of the men who had suffered for their participation in the federation at long last enjoyed benefits from their affiliation. Their unwavering opposition had finally been rewarded by the fall of the Bourbon Monarchy.[58]

[57] AD I-et-V, 2M81, 14 September 1830, *Indicateur historique: contribution des archives à l'histoire du département d'Ille-et-Vilaine de 1789 à 1980*, p. 75; Meyer, *Rennes*, p. 340; Maulion, *Le Tribunal*, p. 39.
[58] AD I-et-V, 2M19, *demandes d'emplois en juillet 1830*.

Chapter 6

The fédérés of Dijon
during the Hundred Days

Dijon in 1815 was a small regional capital with a population of approximately 21,000. It was the administrative centre of the Côte-d'Or and boasted a leading French academy. Its economy was exceedingly diverse and the *boutiquiers* and artisans who comprised fifty-seven per cent of Dijon's active work-force were involved in a variety of trades wholly characteristic of a pre-industrial society.[1]

Local historians have often pointed to the moderation of Dijon revolutionaries.[2] It was due only to the insistence of Bernard, the *représentant en mission* from Paris, that Dijonnais tribunals sent ten men to the guillotine during the Terror. Indeed, during this period one finds Jacobin lawyers and the future *fédérés* Larché and Dézé defending aristocrats. However, moderate behaviour should not be mistaken for indifference to the Revolution. The Jacobin *Société des Amis de la Constitution* remained in control of Dijon well into *Thermidor* and, although dissolved in 1796 after condemnation by the *représentant en mission*, Calès, was refounded after the *coup d'état* of *Fructidor* (4 September 1797). As late as 1798 the leading terrorist, Sauvageot, was elected mayor of Dijon.[3]

Many Jacobins retained their positions of local power under Napoleon. As P. Viard has noted, these men were more dangerous to Bonaparte than local monarchists. Although they accepted *Brumaire* because of Napoleon's popularity with the masses, they did not give up their old convictions. Belonging for the most part to the administrative and

---

[1] G. Chabot, *La Bourgogne* (Paris, 1941), p. 196; J. Richard, ed., *Histoire de la Bourgogne* (Toulouse, 1978), p. 344.

[2] See P. Viard, *L'Administration préfectorale dans le département de la Côte-d'Or sous le Consulat et le Premier Empire* (Paris, 1914), p. 10; P. Perrenet, *La Terreur à Dijon* (Dijon, 1907), p. 7; L. Heguenay, *Les clubs dijonnais sous la Révolution* (Dijon, 1905), p. 6; P. Palau, *Histoire du département de la Côte-d'Or* (Dijon, 1978), p. 35.

[3] Perrenet, *Terreur*, p. 59; Palau, *Histoire*, pp. 36–41; Heguenay, *Les Clubs*, pp. 231–2.

judicial corps, they formed 'une sorte de club' to monopolise local government.[4]

In general, the Empire was a period of prosperity in Dijon. The English blockade did not affect Dijon greatly, and expansion of the Empire opened valuable markets for Burgundian wines. However, 1811 to 1813 were years of famine throughout Burgundy; impoverished Dijonnais were fed 'soupe populaire' and the government made itself unpopular by forcing exports of grain from the Côte-d'Or. Support for Napoleon steadily waned during the final years of the Empire as conscription took its toll on the masses and centralisation of government alienated local administrators. As the Empire collapsed in 1814, many officials simply ignored government orders and the Dijonnais accepted Napoleon's fall as passively as they had accepted his rise.[5]

Louis XVIII soon lost whatever advantage he originally held. Forced closing of shops on Sundays, provocative *fêtes expiatoires*, and the reversal of Artois' promise to end the hated *droits réunis*, produced general discontent. More significantly, the Dijonnais began to fear a return to the *ancien régime* and loss of their *biens nationaux*.[6]

Enemies of the government saw their opportunity. During the months prior to Napoleon's return, drinks were bought at the Café Boulée for soldiers and workers willing to toast the Emperor. When news of the *vol d'aigle* arrived, 'des troupes composées de tout ce que la populace peut offrir la plus vile' gathered at the Café Boulée before spreading revolt throughout the town. Amidst these scenes 'des hommes qui auraient rougi dans d'autres temps de se trouver avec de pareilles gens' could be seen applauding and encouraging the 'enthusiasme populaire'. Little resistance was offered to the crowd and when Ney arrived as Napoleon's emissary, no monarchist overtly opposed his dismissal of Bourbon officials.[7]

Support for Napoleon during the Hundred Days was particularly strong in the east. Along the frontier, where memories of Allied occupation remained vivid, conscription demands were readily met and desertions from the army were rare. In Burgundy and Lorraine, where the plebiscite of the Hundred Days received its most positive response, support for the government was greater in the countryside than in the larger towns and cities. In Dijon, for instance, twenty-three per cent of the electorate voted in

[4] Viard, *L'Administration*, pp. 90–1.
[5] *Ibid.*, pp. 204–7, 221–4, 337; Richard, *Bourgogne*, pp. 336–7; P. de Saint-Jacob, 'La Municipalité de Dijon sous le Consulat et l'Empire', *Annales de Bourgogne*, 4 (1932), p. 220.
[6] S. Fizaine, *La vie politique dans la Côte-d'Or sous Louis XVIII* (Paris, 1931), p. 11.
[7] AD C-d, UV A3, 28 August 1816; P. Gaffarel, *Dijon en 1814 et 1815* (Dijon, 1897), pp. 162–5.

favour of the *Acte Additionnel* (no one voted against it), whereas forty-three per cent of the departmental electorate gave their approval.[8]

Dijon Jacobins joined forces with Bonapartists during the Hundred Days due to force of circumstance, but retained their suspicions of the Emperor, which partly explains why the *Acte* did not fare well in Dijon. Such men were biding their time for an opportunity such as the Hundred Days presented them with. Enjoying freedom of assembly for the first time in several decades, they used the federative movement to re-establish old contacts and forge new ones. However, Bonapartists and Jacobins were united in their opposition to the Bourbon Monarchy. This was apparent in the oath of the Dijon *fédérés*:

Je jure obéissance aux constitutions de l'empire et fidélité à l'empereur, de m'opposer de tout mon pouvoir aux machinations qui tendraient au rétablissement des Bourbons et d'aucun prince de cette famille sur le trône; au rétablissement de l'ancienne noblesse féodale, des droits seigneuriaux, des dîmes, d'un culte privilégié et dominant, et qui pourraient porter atteinte à l'irrévocabilité de la vente des biens nationaux.[9]

Before turning to the political character of the federation, it is useful to know something of who the *fédérés* were, for this helps to explain why they acted as they did.

Descriptions of the social composition of the federation made by prefects of the Côte-d'Or appear to be contradictory. In a report to the Minister of the Interior dated 18 August 1815, Choiseul described the *fédérés* as brigands bent solely on pillage. In the reports of his successor, however, we find a more balanced assessment. Tocqueville realised that the federation had a broad basis of popular support: 'la fédération n'a été dans aucun département plus nombreuse que dans celui de la Côte-d'or'. He also knew that among certain leaders of the association 'le sentiment de jalousie de la bourgeoisie contre la noblesse' was 'une espèce de fureur'. The superiority of Tocqueville's assessment can doubtless be attributed to the fact that he possessed a list of the *fédérés* of Dijon.[10]

The registers of the association had fallen into the hands of Montchinet, a member of the *chasseurs* of the National Guard. The *chasseurs* had been charged with the disarmament of the town on 5 September 1815 and it may well have been then that Montchinet gained possession of them. He made a copy of the registers and drew up his own list of *accusés* in which he

---

[8]   F. Bluche, *Le Plébiscite des Cent-Jours* (Geneva, 1974), pp. 64–7.
[9]   AN, F⁷ 9649, *Liste des Grands Meneurs* (of the Dijon federation).
[10]   *Ibid.*, Prefect to Minister of the Interior, 29 July and 18 August 1815; F⁹ 476–7, Prefect to Minister of the Interior, 26 May 1816.

Table 7. *Occupational groups (Dijon federation)*

Category	Number	% of the 726
1 Liberal professions	91	12.5
2 Merchants	76	10.5
3 Clergymen	6	0.8
4 Proprietors and *rentiers*	38	5.2
5 *Fonctionnaires*	108	14.9
6 Shopkeepers	86	11.8
7 Food and lodging trades	48	6.6
8 Artisans	165	22.7
9 Personal service trades	18	2.5
10 Manual labour	68	9.4
11 Military	22	3.0

named and described the leaders of the association. He sent the documents to the prefecture on 25 October. In November, Montchinet was charged with the repair and redistribution of guns that had been taken from *fédérés*.[11]

Montchinet's copy of the registers informs us of the name, occupation and domicile of each member, enabling us to analyse the socio-professional background of the *fédérés*.[12] Of the 749 members listed, 726 gave their occupation and can be grouped into the categories shown in Table 7.

Given the *fédéré* oath, it is interesting to note the presence of six clergymen. Perhaps this reflected the influence of the Bishop Reymond, a loyal supporter of Napoleon, but it is instructive to note that 530 of the 745 Catholic priests in the Côte-d'Or became *constitutionnels* during the Revolution.[13] The absence of students made the Dijon federation distinct from those of Rennes and Paris. There certainly was a good deal of support for the Emperor among students at the *lycée*, where the *proviseur* formed 'une petite compagnie de canonniers destinée à aider les fédérés dans la défense de la ville'. It would appear, however, that the students were discouraged by the *fédérés* themselves.[14]

That we find only eighteen men in the personal service trades perhaps shows the effect of the Revolution on Dijon. In 1790 it was estimated that

[11] *Ibid.*, F[7] 9649, letter attached to the *Liste des Grands Meneurs*; AM of Dijon, 1D1 1 22, 5 September and 29 November 1815.
[12] The following is based on the list of the *fédérés* of Dijon in AN, F[7] 9649.
[13] Palau, *Histoire*, pp. 22–3.
[14] C. Sadesky, 'La Crise et le relèvement des collèges en Côte-d'Or sous la restauration', *Annales de Bourgogne*, 32 (1960), pp. 35–8.

Table 8. *Dijon* fédéré *taxpayers*

Taxes paid	Number	% of the tax-paying *fédérés*
300–499 francs	74	63.2
500–999 francs	31	26.5
1,000–1,999 francs	7	6.0
2,000 or more francs	5	4.3

there were over 700 domestics in Dijon, yet we find only two in the federation! Perhaps the presence of Trullard, a leading *fédéré*, made domestics feel less than welcome – in 1790 he had proposed that measures be taken by the citizen militia against them due to their reputed aristocratic sympathies.[15] The high number of *fonctionnaires* is striking, especially when we recall that most Dijon Jacobins were drawn from their ranks. It is also part of what appears to be a disproportionately large representation of the middle classes. This impression is reinforced if we consult contemporary census registers.

The voter list of Dijon reveals that ninety-four *fédérés* were entitled to vote in 1817.[16] That the federation held a strong contingent of prosperous men becomes apparent when one considers that the average annual wage for a worker in Dijon was approximately 747 francs as late as 1832.[17] Furthermore, this group includes neither *fédérés* who had left Dijon during the White Terror nor those younger than thirty. We can compensate for this in the former case by consulting a voter list compiled in 1815, and in the latter by checking the list for 1831.[18] In so doing, we uncover another twenty-three eligible voters. As Table 8 illustrates, most of the *fédérés* paid tax amounts that indicate material comfort, but not great wealth.

How wealthy were these men? If we compare the seventy-six Dijon voters in 1817 who had been members of the federation with the 179 who had not, we find that the average *fédéré* had paid 957 francs. Moreover, of the fifty-three voters who paid more than a thousand francs, and therefore can be labelled 'notables', only eight had been *fédérés*. This should not surprise us, however, for taxes fell most heavily during the Restoration on

---

[15] H. Millot, *Le Comité permanent de Dijon* (Dijon, 1925), p. 42.

[16] AD C-d, 2M18, *état des propriétaires.*

[17] Lévêque, *Une Société provinciale: La Bourgogne sous la monarchie de juillet* (Paris, 1983), p. 314.

[18] AD C-d, 2M18 and 2M21, *listes des membres qui composent le collège électoral du département de la Côte-d'Or.*

Table 9. *Occupational groups revised (Dijon federation)*

Category	Number	Voters or *patente* payers removed	% of the 726
1 Liberal professions	91	—	12.5
2 Merchants	76	—	10.5
3 Clergymen	6	—	0.8
4 Proprietors and *rentiers*	38	—	5.2
5 *Fonctionnaires*	108	—	14.9
6 Shopkeepers	76	10	10.5
7 Food and lodging trades	43	5	5.9
8 Artisans	140	25	19.3
9 Personal service trades	17	1	2.3
10 Manual labour	59	9	8.1
11 Military	22	—	3.0
12 Voters or *patente* payers removed	50	—	6.9

landholders; the wealthiest of Dijon landowners were members of the old nobility, none of whom joined the federation.[19]

Employing the same procedure as in our study of Rennes, we can refine our original occupational table by removing *fédéré* voters from the sixth to the tenth categories. Moreover, by consulting *patente* lists we can also identify those who paid taxes on large business properties. If we remove the *fédérés* who either voted in national elections or paid first or second class *patentes* in 1814 from these categories, we are left with Table 9.[20]

We can now draw broad conclusions about the social character of the Dijon federation. Because we cannot be certain as to the social background of the clergymen and *militaires* in our table, we shall leave them out of our calculations. This leaves 698 *fédérés* of whose social status we are relatively certain. If we combine the first, second, fourth, fifth and twelfth categories, we find that 363 *fédérés*, or 52.0 per cent of the 598, were of the middle classes.

The highest registers of Dijon society played little part in the association. There were no members of the old aristocracy in the association, and only eight notables. For the most part, the *haute bourgeoisie* was either hostile

[19] For discussion of Dijon notables and noble landownership, see Lévêque, *Société*, pp. 244, 248.
[20] AD C-d, 2M18, *état des contribuables assujettis à la patente de 1ᵉ et 2ᵉ classe pour 1814 d'arrondissement de Dijon*, 2M21.

or indifferent to the federation. On the other hand, the fact that 117 *fédérés* were at one point or another eligible to vote indicates that many *fédérés* were drawn from the middle ranks of the bourgeoisie. If lawyers, notaries, doctors and bailiffs were integral to the descent of political consciousness to the masses, it is worth noting that these groups were fully represented in the association.[21] However, by no means all Dijon bourgeois were sympathetic to the federative movement; 69.0 per cent of the Dijon voters in 1817 had not been *fédérés*.

If we combine the sixth to the tenth categories, we find that 335 *fédérés*, 48.0 per cent of the 698, were drawn from the lower classes. Thus, it would be inaccurate to term this federation a 'popular' society. The lower classes were somewhat under-represented in the association; 57.0 per cent of the male Dijon population was comprised of artisans and *boutiquiers*. In this group of 335 *fédérés* we find the part of society from which issued the *sans-culottes* – men who possessed enough fortune to be willing to fight for it, but who lived close enough to poverty to be motivated by fear of it. It should be noted, however, that members of this group were by no means of the lowest orders of society. Each of the *fédérés* could state a particular profession and give a permanent address. They were not vagabonds, nor were they part of the 200 indigents whom the municipality sheltered and fed.[22]

It would be equally inaccurate to describe this association as bourgeois or middle-class, at least in terms of total membership. Moreover, as we shall see, there were old Dijonnais *sans-culotte* leaders within the federation. In sum, then, the Dijon federation had a mixed social character. If it is true that revolution was most likely to occur when certain members of the bourgeoisie joined with certain members of the 'people' in a common political enterprise, then it is not at all surprising that monarchists viewed the federation with such trepidation and compared it with the popular societies of 1793.[23]

Were such comparisons merely the product of febrile aristocratic imagination? We can make a rough comparison of the socio-professional composition of the federation with that of its Revolutionary counterpart, the popular society of year II, by using Louis Heguenay's analysis of the latter association.[24] It must be emphasised, however, that we are looking

---

[21] Lévêque, *Société*, p. 475.

[22] Richard, *Bourgogne*, p. 344. For a description of *sans-culottes* which has become definitive, see A. Soboul, *Les Sans-culottes parisiens en l'an II* (Paris, 1962), pp. 405–57; AM of Dijon, 1D1 20, 3 January 1815.

[23] The point that most revolutionary societies were composed of both the 'people' and the bourgeoisie is demonstrated in D. M. G. Sutherland, *France 1789–1815* (London, 1985), p. 157.

[24] Heguenay, *Les Clubs*, p. 157.

for rough correspondences only and cannot claim any great exactitude in such a comparison because some of Heguenay's figures are approximate. Nevertheless, his categories do correspond fairly closely to ours. Because Heguenay did not use the process by which we have made our second table more precise, we shall use our original table in making our comparisons. Heguenay does not cite a single clergyman or *militaire*, and therefore these categories will be left out of our calculations.

Of the 710 club members whose profession is identified by Heguenay, approximately 438, 61.7 per cent, fall into the lower-class categories. This compares with 385, 55.2 per cent, of the *fédérés*. On the other hand, 171, 38.3 per cent, of the club members belong to the middle-class categories, whereas 313, 44.8 per cent, of the *fédérés* fall into these categories. Each association, therefore, drew large numbers from both the middle and lower classes, although the club appears the more 'popular' of the two.[25]

When we consider the age of the *fédérés*, we find that many of them were old enough to have played major roles in the Revolution. However, a few general points must be made before we discuss age statistics. While no age qualification was stated in the constitution of the association, many young Dijonnais had been called to service by the time that the federation was formed. As usual, it is much simpler to gather information on those who possessed wealth than on those who did not, and this probably prejudices our findings by over-representing those who had had enough time to amass wealth.[26] We should not, therefore, conclude too much from the fact that the average age of the 129 *fédérés* of whom we have information was forty-eight. On the other hand, Table 10 clearly indicates that many of the *fédérés* could have been Jacobins. A man of forty-eight in 1815 would have been twenty-two when the Revolution began.

One way of participating in the Revolution was by purchasing lands sequestered from the Catholic Church and *émigré* nobles. If we look at purchases in Dijon alone, we find that no fewer than sixty-one *fédérés* had become owners of *biens nationaux*.[27] It is probable that *fédérés* had purchased property elsewhere and certain that some of them had inherited, or stood to inherit, such properties. This helps to explain why the *fédérés* made explicit reference to *biens nationaux* in their oath and suggests that

[25] In leaving the comparison so broad I have sought to avoid difficulties in assigning too direct a correspondence between Heguenay's categories and mine. When confronted by Heguenay's category of 'jardiniers et vignerons', I have arbitrarily assigned eight *jardiniers* to the 'personal services' category and seven *vignerons* to the 'proprietors'.

[26] With the exception of several citations in court records, relatively few in number, most of our information comes from the census lists previously cited.

[27] AD C-d, Q1159.

Table 10. *Dijon* fédéré *age groups*

Age group	Number	% of the 129
20–9 years	3	2
30–9 years	21	16
40–9 years	45	35
50–9 years	46	36
60–9 years	11	9
70 and older	3	2

at least some support for Napoleon in 1815 was related directly to the question of sequestered lands.[28] There were, of course, more direct ways of participating in the Revolution, as we shall see by turning our attention to the individuals who either led, or were thought to have led, the federation.

The leadership of the federation can be approached in two ways. First, we can discuss the members of the central committee. Second, we can turn to Montchinet's list of *accusés*.

Eleven of the twenty-three committee members were government officials or employees. Gayet was a councillor at the prefecture, where Compérot was a clerk. Peyrard and Mouzin were employed at the *mairie* and Lapertot was on the municipal council. Lerouge and Villeneuve were public prosecutors and Moret was a court clerk. Perrier was a government engineer and Chaussier a tax collector. Four were lawyers: Roy, Bernardin, Gabet and Nardin. Forgeot, Prisset, Villeneuve and Jouvelot were involved in commerce. Richard-Viennot and Duleu were proprietors; Escard was an army officer, and Carion edited the *Journal de la Côte-d'Or*. Ten members voted at one point or another in national elections between 1815 and 1831 (Gayet, Gabet, Forgeot, Prisset, Perrier, Peyrard, Duleu, Jouvelot, Lerouge and Roy).[29]

Thus, Lefebvre's description of the *fédérés* as Jacobin bourgeois appears to fit the committee members well. Carion, Forgeot and Prisset were defrocked priests. Gabet had edited the organ of Dijon's revolutionary society, and during the Hundred Days, in his *Project d'un Pacte Social pour la France*, he argued that the *Acte Additionnel* was provisional and that

---

[28] Etienne Hernoux, for example, inherited *biens nationaux*. For a description of his vast inheritance, see Lévêque, *Société*, pp. 265–6. On the question of *biens nationaux* and Napoleon's popularity, see B. Maurel, 'Vente de biens nationaux et popularité de l'empereur', *Revue d'histoire économique et sociale*, 80 (1975), pp. 428–35.

[29] The names of the committee members are given in AN, F⁹ 476–7, *Fédération Bourguignonne*; AD C-d, electoral lists in 2M18–23.

patriots should busy themselves with deciding what sort of constitution they really wanted. Jouvelot and Duleu were both known for their violence during the Revolution; the latter had led a charge on an equestrian statue of Louis XIV in 1792.[30]

Montchinet's list indicates that there were people of greater influence in the federation. Montchinet was a royalist, so one must read his comments on 118 of the *fédérés* with caution. Nevertheless, his remarks, where verifiable, are borne out by other sources. Montchinet knew the *fédérés* well enough to make distinctions, and from his list we can discern that there were several factions within the federation.

In a letter to the prefect of the Côte-d'Or dated 13 August 1815, the Minister of the Interior warned against the intrigues of the Duke of Bassano and his clientele. While there is no evidence to suggest that the Duke played any direct role in the federation, Montchinet does confirm that Maret's protégés, the Lejéas brothers, were at the centre of the Bonapartist wing of the association. Ties to Maret through marriage had aided both brothers in their careers during the Empire. J. L. Lejéas had been a member of the general council of the department, receiver general of the Côte-d'Or, mayor of Dijon and senator at various points. A. M. Lejéas had also been a tax official. When Ney arrived in Dijon, fresh from his betrayal of the Bourbons, he was met by the Lejéas and given provisions for his troops. The Lejéas themselves had a large clientele in Dijon. Three of their agents (Poulot-Belenet, Chevalot and the lawyer Marinet) had led the agitations at the Café Boulée, and Marinet had gone to take instructions from Napoleon when the Eagle hovered at Lyons. Montchinet cites Mignot, clerk, and the proprietors Causse and Reinhard as belonging to the Lejéas circle, and to this group we can add Naissant, solicitor, Maldant, *conservateur des forêts*, and Lejéas *père*.[31]

This group of Bonapartists was well placed and powerful, but small in number. None of these men were members of the central committee. We should not conclude from this, however, that the federation was dominated entirely by Jacobins. Montchinet cites several *fédérés*, including the president, Gayet, who had joined simply to further their own careers. Moreover, many of the men whom Montchinet terms 'patriots' appear to have feared a return to the *ancien régime* above all else and to have rallied sincerely to Napoleon in 1815. Montchinet places Malardot, clockmaker, and the proprietors Rousset and Guichon in this category. To this list we can add Belin,

---

[30] G. Lefebvre, *Napoléon* (Paris, 1969), pp. 558–9; *Petites Affiches de Dijon*, 11 May 1815; AN, F⁷ 9649, *Liste des Grands Meneurs*.

[31] AN, F⁷ 9649, Minister of the Interior to Prefect, 13 August 1815, *Liste des Grands Meneurs*; Gaffarel, *Dijon*, pp. 163, 165.

commissaire de police, Yon, a bookseller, specialising in anti-royalist tracts, and Locquin, who, though a Jacobin under the Directory, met Napoleon during one of the Italian campaigns and was converted.

The Jacobin circle was larger and contained several of Dijon's leading figures – men whose political principles had often brought them into conflict with Imperial prefects. Vaillant virtually ran the prefecture as its general secretary from the year II to 1815 and was elected to the Chamber of Representatives during the Hundred Days. When the prefect Guillardet sought to have Vaillant removed from office in 1801 he found that he could not do so because Vaillant had powerful connections in Paris. Guillardet's successor, Riouffe, had similar problems with Pierre Jacotot, rector of the Academy. During a dispute over precedence at an awards ceremony, Riouffe had Jacotot summoned to the prefecture. Jacotot responded 'qu'il ignore si M. le préfet a le droit de faire comparaître tout habitant devant lui'. Riouffe attributed the currency of such outmoded egalitarian ideals in 1806 to 'l'appui d'un parti chez lequel le mépris de l'autorité est reduit en système'.[32]

Joseph Jacotot, cousin of Pierre and a professor at the Academy, was another distinguished member of this group. In 1788 he had organised 'la fédération de la jeunesse dijonnaise'. At the age of twenty-one he had already become a professor of the *Collège de Dijon*, but in September 1792 he gave up this post in order to enroll as a volunteer in the army. Three years later he returned to Dijon and began developing a method of instruction based on the principle that 'toutes les intelligences sont égales'. Strongly committed to egalitarianism and the liberties won during the Revolution, Jacotot was viewed with suspicion by Imperial officials. In a report on the academic personnel of Dijon in 1812 that lauded his teaching abilities, one finds the following: 'mais il est malin, frondeur, et se ressent tant peu de son attachement aux principes de la Révolution'.[33]

Fremyet, a retired soldier, owner of *biens nationaux* and a zealous tax collector, was also a member of that 'poignée d'individus . . . encore la terreur des honnêtes gens.' In 1795 he had conducted an anti-royalist campaign in the countryside surrounding Dijon. To this circle of Jacobins can be added Balland, *procureur général*, Liégéard, goldsmith, the doctor Morland, Céron, bureau-chief at the prefecture, the central committee members Villeneuve, lawyer, Gabet, Lerouge and Carion. Carion and Gabet had both edited the Jacobin journal *Le Nécessaire* during the Revolution. Carion went on to edit the *Journal de la Côte-d'Or* under the Empire,

[32] Viard, *L'Administration*, pp. 4, 11, 37, 91, 284.
[33] L.-E. Missinne, 'Un Pédagogue Bourguignon: Joseph Jacotot (1770–1840)', *Annales de Bourgogne*, 26 (1964), pp. 8–9, 11, 15–16.

but he was stripped of the right to publish by the Imperial government in 1811.[34]

This is an imposing collection of leading Dijonnais and their presence in the federation may have caused some anxiety in the Bonapartist camp. However, their appearance could not have caused as much sensation as that of certain ex-terrorists who emerged for the first time from an obscurity they had cultivated since Napoleon's seizure of power.

What were monarchists to make of the presence of Drevon *père*, one of the founders of Dijon's revolutionary society? Had not section meetings been held in his house? More ominous still would be the reappearance of Sauvageot, the *chapelier-poète* mayor of 1792. Sauvageot had led the transformation of the relatively peaceful patriotic society into the extremist popular society and had played a crucial role in preventing the Côte-d'Or from joining the federalist revolt in 1793. With him he brought the old section leader Perrotte, a *cabaretier*, Paillet, a baker, and Vallée, a grocer. All four had been leading *sans-culottes* and terrorists. As late as the year VI, Sauvageot and Perrotte were not above assaulting royalist voters. Despite being denounced by Calès in the Convention, Sauvageot remained popular and had to be removed from the office of mayor by an embarrassed Directory in 1798.[35]

The presence of such men helps to explain why Bonaparte and his officials were wary of the federation. Although they sought to channel this revolutionary *élan*, they were aware that it might get beyond their control. We can appreciate this more fully by considering why the *fédérés* joined the association and what they did while part of it.

There were signs of popular Bonapartism in Dijon. The agitation at the Café Boulée began before Napoleon returned from exile. Busts of Napoleon were paraded repeatedly in the streets during the Hundred Days and an enterprising artist named Pouchetti made them his stock in trade. However, the following description of decorations at a *fédéré* banquet shows how closely republicanism and Bonapartism had come to be bound:

Tapissée d'abeilles au milieu desquelles on voit le monogramme couronné de l'empereur, et de brillans trophées militaires, . . . sur l'estrade où est le bureau, s'élevait le buste de Napoléon qu'on ombrageaient des drapeaux aux couleurs nationales . . . et tout se préparait à imprimer à cette cérémonie le caractère imposant de ces réunions que vit naître l'aurore de la révolution.

[34] The quote is from Montchinet; see also Palau, *Histoire*, pp. 39, 66.
[35] Heguenay, *Les Clubs*, p. 54; J. Brelot, *La Vie politique en Côte-d'Or sous le Directoire* (Dijon, 1932), p. 133; R. Schnerb, 'La mission en Bourgogne du conventionnel Bernard de Saintes', *La Revue de Bourgogne* (1921), p. 374; Perrenet, *Terreur*, p. 101.

The circumstances of the Hundred Days gave the various factions common goals. The experience of occupation cannot be over-stressed as a motivating factor. In part it was simply a matter of wanting to stop the invading hordes from again inflicting indignity and devastation. However, when General Veaux, a *fédéré*, spoke to conscripts of the shame of the treaties of Paris, he struck a chord. Many future *fédérés* had been singled out for especially harsh treatment during the first occupation. The Austrian governor Bartenstein had had Vaillant, Larché, Balland, Fremyet and Joseph Jacotot arrested and transferred to Baume-les-Dames, where they were treated as prisoners of war.[36]

There is little need to repeat here the litany of *maladresses* by which the Bourbons alienated the French populace. It can be noted, however, that *fêtes expiatoires* were well calculated to increase the fears of the many Dijonnais who had purchased *biens nationaux*. During the Hundred Days, Carion argued that although Louis XVIII may have intended to secure such purchases, the nobility eventually would have led him to reverse his policy. Moreover, during a visit to Dijon, Artois rashly announced that the hated *droits réunis* would be suppressed. This proved impossible, however, and when collection recommenced, disturbances broke out which led to thirteen arrests.[37]

General grievances were exacerbated by personal affronts. When Vaillant sought to present an address to Louis XVIII, he was denied a passport. General Veaux had hoped to be given one of the *chevaliers de la croix* that Artois freely distributed and was chagrined when he was not. Boulée was forced to give a dinner in honour of Artois but was not paid for it, on the grounds that he had been a Bonapartist.[38]

The association was a natural resort for those who wished either to secure or to further their careers. Though by no means as reactionary as the Second, the First Restoration gave a clear indication of what the future held. It must have been obvious to Hernoux that he could give up his ambition of becoming mayor while the Bourbons held power. His rival Durande was thoroughly ensconced in the royalist camp and the ties of Hernoux's family to the Revolution would seriously hinder his career. When Ney came to Dijon, Hernoux saw his chance and took it.[39]

Those who chose the side of the Emperor enjoyed immediate benefits. During his first visit, Thibaudeau purged the *mairie* and the municipal

[36] AD C-d, UV A3, 28 August 1816; *Petites Affiches de Dijon*, 2 April and 7 May 1815; BM of Dijon, *Fonds Delmasse*, no. 2218, p. 2; Gaffarel, *Dijon*, p. 38.
[37] Gaffarel, *Dijon*, pp. 132–5, 140; *Petites Affiches de Dijon*, 4 June 1815.
[38] Gaffarel, *Dijon*, p. 116.
[39] *Ibid.*, pp. 165–9; P. Viard, 'Les Fédérés de la Côte-d'Or en 1815', *La Revue de Bourgogne*, 16 (1926), p. 34.

council. The final list of twenty-nine councillors included twenty-four *fédérés*. In addition, the new mayor Hernoux and his *adjoints* Drevon *fils* and Jacob were *fédérés*. Two royalist public prosecutors, Gouget-Michéa and Saverot, were replaced by the *fédérés* Huguet and Lerouge. Villeneuve also became a public prosecutor when Borthon was appointed *juge d'instruction*. Six *fédérés* became members of the *tribunal de première instance*. J. L. Lejéas joined the general council of the Côte-d'Or, while Larché and Gayet were appointed to the council of the prefecture. Locquin-Popelard and Joseph Jacotot became adjoints at the prefecture.[40]

Fédérés also infiltrated the upper ranks of the National Guard. The Guard had had a strong royalist contingent when Napoleon returned, and it was therefore reorganised during the Hundred Days and given a new officer corps. Fourteen of the twenty-three officers of the new Guard were *fédérés*, with Carion-Badelle at the head.[41]

In the official writings of the federation, revolutionary sentiment and Bonapartism are bound inextricably. The first thing to be noted about the Burgundian *pacte* is that it is virtually an exact replica of its Breton counterpart. It may well be that the founders of the Burgundian federation thought the Breton *pacte* so perfect that they dared not alter it, but it is difficult not to suspect that they adopted the original model to assure that their plans to form a federation would be accepted by the government.

To facilitate recruitment, the *pacte* was published along with the address in which Escard first called for a Burgundian federation, and a report made by the committee chosen to organise the association. Escard's address is primarily patriotic and gives little indication of the political beliefs of the *fédérés*. In their report, however, the committee threw down the gauntlet to all those who supported 'superstition, despotism or feudalism'. The clergy was informed that its realm was not of the Earth and the aristocracy was warned that social privilege would no longer be tolerated. The most striking passage of the report concerns the nature of government:

Nous avons dit au monarque: le peuple est le souverain, il vous fait le dépositaire de la suprême puissance. Régnez donc, non plus d'après votre volonté absolue, mais d'après une constitution librement et solennellement acceptée par la nation.

Such a pronouncement would have given Napoleon food for thought. In this statement the issue of how the sovereign people grant supreme power to the ruler is skirted, nor is Napoleon's role as the man who will implement the will of the people questioned. But these are not the words of men who

[40] AM of Dijon, 1D1 1 21, 7 April and 4 May 1815; *Petites Affiches de Dijon*, 26 March and 30 April 1815; AN, Fib II Côte-d'Or 5, 20 May 1815.
[41] P. Viard, 'Les Levées militaires en Côte-d'Or pendant les Cent-Jours', *La Revue de Bourgogne* (1913), pp. 65–6; *Petites Affiches de Dijon*, 13 April 1815.

expected the monarch to pay mere lip service to the principle of popular sovereignty, and this brings us to the central question about the *fédérés*. Did they really believe the Emperor when he claimed to have renounced 'tout esprit de conquête' and that henceforth he would respect the liberty of Frenchmen?[42]

In giving the address of the electoral college of the Côte-d'Or to Napoleon, General Veaux was not above reminding the Emperor of recent promises:

Nous aimons à vous rappeler que les premières paroles de Votre Majesté, en reprenant possession de votre trône, consacrent des principes éminemment libéraux . . . Nous avons reconnu avec satisfaction et avec une sorte d'orgueil que de ce moment tous les actes émanés de votre volonté ont été dirigés par les mêmes principes, et que dans le grand nombre de ceux que nous pouvions rappeler elle s'est empressée de nous rendre la liberté de la presse . . .

Nous aimons surtout à contempler cette magnamine et généreuse declaration de Votre Majesté . . . renonçant a tout système de conquête et d'agrandissement.

In a very real sense, Veaux and the other members of the electoral college were informing Napoleon that their support was based on his promise to respect liberties that had not been respected under the Empire. In fact, praising his resolve to refrain from all conquest and aggrandisement was tantamount to criticising the central policy of the Empire.[43]

Nowhere in France was support for the *Acte Additionnel* stronger than in the Côte-d'Or, and the prefect reported no qualms about the nature of the senate. Yet, how was a determined democrat to interpret the constitution of this body? By wooing the liberals, Napoleon seemed to be turning his back on the more revolutionary of his following, and this probably explains why the *Acte* was much less popular in Dijon than in the surrounding countryside.[44]

During his first visit to Dijon, Thibaudeau found 'une réunion de patriotes, une sorte de comité révolutionnaire, qui avait des relations dans toute la Bourgogne, et qui n'était pas aveuglée par le fanatisme impérial'. The rector Jacotot was a leader of this group. During one of several meetings, Thibaudeau was told that 'l'Empereur se trompe fort . . . s'il imagine que lui seul est la cause, et le but du mouvement populaire . . . s'il croit triompher pour et au nom de l'Empire, il se perdra'. There can be little doubt that this was the circle of Jacobins that had been a thorn in the side of prefects throughout the Empire. Thibaudeau sought to convince them

---

[42] For the Burgundian pact, see AN, F^9 476–7; for its Breton model, see *Le Moniteur Universel*, 29 April 1815.

[43] *Moniteur*, 5 June 1815.

[44] See F. Bluche, *Le Bonapartisme* (Paris, 1980), p. 109.

that under the circumstances the best policy was to throw in their lot with the Emperor. He was told that it was difficult to do so with conviction, and that without conviction the influence they exercised would be lost.[45]

Jacotot and the circle of Jacobins did of course join the federation, but it is quite evident that their support for Napoleon was a matter of expedience. In 1817 Carion was to publish a pamphlet written by Gabet in which Napoleon was described as a despot who systematically destroyed democratic institutions. Such men in 1815 wanted to secure the republic first and foremost; they would deal with the nature of the republic later.[46]

The *fédérés*, therefore, did indeed have equivocal political tendencies, but the Jacobins clearly were in the ascendant. We find more evidence of these divisions when we consider what the *fédérés* actually did.

A cynical observer might report that the *fédérés* devoted themselves primarily to banqueting and singing, but this would not do justice to the purpose that such ceremonies served. The banquets gave *fédérés* a sense of solidarity which increased their resolution. Moreover, they were a means by which links were established with *fédérés* who might otherwise have felt isolated. The *fédérés* went to great lengths to establish contacts throughout Burgundy and beyond. The central committee corresponded with branches of the association in communes such as Is-sur-Tille. They communicated with the federations of Lyons, Dauphiné and Franche-Comté. Gayet and Escard attended a meeting of the Paris federation.[47]

However, the *fédérés* went beyond banquets and song. Indeed, at times they went beyond the wishes of government authorities. Royer drew up a memorandum for Thibaudeau outlining a strategy for creating a network throughout the department of men on whom the government could rely. He suggested that committee sections be formed to advise the government as to who was trustworthy. The plan got as far as the National Archives, but not further. Laguesse presented General Veaux with a proscription list. Was this not the course of action that *sectionnaires* had taken during the Terror when they drew up lists of suspects and made constant denunciations? Veaux ignored the list.[48]

In another act reminiscent of the Terror, the central committee decided to purge the federation of 'toutes les personnes notoirement connues pour avoir des principes opposés au gouvernement existant'. Knowing that the

[45] A.-C. Thibaudeau, *Mémoires 1799–1815* (Paris, 1913), pp. 467–8.
[46] Gabet's pamphlet can be found in AN, BB³ 152–3.
[47] BM of Dijon, *Fonds Delmasse*, no. 2218, p. 8; AD C-d, 3M28, Prefect to president of the *assemblée fédérative* of Is-sur-Tille, 16 June 1815; *Petites Affiches de Dijon*, 4 and 8 June 1815.
[48] AN, F^{ib} II Côte-d'Or 5, 13 April 1815; Gaffarel, *Dijon*, p. 221.

prefect was opposed to any such action, the notary Moyne informed Bercagny of the committee's resolution 'dont vous sentez parfaitement la conséquence'. Bercagny spoke to Gayet, the president, of his opposition to any such move.[49]

The federation was also a vehicle of men involved in a local power struggle. This rivalry of élite groups comes to the fore in a letter which the central committee sent to the prefect on 20 June 1815. In it the *fédérés* demanded that five members of the previous municipal government be made to account for requisitions exacted during the Austrian occupation. The committee also questioned why the previous mayor, Durande, and sub-prefect, Petiot, had taken part in the administration of requisitions when their offices obliged them to remain independent of such tasks in order to protect the interests of the Dijonnais. That the committee expected retribution was made clear when they drew the prefect's attention to a similar case in the Saône-et-Loire in which the administrators had had legal suits brought against them. Bercagny was obviously perplexed as to what action to take. Finally he set up a commission to investigate the matter, but he also wrote to the Minister of the Interior enquiring whether the matter might better be resolved by higher government officials.[50]

As well as involving themselves in political matters, the *fédérés* helped build defence works outside Dijon and became the 'police de la rue' inside. Part of the latter role doubtless involved intimidating royalists, but it would appear that the *fédérés* concentrated on maintaining rather than disturbing public order. Certainly Carion condemned anti-royalist excesses in ringing terms: 'Quoiqu'ils aient été provoqués par une conduite et des propos antérieurs, . . . ils n'en sont pas moins condamnables. La répression n'appartient qu'à la loi, et personne n'a le droit de se faire justice.' Indeed, there appears to have been little need for the *fédérés* to intimidate royalists in Dijon. When a group of the latter shouted 'Vive le Roi' on 28 June 1815, 'le peuple irrité de tels excès' killed several of the royalists. The prefect had to take measures to protect monarchists throughout the town from 'la fureur du peuple'.[51]

Fédérés took part in the military exercises of the National Guard. Perhaps they were led by the thirty-five retired officers among them. The government called on all Dijonnais to deposit their arms at the *hôtel de ville* and the *fédéré* Trullard was assigned the task of visiting local gunsmiths. Bercagny saw to the distribution of some six hundred guns amongst them.

---

[49] AD C-d, 3M28.
[50] AN, F⁷ 9649, Prefect to Minister of the Interior, 25 June 1815.
[51] *Ibid.*, AFIV 1934, bulletins of 28 and 30 June 1815, AFIV 1935, bulletin of 2 July 1815; *Petites Affiches de Dijon*, 7 May 1815.

When Bercagny read news of Waterloo to a tumultuous assembly of the *fédérés*, a call for a *levée en masse* immediately arose. Bercagny rejected the measure as futile for lack of weapons and, although he reported to Carnot that the *fédérés* were willing to fight, Dijon fell to the Allies without a shot being fired.[52]

In sum, then, we can conclude that the Dijon federation had a mixed social and political character. Although leadership was assumed almost entirely by men of the middle classes, membership was divided between the middle and lower classes in roughly equal proportions. Jacobins were clearly in the ascendant in *fédéré* leadership, but there were important Bonapartists within the association and there were numerous signs of popular Bonapartism amongst the rank-and-file members.

Dijon *fédérés* were motivated by their experience of occupation and Bourbon rule in 1814–15. A desire to prevent repetition of this experience brought Bonapartists and Jacobins into a single association. However, Jacobin *fédérés* took a direct interest in local politics, and Bonapartist officials on several occasions had to temper, ignore, or oppose their proposals and initiatives. These proposals and initiatives were directed specifically against Dijonnais monarchists who had held power during the First Restoration, and were part of a power struggle between two rival élite groups. After Waterloo, *fédérés* would find themselves on the defensive in this local power struggle.

[52] AM of Dijon, 1D1 1 21, 7 April and 30 June 1815; AN, F⁷ 9649, *Liste des Grands Meneurs*, Prefect to Minister of the Interior, 2 and 3 July 1815.

Chapter 7

The fédérés of Dijon during the Second Restoration

Many *fédéré* leaders took flight in July and August of 1815. Those closely connected with the Imperial government, such as Hernoux, Royer, Drevon, Jacob and the Lejéas, and the more compromised Bonapartists, such as Chevalot, Marinet and Poulot-Belenet, went into hiding. Carion and Veaux joined Lazare Carnot in hiding at Désiré (Saône-et-Loire). Joseph Jacotot departed Paris and, with his wife, two daughters and a younger sister, found refuge in Belgium. He subsequently lost his position as professor and was removed from the list of legal practitioners. He did not return to France until 1830.[1]

While *fédéré* leaders were taking cover, royalist officials such as Durande and Petitot returned to reclaim their old offices. Mayor Durande prepared an address to the King warning that the 'faction désorganatrice' remained active and advising that clemency would be inappropriate for these 'déstructeurs de tout ordre social'.[2]

Durande was soon presented with a pretext for moving against the *fédérés*. On 12 July a band of thirteen deserters entered Dijon crying 'Vive l'Empereur!' and exchanged gunfire with the National Guard. Several *fédérés* encouraged the deserters, who were not apprehended due to the connivance of sympathetic Dijonnais. Durande immediately ordered that all *fédérés* deliver their arms to the *hôtel de ville* within twenty-four hours. With the help of Austrian soldiers, the National Guard began house searches.[3]

The first order of business for royalist officials was to re-establish the National Guard as a reliable means of repression. Although many *fédérés*

---

[1] P. Gaffarel, *Dijon en 1814 et 1815* (Dijon, 1897), pp. 233–5; P. Gonnet, 'La Société Dijonnaise au XIXe Siècle', Ph.D. thesis (University of Paris, 1974), pp. 381–2; L.-E. Missinne, 'Un Pédagogue bourguignon: Joseph Jacotot (1770–1840), *Annales de Bourgogne*, 36 (1964), pp. 18, 39.

[2] AM of Dijon, 1D1 1 22, 30 June 1815.

[3] *Ibid.*, 13 July and 5 September 1815.

had entered the Guard, it appears to have remained predominantly monarchist in its sympathies during the Hundred Days. Indeed, *fédérés* in control of the distribution of arms at the *hôtel de ville* had refused to supply Guardsmen who were not *fédérés*. Nevertheless, the Guard was purged of *fédérés*; its officers corps was completely reorganised, and by 18 August the prefect, Choiseul, thought it reliable.[4]

Simultaneously, preparations were made for another administrative purge. On his first attempt to reconvene the municipal council of the First Restoration, Durande found that only five members attended. When they did heed his summons, a majority of the council refused to sit with members who had rebelled against the Bourbon government. Therefore Durande drew up a list of men he thought appropriate for a new council and submitted it to the prefect.[5]

Due to the breadth of support for Napoleon amongst officials and *fonctionnaires*, the royalist government had to move slowly. They simply could not dismiss every government employee, nor was the degree of culpability always evident. Vaillant appears to have been the first *fédéré* to fall; he was removed officially on 15 July 1815. At about the same time, Perrier lost his post as government engineer and Balland was replaced as *procureur général* by Riambourg. Lejéas, receiver general, was dismissed on 31 August; Royer had been removed from the prefecture two weeks previously. Compérot and Darbois were removed from the bureaux of the prefecture in September and Céron followed them one month later. Dupont, police officer, was dismissed on 24 November. Ten days later, the tax collectors Hecquet and Fremyet lost their posts. Lévêque, head clerk at the *cour royale*, was retained by an act of the King on 29 November, but was subsequently replaced by 'un absolutiste de la congrégation' due to the intervention of Riambourg.[6]

The reformed municipal council was not officially appointed until 16 November 1815. Of the twenty-five members, only Morizot, who alone had steered clear of the federation, had been retained from the council of the Hundred Days. Jacob and Drevon *fils* were dismissed as *adjoints* at the *mairie*, and the magistrature was purged by the removal of Borthon, Huguet, Balland and Larché.[7]

The problems faced by royalist officials in Dijon could not be solved by administrative purges alone. Although the arrival of Allied troops put an

---

[4] *Ibid.*, 30 June 1815, *Petites Affiches de Dijon*, 11 May 1815; AN, F[7] 9649, Prefect to Minister of the Interior, 18 August 1815.
[5] AM of Dijon, 1D1 1 22, 26 July 1815.
[6] *Ibid.*, 22 and 24 November 1815; AD C-d, K 6 5, 1M 7/1, 9/1, and 15/1.
[7] AM of Dijon, 1D1 21 and 22, 4 May and 16 November 1815; S. Fizaine, *La vie politique dans la Côte-d'Or sous Louis XVIII* (Paris, 1931), p. 51; Gonnet, 'Société', p. 386.

end to federation assemblies, this did not stop *fédéré* chiefs from maintaining contact with their followers. As late as July 1816, *fédéré* leaders continued to agitate and the prefect noted that the worse communes 'renferment le plus de chefs de fédérés'. Even peasants closed their doors when they heard shouts of 'Vive le Roi!' It was therefore imperative to separate *fédéré* leaders from those who were 'susceptible' and silence the former whenever possible. Cafés that were meeting places for opponents of the monarchy were therefore closed. The *Journal de la Côte-d'Or* was removed from Carion and its supplement, the *Petites Affiches de Dijon*, was suppressed. The Jacotots, Brun, Lefevre and Prudhon were dismissed from the Academy.[8]

The authorities were willing to take more extreme measures. General Colloredo had Vaillant arrested and marched on foot to Autun in August 1815. Durande tricked General Veaux into returning to Dijon so that the latter could be arrested, along with Hernoux, Royer and J. Lejéas, on charges of conspiracy.[9]

The subsequent trial caused much controversy and ultimately led to a serious defeat for the government. All four were prosecuted for plotting to aid the return of Bonaparte. Accounts of the gatherings at the Café Boulée were given and the actions of the four at the time of Ney's visit were noted. For their part, the defendants pleaded that they had not been involved in any conspiracy to bring Napoleon back and defended their actions as necessary to secure public order. The charge of conspiracy was poorly chosen. The prosecution was unable to prove any connection between the four and the Café Boulée, while the rest of the events had not occurred until after Napoleon had reached Lyons.

Riambourg had not helped the prosecution's cause by transferring the four defendants to Besançon while they awaited trial. His suspicions of a conspiracy to free the prisoners were groundless, and the four were treated badly while in Besançon, where Hernoux had to be put under guard at a hospital. This gave the distinct impression that the four were being persecuted.[10] Sympathy for the defendants grew as the trial dragged on. While the jury was out, *fédérés* and *demi-soldes* gathered outside the courts, obliging the prefect to take measures to ensure that the four were not carried in triumph to their homes by the crowd. It was no

---

[8] AN, F⁷ 9649, Prefect to Minister of the Interior, 29 July 1816 and 13 February 1817; *Journal de la Côte-d'Or*, 12 August and 20 December 1815; C. Sadesky, 'La Crise et le relèvement des collèges en Côte-d'Or sous la restauration', *Annales de Bourgogne*, 72 (1960), pp. 37–8.

[9] Gaffarel, *Dijon*, pp. 234–5, 277.

[10] AN, BB³ 152.

surprise when the defendants were acquitted of all charges in late August 1816.[11]

Government prosecutors enjoyed slightly more success in a companion trial of Marinet, Chevalot and Poulot-Belenet. In December 1816 the latter two were cleared entirely of conspiracy charges, but Marinet, who had met Napoleon in Lyons, was sentenced to death *in absentia*. The difficulty lay in proving conspiracy to jurors inclined to clemency. However, in a case resulting from the invasion of Dijon by thirteen army deserters, the government could present hard evidence of sedition and consequently two *fédérés* who had encouraged the soldiers were banished from Dijon for six years.[12]

Other *fédérés* left themselves open to repressive measures by committing similarly imprudent acts. When Bishop Reymond was ordered to give his residence to the Austrians, his valet Amiot intentionally left behind a eulogy of Bonaparte and was banished to Longvic for his folly. Pierre Morey, 'un très mauvais sujet', attacked a Hungarian grenadier and had to take flight. One of the federation *commissaires*, Bernardin, fell foul of the authorities in Chaumont. Bernardin appears to have been a popular figure at a café where patriots continued to shout 'Vive l'Empereur!' as late as 29 July 1815. Acting on the request of the mayor, and the demand of the commander of the local Allied forces, the prefect of the Haute-Marne banished Bernardin to a village in the Vosges. On 25 January 1816, Bernardin returned without permission to a village close to Chaumont and claimed that the general law of amnesty had freed him. The prefect immediately had him arrested and requested permission of the Minister of Police to have Bernardin placed under police surveillance in some department that was not adjacent to the Haute-Marne.[13]

The sedition acts of 29 October and 9 November 1815 enabled authorities to extend their persecution to any individual who defamed a member of the royal family. Five *fédérés* were convicted under these acts, with penalties ranging from three months to three years of imprisonment. The lawyer Genret was sentenced to six months imprisonment, a two hundred franc fine and two years of police surveillance. At the time of a visit of the Duchess of Angoulême to Dijon he had had the 'impudence' to state to a certain Madame Charbonnier that 'Si Bonaparte revenait, je rejeunirais de quarante ans.' Madame Charbonnier duly reported these offensive words to the authorities. Duroc, a *menuisier*, was sentenced to three months

---

[11] *Ibid.*, F[7] 9649, Prefect to Minister of the Interior, 29 August 1816; BB[3] 152; AD C-d, UV A3.
[12] AD C-d, UVB 76–90, UV A3.
[13] Gaffarel, *Dijon*, pp. 262–3; AM of Dijon, 1D1 22, 13 October 1815; AN, F[7] 9678, Prefect to Minister of the Interior, 1 August 1815 and 25 January 1816; Prefect to Minister of Police, 25 January 1816.

imprisonment, a fifty franc fine and two years of police surveillance for shouting 'Vive l'Empereur!' It would appear that Genret was given the more severe penalty because his position was thought to entail greater authority and, hence, required greater responsibility.[14]

After the abortive uprising in Grenoble led by Didier, Tocqueville used the laws of sedition to round up old leaders of the federation during April and May 1816: Peyrard, Buvée, Chauvot, Nardin, Drevon, Morland and Panisset were arrested. Morland, Balland and Rousset were later put under surveillance; Peyrard and Panisset were banished from Dijon. Huguet, Yon and Carion managed to go into hiding before they could be apprehended.[15]

Carion attracted particular attention. In August 1815 the Austrians destroyed his printing press and the Bourbon authorities suppressed his journal. From his place of hiding Carion sent a memorandum to Mayor Durande requesting an indemnity for his losses. The request went unheeded. After a second unsuccessful attempt to arrest him in July 1816, the authorities impounded Carion's new printing press. Carion responded by having a pamphlet published in which he charged the authorities with making a travesty of justice. The National Guardsmen sent to arrest him certainly reduced his wine stock! Several weeks prior to the election of 1817, Carion published a pamphlet written by Gabet which was designed to rally liberals in the Côte-d'Or and give them a political programme. Riambourg considered prosecuting the two for sedition but, after several communications with the Minister of the Interior, decided that such a procedure would probably do more harm than good.[16]

There were other means of punishing men thought to be in opposition to the government. Assessments were made of the 'morality' of *demi-soldes*, and those of 'familles fédérés' were the least likely to be fully reinstated. Requisitions could be made the pretext for vengeance. Reymond and Girarde, constitutional clergymen, were especially ill used, but others such as Larché, Drevon and Lejéas were also forced to make excessively large contributions. It is not surprising, therefore, to find that fourteen *fédérés* applied to the mayor for permission to leave Dijon in the latter half of 1815 and the early months of 1816. It is to be presumed that others left without requesting permission.[17]

Fédérés bore the brunt of White Terror because they were thought to hold influence over others. The Marquis de Tessières, Vaillant's replacement at

[14] AD C-d, UIII Ca 4 and 6.
[15] AN, F⁷ 3028, 3274, 9881, 9884; Gonnet, 'Société', p. 391.
[16] Gaffarel, *Dijon*, pp. 278–80; BM of Dijon, Ms. 1697; Fizaine, *La Vie*, pp. 136–7.
[17] AD C-d, 12 R 2, 5 January 1816; Gaffarel, *Dijon*, pp. 258, 261, 290; Gonnet, 'Société', p. 383; AM of Dijon, 1D1 1 22, July–December 1815.

the prefecture, identified Buvée, Chauvot and Gabet as especially worthy of attention, and the government acted against them when it found opportunity. Taking legal action against *fédérés* was not a simple matter however. For one thing, information that might have been used against *fédérés* tended to disappear – even from the mayor's desk! When evidence was provided, the judges, many of whom had been *fédérés* but had been left in office due to a shortage of alternative candidates, inclined to leniency. Moreover, *fédéré* lawyers, such as Gayet, Etienne Cabet and Lerouge, defended the *fédérés* tried for sedition. Although they could no longer assemble, *fédérés* continued to help each other as best they could, and thus avoided isolation.[18]

Certain *fédérés*, whose actions during the Hundred Days were not deemed especially culpable, were allowed to retain or return to their old positions. Eventually the government brought Lévêque and Arnollet back into the prefecture. A man such as Proudhon was not easily replaced, so in time he was reinstalled at the *lycée*. Nevertheless, the prefect remained suspicious of Proudhon's influence over students, who repeatedly demonstrated their opposition to the Monarchy. In February 1817 law students clashed several times with royalist soldiers at the theatre; in December 1818 they were denied permission to hold a banquet in celebration of the end of Allied occupation because they refused to toast the King. Well aware that in 1815 Proudhon had led students in a march behind a bust of the Emperor, the prefect called Proudhon in for a discussion in December 1818, but found him neither frank nor repentent. Although there was no evidence to warrant action, the prefect fretted over Proudhon's influence on future generations. By February 1818, Carion was back to publishing a journal. In 1823 he was again incarcerated, this time for his opposition to the war with Spain and, true to form, in 1824 he attacked the indemnity granted by Charles X to nobles who had lost their lands during the Revolution.[19]

The most striking evidence of the continuing influence of *fédéré* leaders can be seen in their domination of the Liberal Opposition in Dijon. Realising that they no longer could hope to be appointed to government administrative posts, *fédérés* turned to the arena of national elections.

[18] P. Viard, 'Une Enquête politique dans l'arrondissement de Dijon en 1816', *Annales Révolutionnaires*, 14 (1922), p. 403; AM of Dijon, 1D1 1 22, 21 September 1815, AD C-d, UIX Cd 16.
[19] R. Durand, 'La Révolution de 1830 en Côte-d'Or', *Revue d'histoire contemporaine* (1931), p. 164; AN, F⁷ 9649, Prefect to Minister of the Interior, 13 February 1817 and 7 December 1818; Fizaine, *La Vie*, p. 155; P. Palau, *Histoire du département de la Côte-d'Or* (Dijon, 1978), p. 69; J. Pidancet, 'L'Indemnité aux émigrés en Côte-d'Or', *Annales de Bourgogne*, 23 (1951), p. 169.

Despite the efforts of the prefect Choiseul, Hernoux and P. Jacotot both received a significant number of votes in the elections for the Chamber of Deputies in 1815. With the support of Larché, Gabet stood as a liberal candidate in 1816, but the prefect again intervened on behalf of ultra-royalist candidates and Gabet was unsuccessful.[20]

Matters changed significantly after Louis XVIII dismissed the *Chambre Introuvable*. Girardin, a moderate monarchist, became prefect of the Côte-d'Or, and, in order to reduce the influence of ultra-monarchists, tacitly supported Dijonnais liberals by refusing to influence elections and allowing the opposition to organise. In 1817, a liberal meeting in Dijon was addressed by four *fédérés*, Gayet, Larché, Moreau and Gabet, and Hernoux was selected as one of three liberal candidates for the Côte-d'Or. Hernoux finished second in a field of seven candidates, receiving 629 votes from the 1,213 electors who participated. This measure of support (fifty-two per cent) was roughly equivalent to that of the plebiscite of the Hundred Days (forty-eight per cent). Numerous banquets were given in honour of Hernoux and his two victorious liberal colleagues. The first was held at the Café Boulée. However, Proudhon, doyen of the law faculty at Dijon, had less success in his attempts to become a deputy of the Doubs. Proudhon had been a co-founder of the federation at Besançon and relied on fellow *fédérés* such as Violand to rally sufficient liberal support. But the Doubs proved more conservative than the Côte-d'Or, and Proudhon ran aground in 1819 and 1820.[21]

Hernoux's success in 1817 was due partly to the ability of Dijonnais liberals to organise rapidly. This in large part resulted from the fact that they were accustomed to working together. P. Gonnet, in his study of Dijon society in the nineteenth century, has identified twenty-five leaders of the Dijonnais Liberal Opposition. Twenty of these men were old *fédérés*. Thirteen of these *fédérés* were eligible to vote in 1817, but the liberals distinguished themselves from ultra-monarchists by recruiting supporters who were not so entitled. Among the seven liberal leaders who could not vote were Jacotot and five members of the federation central committee, who dominated the radical wing of the Liberal Opposition. At a banquet given at the Chapeau Rouge for liberal deputies, about a quarter of the 210 tables were occupied by non-electors, one of whom left behind a tri-coloured ribbon. Among twenty-one individuals noted for their exceptional enthusiasm during a visit of the liberal deputy Chauvelin, eleven were old *fédérés*, only two of whom had the vote. While such men were

[20] Fizaine, *La vie*, p. 57; Gonnet, 'Société', pp. 329, 394.
[21] Gonnet, 'Société', pp. 397, 406; Fizaine, *La vie*, pp. 142, 145–6, 163; H. Weiss, *Journal 1815–22* (Paris, 1972), pp. 55, 256–8, 303.

eager to cry 'Vive Chauvelin!', 'Vive la Liberté!', and 'Vive le défenseur de nos libertés!', few were willing to shout 'Vive le Roi!' Liberal reticence regarding the King was also apparent in that no toasts were given to the Monarch at their banquet. Girardin was well aware of this and the fact that liberals greatly outnumbered ultra-royalists in the department. In a report to the Minister of the Interior in May 1819, he attributed Liberal Opposition to the Monarchy to the persecution that had followed the Hundred Days and argued that the way to rally liberals was to remove reactionaries currently in office. He did not, however, remain prefect long enough to implement any such policy.[22]

Liberal meetings were held at Gevrey in the home of Belot, an old *fédéré*. In Dijon, liberals could read opposition newspapers in the salon of Yon or at the Café Boulée. Carion's *Journal d'Annonces* became the local liberal newspaper. With the able support of Vaillant, who remained highly influential among government *fonctionnaires*, Hernoux emerged as the leading Dijon liberal. Although careful not to compromise himself, Hernoux maintained friendly relations with Dijon republicans and democrats. He became a champion of freedom of the press and supported mutual schools in order to combat clerical influence manifested in a school of the *Frères de la Doctrine Chrétienne*.[23]

During the period of reaction that began in 1819, Girardin was replaced by two successive ultra-royalist prefects – Séguier and Arbaud-Jogues. Extensive liberal agitation exacerbated tensions and led the ultra-royalist municipal council of Dijon to denounce 'cette secte impie qui aspire également à la ruine de la religion de nos pères et à celle au trône auguste', a description similar to previous fulminations against the *fédérés*. A petition opposing changes in the electoral laws was kept at the office of the notary Lapertot, a member of the federative central committee in 1815. It gained 426 signatures in Dijon alone, and was later presented to the Chamber of Deputies by Hernoux. In January 1820 Carion was brought to trial for publishing an article which predicted that owners of *biens nationaux* would be forced either to give up their lands or pay an indemnity to previous owners. Trial by jury disappointed the authorities once again, however, and the old *fédéré* was acquitted. Passage of the law of the double vote in 1820 had the effect of driving moderates into an increasingly radical liberal camp. Old *fédérés* such as Weiss, Blum and Eschalié became active supporters of the liberals. These men were merchants and the law of the double vote alienated them by favouring landed interests. Nevertheless,

---

[22] Gonnet, 'La Société', pp. 406–8; AN, F^7 9649, prefectoral reports of 13 October and 19 November 1818, 2 May 1819 and 13 July 1820.

[23] Gonnet, 'Société', pp. 404–6, 408, 416–18; Palau, *Histoire*, pp. 66–7.

liberal fortunes declined in the short term as prefects took care to intimidate government employees and ensured the success of ultra-monarchist candidates. Many liberals abstained from voting.[24]

With government posts reserved for ultra-monarchists and electoral opportunities blocked, *fédérés* turned to illegal means of opposing the government. Thus we find that seven of twelve presidents of Carbonari lodges uncovered by Dijon police in 1822 had been *fédérés* (Lerouge, Prisset, Yon, Duleu, Michel, Sarrau and Silvestre). Indeed, the entire organisation of the Carbonari is remarkably familiar. In it, Dijon was the centre of a federation that covered the Haute-Saône, Saône-et-Loire and Côte-d'Or. The federation itself was part of the division of Lyons. At a general assembly of the Carbonari of eastern France, Lerouge represented the Côte-d'Or and the departments federated to it. Of course the most famous of Dijon *fédérés* who became a Carbonaro, Etienne Cabet, was a member of the *vente suprême* at Paris.[25]

Reports made by officials of both the Côte-d'Or and the Saône-et-Loire indicated that local Carbonari remained active until at least June 1823, when a meeting, reputedly presided by Hernoux, took place at Dijon. Representatives of the *loges* of the Côte-d'Or and neighbouring departments supposedly voted in favour of a future rebellion at Dijon, provided that the *vente suprême* at Paris approved. No such revolt took place however, perhaps because the Parisian directors disapproved, or perhaps because police information was inaccurate. Certainly the prefect of the Côte-d'Or was sceptical of the possibility of an uprising at Dijon; nevertheless, he had little doubt as to the existence of Carbonari plotting and kept close watch over the movements of Hernoux and Cabet. In the event, Carbonari attempts at revolution, made principally in the west, failed miserably, and gradually the entire network fell apart. Dijonnais *fédérés* then joined other clandestine organisations equally suspect in the eyes of the authorities. Gabet became a *phalanstérien*, and Carion, Larché, Duleu, Milsand and Chocarne became leading freemasons. Indeed, masonic lodges provided liberals with a cover for their continuing opposition to the government.[26]

[24] Gonnet, 'Société', pp. 327–8, 398–403; H. Baumont, 'Stanislas de Girardin', *La Révolution Français*, 55 (1908), pp. 227–8; AN, F[7] 6740 (dossier Côte-d'Or), Prefect to Minister of the Interior, 26 November and 26 December 1819, 20, 27 January and 7 February 1820.
[25] Gonnet, 'Société', pp. 414–15; Fizaine, *La Vie*, pp. 220–1; C. Johnson, *Utopian Communism in France: Cabet and the Icarians, 1839–1851* (Ithaca, N.Y.), p. 24.
[26] P. Lévêque, *Une Société provinciale: La Bourgogne sous la monarchie de juillet* (Paris, 1983), pp. 424, 531; Gonnet, 'Société', pp. 410–11; AN, F[7] 6686, Prefect of the Côte-d'Or to Minister of the Interior, 8 and 19 June 1823, Prefect of the Saône-et-Loire to Minister of the Interior, 9 June 1823.

As elsewhere, electors in the Côte-d'Or responded to the Carbonari revolts by voting for conservative candidates, leaving the department without an opposition deputy in 1824. By September 1826 the Liberal Opposition had begun to recover however, due partly to middle-class anger at government legislation compensating *émigrés* stripped of their lands during the Revolution. Inveterate enemies of the Monarchy remained true to their cause. According to the prefect, 'les deux factions révolutionnaires, la républicaine et la Bonapartiste, ont conservé de nombreux et incurables partisans'. One of the most 'audacieux' of these partisans was the *fédéré* Nanteuil, who had recently been arrested for distributing daggers with suspicious markings. Liberal resurgence continued in 1828, and the prefect reported that most merchants, particularly those involved in small-scale commerce, had joined the ranks of the opposition. By July 1828 the prefect was clearly worried by this development. Within the electorate there was a marked division between landed proprietors and the 'classe industrielle'. The latter group, composed of industrialists, merchants and men in the liberal professions, was infected by a democratic spirit and demanded increased liberties. In the following passage, the prefect cited a more specific cause for apprehension:

Elle est, certes, bien éloignée du dessein . . . de renverser le Gouvernement Monarchique, et de retrograder vers des tems du despotisme militaire ou d'anarchie populaire; mais sans la sagesse et la fermeté du Gouvernement, quelques vétérans de la révolution, qui se sont ses chefs et ses organs, et que leur conduite exagérée en démocratie sous la république, comme en servitude sous l'Empire, ont rendus vraiment ennemis de l'ordre actuel et légitime, ne pourraient-ils pas égarer, à son insu, dans les voies les plus dangereuses, une jeunesse impétueuse et de bonne foi, qui ne se nourrit, dans les seuls journaux hostiles, que des plus funestes doctrines politiques et religieux?

These influential veterans, former Jacobin and Carbonari leaders, were 'l'excès, la honte et pourtant les agens du parti libéral dans les tems d'agitations et des élections'.

One of these old Jacobins was, of course, Carion, who remained the leading opposition journalist in Dijon. During a by-election held in 1829, he again angered officials with an address published in support of Hernoux. The address attacked the Polignac Ministry as a threat to 'institutions constitutionnelles' and a danger to the security of the throne itself. Voters were to set an example for the rest of France by demonstrating their rejection of the recently appointed Ministry. Despite being convinced that Carion was guilty of sedition, the Crown General Prosecutor was equally certain that trial by jury would not produce a guilty verdict. Moreover, action against Carion would probably increase support for Hernoux, and thus it was better to let the matter pass. Such discretion did not, however, prevent Hernoux from triumphantly returning to the Chamber of Deputies.

As a member of the *Aide-toi, le Ciel t'aidera*, Hernoux established a Burgundian version of Beslay's *Association Bretonne* and in late 1829 headed a list of citizens who vowed to refuse payment of direct taxes if they were not voted by Parliament. Naturally, Carion's *Journal* gave full publicity to the association and printed lists of members to encourage recruitment. This was both the warning shot in the looming battle against governmental 'counter-revolution' and a useful means of organising opposition to the Polignac Ministry before Parliament actually met in 1830. In March 1830 Hernoux supported, and had the pleasure of delivering, an address of 221 deputies to the King, in which Charles X was called on to dismiss the reactionary Polignac Ministry. The King refused, of course, and instead called for new elections. As subsequent events were to prove, the prefect of the Côte-d'Or was correct when he reported that the electorate of his department was hostile to the Ministry.[27]

The Revolution of 1830 was warmly welcomed at Dijon. Officials at the prefecture decided to suspend liberty of the press on 18 July, but Carion went ahead and published the royal ordinances despite the proscription. This proved unfortunate for the Duchess of Angoulême, who had to cut short a visit to the theatre and was followed to the prefecture by a crowd chanting 'Vive la Charte! Vivent les 221! Vive la liberté de la presse! Vive la liberté!' On the following day, the crowds turned into angry mobs; troops were called out, but they soon retired after getting the worst of violent clashes with the populace. When news of Parisian resistance arrived, constitutional slogans rapidly gave way to chants which underlined the anti-Bourbon nature of opposition: 'Vive la Charte! A bas les rats! A bas les royalistes! Vive l'Empereur! Vive Napoléon II! Vive la République!' Thus, while there were no signs of support for Orleans, the old mixture of Bonapartism and republicanism was still very much in evidence. When the establishment of a provisional government was made known on 31 July, crowds sang the *Marseillaise* and demanded that the beloved tricolour be raised – flags were uncovered from hiding places

---

[27] Information on the Liberal Opposition has been collated from: Gonnet, 'Société', pp. 405, 429, 435; C.-H. Pouthas, *Guizot pendant La Restauration* (Paris, 1923), p. 429; P. Pilbeam, 'The Growth of Liberalism and the Crisis of the Bourbon Restoration, 1827–30', *The Historical Journal*, 25, 2 (1982), pp. 363–4; AN, F⁷ 6768 (dossier Côte-d'Or), Prefect to Minister of the Interior, 1 September 1826, 28 February and 6 July 1827, 5 July 1828, and 24 March 1830, F⁷ 6740 (dossier Côte-d'Or), Prefect to Minister of the Interior, 25 September 1829.

chosen in 1815. Significantly, popular euphoria came to an immediate halt when the proclamation making Louis-Philippe King arrived.

Amidst the tumult that was, except for the odd incident of anti-clericalism, relatively non-violent, liberals, led by old *fédérés*, seized the initiative. Hernoux headed a provisional administration of the department, and a provisional municipal commission, including Proudhon, Lerouge, Monnet and Varemby, was established. This was all the more necessary and simple in that Bourbon authorities, knowing the majority to be enthusiastically in support of the Revolution, offered no resistance of consequence. A new National Guard was founded. Popular as an institution because of its revolutionary associations, the Guard was necessary to maintain domestic order and ward off the Allied invasion that many Dijonnais thought must be imminent. Indeed, it was above all else the necessity of preserving the Revolution that led Dijon republicans to accept the compromise that was the July Monarchy.[28]

Fédérés were quick to profit from the Revolution of 1830. Hernoux became mayor in August 1830 and Détourbet became one of his *adjoints*. Jacob and Lévêque returned as councillors at the prefecture. Lejéas, Arnollet, Morland, Lapertot, Muteau, Huguet, Mazeau and Gleise joined the new municipal council. Hernoux and Lejéas became members of the general council of the department and Lamblin, Peyrard and Liégéard became members of the council of the *arrondissement*. Varemby became *avocat général* and Buvée was reinstalled as a judge of the peace.[29]

Opposition to the Bourbon Monarchy was the bond that had held together the various groups within the federation. It should not surprise us, therefore, to find that after 1830 *fédérés* emerged as leaders of opposed factions. Certain *fédérés*, such as Weiss, Lerouge, Lévêque and Huguet, were loyal Orleanists under the July Monarchy. Carion, after waxing lyrical over 'the triumph of the people over the ordinances which had tried to steal away their rights', soon began to view with disfavour the government that had issued from the Revolution. In reaction to legitimist manifestations in 1831, Carion and Hernoux became committee members of Dijon's version of the National Associations that spread throughout France and bore marked similarities to the federations of 1815. Although organised to oppose legitimist subversion and ward off Allied invasion still thought to be forthcoming, the Associations were hostile to the conservative Périer Ministry and the Dijon Association was not above declaring 'the desir-

---

[28] Lévêque, 'Société', pp. 486–9; P. Pilbeam, 'The "Three Glorious Days": the Revolution of 1830 in Provincial France', *The Historical Journal*, 26, 4 (1983), pp. 835–412.
[29] Durand, 'La Révolution', p. 170; J. Laurent, 'Mélanges: Un Témoinage sur la révolution de juillet à Dijon', *Annales de Bourgogne*, 2 (1930), pp. 374–5; AD C-d, 1M2; Gonnet, 'Société', p. 835; Gaffarel, *Dijon*, p. 39.

ability of the creation of republican institutions within the popular monarchy'. By April 1831, the iron fist of Périer had begun to smash these
Associations, driving at least some members into full-blooded republicanism. Among the old *fédérés*, Hernoux, Belot and Eschalié became
leaders of the local *parti du mouvement* which, at least ostensibly, opposed
the conservative policies of the government, but not the Monarchy
itself.[30]

A good number of *fédérés*, however, emerged as uncompromising republicans after 1831. Etienne Cabet, whose mentor had been the Jacobin
Joseph Jacotot, successfully ran in the Côte-d'Or as a liberal candidate for
the Chamber of Representatives in 1831. He had been enabled to do so by
a timely property transfer conducted by the Bonapartist Lejéas family. One
year later, disillusioned by the new government, he became a republican.
During his frequent visits to Dijon, Cabet helped organise several republican societies. His brother, a cooper, and Vallée, both *fédérés*, were also
leading Dijonnais republicans thought to be influential with the working-
classes. Indeed, in 1832 members of the republican society 'amis du peuple'
decided to create a new federation. Little appears to have come of this plan,
but the society became part of the republican 'Société des Droits de
l'Homme', a force to be reckoned with in Dijon in the 1830s. François
Monnet, old friend of Prieur de la Côte-d'Or and inheritor of most of his
fortune, was president of the central committee of the *Droits de l'Homme*
at Dijon. However, this society, which numbered some 300 members, was
never as large or as influential as the federation of 1815.[31]

One republican *fédéré* who made his mark outside Dijon is, perhaps,
worthy of particular mention. After being released from arrest in 1815,
Pierre Morey was again arrested for conspiring against the Bourbons in
1817. Fortunate enough to be set free a second time, he then moved to Paris
in search of anonymity. He lived in obscurity until the Revolution of 1830
brought him a *medaille de juillet* for his part in the street fighting. An old
Jacobin of the Robespierrist variety, Morey watched in anger as the July
Monarchy destroyed republican hopes. A reader of Cabet's *Le Populaire*,
he then joined the *Société des Droits de l'Homme* which put him in contact
with leading republicans such as Godefroy Cavaignac, Bastide and Recurt.
He kept the latter informed in 1835 as he master-minded the Fieschi
assassination attempt of 28 July which left some eighteen dead, twenty-two
injured and Louis-Philippe still on his horse. Made of sterner stuff than the

---

[30] P. Gonnet, *La Correspondance d'Achille Chaper (1831–1840)* (Dijon, 1970), pp. 93, 236;
Gonnet, 'Société', p. 862; P. Pilbeam, 'The Emergence of Opposition to the Orleanist
Monarchy, August 1830–April 1831', *English Historical Review*, 85, 334 (January 1970),
pp. 19–28; Pilbeam, 'The "Three Glorious Days"', p. 844.

[31] Johnson, *Utopian*, pp. 31–2; Lévêque, 'Société', pp. 496–501; Gonnet, 'Société', p. 862.

loquacious Fieschi, Morey refused to reveal the identity of his fellow conspirators and, by taking his secret to the grave, made himself a republican hero and martyr.[32]

Thus one can trace a continuity in the opposition to the Bourbon Monarchy which spanned the revolutions of 1789 and 1830. The *fédérés* were at the centre of this opposition. The federation was a nexus; it brought together the various dissident elements.

We have seen that the federation was at times an uneasy coalition of men who might otherwise have been adversaries. During the Empire, influential Jacobin leaders such as Vaillant and Jacotot had been willing to serve under the Bonapartist regime because, in truth, there was little alternative if they wanted to maintain their positions of local power. That they were dissatisfied with Napoleonic dictatorship was well known to Imperial prefects. Nevertheless, Bonapartist officials found men such as Vaillant useful. During the Hundred Days, the two sides found themselves mutually dependent.

After Waterloo, *fédérés* had to endure a period of reaction which served to remind them of what they held in common. They emerged from this period still united by their desire to regain local power by whatever means necess-ary. Moreover, government persecution made local heroes of men such as Carion and Hernoux.

After the White Terror ended and government became more moderate, middle-class *fédérés* rapidly reorganised within the Liberal Opposition. During the period of 1817–20, when constitutional means of opposition were available to them, they achieved notable success in electing Hernoux to the Chamber of Deputies. However, after 1820 the means of constitutional opposition were severely restricted and *fédérés* such as Lerouge and Cabet resorted to the illegal means of organising a revolutionary society. Although the Carbonari achieved little success, this was a clear indication of the lengths to which *fédérés* were willing to go. Moreover, support for the liberals continued to grow as moderates became alienated by government policies that included election manipulation in favour of landed interests. By 1827, most of the Dijon electorate was liberal, and this was manifested two years later by the triumphant return of Hernoux to the Chamber of Deputies.

When news of revolution came from Paris in 1830, middle-class Dijonnais readily accepted it, and the populace showed general enthusi-

---

[32] J. Lucas-Dubreton, *Louis-Philippe et la machine infernale (1830–1835)* (Paris, 1951), pp. 237–40, 274–9, 293, 360–3.

asm as *fédérés* at last regained the offices they had lost in 1815. Only after the removal of the Bourbon Monarchy in 1830 did the divisions apparent among *fédérés* during the Hundred Days again manifest themselves.

Chapter 8

The fédérés of Paris
during the Hundred Days

As we have seen in the previous chapters, Dijon and Rennes each produced a single federation. This was the case throughout France, except for the capital. Paris and its *faubourgs* spawned four federations. However, two of these associations became part of a third so that there were, in essence, only two federations in the capital. As K. D. Tönnesson has noted, this confused contemporaries and, subsequently, historians.[1] Unfortunately, Tönnesson has also given a somewhat misleading account of the *fédérés* of Paris. For this reason, it is important to begin by discussing the development of the federative movement in Paris and its *faubourgs*.

Perhaps much of the confusion over the *fédérés* resulted from the rapidity with which the movement was organised. The federation of the *faubourgs* Saint-Antoine and Saint-Marceau was founded on 10 May 1815. In their initial address, these 3,000 *fédérés* called on the government to organise and arm them for defence of the capital. On 15 May a similar association was founded in the *faubourgs* of Saint-Martin, Saint-Denis and Temple. If these *fédérés* drew up an address, we do not know of it. Be that as it may, on 18 May they affiliated with the federation of the *faubourgs* Saint-Antoine and Saint-Marceau, and it may be assumed that they held the same objectives. Perhaps they were influenced by an Imperial decree of 15 May which announced the creation of twenty-four battalions of *fédérés-tirailleurs* which would be armed and organised as part of the National Guard. The decree was Napoleon's response to the request of the *fédérés* of the *faubourgs* of Saint-Antoine and Saint-Marceau. On 17 May a final association, the federation of Paris, was formed.[2]

---

[1] K. D. Tönnesson, 'Les Fédérés de Paris pendant les Cent-Jours', *Annales historiques de la Révolution Française*, 54 (1982), pp. 395–6.

[2] *Le Moniteur Universel*, 9 and 12 May 1815; *Patriote de '89*, 14, 19, 20, 21 and 24 May 1815; *L'Indépendant*, 14 May 1815; *Journal de l'Empire*, 18 and 26 May 1815; AN, AFIV 1935, *Pacte Fédératif des Parisiens*; J. Tulard, *Nouvelle Histoire de Paris: le Consulat et*

Tönnesson has improved our understanding of the federative movement in the capital in one especially important respect. In referring to the federation of Paris, he states: 'Il importe de distinguer cette société politique et bien bourgeoise de la "fédération ouvrière" [the federation of the *faubourgs*] et de l'organisation militaire des fédérés-tirailleurs.' He then cites a letter written by Darricau, commander of the *fédérés-tirailleurs*, stating that his organisation and the Parisian federation were separate institutions. Tönnesson is correct in stating that the Paris federation was distinct from the *fédérés-tirailleurs*. However, General Darricau did not distinguish between the 'fédération ouvrière' and the *fédérés-tirailleurs*, a point which Tönnesson entirely overlooks. Moreover, while Tönnesson does give an account of the initial proclamation of the *fédérés* of the *faubourgs* and their parade before the Emperor, he gives very little consideration to how closely linked this organisation was to the *fédérés-tirailleurs*.[3]

The formation of the *fédérés-tirailleurs* put an end to the associations of the *faubourgs* as independent entities. There is no evidence of these federations holding assemblies or issuing proclamations after 20 May. On 24 May the following notice to the *fédérés du quartier et faubourg Saint-Marceau, et des quartiers Saint-Jacques, Observatoire et Jardin des Plantes* was published by the mayor of the twelfth arrondissement:

Fédérés

Vos offres et votre dévouement à la patrie ont été acceptés; plein de confiance dans votre démarche patriotique, S.M. a rendu un décret qui ordonne la formation de vingt-quatre bataillons de tirailleurs de gardes nationales.

Vous ferez donc partie essentielle de cette garde.

Unfortunately, it is not possible to determine how many of the original *fédérés* joined this institution, but given that it was created for them on their request, it is logical to assume that most of them did join. We do know that the *charbonniers* who joined the federation of the *faubourgs* Saint-Antoine and Saint-Marceau became part of the *fédérés-tirailleurs* of the ninth arrondissement.[4]

On the other hand, the Parisian federation met frequently in general assemblies after the creation of the *fédérés-tirailleurs*, and these *fédérés* took pains to inform others that they were separate from the latter institution. Thus, the Parisian *fédérés* maintained a degree of independence

l'Empire (Paris, 1970), pp. 400–1; E. Le Gallo, *Les Cent-Jours* (Paris, 1924), pp. 310–11; *Correspondance de Napoléon I*, published by order of Napoleon III (Paris, 1859), vol. XXI, pp. 127–8.
[3] For Darricau's letter, see *Indépendant*, 27 June 1815; Tönnesson, 'Fédérés', pp. 397–8.
[4] *Patriote*, 21 and 24 May 1815; APP, A A/330, 50–2.

from governmental control which *fédérés* of the *faubourgs* did not.[5] For this reason, the two organisations will be considered separately.

Although it is now clear that the Parisian federation and the *fédérés-tirailleurs* were separate, this point was lost on most contemporaries. However, any Parisians who might have compared the addresses and pacts of the federation of the *faubourgs* and the Parisian association would have noticed appreciable differences. As we shall see shortly, the *fédérés* of the *faubourgs* caused much alarm by calling for the use of terror, but the essential element of their initial address was their request of arms and organisation. The Parisian *fédérés* made no such request of the Imperial government. Instead they devoted themselves to collecting funds for defence of the *patrie*. The sixth article of their pact specified that joining the association did not enable a member to dispense with his usual military or civil obligations. Clearly, this association was not a government institution.[6]

It is difficult to find information concerning the social character of the Parisian federation, but the little we do possess indicates that it was middle-class. Police reports occasionally identified the occupation of a member. From this source we learn that the association included an employee at a bureau of weights and measures, an inspector at the Port Saint-Nicolas and his *adjoint*, a professor at the *collège de Charlemagne*, and a soldier. The *Patriote de '89* printed a list of Paris *fédérés* who contributed *dons patriotiques*. The list informs us that the federation included four *militaires*, a merchant, a *négociant*, an *agent de commerce*, a surgeon and three government *fonctionnaires*.[7]

Le Gallo has stated that the Parisian federation was born 'au sein de la garde nationale' without giving a source which supports this contention. Given the apparent middle-class nature of the association, this is perhaps a reasonable conjecture, but there is some evidence that argues against it. On several occasions the central committee of the association requested permission to parade before the Emperor. This at least suggests that the *fédérés* were sufficient in number to make a decent parade. However, one must question why the *fédérés*, if they were members of the National Guard, should wish an opportunity to march before the Emperor, given that they had already done so. Whatever the case, no such parade took place.[8]

---

[5] *Moniteur*, 26 June 1815.
[6] For the original address and subsequent Parisian pact, see BN, Lb[41] 303, *Fédération Parisienne; Patriote*, 24 May 1815; AN, AFIV, *Pacte Fédératif des Parisiens*.
[7] AN, F[7] 6630–3, *notes de police*, 267, 341, 367, 1511; *Patriote*, 3 June 1815.
[8] Le Gallo, *Les Cent-Jours*, p. 310; for the request, see AN, AFIV 1948, letter of the central committee of the Paris federation to the Emperor, 9 June 1815. See also *Journal de l'Empire*, 20 and 22 May 1815.

The general assemblies of the association and the particular interest that *fédérés* took in military matters have been discussed previously. At the third such meeting, on 30 May, president Carret took up the question of the nature of the Parisian federation:

On voudrait . . . nous présenter comme formant un club; tout le monde a pu voir que nous ne nous occupons d'aucune matière politique; nous ne traitons aucun des sujets qui sont exclusivement réservés à l'assemblée qui doit nous donner des lois: nous sommes ici en famille; nous réunissons les moyens dont chacun de nous veut faire hommage à la patrie, et dont le gouvernement doit avoir la direction. Les hommes instruits payeront leur tribut en lumières et en conseils utiles, les riches en offrandes patriotiques, et les pauvres eux-mêmes apporteront au foyer commun le faible mais glorieux hommage de leur dévouement.

Carret's harangue was doubtless intended to reduce fears about *fédéré* intentions. His reference to 'l'assemblée qui doit nous donner des lois' was a clear signal that the association was liberal in political character, rather than revolutionary. His reference to rich and poor *fédérés* was perhaps a clue that the association had a mixed social character, in contrast to the federation of the *faubourgs*.[9]

At the same assembly, a deputy from an artillery battalion composed of students of the *école de médecine de Paris* sought and gained permission for the members of the battalion to join the association. At that point, the entire assembly rose and vowed to defend France and the Emperor 'contre les monstres qui veulent diriger le fer de l'étranger dans le sein de nos familles'. Knowledge of this avowal may well have made certain Parisians doubly nervous, in spite of Carret's reassurance.

After this arresting scene, the *fédérés* began to discuss the possibility of creating their own journal, to be entitled the *Journal central des Fédérés de l'Empire*. It was generally agreed that such a journal would prove useful and a prospectus read by a M. Bazin was received favourably. Bazin proposed that 'des bureaux d'abonnements près toutes les fédérations des départements' could be established and suggested that the funds earned by the journal could be used to raise a free corps. Although the *fédérés* wished to establish a free corps, they made no mention of providing the rank and file. Nothing appears to have come of this proposal, probably because the government fell shortly thereafter, but the mere suggestion of such a journal indicates that the Parisian *fédérés* harboured plans for strengthening ties between the provincial federations and that of the capital. In this they were following a precedent established by the Jacobins. Did the Parisian *fédérés* have visions of creating a 'mother federation'?

---

[9] *Patriote*, 31 May 1815.

Certainly they were concerned with establishing contacts with the provincial associations. The seventh article of their pact stated that deputies would be sent to the 'fédérations des départements' in order to 'se concerter sur les moyens d'une réunion'. During the eventful assembly of 30 May, they received two deputies from the Burgundian federation and fervently applauded a 'chanson patriotique bourguignonne'. Although the Parisians had not initiated the federative movement, they appear to have been eager to put themselves at the centre of it.[10]

Perhaps the most significant action of the Parisian federation was their offer to provide a guard for the Chamber of Representatives. During a meeting of the Chamber on 25 June, the representative Dumolard stated a request of the Parisian *fédérés* that they be permitted to serve either at the frontier or in the interior. Bori de Saint-Vincent suggested that the entire address be read. A member of the administrative commission then stated that it recommended that 'il convient d'adjoindre 25 fédérés à la garde de la chambre'. Lanjuinais, president of the Chamber, opposed the reading of the address, stating that there were several such petitions and that if one were read all would have to be read. Cambon and Arnault (of the Seine) then joined Bori de Saint-Vincent in demanding that the address be read. The latter had their way, and Dumolard did the reading. The address is worthy of extensive quotation:

La patrie était menacée, les Bretons, les Lyonnais, les Bourguignons se sont fédérés pour repousser nos agresseurs. Mûs par les mêmes sentimens, les Parisiens . . . se sont levés aussitôt, et indépendamment des fédérations de Saint-Antoine et Saint-Marceau, la capitale a vu se former dans son sein la fédération parisienne . . .

De grandes événements viennent d'éclater, de plus grands peut-être se préparent . . . Les représentants de la nation appellent à la défense de la patrie tous les Français capables de porter les armes. La fédération parisienne a entendu cet appel, la fédération se presente toute entière . . . Les fédérés sollicitent des armes, une organisation militaire, et l'honneur de servir utilement leur pays, soit aux frontières soit sur les hauteurs, ou dans l'intérieur de la capitale, pour veiller au maintien de l'ordre que la malveillance chercherait vainement à troubler.

La fédération parisienne manifeste un vœu unanime, elle ne connaît point d'efforts au-dessus de son zèle pour la sainte cause de la liberté.

The timing of this address could hardly have been more significant; it occurred one week after Waterloo, and after Napoleon's second abdication.[11]

The offer to bear arms at the frontier was quite extraordinary in itself, but it was doubly significant in that no such offer had been made while

---

[10] *Ibid*, AN, AFIV 1935, *Pacte Fédératif des Parisiens.*
[11] *Moniteur*, 26 June 1815.

Napoleon reigned. It may well be that the offer was largely a product of the desperate circumstances in which France now found herself, but when combined with the evidence of liberal inclinations previously noted, this would appear to suggest that the primary allegiance of the Parisian *fédérés* was to the Chamber of Representatives.

In their address, the Parisian *fédérés* took pains to dissociate themselves from the federations of the *faubourgs*. The loyalty of the *fédérés-tirailleurs* to Bonaparte was not doubted and many who sought a second abdication, including Fouché, feared that Napoleon might use them to disband the two Chambers.[12] Given these circumstances, the offer of the Parisian *fédérés* to protect the Chamber of Representatives must have been highly welcome. Had Napoleon reversed his decision to abdicate and sought to overpower the two Chambers, the two federations might have found themselves in confrontation.

The address of the Parisian federation caused further consternation amongst Parisians who once again confused the two associations. In order to clarify the situation, General Darricau had the following letter published in several newspapers:

Les fédérés parisiens ayant fait à la chambre des représentants une pétition tendante à demander une organisation militaire et des armes pour combattre les ennemis de notre indépendance, des malveillans ont profité de cette démarche pour répandre d'injustes alarmes parmi les citoyens paisibles. Ils ont montré l'immense population des faubourgs armée de fusils et de piques, formant un corps distinct des autres habitants de la capitale. Ils ont rappelé des souvenirs désastreux, et des horreurs que personne ne pense à renouveler. Je m'empresse, Monsieur, de calmer ces inquiétudes en vous priant de vouloir bien annoncer que messieurs les fédérés parisiens . . . ne doivent pas être confondus avec les tirailleurs de la garde nationale.

Darricau's letter perhaps restored a degree of calm in the minds of some Parisian liberals, and it should have made the difference between the two associations apparent. However, with its allusions to an armed populace in the *faubourgs* and sad memories of the past, it probably did not instill much faith in the *fédérés-tirailleurs*.[13]

No confrontation between the two federative associations did take place of course, and the rapid restoration of the Bourbon government left *fédérés* of both associations sorely aggrieved and again united in their opposition to the returned monarchy.

Because the *fédérés* of the *faubourgs* came so rapidly under the direction of the government, it is difficult to speak of them as an independent

---

[12] L. Madelin, ed., *Les Mémoires de Fouché* (Paris, 1945), pp. 488–9.
[13] *Indépendant*, 27 June 1815.

association comparable to the Parisian federation. Tönnesson has suggested that Réal, the prefect of police, was involved with the association from its foundation. If such was the case, Réal did not make his preparations as well as might have been expected.[14]

From its very inception, the federation of the *faubourgs* caused a good deal of concern both to the government and the general populace. In part this was due to the fact that the association was composed almost entirely of artisans and workers of the *faubourgs* Saint-Antoine and Saint-Marceau. Contemporaries who watched the *fédérés* march before Napoleon commented on this. While Madame de Chastenay gave voice to the fears of middle- and upper-class Parisians by noting the presence of old revolutionaries in their midst, the Englishman Hobhouse more shrewdly noted the large number of old soldiers in their ranks. If Barante truly thought the parade of the *fédérés* little more than a farce, Sismondi took matters seriously enough to observe that the *fédérés* might support the Emperor at present, but could well prove his undoing in the future.[15]

The popular social character of the federation of the *faubourgs* has never been subject to doubt. Indeed, in the preamble of their pact, the workers and citizens of the *faubourgs* of Saint-Antoine and Saint-Marceau stated that their association was designed to unite all able-bodied men who were not eligible to join the National Guard. They further stated: 'Nous ne portons point envie à la garde nationale, qui a sur nous l'avantage de pouvoir consacrer son temps à un service journalier, mais nous voulons avoir notre part à la défense commune.' The *fédérés* took care to specify that they wished to be auxiliaries of the National Guard, but not rivals. Doubtless this was intended to assuage the anxiety of the higher social orders.

But other parts of their preamble increased such fears, and this must throw a good deal of doubt on assertions that Réal was managing the association. The following avowal drew particular attention: 'Nous voulons aussi par notre attitude frapper de terreur les traîtres qui pourraient désirer encore une fois l'avilissement de leur patrie.' This was but one of several passages that had an especially revolutionary resonance. While avowing 'obéissance sans bornes' to Napoleon because 'la cause du peuple' was 'inséparable de celle de notre immortel Empereur', the *fédérés* directed their appeal to the workers of the *faubourgs*

[14] Tönnesson, 'Fédérés', pp. 398–9.
[15] A. Roserat, ed., *Mémoires de Madame De Chastenay* (Paris, 1896), II, p. 520; J. Camden Hobhouse, *Last Reign of Napoleon* (London, 1816), I, pp. 210–13; A. De Barante, *Souvenirs* (Paris, 1892), II, p. 146; 'Lettres de Sismondi', *Revue historique*, 4 (1877), p. 355, 90 (1906), p. 276.

who 'dans tous les temps ont montré leur dévouement à la cause du peuple'.[16]

At the review, an old soldier read Thuriot's address to the Emperor on behalf of the *fédérés*. Although ardently patriotic and bellicose, it was much less revolutionary in tone than the initial appeal. Indeed, one passage stated:

Donnez-nous, Sire, des armes en son nom [France]: nous jurons entre vos mains de ne combattre que pour sa cause et la vôtre. Nous ne sommes les instruments d'aucun parti, les agens d'aucune faction; nous n'avons pas été soulevés par l'éloquence d'un tribun.

The necessity of such assurances spoke volumes for the fear that this association inspired. When the *fédéré* orator went on to describe the oncoming war as one of liberation for the enslaved people of the Allied Nations, he probably destroyed whatever good effect he may have created previously. Le Gallo was correct in calling this the language of the Convention in late 1792.[17]

There is much evidence in contemporary Parisian newspapers of the anxiety caused by the *fédérés*. Napoleon himself used the *Journal de l'Empire* to disavow some of the less fortunate revolutionary songs and chants of the *fédérés*. While ostensibly praising the desire of the *fédérés* to support the government as part of the National Guard, an editor of the *Aristarque* fervently expressed his hope that the association did not become a 'club de frères et d'amis!' A similar note of alarm was struck in the liberal *Indépendant*, the journal of Fouché. After lauding the *fédérés*' desire to defend the *patrie*, the editor stated his opinion that their zeal had carried them too far in their initial address. He added 'Nous voulons la liberté, mais non celle de 1793.' Referring to the *fédéré* evocation of terror he stated:

Dans un état libre et soumis à des lois justes, la loi seule doit frapper de terreur les traîtres quels qu'ils soient. Les citoyens armés ne doivent qu'être les instruments de la loi, et les protecteurs de l'ordre et des propriétés. Ce mot de terreur rappelle de souvenirs affligéants. Il serait peut-être plus convenable de former en compagnies les ouvriers dont le patriotisme n'est point équivoque.

Not surprisingly, the *Indépendant* expressed no such reservations about the Parisian federation.[18]

Other newspapers wer? more sympathetic to the federation of the

[16] All of these passages are taken from the *Moniteur*, 12 May 1815.
[17] *Indépendant*, 15 May 1815; Le Gallo, *Les Cent-Jours*, pp. 304–5.
[18] Hobhouse, *Last Reign*, I, p. 211; *Journal de Paris*, 15 May 1815; L. Madelin, *Fouché* (Paris, 1901), II, p. 354; *Indépendant*, 12 May 1815.

faubourgs. This was especially true of the *Patriote de '89*. An editorial entitled 'Sur la Terreur' began as follows:

Des grandes craintes, répandues avec affectation, s'étaient élevées sur la confédération des faubourgs Saint-Antoine et Saint-Marceau. Les incorrigibles affectaient de voir, dans la réunion de leurs paisibles citoyens, le germe des fureurs populaires.

The editor then blamed the excesses of the terror on 'la résistance imprudente de quelques privilégiés' and the egoistic opportunism of 'le farouche Robespierre'. Admitting that the Jacobin Society had been led astray by several powerful orators, the editor nevertheless argued that the original clubs had been ardent foyers of principle, enlightenment and sagacity. Furthermore, he opined that the French populace had learned from the errors of the Terror and was now ready again to renovate its constitutions and enjoy liberty. He described the *fédérés* as 'honnêtes chefs de familles que l'intérêt de la patrie fait seul mouvoir'. If such men sang 'les chants nationaux précurseurs, en 1792, de nos premières victoires', it was because the *patrie* was again in danger.[19]

Without going to the extremes of the *Patriote*, the *Journal de l'Empire* also published a sympathetic editorial. Once again, responsibility was laid squarely on the shoulders of a privileged minority 'qui aima mieux verser des flots de sang que de sacrifier un seul de ses prétendus droits'. Referring to the federations of 1789, the editor warned all those who wished to spread 'les germes de discorde et révolte' to renounce their criminal aspirations. Royalist plotters were leaguing against the people once again and therefore 'le peuple se ligue contre eux'. Federations were the means by which the 'people' protected its liberty.[20]

Reaction to the *fédérés* of the *faubourgs* appears to have been as divided amongst government ministers as journalists. The liberals of Napoleon's entourage feared that the *fédérés* might be used against them. Certainly Fouché, who termed the *fédérés* 'de la plus vile populace', was of this opinion. The crucial decision as to whether to arm the *fédérés* of course rested with Napoleon.[21]

Bonaparte's attitude in this regard remains a mystery. Madelin may well have been correct in conjecturing that Napoleon's suspicions of the loyalty of the National Guard led him to see the *fédérés* as a possible counterbalance to the Guard.[22] We shall see later that he could have used them for

[19] *Patriote*, 20 May 1815.
[20] *Journal de L'Empire*, 22 May 1815.
[21] L. Madelin, *Les Cent-Jours, Waterloo* (Paris, 1954), p. 137; Madelin, *Mémoires de Fouché*, pp. 488–9.
[22] Madelin, *Les Cent-Jours*, p. 137.

this purpose, if he had armed them sufficiently, but ultimately chose not to do so. Whatever the case, Napoleon's decree of 15 May officially organised the *fédérés* as part of the National Guard. Each *arrondissement* of the capital was to have two regiments of 720 *fédérés-tirailleurs* for a total of 17,800 men.

The essential dispositions of the decree were as follows. The tasks of the *fédérés-tirailleurs* were to help in the building of fortifications and, in case of need, to defend the capital from these positions. Thus the *fédérés-tirailleurs* were not to take part in the maintenance of public order within the city. They were to be trained and commanded by a lieutenant-general and six marshals. The colonels, lieutenant-colonels and officers of the battalions were to be selected from officers of the troops of the line, who would be required to install themselves in the *arrondissements* of their battalions. Under-officers would be chosen from the volunteers and would be selected by them. The *fédérés-tirailleurs* would assemble each Sunday for military instruction and their participation would be noted on muster rolls.[23]

Several important issues concerning the *fédérés-tirailleurs* have recently been discussed by Tönnesson. The first of these involves the question of the number of *fédérés-tirailleurs*. Tönnesson has placed great emphasis on the fact that the government was unable to find the required 17,800 men, arguing that this indicated that the people of Paris remained politically apathetic in 1815. Firstly, we can be more specific than Tönnesson's estimate that there were approximately 13,000 *fédérés-tirailleurs*. The final count of the *fédérés-tirailleurs* available to us is that of 19–20 June, which indicates that 13,725 men had been enrolled by that time.[24]

The *fédérés-tirailleurs* existed officially until 6 July 1815. Whether numbers increased after 20 June we cannot say with absolute certainty. However, numbers had been increasing steadily throughout the month of June. There were 8,414 *fédérés* by 29 May; 11,786 by 5 June; and 13,021 by 15 June. Moreover, the report of 20 June indicates that there were 813 *fédérés-tirailleurs* in the second *arrondissement* at that time. However, lists in the Archives of the Prefecture of Police, which are not necessarily complete, indicate that the final total in the second *arrondissement* was at least 892. This suggests that recruitment continued steadily through the final ten days of June.[25]

If we look closely at recruitment figures, we find that the number of

---

[23] The decree was published in the *Journal de L'Empire*, 26 May 1815.
[24] Tönnesson, 'Fédérés', pp. 414–15, AN, F⁹ 661–2, *situation des fédérés-tirailleurs* of 19 and 20 June 1815.
[25] AN, F⁹ 661–2, *situations* of 29 May, 5 and 15 June 1815; APP, A A/331.

fédérés-tirailleurs actually declined from 12,455 to 11,786 between 3 and 5 June. As early as 2 June, General Darricau had begun to forward to General Durosnel complaints that officers of the National Guard were using *fédéré* registers to recruit men into their own institution, thereby reducing the number of *fédérés-tirailleurs*. General Durosnel therefore instructed his officers to cease such activities. Nevertheless, on 5 June, Darricau again wrote to Durosnel complaining of this unscrupulous practice and blamed the decline in the number of his men on the National Guard officers. He warned that organisation of the *fédérés-tirailleurs* would become impossible if severe measures were not taken. Whatever measures Durosnel may have taken must have proved effective, for on 6 June Darricau could report that National Guard raiding had diminished, and that the number of recruits had increased to 12,895. Nevertheless, the colonel of the eleventh regiment of the *fédérés-tirailleurs* continued to complain of the activities of Guard officers. This rivalry between the National Guard and the *fédérés-tirailleurs* is a theme which will be developed more fully later, but for the moment it should be noted that recruiting problems were not simply the result of popular apathy.[26]

Tönnesson has used the materials in the Archives of the Prefecture of Police to discuss the nature of recruitment practices. Doubtless he is correct in concluding that, while enrolment was by no means obligatory, certain recruiting agents did employ 'pressions morales ou autres' on prospective members. It was, after all, in the interests of members of the *comités des quartiers* in charge of recruitment to fill the quotas set for them by the Imperial government if they wished to be viewed favourably by that government. But the mass of evidence contained in the reports of police officers points to the conclusion that Parisian workers had the final say in the matter. Numerous police officers stated that enrolment was entirely voluntary. In the second *arrondissement*, some 1,200 men were requested to attend a meeting at the Bibliothèque Impériale. Only some 400 actually attended and were recruited. There is no evidence that any further measures were taken regarding the other 800. Moreover, the police officer who acted as recruiting agent in the *quartier du Mail* visited several *ateliers* and could report no success whatsoever. Perhaps the members of the committee of the *quartier* Saint-Michel were wise when they decided that the presence of police officers was to be avoided during recruitment. Curiously, the name of Etienne-Denis Pasquier somehow appeared on a *fédéré* muster roll and the future Chancellor was ordered to appear at the Saint-Denis parade ground to start training. Although he obtained no satisfaction from the

---

[26] AN, F⁹ 661–2, *situations* of 3, 5 and 6 June 1815; General Darricau to General Durosnel, 2, 5 and 6 June 1815; Durosnel to Darricau, 3 June 1815.

mayor or his district, Pasquier was able to contact General Darricau and have his name struck off the rolls.[27]

It does not appear that all officials acted with great zeal in furthering recruitment. On 27 May, Darricau wrote that he had had to press the mayor of the eighth *arrondissement* to follow instructions. Durosnel forwarded complaints to Réal of 'l'insouciance extraordinaire de la partie des autorités municipales' of the ninth *arrondissement*. The prefect of the Seine, Bondy, also proved a consistent source of difficulty for Darricau. On 6 June, Bondy raised problems over the payment of under-officers elected by the *fédérés-tirailleurs*. He failed to answer numerous letters from Darricau enquiring where guns for the *fédérés-tirailleurs* could be stored. Under Bondy's direction, the city of Paris failed to fulfil financial obligations to provide dress and equipment. Finally, as we have seen, National Guardsmen on the recruitment committees often proved a serious liability.[28]

While it is probably true that certain recruiting agents pressured workers to enroll, we should not conclude from this that all men, regardless of ability, were accepted as *fédérés-tirailleurs*. Workers who were either too feeble or too small were not allowed to enroll in the *quartier* Saint-Germain. Unsuitable men who had enrolled were removed from the lists in the *quartiers* Feydeau and Chausée d'Antin. On 15 June, Darricau reported that three men had been removed from the ninth regiment because they were more than forty years of age. Nevertheless, reports that certain *fédérés-tirailleurs* were not sufficiently fit led Davout to urge Darricau to take further measures to ensure that all his men were capable of rendering good service.[29]

In sum, then, we must conclude that Tönnesson has given a false impression of *fédérés-tirailleurs* recruitment. The final figure was definitely higher than he has suggested, and the evidence points to the conclusion that recruitment difficulties arose more from the officials involved than from apathy on the part of the masses. Finally, enrolment figures were not so disappointing that officers could not afford the luxury of being selective about whom they recruited.

The other central issue regarding the *fédérés-tirailleurs* concerns the distribution of arms. It is well known that Napoleon's ministers were divided over whether the *fédérés-tirailleurs* should be given guns. Fouché and

---

[27] Tönnesson, 'Fédérés', p. 402; APP, A A/330, 8, 11, 12, 16, 23, 53, 59, 63; E.-D. Pasquier, *The Memoirs of Chancellor Pasquier* (London, 1967), pp. 244–5.
[28] AN, F⁹ 661–2, Darricau to Durosnel, 27 May and 13 June 1815; Prefect of the Seine to Darricau, 6 June 1815; APP, A A/330, 48.
[29] APP, A A/330, 24, 56, 57; AN, F⁹ 661–2, report of 14–15 June 1815; AG, 1K 47 (*Papiers Davout*), Minister of War to Darricau, 18 June 1815.

Durosnel were opposed to such a measure; Carnot and Davout were in favour. It would appear that Napoleon never could make up his mind about whether to arm the *fédérés-tirailleurs*. He certainly had fears about what these men might do if provided with guns. But it is difficult to believe that he went to the length of organising the *fédérés-tirailleurs*, assigning them precious officers of the line, and training them for combat, simply to intimidate the National Guard. It seems more likely that he planned to use them against the Allies if the proper situation arose, but that situation never did arise.[30]

The Emperor's first steps in arming the *fédérés-tirailleurs* were cautious enough. On 10 June he decreed that 100 *fusils* per battalion be provided for training, despite warnings from Durosnel of the grievous effect that this would have on the National Guard. Davout informed Bonaparte of Durosnel's position while clearly stating that neither he nor Carnot agreed:

Je dois à cet égard faire connaître à Votre Majesté la répugnance du Général Durosnel. Il craint que cela produira un mauvais effet sur la Garde Nationale. Il avait cherché à donner cette opinion au Ministre de l'Intérieur; mais aux premières observations que je fis à M. le Comte Carnot, il se rendit à mon avis, qui est que cet armement ne peut produire un mauvais effet que sur les gens mal intentionnés, et que si on déposait les armes chez les maires, ce serait témoigner aux fédérés une défiance que ne pourrait que les indigner ou les décourager.

Nevertheless, the guns issued were to be used for the purpose of training all the *fédérés-tirailleurs* and were to be turned in to the *mairie* at the end of each exercise. It is tempting to see in this measure a token gesture on the part of Bonaparte to give the impression that he was keeping his promises to the *fédérés*. But one should not overlook the fact that *fusils* were a scarce commodity during the Hundred Days, and that Napoleon's priorities lay with ensuring that forces on the frontier were sufficiently armed. On 9 June, the Emperor wrote to Davout:

Les armes sont aujourd'hui la grande question. Avant de donner des armes aux fédérés de Paris, je voudrais en donner dans les Vosges, en Alsace, dans le pays messin, dans le Jura, dans le Dauphiné, puisque là, elles seraient d'un si grand résultat. J'attendrai, pour donner les derniers ordres, que j'aie l'état exact des armes.

Napoleon sent similar instructions from Avesnes on 14 June.[31]

If there was one thing that the *fédérés-tirailleurs* did not wish to do for

---

[30] H. Houssaye, *1815 – Les Cent-Jours* (Paris, 1901), p. 624; AG, 1K 48, Minister of War to the Emperor, 7 June 1815; Fleury de Chaboulon, *Memoirs of Napoleon in 1815* (London, 1820), pp. 412–16.

[31] AN, AFIV 1936, Minister of War to the Emperor, 7 June 1815; A. Chuquet, ed., *Inédits Napoléoniens* (Paris, 1913), I, pp. 452–3; *Correspondance de Napoléon I*, XXVIII, p. 323.

Napoleon, it was to fight at the frontier. Fears that they might be assigned such a task hurt recruitment. Indeed, Darricau found it necessary to take measures against rumours that the *fédérés-tirailleurs* would be sent to the frontier by publishing denials in Parisian newspapers.[32]

The question of the distribution of arms was, of course, a burning issue with the *fédérés-tirailleurs* themselves. They were displeased when they learned that their *fusils* would have to be kept at the *mairie*. An official at the Bibliothèque Impériale expressed fears that disgruntled *fédérés-tirailleurs* might seize the arms stored there, and measures were taken to assure that this did not take place.[33]

As late as 23 June, promises of arms were still being made by *fédéré-tirailleur* officers to their men. This confirms that Napoleon, even after his return from Waterloo, could not bring himself to order a complete arming of the *fédérés-tirailleurs*, despite the pleas of Davout, Carnot and Lucien Bonaparte. Davout even went so far as to advise using the *fédérés-tirailleurs* to disperse the Chambers of Peers and Representatives, when members of the latter two bodies were pressing Bonaparte for a second abdication. This suggests that Davout was responsible for the fact that ultimately some 6,348 *fusils* were distributed to the *fédérés-tirailleurs* by 2 July 1815.[34]

During the critical first week of July, the *fédérés-tirailleurs* saw active service, primarily at the barriers in the north-east sector of Paris (the *faubourg* Saint-Antoine). They were at this stage allowed to retain the guns distributed to them. As we shall see in the following chapter, many *fédérés-tirailleurs* chose to keep their guns after learning of the capitulation of 3 July.[35]

Napoleon ultimately refused to arm the *fédérés-tirailleurs* fully because he thought their hatred of the bourgeoisie and nobility might lead them to provoke civil war. There is a good deal of evidence that the Emperor was correct in his assessment of the situation.[36] Relations were always tense between *fédérés-tirailleurs* and National Guardsmen. We have previously noted Darricau's complaints regarding National Guard recruit raiding and Durosnel's opposition to arming the *fédérés-tirailleurs*. An equally significant clash between the two generals arose over a question of funds. An apparently significant amount of money had been collected from *dons*

[32] APP, A A/330; *Patriote*, 24 May 1815; *Indépendant*, 13 June 1815.
[33] AN, F⁹ 661–2, reports of 31 May, 16–17 June and 4 July 1815.
[34] *Indépendant*, 24 June 1815; Madelin, *Les Cent-Jours*, p. 301; E. Le Gallo, 'Carnot et Napoléon pendant les Cent-Jours', *Revue des études napoléoniennes*, 38 (1934), p. 79; APP, A A/331, 38. See also the *Patriote* of 3 July 1815, which cites the figure of 7,000.
[35] Tönnesson, 'Fédérés', p. 406.
[36] Fleury de Chaboulon, *Memoirs*, p. 421.

patriotiques given by members of the Guard. These funds were designated initially by the Emperor for provisioning the *fédérés-tirailleurs* with uniforms and equipment. However, when Davout informed Durosnel that he would not be able to supply the National Guard with *fusils*, Durosnel decided that the funds from the *dons patriotiques* might better be used to complete the armament of the Guard. When Darricau learned, on 14 June, of Durosnel's intentions, he wrote a letter of complaint to the latter. Durosnel, however, wrote to Carnot on 16 June, requesting that the change in the destination of the funds be ratified. On 19 June, Carnot put the matter to rest: the funds would continue to be used for provisioning the *fédérés-tirailleurs*.[37]

Although relations between Durosnel and Darricau appear to have been cordial at the end of May, when Darricau accepted the former as his superior officer without complaint, it appears that they deteriorated significantly as the month of June progressed. The strain on their relationship is most evident in an exchange of letters written towards the end of the month. On 27 June, Durosnel's secretary forwarded to Darricau a letter in which the commander of the twelfth legion of the National Guard complained of the conduct of *fédérés-tirailleurs* working on fortifications. According to the letter, very few *fédérés-tirailleurs* had turned up for work, and even those who had done so removed their uniforms and insulted passers-by. Darricau in turn forwarded the complaints to Beaupoil Saint-Aulaire, who commanded the *fédérés-tirailleurs* of the twelfth regiment. Beaupoil responded that these complaints were totally unfounded and added that Talleron, author of the original letter, must have been misinformed by someone who wished to slander the *tirailleurs*. He proceeded to laud the efforts of his men and added 'beaucoup d'entre les tirailleurs ayant servi, il serait plus aisé de les discipliner que la Garde Nationale elle-même, s'ils étaient armés et habillés'. He then lodged a complaint of his own: 'nous aurions eu un bien plus grand nombre de ces hommes, si l'on ne s'était empressé de les agréger à la Garde Nationale dont ils ne feraient pas partie avant la formation des bataillons de tirailleurs'. On 29 June, Darricau sent Beaupoil's report to Durosnel and gave it his full support. Moreover, in regard to Talleron, he stated: 'si ce chef de Légion avait senti que les devoirs qu'il a remplir lui imposent d'assez grandes obligations, il se sera borné dans ses attributions et ne se serait pas chargé de redresser des torts d'une troupe dont le commandement est confié à un excellent officer'. Relations between the two organisations were growing

---

[37] See the correspondence between the two generals in AN, F⁹ 661–2, 15–16 June 1815 and Minister of the Interior to Durosnel, 19 June 1815.

tense, and this was reflected by the friction between the two commanders.[38]

After Napoleon's second abdication and, more particularly, after the provisional government's capitulation to the Allies, rivalry between the two organisations turned into outright hostility. The *fédérés-tirailleurs* were outraged by the capitulation and, as we shall see, gave evidence of their displeasure at this second 'betrayal'. The government thereupon turned to the National Guard to disperse groups of angry *fédérés-tirailleurs*, a step which proved to be the first in a process that ultimately led to straightforward repression. This process will be considered in the following chapter, in which the essential differences between these two institutions will be examined, and the fate of the Parisian *fédérés* after the Hundred Days will be discussed.

In conclusion, there were essentially two distinct federations in the capital. The *fédérés* of the *faubourgs* became part of the *fédérés-tirailleurs*, thus entering a paramilitary force organised and trained by the government. Despite problems caused largely by government officials and members of the National Guard, recruitment reached a figure that was probably somewhat greater than 14,000. The *fédérés* of the *faubourgs* were lower-class in social character and, despite their revolutionary rhetoric, devoted to the Emperor. Nevertheless, Napoleon ultimately refused to arm these *fédérés* because he feared this might lead to civil war.

On the other hand, the Parisian *fédérés* did not become part of the *fédérés-tirailleurs* and showed no great willingness to risk their lives in combat until after Napoleon had abdicated. They were part of what appears to have been a middle-class political association that was liberal in character. Thus the capital gave birth to two separate federations which were fundamentally different.

[38] *Ibid.*, Darricau to Durosnel, 24 May and 29 June 1815; Marshal Borelli to Darricau, 27 June 1815; Beaupoil Saint-Aulaire to Darricau, 28 June 1815.

Chapter 9

The fédérés of Paris
after the Hundred Days

In the previous chapter, the differences between the federation of the *faubourgs* and the Paris federation were investigated, and it was noted that members of the former association joined the *fédérés-tirailleurs*, while members of the latter did not. The focus of the present chapter will first be on the *fédérés-tirailleurs*: that these men were almost entirely lower-class will be confirmed, and that they lived in all parts of Paris (not just the *faubourgs*) will be demonstrated. Then the deteriorating relations between the National Guard and the *fédérés-tirailleurs* will be further examined, paying particular attention to the attitude of *fédérés-tirailleurs* to Napoleon. By way of conclusion, repression of *fédérés* of both associations by the Bourbon government will be discussed.

Analysis of regiment lists does indeed indicate that the *fédérés-tirailleurs* had 'une composition populaire, sans-culotte'.[1] The Restoration government, in its attempt to regain guns distributed to the *fédérés-tirailleurs*, sought out lists of the *fédérés-tirailleurs*. Though officials were unable to collect all such muster rolls, they did gain many, some of which cited the occupation and age of the men involved. By sorting through these lists, we can determine that 2,435 of the 13,725 *fédérés-tirailleurs*, 17.7 per cent, fell into the occupational categories shown in Table 11.[2] These figures are what one might expect of an organisation recruited specifically from men who were ineligible to join the National Guard. If we combine the sixth to the tenth categories, which can be identified with the lower classes, we find that this group comprised 93.3 per cent of the *fédérés-tiraillauers*.

Because *fédéré-tirailleur* officers in the second and sixth *arrondissements*

[1] K. D. Tönnesson, 'Les Fédérés de Paris pendant les Cent-Jours', *Annales historiques de la Révolution Française*, 54 (1982), p. 408.
[2] The lists of the *fédérés-tirailleurs* can be found in the APP, A A/331. I have cited the figure of 13, 725 because it is exact, but there were probably more *fédérés-tirailleurs* than this. This would not, however, affect our calculations in any significant way.

Table 11. *Occupational groups (Paris* fédérés-tirailleurs*)*

Category	Number	% of the 2,435
1 Liberal professions	19	0.7
2 Merchants	50	2.1
3 Clergymen	—	—
4 Proprietors and *rentiers*	3	0.1
5 *Fonctionnaires*	89	3.7
6 Shopkeepers	153	6.3
7 Food and lodging trades	38	1.6
8 Artisans	915	37.6
9 Personal service trades	95	3.9
10 Manual labour	1,068	43.9
11 *Militaires*	3	0.1
12 Students	2	0.1

were particularly efficient in filling out the registers of their regiments, most of our information comes from these two *arrondissements.* Of the 777 *fédérés-tirailleurs* in the second *arrondissement* of whom we know the occupation, 90.7 per cent fall into the sixth to the tenth categories. Of the 654 in the sixth *arrondissement,* 94.2 per cent fall into these categories.

Given that these two *arrondissements* contained 1,431 of the 2,425 *fédérés-tirailleurs* of whom we know the occupation, it is important to determine whether figures for the other *arrondissements* differ significantly. This does not prove to be the case. In the ninth *arrondissement,* 97.6 per cent of the 294 *fédérés-tirailleurs* of whom we know the occupation were from the lower-class categories; in the eleventh *arrondissement,* 96.6 per cent of the 290 *fédérés-tirailleurs* were from these categories.

The registers also inform us of the age of 1,163 *fédérés-tirailleurs.* As Table 12 indicates, they were relatively young men, fully capable of prolonged military service. Thus, while it is quite possible that most of these men had served in Imperial armies, relatively few could have played significant roles in the Revolution.

It would be interesting to know which of the Parisian *arrondissements* contributed most to the *fédérés-tirailleurs.* See Table 13 for the regimental muster rolls of 19–20 June 1815 regarding the 13,725 men enrolled at that time. Although these figures appear to indicate that the *fédérés-tirailleurs* were distributed fairly evenly throughout the capital, recruitment reports suggest that the *fédérés-tirailleurs* did not necessarily serve in the regiment of the *arrondissement* in which they resided. A report from the Les Invalides quarter, for instance, stated that recruits came from all the

Table 12. Paris fédérés-tirailleurs age groups

Age	Number	% of the 1,163
up to 29 years	646	55.5
30–9 years	316	27.2
40–9 years	149	12.0
50–9 years	58	5.0

arrondissements of the city. Given that many fédérés-tirailleurs were recruited in their ateliers, it is reasonable to conclude that they served in the regiments of the arrondissements in which they worked rather than resided. However, it is quite likely that officials attempted to balance the regiments as much as possible. This is suggested by the figure of 1,092 for the ninth arrondissement. Recruitment reports continually cited a poor response in this area, and therefore it seems likely that many of the 1,092 were drawn from the nearby seventh, eighth and twelfth arrondissements.[3]

Thus, although we cannot say precisely where in Paris most of the fédérés-tirailleurs resided, we can state that they were drawn almost entirely from the lower classes. This, of course, made them quite distinct from the National Guardsmen, most of whom were drawn from the middle classes. Guardsmen could accord the time and expense to be part of an organisation that served on a regular basis without pay, and armed, dressed and equipped itself; the fédérés-tirailleurs could not. Social position, however, was not the only important difference between these two groups.[4]

Although the Guard was not monarchist, neither was it Bonapartist. During the Hundred Days it sought to maintain a studied neutrality in politics, although Guardsmen repeatedly gave Napoleon a cold reception when he reviewed them. Tönnesson has noted that there were conflicts within the Guard, while arguing that differences between Guardsmen and fédérés-tirailleurs have been overestimated by historians. But it is instructive to note that in pursuing this argument he can cite only a single example of republicanism within the Guard, while citing two instances of royalism.[5]

---

[3] AN, F⁹ 661–2, situation of 19–20 June 1815, APP, A A/330, 40, 48.
[4] On social differences between the two groups, see L. Madelin, Les Cent-Jours, Waterloo (Paris, 1954), pp. 16, 137; E. Le Gallo, Les Cent-Jours (Paris, 1923), pp. 301–2; J. Tulard, Napoleon (London, 1984), p. 336.
[5] See L. Girard, La garde nationale, 1814–1871 (Paris, 1964), pp. 46–7; Tulard, Napoleon, pp. 332, 336; Tönnesson, 'Fédérés', p. 409.

Table 13. Fédérés-tirailleurs recruitment by arrondissement

Arrondissement	Number	% of the 13,725
First	840	6.1
Second	813	5.9
Third	1,051	7.7
Fourth	971	7.1
Fifth	1,588	11.6
Sixth	1,307	9.5
Seventh	1,576	11.5
Eighth	1,103	8.0
Ninth	1,092	8.0
Tenth	1,538	11.2
Eleventh	813	5.9
Twelfth	1,033	7.5

There was no such ambivalence on the part of the *fédérés-tirailleurs*. On 11 June 1815, groups of *fédérés-tirailleurs* marched under Napoleon's windows at the Tuileries to salute him before his departure to the frontier. Such manifestations continued after he returned from Waterloo. Indeed, as Napoleon pointed out to Benjamin Constant, he could have put a rapid end to Fouché's intrigues in the Chamber of Representatives by unleashing the *fédérés-tirailleurs* on that institution. On 21 June, when the Chamber declared itself to be in permanent session, groups of *fédérés-tirailleurs* began to cluster about the Elysée to voice their disapproval. Fears among deputies that the *fédérés-tirailleurs* would be used to attack the Chamber led to the posting of some 500 National Guardsmen around the Elysée. Rather than risk civil war by arming *fédérés-tirailleurs* who gathered daily at the Tuileries, Napoleon, on 22 June, once again chose to abdicate. On learning of the Emperor's decision, angry *fédérés-tirailleurs* ran through the streets crying 'L'Empereur ou la mort!' and the National Guard repeatedly had to intervene to stop battles between *fédérés-tirailleurs* and royalists. On 23 June, a column of *fédérés-tirailleurs* marched to the Elysée, causing panic among authorities. However, no clash took place.[6]

On 28 June Paris was placed under siege and the *fédérés-tirailleurs* were assigned the task of serving as auxiliaries to the troops of the line stationed outside the city barriers. This at least was a means of getting them out of the

[6] *Journal de L'Empire*, 12 June 1815; Tulard, *Napoleon*, p. 339; Madelin, *Cent-Jours*, pp. 312, 320; H. Houssaye, *1815 – La Seconde Abdication* (Paris, 1909), pp. 37–8, 79–80; Girard, *Garde*, p. 51; AN, AFIV 1934, bulletin of 24 June 1815.

city. On 30 June several detachments of *fédérés-tirailleurs* were reviewed by Masséna at the Place Vendôme. At about this time, some 6,348 *fusils* were assigned for use by the *fédérés-tirailleurs*, of which 1,543 appear never to have been used. Tönnesson has concluded from the latter fact that only 4,805 *fédérés-tirailleurs* were actually willing to fight for the defence of the capital, which indicates how apathetic the 'people' of Paris were in 1815. This is a very dubious assumption. Given that guns were only distributed to *fédérés-tirailleurs* deemed to be of 'bonne volonté', and given previous *fédéré-tirailleur* manifestations of hostility to the provisional government, it seems much more likely that the guns were not distributed due to official fears. This would help explain why several hundred *fédérés* served without the benefit of guns. It would also explain the following excerpt from the *Patriote de '89* of 3 July 1815:

Ceux qui s'imaginaient que nous n'avons pas de forces suffisantes pour combattre l'ennemi, ne font pas assez attention aux efforts que l'on est obligé de faire pour arrêter le zèle de ces hommes qui solicitent en vain l'honneur de défendre la patrie. La séance d'hier a fait voir des citoyens obliger de soliciter du corps-législatif la permission de combattre, que leur refuse les chefs de la garde nationale auxquels ils obéissent. Les faubourgs surtout renferment une masse terrible d'hommes dont le courage et l'ardeur seraient de la plus grande utilité, si le gouvernement eut cru en avoir besoin.

The problem was, of course, that officials were not certain that the *fédérés-tirailleurs* would content themselves with firing on the foreign enemy.[7]

When the provisional government capitulated on 3 July 1815, the *fédérés-tirailleurs* felt betrayed. Some of them continued to engage the enemy on 4 July, and two English officers were attacked by *fédérés-tirailleurs* when they brought news of the capitulation to an outpost. Despite a report in the *Indépendant* that shots fired by *fédérés-tirailleurs* during the nights of 3 and 4 July were merely expressions of joy, police reports clearly indicate that *fédérés-tirailleurs* were anything but pleased at the recent turn of events:

La soirée d'hier avait été orageuse, des coups de fusil tirés dans beaucoup de rues par des fédérés-tirailleurs . . . avaient jetté l'alarme dans tous les quartiers, mais à onze heures du soir la garde nationale étant sur pied, le calme se rétablit.

By the evening of 4 July, the *fédérés-tirailleurs* had to recognise that their cause was lost and began to depart from their defence posts. Four hundred

---

[7] *Le Moniteur Universel*, 29 June 1815; Houssaye, *1815 – La Seconde Abdication*, pp. 256–7; *L'Indépendant*, 1 July 1815; Tönnesson, 'Fédérés', pp. 405–7; *Patriote de '89*, 3 July 1815.

of them returned in a single column, marching behind a bust of Napoleon. Along the way, they exchanged gunfire with the National Guard.[8] As part of the treaty of 3 July 1815, policing of the city of Paris was assigned to the National Guard. The essential task of the Guard became that of dispersing *fédérés-tirailleurs* who wished to continue the fight against the Allies. This could only have worsened relations between the National Guard and the *fédérés-tirailleurs*, which were already bad:

Il résulte de rapports qui parviennent au Préfecture de Police que les fédérés-tirailleurs donnent de vives inquiétudes aux habitants de Paris. Ils tiennent des propos alarmans et menaçient la vie des individus qu'ils supposent royalistes ou qu'ils désignent comme tells. Ils montrent surtout une haine profonde et des intentions hostiles contre la garde nationale.

Given that this report was filed on 27 June 1815, it is not at all surprising that only 4,805 *fédérés-tirailleurs* were thought sufficiently trustworthy to be given guns.[9]

This antagonism between the *fédérés-tirailleurs* and National Guardsmen must have greatly increased when the convention of Saint-Cloud, 15 July 1815, assigned the latter group the task of disarming the former. On 5 August a bulletin of the Interior stated:

Les ressources des ouvriers s'épuisent . . . leur mécontentement est certain. La présence de la Garde Nationale a suffi constamment pour dissiper les groupes et imposer silence aux provocateurs. On a surtout pris soin d'isoler les fédérés.

Nevertheless, workers continued to gather at the Tuileries and on 7 August six of them were arrested for shouting seditious slogans. On 9 August, a *fédéré* wounded a Guardsman seeking to arrest him and, on 23 August, a *fédéré* killed a royalist.[10]

These were the most visible signs of *fédéré* hatred of the Bourbon government and those associated with it. To better understand this hatred, and how it came to be directed particularly at the National Guard, the repression of *fédérés* by the Second Restoration government must be examined.

Repression took place in two stages. The first involved disarmament of the *fédérés-tirailleurs* by the National Guard and, for the most part, this

---

[8] Houssaye, *1815 – La Seconde Abdication*, pp. 305, 308–9; AN, AFIV 1934, bulletin of 5 July 1815; *Indépendant*, 5 July 1815; J.-B. Regnault de Warin, *Cinq mois d'histoire de France* (Paris, 1815), p. 441; Girard, *Garde*, p. 52.
[9] *Moniteur*, 5 July 1815; M. A. Thiers, *History of the Consulate and the Empire* (London, 1861), XX, pp. 276–8; AN, AFIV 1934, bulletin of 27 June 1815.
[10] AN, F⁷ 3786, bulletin of 5 August 1815; F⁷ 3735, bulletins of 8, 10, and 24 August 1815.

operation was conducted with little difficulty. Most *fédérés-tirailleurs* realised that further opposition to the Allies and the Bourbon government would prove futile and willingly submitted. However, the number of unco-operative *fédérés-tirailleurs* proved sufficient to convince officers of the Guard that the police would have to be called into play. This began a second stage of repression that consisted of numerous house searches and constant surveillance of *fédérés* thought to be incorrigibly opposed to the Bourbon regime. This latter group of 'incorrigibles' included both *fédérés-tirailleurs* and members of the Parisian federation. As we shall see, such men were subjected to a process of harassment very much akin to that meted out to Parisian *sans-culottes* during *Thermidor* and subsequent periods of the Revolution and Empire.[11]

As a first step in disarmament, *fédéré* under-officers were instructed to deliver arms in their possession to either the local commander of the National Guard or the police station of their quarter. They were also instructed to direct the *fédérés* of their company to do likewise. By 25 July 1815, 3,600 of the 6,400 arms distributed had been retrieved in this manner. Nevertheless, many *fédérés* had refused to deliver their arms and Count Dessolle, noting that National Guard officers lacked sufficient legal coercive authority, requested the Prefect of Police to direct his officers to aid in the process. Consequently, on 3 August, a circular was sent by the Prefect to all police officers instructing them to aid Guard officers in the search for arms and to arrest unco-operative *fédérés*. On 10 August, the Prefect ordered all *fédérés-tirailleurs* who had not yet returned their arms to do so within twenty-four hours and threatened recalcitrants with 'les peines les plus sévères'. However, on 14 August, Count Dessolle decided to take further measures to hasten disarmament. Noting that many *fédérés* stated they had left their arms behind at the barriers, he ordered that each *tirailleur* who could not produce a *fusil*, or a certificate vouching that he had already done so, be examined. The recalcitrant *fédérés* of each company were to be summoned by Montjardet, former *chef-d'état-major* of the *fédérés-tirailleurs*, to a meeting at their local *mairie*. Each *fédéré* would then be asked to justify his inability to return a *fusil* and officers of the National Guard would comment as to the veracity of the *fédéré*'s account. A report of each discussion would then be sent to Dessolle, who would determine whether the *fédéré* in question should be arrested. Those who did not attend the meeting would be subject to arrest.[12]

In effect, the *fédérés-tirailleurs* who could not or would not produce their

---

[11] On repression of the *sans-culottes*, see R. Cobb, *The Police and the People* (Oxford, 1970), pp. 131–69.
[12] APP, A A/330, 68, 69, 81, 82.

arms were to be tried by officers of the Guard whom they despised. However, it does not appear that this procedure led to massive arrests. On 30 October 1815 the Duke de Mortemart, lieutenant-general of the National Guard, reported to the Prefect of Police that some *fédérés-tirailleurs* had returned their arms and that some had offered adequate justification of their inability to do so. However, others had only given vague explanations or failed to attend the meetings. Lists of the latter were therefore sent to police officers, and house searches began in earnest.[13]

These measures were simply a matter of giving improved organisation to a process that had been going on since the start of August. There are numerous reports of house searches conducted before 14 August. Because such reports are fairly uniform in content, we shall limit ourselves to citing the following brief but representative examples. From 9 to 11 August, a police officer of the *quartier du Mail* called on sixteen *fédérés-tirailleurs*. Thirteen stated that they had either left their *fusils* at the *butte* Chaumont or had turned them in at the *mairie* between 4 and 6 July. Many claimed to have signed a register at the *mairie*, but the register had apparently been lost. One reported that his *fusil* had been seized by the National Guard while he was returning from the barrier and that he had been imprisoned for nine days at that time. Three of the sixteen *fédérés* had moved elsewhere and could not be traced from their original locality. Although the police officer was unable to find any guns, he did find numerous cartridge-pouches, shakoes and articles of military attire. In conclusion, the officer reported that the *fédérés* had proved helpful and were not a source of concern. Moreover, he added that there had been much confusion during the return of arms and thus supported *fédéré* claims about signing a register at the *mairie*.[14]

Not all *fédérés-tirailleurs* proved so accommodating. In the *quartier du faubourg Saint-Denis*, Lettu, a *salpêtrier*, first sought to convince a police officer that he had left his *fusil* behind when he left camp. After an hour of interrogation, however, he admitted to having hidden the gun and promised to turn it in. On 20 August 1815, a police officer of the Saint-Eustache quarter filed reports on visits to twenty *fédérés-tirailleurs*. He also found that most of the *fédérés* claimed either to have left their arms at the *butte* Chaumont or to have been disarmed by the National Guard while returning to Paris. He was unable to uncover any *fusils*, but did manage to collect several shakoes. Only one of the *fédérés*, a knife-cutter named Desroche, merited special attention, for he was reputed to be strongly attached to the Emperor and given to seditious utterances. In one instance a *fédéré-tirailleur*, named Gallois, wrote to the Prefect that he had sold his *fusil* because he was unemployed and destitute. Because he was able to cite

---

[13] *Ibid.*, A A/331, 4.   [14] *Ibid.*, A A/330, 367–74.

the purchaser, a *brocanteur*, he was treated with leniency and allowed to go free. Other *fédérés* were found in possession of their *fusils*. On 12 August, a search of the apartment of Nicolas Louis, a mechanic who was away in the countryside working on the harvest, netted a gun, cartridge-pouch and bayonet. In May 1816, François Basania, a dockworker, was found to possess a *fusil*, bayonet, shako, *cocarde tricolore*, cartridge-pouch, knapsack, 'balles de plomb et autres munitions', and a silver plaque with the Imperial eagle on it. A search of the domicile of the mason Pierre Noël revealed nothing, but he was unable to justify his failure to produce a gun and consequently was arrested.[15]

It does not appear that a great number of *fédérés-tirailleurs* suffered the same fate as Pierre Noël. Instead, the authorities contented themselves with putting suspected troublemakers under close surveillance and bringing them repeatedly to the police office for questioning. This was a means of intimidating enemies of the regime which probably succeeded in most cases.[16]

In the lists of Parisians arrested for political crimes during the period of August 1815 to January 1818, there are numerous references to *fédérés*. Unfortunately, whether these men were *fédérés-tirailleurs* or members of the federation of the *rue* de Grenelle is specified only occasionally. Nor can we assume that arrested *fédérés* were identified as such. Nevertheless, these lists do indicate that arrested *fédérés* were generally placed under surveillance, but not imprisoned. Of the seventy-six men cited as *fédérés*, fifty-five were placed under surveillance, six were imprisoned and three were exiled from Paris.

The list of arrested Parisian *fédérés* tells a good deal about whom the authorities thought worth watching. Of the seventy-six, twenty-eight were cited as *fédérés-tirailleurs* and five as members of the federation of the *rue* de Grenelle. Thirteen were small-scale merchants, either of wine, tobacco or beer. They, like two bakers, one *charcutier* and a hotel-keeper, were suspected of holding meetings with other *fédérés*. Five coach drivers received attention because they were thought to carry messages between Parisian and provincial *fédérés*. Eight workers, apprentices and artisans were apparently prone to making seditious statements.[17]

We can determine other things about the *fédérés* by making judicious use of police notes. Richard Cobb has given a description of how misleading these reports can be, and the caution that he prescribes is pertinent to our

---

[15] *Ibid.*, 375, 190–3, 177–85, 260, 224–31, 386–96.
[16] *Ibid.*, 120.
[17] AN, F⁷ 3028–30, *extrait des arrestations politiques*, March 1815–January 1818.

consideration. There is, for instance, a certain uniformity in the police notes that arouses suspicion. Nevertheless, simply knowing whom the police thought worthy of repression tells us a good deal. Moreover, as will be seen in the following chapter, Parisian police knew what they were about when they were chasing provincial *fédérés*. Finally, given that the police had access to lists of the *fédérés-tirailleurs*, it can safely be assumed that they were accurate when they cited a suspect as a *fédéré-tirailleur*.[18]

Numerous *fédérés* were reputed to have had revolutionary sentiments. Raimond, a wine merchant, was termed a revolutionary, as was Corval, a soldier. Tallard, tax collector, Rimbaud, wine merchant, and Français, goldsmith, were all labelled Jacobins. Certain *fédérés* were honoured with more specific appellations. Vitry, *concierge*, Courfier, locksmith, and Dorlet were cited as old *septembriseurs*. Finally, Davianc, a member of the Paris federation, was said to have been a judge of the revolutionary tribunal at La Rochelle.[19]

Other *fédérés* were noted for their loyalty to Napoleon. Vacher, master carpenter, Meunier, tobacconist, and Fessigny, coal inspector and member of the federation of the *faubourg* Saint-Antoine, were described as Bonapartists. Lamotte, a locksmith, was found to possess a cross of the Imperial Legion of Honour, a medal with Napoleon's effigy on it, and buttons with the emblem of the eagle. Drigny, placed under surveillance at Passy, had paraded a bust of the Emperor during the Hundred Days. In the spring of 1816, *fédérés* of the *faubourg* Saint-Marceau were reported to be predicting a return of Napoleon 'pour les cerises'.[20]

Police reports also cite several employers thought to have aided in the organisation of the *fédérés-tirailleurs*; these men were naturally suspected of having a bad influence on their employees. Taleron, a wealthy pottery manufacturer in the *faubourg* Saint-Marceau and member of the Imperial Legion of Honour, was reported to have forced his workers to enlist. Similarly, the brothers Ditans were suspected of inciting their workers to cry 'Vive l'Empereur!' and sing seditious songs. According to police reports, Vacher had encouraged his employees to enlist, and La Rue, a tax administrator, had aided in the distribution of arms. But the two employers who attracted most attention were the manufacturers Robillard and Richard (of Richard-Lenoir), both reputed to have been leaders of the federation of the *faubourg* Saint-Antoine. Both men were said to have drunk toasts to the Emperor at the Café Montasier, a notorious *fédéré*

---

[18] For Cobb's warnings against interpreting police reports too literally, see his *Police*, pp. 5–45.

[19] AN, F⁷ 6630–3, *notes de police*, 152, 618, 117, 188, 114, 219, 367.

[20] *Ibid.*, 193, 226, 1116, 519, 62, 1137, 738.

meeting place. Three of Richard's employees, including Pinotel, the son of a judge in the eighth *arrondissement*, were reputed to have been leaders of the federation of the *faubourgs*.[21]

That Richard was a Bonapartist is well known. One of the great entrepreneurs of the French textile industry, it is highly probable that he encouraged his workers to join the federative movement. According to the police, Richard was the 'protecteur' and close friend of Baudoin, a leading *fédéré-tirailleur*, official hat-maker of Joseph Bonaparte, and an employer of five workmen. It is difficult not to suspect that Baudoin's alleged connection with Richard was the reason that he was honoured with the full-time surveillance of a paid informant. Baudoin had been arrested and imprisoned in October 1815 because of his role in the *fédérés-tirailleurs*. Despite frequent warnings, he continued to hold meetings with other *fédérés* such as Vachot, who had also been arrested for conspiring against the monarchy, and hence was kept under close surveillance at least until June 1816, after being arrested for a third time on 24 May 1816. Friends of Baudoin were also viewed with suspicion, and two of them, Caron and Patrin, were presented with search warrants.[22]

All of these men lived either in or close to the *faubourg* Saint-Antoine, and this partly explains why they attracted so much interest. Police notes are full of general reports on public opinion in the revolutionary *faubourg*, and no other part of Paris received comparable attention. The workers of Saint-Antoine were thought to have subversive political principles in general. Wild rumours, such as one that Richard would lead a Bonapartist uprising in February 1816, circulated both inside and outside Richard's *ateliers*. Rumour-mongering appears to have reached a peak in March 1816, one year after Napoleon's *vol d'aigle*. After this matters appear to have calmed down somewhat and there was a temporary lull during the summer of 1816. By October 1816, however, rumours were again flying, royalists were being threatened and, worst of all, unemployed workers were complaining about the price of bread. One of the rumour-mongers proved to be the *fédéré* Thiolle, an *ouvrier de filature* who, from August 1815 to April 1817, proved himself to be one of the most ardent and foolish of Bonaparte's supporters.[23]

How reliable are such reports? Without placing too much emphasis on individual reports, they can be used as a barometer of the general state of

[21] *Ibid.*, 91, 168, 266, 789, 1116, 522.
[22] *Ibid.*, 682, 1083; APP, A A/330, 99–152, 292–301; on Richard, see Tulard, *Napoleon*, p. 202; for both Richard and Robillard, see R. Monnier, *Le Faubourg Saint-Antoine 1789–1815* (Paris, 1981), pp. 180–8, 280–4.
[23] AN, F⁷ 6630–3, *notes de police*, 739, 522, 575, 696, 486, 496, 839, 909; APP, A A/330, 342–66; Tönnesson has described Thiolle's seditious career in 'Fédérés', pp. 412–13.

public opinion. When warnings of unrest dramatically increase in frequency, as they do in the spring of 1816, one can safely assume that the authorities had some cause for concern. This was, after all, the period when both the Didier and 'Patriots of 1816' conspiracies came to light. The initial effect of these conspiracies was to give hope to opponents of the regime that some sort of successful uprising would eventually take place. When this did not occur, and those involved in the conspiracies were duly and harshly punished, these hopes diminished. Looking back on the period, it seems quite obvious that there never was much chance of the *fédérés* stirring the populace of Paris into serious rebellion. Contemporary authorities could not have known this, of course, and the care they took to intimidate potential leaders of rebellion was doubtless prudent. However, the essential point to be derived from police notes is that a significant number of Parisian workers continued to long for the fall of the Bourbon Monarchy and the restoration of the Imperial government. Moreover, *fédérés* played a significant role in keeping hopes for such a change alive. For this reason, authorities took pains to punish those who overtly manifested their political sentiments.

Several *fédérés* revealed their aspirations to the authorities by foolhardy actions. The student Jean-Baptiste L'Abesse was not particularly wise to keep a brochure entitled 'Le bouquet de violettes' and a seditious song in his apartment. François Noël became involved in a brawl and a subsequent search of his domicile led to the uncovering of a *fusil*, bayonet and shako. Perhaps the most foolish of all were the brothers Lefevre. After a serious bout of drinking in the Quinze-Vingts quarter, they accosted four gendarmes while shouting: 'nous sommes malhereux à présent, mais le petit Caporal reviendra, les fédérés ne sont pas morts, . . . nous enverrons le grand Cochon manger des pattates en angleterre, nous avons été fédérés et vive la fédération!' They were rewarded with a trip to the prefecture of police, where they were reprimanded and then sent home.[24]

Reports of clandestine meetings of *fédérés* continued to be made throughout the summer of 1816. Authorities became particularly concerned when *fédérés* were seen in the company of soldiers. Judging by the diminished frequency of police notes on the *fédérés*, however, it would appear that the *fédérés* were no longer a source of great concern after this period. Perhaps they had finally given up hope one year after the second exile of Napoleon.[25] The abortive uprising of the 'Patriots of 1816' probably contributed greatly to this disillusionment.

The minutes of the trial of the Patriots inform us that at least eight of the

---

[24] APP, A A/330, 203–23, 283–6, 241–6.
[25] AN, F⁷ 6630–3, *notes de police*, 971, 995, 1083, 909.

twenty-seven men tried for conspiracy had been *fédérés*, and that the Patriots had hoped to convince a sufficient number of *fédérés* that an assault on the Tuileries would bring an end to the Bourbon Monarchy. A police list of suspects in the affair actually included Richard and Count Beaupoil de Saint-Aulaire, who had been a colonel of the *fédérés-tirailleurs*. Tolleron and Edouard Martin, both *fédéré* officers, were arrested subsequently. Martin was reported to have distributed the triangular cards used to recruit Patriots. If this was so, the police had no evidence to prove it, and Martin was not involved in the trial of twenty-eight Patriots. Perhaps the police had simply become frustrated with their inability to catch Martin in some intrigue. They had been following his movements since July 1815. Tolleron, however, was one of two *fédérés* executed for conspiring against the Monarchy. Five other *fédérés* were given prison sentences. One of them, Jean Charles, who printed the proclamation of the Patriots, had printed the pact of the Parisian federation. One of the Patriots who actually drew up a plan for bombing the Tuileries, Drevin, had been a *fédéré*.[26]

The police were aware of the plot from its very beginning, and it would appear that *agents provocateurs* may have been involved. Whatever the case, the plot was a complete disaster for the *fédérés* and soldiers involved, and must have served notice to other *fédérés* that any return of the Emperor would have to be brought about by the man himself.[27]

Unfortunately, it is not possible to trace the subsequent history of the *fédérés* of Paris. Because no list of the *fédérés* of the *rue* de Grenelle has ever been found, either by government authorities or historians, we cannot say what became of them. This is all the more regrettable in that the Parisian federation was middle-class. As we have seen in our studies of Dijon and Rennes, it was middle-class *fédérés* who went on to become members of the Liberal Opposition and joined the revolutionary societies of the 1820s. As we shall see in the following chapter, at least one member of the Parisian federation became a revolutionary and it may be that others also did, but we will probably never know whether the case of Cugnet was typical.

Although lists of the *fédérés-tirailleurs* are available to us, these men, because they were lower-class, were not apt to have participated in the

---

[26] BN, Lb⁴⁶ 598, *Procès des auteurs et fauteurs de la conspiration de 1816*, pp. 11, 13, 19, 35; AN, F⁷ 6632, *notes de police*, 1012, AFIV 1935, *Pacte Fédératif des Parisiens*; APP, A A/330, 267–71.

[27] On the Patriot conspiracy, see A. Spitzer, *Old Hatreds and Young Hopes* (Cambridge, Mass., 1971), pp. 24–5; J. Vidalenc, *Les Demi-Soldes* (Paris, 1955), p. 185; J. Lucas-Dubreton, *Le Culte de Napoléon, 1815–1848* (Paris, 1960), pp. 75–6. The entire proceedings of the trial can be followed in daily reports of the *Journal des débats*, commencing on 4 July 1816.

Liberal Opposition. Moreover, after the disastrous affair of the 'Patriots of 1816', Paris was not the scene of lower-class rebellion. Government repression, and particularly disarmament, had succeeded in removing the *fédérés-tirailleurs* as a source of danger. This, however, did not indicate any change in the political opinions of *fédérés-tirailleurs*. The *fédérés-tirailleurs* simply had to recognise that the cause of Napoleon was lost as long as the Emperor remained securely imprisoned on the island of Saint Helena.

We have seen that the *fédérés-tirailleurs* revealed themselves to be Bonapartist by their actions during and immediately after the Hundred Days. Moreover, the *fédérés-tirailleurs* were enraged when liberals and monarchists forced Napoleon to abdicate after Waterloo. Their suspicions of betrayal were confirmed when the provisional government capitulated without a fight, thereby paving the way for the second restoration of Bourbon rule.

Until the death of Bonaparte, opposition to the Bourbon Monarchy was very much a middle-class affair in Paris. The liberals who took the lead in opposing the government of Louis XVIII could not command the support of lower-class Parisians whose dislike of the Bourbons did not cause them to forget the part the liberals had played in deposing Napoleon in 1815. This is not to say that the Parisian masses became politically apathetic after 1815. In his study of Parisian workers during the Empire, M. Sibalis has concluded that the Parisian lower classes had achieved political consciousness, although they had not achieved class consciousness. Our study of the two Parisian federations tends to confirm this. When middle-class members of the Parisian federation went to the barriers to help build fortifications, they were soon joined by lower-class *fédérés-tirailleurs* who wished to express their sense of fraternity. The two groups then paraded before a bust of the Emperor. As long as the two groups shared a common willingness to support the Emperor, there was no conflict between them.[28]

However, our examination of relations between the middle-class National Guard and the lower-class *fédérés-tirailleurs* demonstrates that hostility could arise between the two classes. Conflict was not a result of class consciousness however; the issue at stake was support for Napoleon. *Fédérés-tirailleurs* were unwilling to compromise over who should rule France, whereas Guardsmen, by their actions in 1815, proved themselves quite willing to support either the provisional government or the government of Louis XVIII, so long as civil order was maintained.

It would appear that the *fédérés-tirailleurs* were typical of the Parisian

[28] M. D. Sibalis, 'The Workers of Napoleonic Paris', Ph.D. dissertation (Concordia University, 1979), p. 446; *Patriote*, 21 June 1815.

masses in their devotion to Bonaparte. If anything, Bonaparte's popularity actually increased after the Hundred Days, most notably in the *faubourg* Saint-Antoine. The seeds of popular Bonapartism had been sown in 1814 by the Allies and the Bourbon Monarchy. Bonaparte had exploited this during the Hundred Days by posing as the defender of the Revolution. Moreover, even after Waterloo, he had been willing to carry on the fight against the Allies. In the eyes of the populace, this was more than one could say of the liberals in the two Chambers, compromised by their capitulation.[29]

This helps to explain why the Carbonari of Paris recruited very few lower-class Parisians. The ties between leading liberals, such as Lafayette, and the Carbonari were very close. Certainly the Carbonari had little to offer lower-class Parisians who wanted nothing less than a return of Bonaparte. Moreover, it would appear that the liberals and lower-class Parisians viewed each other with mutual distrust. As E. Newman has shown, liberals were not sure what to make of lower-class support when it emerged in the late 1820s. This, of course, occurred after Napoleon had died, and the liberals were the only possible leaders of opposition to an increasingly reactionary Bourbon government.[30]

[29] See Monnier, *Saint-Antoine*, pp. 286–9 and Sibalis, 'Workers', pp. 430–3.
[30] Spitzer, *Hatreds*, pp. 281–94; on relations between liberals and the Paris populace, see E. Newman, 'The Blouse and the Frock Coat', *Journal of Modern History*, 46 (1974), pp. 26–59.

Chapter 10

The fate of the fédérés
– White Terror

Having concluded our case-studies of the *fédérés* of Rennes, Dijon and Paris, it is now time to return to the movement as a whole, taking up where we left off at the end of the third chapter. The second reinstallation of the Bourbon government rapidly brought federative assemblies to a close; it was hardly possible to continue denouncing the King and his followers in public. In this sense, the federations came to an end. Previous accounts of the federative movement have generally concluded at this point, but in the present study our subject is not so much the federations as the *fédérés* themselves. How did *fédérés*, individually and collectively, respond to the return of Louis XVIII?

Once their cause was lost, *fédérés* might have been expected to admit defeat and make the best of a government buttressed by the twice victorious Allies. It was perhaps too much to expect them to alter their opinions, but it could at least be hoped that they would cease actively opposing the Monarchy. Yet, overwhelming evidence points to the conclusion that they continued to work for the triumph of some alternative regime. After losing the battle against restoration, they set about undermining it. There were many reasons for this obstinate resistance, not least of which was the belief of some *fédérés* that a second *vol d'aigle* could be made to match a second restoration. Not all *fédérés* laboured under such an illusion, however, and there were signs that some of them were willing to make peace with a constitutional Bourbon Monarchy. Such men soon found themselves ostracised by Bourbon government and society, and this drove them back to an opposition which they learned to make covert.

Given the way in which the *vol d'aigle* had exposed the fragility of the First Restoration, and given the many manifestations of hostility to the Second, it was entirely natural that the Bourbon government should set about assuring that authority was placed exclusively in loyal hands. Even moderate royalists were convinced they were fighting for the survival of the throne; there was no reason for them to assume that a second crisis would

219

not occur. *Fédérés* could plead temporary insanity as often as they pleased; their actions during the Hundred Days gave eloquent testimony of how much faith could be placed in their avowals of loyalty to the King. As a result, they were the first to go in a systematic purge conducted at all levels of government. Reasonable as this was, it was not the way to bring sheep back into the fold.

But the government went much further than mere dismissal from office. Betraying its insecurity, it put into practice a host of repressive laws voted by the ultra-royalist *Chambre Introuvable*. Although it is true that the extremism of the latter body made it as much a liability as an asset to the Monarchy, it should be understood that while it was the *Chambre Introuvable* that forged the instruments of repression, it was the government that used them. *Fédérés* found themselves under the constant observation of police officers, spies and informants; the slightest hint of lingering opposition could lead to fines, imprisonment and internal exile. Rank-and-file *fédérés* proved especially susceptible to the temptation to cry 'Vive l'Empereur!' in public; they were severely punished for it. For middle-class leaders too shrewd to manifest overtly their sentiments, there was always guilt by association; D'Allonville was not the only prefect to use the laws of exception when he lacked sufficient proof to present in court. Where there was sufficient evidence, *cours prévôtales* could serve the causes of vengeance and repression. All of this was designed to suppress public demonstrations of hostility in the hope that the appearance of stability would persuade opponents to view their cause as lost and renounce their culpable ambitions; it also served to bind a massive number of *fédérés* in obloquy.

Legal repression and harassment came to be viewed by its victims as part and parcel of a White Terror which included mass violence in the south. Contemporary accounts of murder and pillage in the south soon took on mythical proportions which historians have only begun in recent decades to bring back into line with what actually took place. Although appalling in some instances, mob violence was isolated to certain departments and not typical of most. Nevertheless, it provided more than enough tales of atrocity for fleeing *fédérés* to fill their compatriots elsewhere with horror. This was all the more unfortunate for the Monarchy in that opponents of the regime seldom took the trouble to distinguish between the actions of central government officials, struggling to bring an end to anarchy, and the extremist agents of the Duke of Angoulême who did little to stop it. Events in the south undermined the more constructive efforts of Bourbon officials who assured that blood was not shed in the west.

Because the *fédérés* of our case-studies were not subjected to the most extreme forms of White Terror, we shall want to look at the south in detail.

Fédérés, whose support for Napoleon had been public, were the leading victims of mob violence, and by studying their fates we can learn much about why this bloody White Terror broke out in some places and not in others. Elsewhere in France, the experience of *fédérés* was not substantially different from that of their compatriots in Dijon, Rennes and Paris, and by analysing the way in which Bourbon officials sought to deal with *fédérés* we can demonstrate the point. By way of introduction, we shall discuss police measures taken against provincial *fédérés* seeking refuge in the capital.

The police of Paris had their hands full during the early stages of the Second Restoration. Not only did they have to keep an eye on Parisian *fédérés*, they also had to track down *fédérés* who had fled from the provinces in search of anonymity. Their notes are full of reports on provincial *fédérés*, and these are sufficiently accurate to confirm that provincial authorities made a policy of notifying the Minister of Police whenever a *fédéré* leader was thought to have gone to Paris. Séré, for instance, was spotted on the very day he arrived from the Haute-Garonne, as was Matthieu de Vier, one of the most active *fédérés* of Rive-de-Gier (Loire). Many names by now familiar to us are to be found in the correspondence of the Parisian police. Huguet and Viennot from Dijon, Jollivet, Leroy and Milet from Rennes, Puthod and Butignot, members of the central committee of Lyons, Azaiis from Nancy, and Banon, a founder of the federation of Toulon, are all cited.[1]

For the most part, Parisian police officers contented themselves with determining the address of visiting *fédérés* and watching to see whether they kept contacts with other provincial or Parisian *fédérés*. Such men were seeking anonymity and were not likely to cause trouble in a city where they were unknown to all but the authorities. Nevertheless, they were suspected of plotting uprisings in their native provinces, and therefore the police were quite interested in their correspondence. One policy spy suggested that Parisian *fédérés* were sending directions to Breton *fédérés*. Raymond Maurette of Toulouse was suspected of holding dinner parties for *fédérés* of the Midi, and of acting as a liaison between Toulousain and Parisian *fédérés*. One enterprising spy hoped to obtain a key to Maurette's chambers in order to peruse his letters.[2]

The police were interested in provincial *fédérés* particularly because they were suspected of abetting Parisian *fédérés* in spreading rumours of

---

[1] AN, F⁷ 6630–1, 363, 1173, 851, 783, 1128, F⁷ 3028–30, 160, 163, 112, 783, 101, 198, 611.
[2] *Ibid.*, F⁷ 6630, 611, 456, 113, 316, 571.

uprisings in the provinces. Few of these reports, however, led to more than periodic surveillance. One stated that there was no evidence that Barthe of Toulouse was involved in such intrigues. Another noted that Butignot was keeping a low profile. Nevertheless, Milet, who had been banished from Rennes, was directed to continue his journey to Montpellier, by no means an attractive destination for a *fédéré*.[3]

Although virtually every department was represented by a *fédéré* hiding in Paris, there was an unusually high concentration of men from the south. Reports on Toulousain *fédérés* were particularly numerous; there were also reports on Agricole Moreau, Vinai, Guillon and Tissot, all of whom had been active in the federation of Avignon. This large concentration of *fédérés* from the south is readily explained by the violence of the White Terror in that region.[4]

White Terror did not break out with equal virulence in all parts of the south. While the Gard was the scene of some of the worst excesses, certain communes of the department, such as the Vaunage and the Gardonnenque, escaped relatively unscathed. Elsewhere there was much violence in Toulon, but Draguignan remained fairly peaceful. Marseilles and Nîmes saw repeated scenes of savagery which were not duplicated in Montpellier and Rodez.[5]

In part, mob violence was unevenly distributed because some potential victims were able to defend themselves. This was the case in the Vaunage and the Gardonnenque. Indeed, when a squadron of the *chasseurs d'Angoulême* attempted to travel from Nîmes to Alais on 23 August, they were confronted and forced to retreat by a band of peasant *fédérés* bolstered by *fédérés* from Nîmes, Avignon, Arles and Tarascon, and army deserters. The fact that Austrian troops had to be called in to disperse the rebels suggests that this was not an area suitable for royalist reprisals. Foreign troops could also help to reduce carnage, as did Austrians in the Gard when they finally realised exactly what was taking place around them.[6]

One of the few truths contained in the *Précis de ce qui s'est passé en 1815*

[3] *Ibid.*, 522, 379, F⁷ 6631, 935, 783.
[4] APP, A A/331, 400–24.
[5] G. Lewis, *The Second Vendée* (Oxford, 1978), pp. 204–15; C. Alleaume, 'La Terreur Blanche dans le Var', *Bulletin de la société d'études scientifiques et archéologiques de Draguignan*, 45 (1944–5), pp. 5–7; P. Gaffarel, 'La Terreur Blanche à Marseille', *Revue historique*, 122 (1916), pp. 240, 287; D. Resnick, *The White Terror and Political Reaction after Waterloo* (Cambridge, Mass., 1966), pp. 20–37, 41–61. Montpellier and Rodez will be discussed later.
[6] Lewis, *Second Vendée*, pp. 187–8, 217; E. Daudet, *La Terreur Blanche* (Paris, 1878) p. 125.

dans les départements du Gard et de la Lozère of René de Bernis is the author's contention that enemies of the Bourbon Monarchy occasionally provoked reprisals by their own actions. The opponents of the government in towns such as Bandol, Beausset and Castellet (in the Var), actually went on the offensive and attacked royalists well after Louis XVIII had returned to Paris, leading to some fifty arrests. However, it is unlikely that this was predominantly a matter of political opposition; the men under attack were mostly tax-collectors.[7]

The claim of de Bernis that royalist officials uniformly did their utmost to prevent pillage and massacre was false. As G. Lewis has demonstrated, *commissaire extraordinaire* de Bernis and the officials he appointed were often implicated in acts of violence committed by royalists. Royalist officials in Grasse did their best to create trouble in order to further their own interests by wiping out the competition.[8]

Perhaps the most risible of Bernis' claims was that religion had little to do with the violence that broke out in 1815. There can be little doubt that members of the Catholic and Protestant faiths lined up on opposite sides in 1815. Bernis was correct, however, in pointing to the complexity of factors leading to violence. Clashes between the citizens of Moustiers and Aiguines, for instance, probably had as much to do with communal rivalry as political or religious differences.[9]

Lewis has demonstrated that White Terror in the south was the product of personal and group rivalry, and religious, social and political animosity; it was the culminating blow in a power struggle which had been going on at least since 1789.[10] *Fédérés* were first in the line of attack because they were obvious targets for reprisal. There was nothing secretive about the federative movement in 1815, and those who participated in it were well known to their enemies. They knew this, and consequently many took flight when Bourbon government was restored. But those who could not, or would not, were left in a vulnerable position.

As soon as royalist forces gained control of the Basses-Alpes, in the first week of July, *fédéré* central committee members were rounded up at Digne and sent off to be kept under guard at Barcelonnette. Fortunately for these men, this was not a region where repression was characterised by brutality, and they were eventually freed of imprisonment, as well as the burden of their administrative positions (most of them had been tax-collectors). Few

---

[7] R. de Bernis, *Précis de ce qui s'est passé en 1815 dans les départements du Gard et de la Lozère* (Paris, 1818), pp. 4–5; Alleaume, 'Terreur', p. 12.
[8] De Bernis, *Précis*, pp. 4–5; Lewis, *Second Vendée*, pp. 182, 192–3, 204, 210; Alleaume, 'Terreur', pp. 5–7.
[9] De Bernis, *Précis*, p. 5; Alleaume, 'Terreur', p. 11.
[10] This is central to Lewis' *Second Vendée*, but see pp. 187–219 in particular.

fédérés could have emulated the audacity of Beau, author of the local federative pact, who in October 1815 presented himself at the prefecture announcing that he was ready to retake his old position and claiming to be 'un des plus dévoués du trône'. Everyone at Digne, most particularly the prefect, knew that Beau had been 'un des partisans les plus déterminés de l'usurpateur' and, of course, the *ex-inspecteur des contributions directes* was sent packing. This curious episode illustrates several aspects of the White Terror in this part of the south. Firstly, repression was official in character, but not bloody. Secondly, men such as Beau valued their positions above all else and might have been drawn away from opposition had the Bourbon Monarchy been able to accommodate their career aspirations. Finally, such men had compromised themselves far too much for Bourbon officials to risk returning them their old positions; this was to prove unfortunate in the long run, for it confirmed such men in their opposition.[11]

In places where the authorities did not intervene, the fate of *fédérés* could be grim. In towns such as Nîmes, Avignon and Montpellier, *fédérés* had to a certain extent brought this on themselves by their violent actions during the Hundred Days, but in the latter town government officials took pains to maintain order and succeeded. The confessional element was largely missing at Montpellier, but religion does not appear to have been an important factor in places such as Marseilles. Hence, the attitude of government officials was vital. Timely imprisonment perhaps saved the lives of some *fédérés*. However, arbitrary arrest and imprisonment merely simplified murdering them in Nîmes and Uzès. Nor did release from prison improve their safety, as fifteen murders in Nîmes proved in August 1815.[12]

We do not propose to recount all of the atrocities committed against *fédérés*, which would require several dismal volumes. Rather, we shall focus on certain centres in order to assess the degree of violence inflicted. While taking the virulence of White Terror into account, it should be kept in mind that news of this soon reached other parts of France. The inability or unwillingness of certain officials appointed by the Duke of Angoulême to control anarchy in the south would do much to undermine the more constructive efforts of officials elsewhere.[13]

---

[11] C. Cauvin, 'Le Retour de l'Ile d'Elbe et les Cent-Jours dans les Basses-Alpes', *Bulletin de la société scientifique et littéraire des Basses-Alpes*, 22 (1928), p. 73.

[12] Lewis, *Second Vendée*, pp. 177–86, 194–5, 200–2, 210, 212–13; J.-P. Thomas, *Précis historique des événements arrivés à Montpellier pendant les Cent-Jours de l'Interrègne* (Paris, 1976); J.-J. Hémardinquer, 'Un Libéral: F.-B. Boyer-Fonfrède (1767–1845)', *Annales du Midi*, 73 (1961), pp. 178–82.

[13] See G. Ribe's comments on the impact of southern White Terror in the east in his *L'Opinion publique et la vie politique à Lyon lors des premières années de la Seconde Restauration* (Paris, 1957), p. 212.

Some of the worst outrages were committed in Marseilles, but as there was no federation in that city, we shall focus our attention elsewhere. Not having sated themselves in Marseilles, royalists marched to Toulon, which had been evacuated by Marshal Brune and his troops in early August. No longer intimidated by Bonapartist soldiers, royalist officials in Toulon purged the National Guard and began house searches. Numerous arbitrary arrests took place and Aurel and Gosse, who had helped draw up the federative pact, were among the victims. Angry mobs began to pillage and some one thousand citizens fled Toulon. The Marseillais who established themselves in Beausset, a suburb of Toulon, attacked *fédérés*, but local authorities intervened to save the latter. *Fédérés* seeking to return to Toulon in October 1815 were subject to mass attack. Some of these *fédérés*, having left their livelihoods behind, turned to brigandage on the roads to Marseilles and Draguignan. In December 1815 this led the police commander of Toulon to suggest lifting all proscriptions on *fédérés* so that they would return home, where they could be kept under close watch. Other officials objected, however, arguing that this would lead to further disturbances. In the third week of December, the mayor of La Cordière, just outside Toulon, learned of a meeting of *fédérés*. A detachment of National Guardsmen sent to arrest the participants exchanged gunfire with them, but the *fédérés* escaped through a back door into a nearby wooded area. Toulon returned to an uneasy calm in 1816, despite various rumours threatening massacre of all *fédérés*. News of the Didier conspiracy of Grenoble, however, led to the expulsion of five Bonapartists, and as late as September 1816 the mayor of La Cordière was protecting royalists who destroyed the property of *fédérés*.[14]

Although a *fédéré* named Barbot assaulted a monarchist on 3 August 1815, and subsequently was found to possess a tricolour embroidered with the words 'L'Empereur ou la mort!', Draguignan remained relatively calm. Nevertheless, royalists were known to run the streets yelling 'à bas les fédérés', and the prefect believed that to have forced *fédérés* to return from their hideouts in the countryside would have been tantamount to signing their death warrants. In April 1816, measures were still being taken to stop young men from threatening *fédérés* with slaughter. Intimidation was one thing, however, bloody reprisals were quite another.[15]

Many *fédérés* shared the sad fate of Marshal Brune in Avignon. As late

[14] Gaffarel, 'Marseille', pp. 240–87; Resnick, *Terror*, pp. 7–15; Alleaume, 'Terreur', pp. 7–10; AN, F^7 3735–6, bulletins of 2 October and 17 December 1815, 3 January and 22 February 1816, F^7 3737, bulletins of 22 April and 29 May 1816, F^7 3738, 22–3 September 1816.

[15] AN, F^7 3735, bulletin of 14 August 1815, F^7 3736, bulletin of 20 January 1816, F^7 3737, bulletin of 7 May 1816, F^7 3786, bulletin of 6 October 1816.

as 13 July 1815, soldiers and the *fédérés* of Avignon, reinforced by recruits from nearby Protestant communes, remained in control of the city, despite a hostile populace. When General Cassan learned of the return of Louis XVIII to Paris, he met with the *fédérés* and proposed recognition of the royal government. When the *fédérés* refused, he and his troops evacuated the city, taking most of the saner *fédérés* with them. Those foolish enough to remain experienced three months of arbitrary arrest, pillage and assassination. Royalist *miquelets* systematically slaughtered *fédérés* both inside and outside the city. By 27 July, at least 130 reputed *fédérés* had been arrested and imprisoned by men who held no civil authority. Several *fédérés* were executed before reaching prison. One officer of the National Guard claimed to have trained his horse to walk on *fédérés* and bragged of having murdered seventeen of them. Such men were able to act with impunity because royalist officials were either unwilling or unable to restrain them.[16]

It is difficult to believe a report of the prefect of the Vaucluse that *fédérés* were still bringing about reprisals by their provocative actions as late as 21 August. On the other hand, his report that disarmament of *fédérés* in the countryside was being conducted with alacrity is entirely credible. *Fédérés* were reported to be in danger as late as December, although they had submitted fully to the authorities. Arbitrary arrests were still being conducted by unauthorised members of the National Guard. In January 1816, the authorities continued to wring their hands at their inability to stop popular vengeance against *fédérés*. Of course most leading *fédérés*, including Agricole Moreau, had long since departed. Even so, their reputations continued to dog them. Moreau had taken flight for the Drôme, from whence he was expelled by the commander of the *gendarmerie*. Having returned to his residence in Paris he was, in April 1816, banished to Rouen, where he was kept under the surveillance of a prefect fully informed of his past.[17]

Perhaps life for *fédérés* was even more perilous in Nîmes or Uzès during this period. In Nîmes, the *commissaire de police* was certainly implicated in the atrocities committed by the notorious Trestaillons. In Uzès, Quatretaillons went about the grisly business of slaughtering *fédérés*, Bonapartists and Protestants with no hindrance from the authorities whatsoever. Both of these gentlemen expanded their theatre of operations into nearby communes, using *miquelets* who had entered the National Guard in support. Repeated scenes of arbitrary arrest, pillage and murder took place through-

[16] Resnick, *Terror*, pp. 18–19; H. Houssaye, *1815 – La Terreur Blanche* (Paris, 1909), pp. 350–61; AN, F⁷ 3786, bulletins of 3 and 8 August.
[17] AN, F⁷ 3786, bulletin of 27 August 1815, F⁷ 3735, bulletins of 17 November, 6 and 11 December 1815, F⁷ 3736, bulletins of 15 and 27 January 1816; APP, A A/331, 400–24.

out the Gard from July to December 1815. Protestants and *fédérés* fled
Nîmes and Uzès *en masse*. Naturally the café *L'Ile-d'Elbe*, favoured
watering-hole of the *fédérés* of Nîmes, was sacked. While pamphlets
circulated calling for vengeance on *fédérés*, *gardes royales* used orders for
disarmament of *fédérés* as a pretext for pillage, and owners of *biens
nationaux* had their lands seized. 'Royalists' from Bouillarques and Garons
travelled to the villages of Générac and Beauvoisin, 'habités par des
hommes notoirement connus par leur haine contre la royauté et leur
dévouement à Napoléon ou à la fédération' in order to demand a 'contribution' of 20,000 francs, half of which was promised. Members of the
National Guard of Nîmes claimed fifteen victims on 1 August, but failed to
execute their plans for a prison massacre. The *commissaire de police*
explained that assassinations were motivated by 'le défaut de punition des
prisonniers chefs de fédéralistes'. *Miquelets* in Uzès enjoyed greater success, shooting six defenceless *fédérés* whom they had taken from prison.
Later in the month, sixteen men just released from prison were murdered
in Nîmes. At the same time, *fédérés* were slaughtered in Générac;
apparently the ransom money had not sufficed. One Nîmes *fédéré* was
somewhat more fortunate than the rest. Despite being dragged from his
home into the street, robbed, stabbed with sabres and left for dead, he
managed to recover in prison after being found by a police officer. The
president of the federation, Etienne Paris, was more fortunate still, for he
was only imprisoned and then put under police surveillance outside the
Gard.[18]

Fualdès, organiser of the federation of the Aveyron, was not so fortunate.
Rodez, capital of the department, was not the scene of massacres during the
White Terror; indeed, the populace was largely Bonapartist. Although he
had several dangerous enemies, Fauldès was able to survive until April
1816 with only the loss of his position as *procureur* and the office of
municipal councillor. Because threats had been made on his life, he did not
leave his house during the evening. But on one fatal occasion he fell into a
trap set for him by royalist *égorgeurs* who slit his throat and threw his
corpse into the Aveyron. With the apparent complicity of the Minister of
Police Decazes, royalist officials arranged a subsequent trial which led to
the conviction and execution of three innocent men, allowing the actual
murderers to go free. Subsequent trials produced results that were no more
just.[19]

---

[18] *Ibid.*, F⁷ 3735, bulletin of 5 December 1815, F⁷ 3786, bulletins of 2 and 21 August 1815;
Lewis, *Second Vendée*, pp. 194–5, 197, 200–8, 222; Daudet, *Terreur*, pp. 366, 375, 377–8,
384.
[19] H. Enjalbert, ed., *Histoire de Rodez* (Toulouse, 1981), pp. 210, 214–24.

Montpellier was a place where mass reprisals might have been expected; here *fédérés* were a small minority in a royalist bastion. Moreover, in June and early July *fédérés* themselves had murdered and pillaged. But royalist officials took pains to prevent confrontation and sought to repress opponents of the regime by legal means. An order of the Marquis de Montcalm, *commissaire du roi*, cited a list of men to be imprisoned and appeared to herald rough justice:

considérant qu'il est notoire que plusiers *fédérés* de la ville de Montpellier et du département ont, dans les journées des 27 juin et 2 juillet derniers, fait feu sur des citoyens paisibles et sur des femmes, que d'autres se sont renfermés dans la citadelle avec les rebelles, qu'ils ont participé à la défence contre l'autorité légitime.

The order was subsequently annulled, but many of the men listed were thereafter tried by the *cour prévôtale* of Montpellier.

M. Vidal has neatly summarised the *raison d'être* of the *cours prévôtales* as follows: 'il s'agit de mener à bien une vaste opération de police politique contre les hommes de Cent-Jours et d'enricher l'arsenal des mesures de répression'. At Montpellier the court was to prove first and foremost an instrument of reprisal. Among thirty-nine men from Montpellier who were judged, fourteen *fédérés* suffered the harshest verdicts. Five were condemned and executed. One was sentenced to perpetual forced labour and another received ten years imprisonment. Five others were meted out fines and ten years of police surveillance; among them was Demoulin, central committee member. Thus, the severity of the judgements gave Montpellier authorities a black reputation which largely negated the positive effects of having prevented mass violence. Neither Bonapartist nor republican agitation in the Hérault ceased as a result; the latter cause was probably aided by the *fédéré* who shouted 'Vive la République!' immediately before decapitation. The spirit of the exiled Cambon lived on.[20]

Miquelets were able to operate with such abandon in Nîmes, Uzès and Avignon because many royalist officials were in league with them. Indeed, both groups acted under the direction of ultra-royalists based in Toulouse. Nevertheless, Toulouse was not the scene of comparable atrocities. Despite the fact that General Ramel was assassinated, perhaps due to the instructions of a Toulousain royalist committee, Toulouse *fédérés* were subject to no more than beatings and imprisonment.[21]

This was all the more significant in that General Decaen had kept

[20] M. Vidal, 'La Cour Prévôtale du département de l'Hérault', *Annales du Midi*, 87, 123 (July–September 1975), pp. 290–311; Thomas, *Montpellier*, pp. 44–5; G. Weill, 'L'idée républicaine en France pendant la Restauration', *Revue d'histoire moderne*, 2 (1927), p. 327.
[21] Lewis, *Second Vendée*, p. 191.

Toulousain royalists in a state of terror even after the Provisional Government had capitulated to the Allies and Louis XVIII had returned to Paris. *Fédérés* themselves had not been entirely free of violent actions.[22] Although he referred to the federation as 'un club incendiare compris de quelques forcenés qui s'etoient associé sous le nom des *fédérés* toute la plus vile canaille', Prefect Rémusat ultimately emerged as something of a moderating influence in Toulouse. However, during the period of 17 July–13 August, Rémusat exercised no authority whatsoever; government was directed by an ultra-royalist committee attached to the Duke of Angoulême, whom the King had granted extraordinary powers in the Midi. One of the central figures of the ultra-royalist committee, Léopold de Rigaud, published several proclamations on 17 and 18 July. The first gave a good indication of what was to come:

> Vous avez vu, Braves habitants du Midi, comment ces hommes pervers ont trompé sa clémence; vous les avez vus, couverts du sang des amis du Trône et de l'Autel, s'envelopper pendant dix mois du voile de l'hypocrisie, pour venir achever les débris échappés à leur rage. Vous avez vu les satellites du monstre, après avoir ravagé sous ses ordres les plus belles contrées du Monde, appeler sur notre Patrie la vengeance des Nations.

In case there was any doubt as to the identity of these 'hypocrites' who had abused the 'clemency' of Louis XVIII during the First Restoration, a second proclamation clarified matters:

> Considérant que les corps armés, connus sous le nom des *fédérés*, formés pendant les trois mois d'anarchie qui viennent de déchirer la France, sont justement regardés comme les auteurs et les principaux fauteurs de tous les désordres qui ont accompagné ces temps de désastre, et que la plupart des membres qui composent ces corps, restent encore munis des armes que la trahison mit dans leurs mains.

Fédérés were then ordered to turn in their guns within twelve hours; failure to comply led to immediate arrest and trial. *Fédérés* who did not possess arms were ordered to register the fact at the *mairie*, also within twelve hours. Thus *fédérés* were signalled as the principal targets of reaction.[23]

Boyer-Fonfrède, president of the federation of the Midi, immediately protested against de Rigaud's ordinance, calling for an orderly disarmament which would not prove a pretext for revenge; he then had the good sense to go into hiding. From his hiding place, he had the mixed pleasure of listening to crowds calling for him to be hanged; not far away his house was

---

[22] *Ibid.*, p. 194; Resnick, *Terror*, pp. 29–30; Houssaye, *1815 – La Terreur Blanche*, p. 474; AN, F⁷ 9659, Prefect to Minister of the Interior, 16 July 1815.

[23] The proclamation of de Rigaud can be found in AN, F⁷ 9569; see also Prefect to Minister of the Interior, 20 July 1815.

being ransacked. He was able to get a letter to Fouché, who in turn instructed Rémusat to put Boyer-Fonfrède under his protection. Rémusat, after conferring with Mayor Joseph de Villèle (a member of the ultra-royalist committee), therefore threw Boyer-Fonfrède into prison.

During the period when the Duke's men were in control, pillaging and unauthorised arrests were very much the order of the day, and *fédérés* who wished to avoid physical assault remained behind locked doors, though this did not always suffice. A military commission was set up to judge *fédérés*, who were arrested *en masse* by members of the *corps secrets*, a makeshift royalist army rapidly mobilised after Decaen had departed Toulouse. The *verdets*, as they became known after they had donned uniforms in the Duke's colours, executed the directives of the ultra-royalist committee with such excessive enthusiasm that even moderate royalists began to take fright. General Ramel went so far as to criticise *verdet* leaders for their actions and refused their demands for guns, cannons and salaries because he did not consider them part of the King's army; in consequence, he was assassinated in brutal fashion. When news finally arrived on 13 August that Angoulême's extraordinary powers had been terminated and that his appointments were no longer valid, the King's representatives began the process of restoring order to an anarchic Toulouse.[24]

Part of Rémusat's problem thereafter lay in the fact that local officials remained inclined to follow the directions of the ultra-royalist committee rather than those of the King's prefect. Moreover, ultra-royalists could still rely on the *verdets* to carry out their orders. When judges failed to reach suitable verdicts, for example, they were threatened by *verdets* in a way which convinced them of the necessity of rigour. All of this gave Rémusat ample fodder for continuous lamentations to the Minister of the Interior, but it should be noted that while the prefect was far from condoning the *verdets'* more extreme actions, he nonetheless thought the *verdets* useful.

In several replies to ministerial inquiries about the possibly grievous effects of White Terror in Toulouse, Rémusat took pains to clarify what his policy had been during the initial four months of his tenure. On his arrival in mid-July, he had found that 'une faction bien exaltée et très dangereuse venait d'être comprimée par l'heureux retour du roi. Il était d'une indispensable necessité de la tenir dans cet état de compression.' As he lacked the normal means of maintaining this 'compression', he had not taken any actions against the *verdets*, because they inspired 'un juste effroi aux ennemis du gouvernement royal'. This remained Rémusat's strategy until

---

[24] Hémardinquer, 'Boyer-Fonfrède', pp. 177–9; J. Loubet, 'Le gouvernement toulousain du duc d'Angoulême après les Cent-Jours', *La Revolution Française*, 64 (1913), pp. 149–65, 337–66.

at least late December 1815:

> Je ne saurais, monseigneur, trop le répéter, l'audace du parti révolutionnaire est extrême, elle n'a été jusqu'à présent comprimée que par la terreur que lui ont inspirée les associations formées pour le triomphe de la cause royale; et si pour ramener l'ordre légal on avait à sévir contre les personnes qui ont fait partie de ces associ-ations, il n'y a pas de doute que les factieux n'en tirassent un grand avantage.

Thus, even the King's man saw fit to leave opponents of the Bourbons largely to the tender mercies of the *verdets* and their directors.[25]

Bertier de Sauvigny's contention that bloodshed was avoided in Toulouse 'because the officials had the good idea to throw into prison all those who might have been the objects of reprisal' seems highly doubtful. Incarceration may well have served to protect Boyer-Fonfrède during the first weeks of August, but thereafter it was an excuse for ignoring Fouché's demands that the president of the federation be released. Nor could 'pro-tection' have been the cause of detaining the *fédérés* Peloux, Projet and Roussel until December 1816. In truth, imprisonment of leading *fédérés* in Toulouse served the same end as elsewhere in France – political repression. Moreover, prisons were not a great barrier to royalist mobs elsewhere in the south, and Rémusat's correspondence made clear that his authority was insufficient to stop *verdets* from doing pretty much what they wanted. Equally clear from his correspondence was his fear concerning the strength of the opposition, and herein we can find a reason for the absence of mass murder in Toulouse.[26]

It would have been difficult to ensure the safety of some 1,800 *fédérés*, many of whom retained their arms, through imprisonment. On the other hand, attempts at mass slaughter would have run the risk of serious reprisals from a large and dangerous force. Local Toulousain officials, such as Villèle, did not want this, nor was it in the interests of *verdets* to provoke a *guerre à l'outrance* which would have produced serious losses on both sides. It was one thing to harass individual *fédérés* and extort money from them, it was another to attack the opposition *en masse*. Moreover, two vital components of White Terror were absent at Toulouse. Firstly, the com-bustive religious element was lacking; there were no indications of a strong

[25] AN, F⁷ 9659, *Président du Collège d'Arrondissement de Toulouse* to Minister of the Inte-rior, 16 August 1815 and Prefect to Minister of the Interior, 9, 10, 11, 21, 28 November, 14, 16, 19 and 23 December 1815.

[26] G. de Bertier de Sauvigny, *The Bourbon Restoration* (Philadelphia, 1966), p. 119. See also H. Ramet, *Histoire de Toulouse* (Toulouse, 1935), p. 850, the correspondence concerning Boyer-Fonfrède in AD H-G, 4M35, and 4M40, Minister of Police to Prefect, 24 October 1816.

Protestant element within the Toulouse federation. Secondly, Toulouse had not inherited a particularly bloody tradition from the Revolution, despite the fact that it had been a republican stronghold until the *coup d'état* of *Brumaire*. Rather like the Dijonnais, Toulousains had been wise enough to avoid mass bloodshed throughout the Revolutionary period and, with few exceptions, *fédérés* had acted within this tradition even while exercising Terror. As a result of all these factors, *verdets* carried out White Terror within certain historically defined bounds, and we should not allow ourselves to be misled by the assassination of General Ramel into thinking that Toulouse was comparable to Nîmes, Marseilles or Avignon in the period following the Hundred Days.[27]

While gradually bringing the *corps secrets* under control by incorporating them into the National Guard, Rémusat conducted the usual administrative purge, convinced that clemency should not be extended to those whose positions gave them influence within society. He was particularly determined to weed out judges who were inflicting unduly harsh sentences due to fear and desire to maintain their positions. The prefect's policy was neatly summarised in a circular dispatched to the communal mayors:

> Vous connaissez, Messieurs, la conduite qu'a tenue chacun de vos administrés. Les événements du mois de mars et leur funeste suite ont mis a découvert les principes politiques de chaque individu, et l'on ne peut plus se méprendre sur les habitants qui sont restés fidèles et sur ceux qui ont trahi leur devoir, soit avec une volonté déterminé, soit par faiblesse.
>
> Mais ne vous y trompez pas, Messieurs, le respect que l'on doit avoid pour la Loi d'amnistie n'exclu pas une surveillance attentive et sévère à l'égard des personnes dont le royalisme n'est pas bien reconnu; leurs démarches, leurs actions, leurs relations, leurs propos doivent être soigneusement observés, afin de distinguer les répentents des incorrigibles. Indulgence pour les premiers, inflexible sévérité pour les autres.

This was plain speaking; men would be judged by their actions during the Hundred Days and those who had chosen the wrong side would not just be removed from authority, but also kept under close watch. Men who had not been royalists prior to the First Restoration, but had not compromised

---

[27] On the relatively moderate behaviour of Toulousains during the Revolutionary period, see M. Lyons, 'The Jacobin élite of Toulouse', *European Studies Review*, 7, 3 (July 1977), p. 261 and P. Wolff, ed., *Histoire de Toulouse* (Toulouse, 1964), pp. 389–431. Money appears to have motivated the *verdets* at least as much as royalism. Ramel, if anything a moderate royalist, was assassinated after refusing to agree that the *verdets* should be paid as part of the Army. Lasmartier, 'because he had been a *fédéré*', was forced to disgorge 600 francs; Rémusat viewed this as simple robbery. See the correspondence concerning the assassination of Ramel in AN, F^7 9659, and Prefect to Minister of the Interior, 9 and 13 January 1816.

themselves during the Hundred Days, would be given every encouragement to confirm their loyalty. Such a policy was good news for those owners of *biens nationaux*, civil servants and soldiers who had been shrewd enough not to support the Emperor, but it held little solace for *fédérés* – whose opinions had been all too apparent. Not surprisingly, then, such individuals continued to dream only of 'la République ou le règne de l'Usurpateur'.[28]

Ultimately, Rémusat was successful in bringing order back to Toulouse, in part because he was wisely sceptical of the numerous personal denunciations accepted by military officials. But, as his replacement noted in May 1817, not all of the results of Rémusat's administration were fortunate. Many of the officials appointed by Rémusat were ultra-royalist extremists little inclined to follow the path of moderation. The nobility and clergy had regained their old ascendancy and were inclined to ignore the directions of the King's representative; witnesses to the assassination of General Ramel were still being threatened by *verdets*. Students, especially student *demi-soldes*, had emerged as a constant source of trouble and, more importantly, as late as November 1817 Toulouse remained divided, though war was now waged through songs and parodies. Attempts to reconstruct unity had obviously failed, and every café and billiard hall was the exclusive terrain of one of the various parties – ultras, constitutional monarchists, Bonapartists or republicans.[29]

There are few indications of mass reprisals in other parts of south-western France. There appears to have been some hostility in Perpignan, where petitions against *fonctionnaires* who had signed the federative pact or owned *biens nationaux* were being circulated. Several leading *fédérés* were brought to trial in January 1816; others had chosen to go into hiding, but there is no mention of mob violence in police reports.[30]

At Albi, one of the first actions of the prefect J.-L. Decazes was to have *fédéré* membership investigated throughout the Tarn. Several arrests resulted and a commission was established to interrogate suspects, but the authorities could never quite place their hands on *fédéré* registers. The mayor of Albi could not say what had become of them, nor could his *adjoint* who, curiously enough, disappeared the morning after being questioned by the committee. Local wags commented that he had been struck by 'Terreur Panique' and that he suffered from 'Bonapartisme chronique';

[28] AN, F⁷ 9659, Minister of the Interior to Prefect, 30 November 1815 and Prefect to Minister of the Interior, 14 and 16 December 1815, 18 January and 23 April 1816.

[29] *Ibid.*, Prefect to Minister of the Interior, 14 May 1816, 28 May, 12 November and 1 December 1817.

[30] *Ibid.*, F⁷ 3736, bulletins of 24 January and 4 February 1816, F⁷ 3737, bulletin of 15 June 1816.

doubtless he had gone off to burn the registers. Fabre, when called before the commission, claimed that although he had been the *fédéré* secretary, he had never actually fulfilled that function and, moreover, the *fédérés* had never been armed. He was playing fast and loose with the truth in the latter regard and it is perhaps permissible to suspect that he was being excessively modest in the former. Despite the diffidence of other *fédérés* who claimed they had been forced to join by the Imperial prefect, the federation remained a symbol of opposition throughout the White Terror. In May 1816, placards were posted at Gaillac reading 'Vive Napoléon II, vivent les fédérés! A mort les nobles!' Protestants and Catholics clashed outside a café in Mazamet after a group of the latter had shouted 'A bas les fédérés!', but the fight was easily broken up by the *gendarmerie* and neither the police nor the prefect saw fit to arrest any of the combatants. The *fédérés* of the Tarn had remained circumspect during the Hundred Days and this goes a long way towards explaining why the department saw none of the violence experienced in the Gard, but we should also note that Bonapartism was rife amongst the masses. Royalism here lacked the necessary popular base.[31]

Matters were much the same in the Dordogne. On his arrival, the royalist prefect du Hamel described Périgueux as a 'petite ville où il y a beaucoup de fédérés, et surtout un esprit très douteux'. Nor did he think highly of 'le tribunal de Sarlat en entier', which offered 'encore le pénible spectacle d'une réunion de fédérés buonapartistes investis du droit de défendre la cause des Bourbons'. Naturally, the prefect's suspicions also fell on soldiers and officers stationed in Périgueux. At least in regard to the capital, the prefect was well informed as to the identity of the most active and enthusiastic *fédérés*; as they had departed their assemblies the police officer Lavergne had taken care to jot down the names of the more vociferous. The department had rallied almost uniformly to the Emperor during the Hundred Days and there could be no question of any violent mass reprisals, so ultra-royalists bent on revenge had to rest content with the standard administrative purge. A fanatic royalist secret agent named Chrysostome kept the prefect well supplied with suggestions. Documentation was compiled on all the administrators of the department; one of the leading lines of investigation was whether an individual had been a *fédéré*. Among those to fall were Galaup, sub-prefect at Ribérac, and de Lacroiselle and de Belleyme,

[31] *Ibid.*, F⁷ 3737, bulletin of 25 October 1816; J. Vanel, 'Le Mouvement fédératif de 1815 dans le département du Tarn', *Gaillac et le pays tarnais, 31ᵉ congrès d'études de la fédération des sociétés académiques et savantes de Languedoc-Pyrénées-Gascogne* (Gaillac, 1977), pp. 387–95; L. Curie-Seimbres, 'Joseph-Léonard Decazes et les derniers bonapartistes tarnais (1815–1819)', *Revue du Tarn, 3ᵉ série*, no. 81 (1976), p. 75.

councillors at the prefecture. Giry was kept under surveillance at Périgueux and Paul Dupont was exiled to Paris.[32]

In late December 1815, the prefect apparently gained information regarding a plot against leading government officials and ordered disarmament of the *fédérés* of Forges and Robier (both in the *arrondissement* of Périgueux). As a result, the doctor Dupuis was found to possess a hidden cache of three guns, several pistols and sabres, and a store of cartridges. If he was arrested, Dupuy was not long imprisoned, for there is a subsequent report of his activities in January 1816.[33]

Despite du Hamel's good intentions, he only made a nuisance of himself in trying to persecute men he suspected. By March 1816 he had been replaced by Baron Montureux, who commenced his tenure by drawing up a list of suspects 'les plus dangereux du département de la Dordogne et qu'il conviendrait d'envoyer en surveillance dans un autre département'. Among the list of seventeen exiled from the department, nine men were specifically identified as *fédérés*.[34]

In March 1816, Montureux had the anniversary of the death of the Duke of Enghien marked by a funeral service. Liberty trees in the department had already been uprooted and replaced by busts of the king. Despite such measures, and a *cour prévôtale* in Périgueux which meted out severe sentences to opponents of the regime, the *fédérés* of the Dordogne do not appear to have been intimidated by the government. More will be said on this subject in the following chapter. Ultimately, Montureux succeeded only in making himself as unpopular as his predecessor and, fortunately for the Dordogne, he was soon thereafter replaced by Pépin de Bellisle, who rapidly put an end to White Terror.[35]

Having discussed why royalist mob violence in the south was largely confined to Provence and the eastern extremities of Languedoc, an obvious question yet remains: why did violent White Terror not break out in other parts of France? After all, other regions inherited equally violent revolutionary legacies. Though not exactly a matter of confessional divisions, religion had certainly been an important factor in the battles between blues and whites in the west. This question can be broached by looking at the example of Lyons in the east, and the western departments in general.

Lyons offers a particularly instructive example of why *fédérés* in the east

---

[32] J. L'Homer, *Les Cent-Jours et la Terreur Blanche* (Paris, 1904), pp. 13–15, 18, 22–3; G. Rocal, *De Brumaire à Waterloo en Périgord* (Paris, 1942), I, pp. 253–4.

[33] G. Rocal, *La Seconde Restauration en Périgord* (Angoulême, 1956), pp. 19–33; F[7] 3735, bulletin of 31 December 1815, F[7] 3736, bulletin of 2 February 1816.

[34] L'Homer, *Les Cent-Jours*, pp. 28–34.

[35] *Ibid.*, pp. 34–7; Rocal, *Seconde Restauration*, pp. 33–9.

and north-east were not the victims of popular violence. Unlike Dijon, Lyons had experienced a great deal of brutality during the Revolution, and ultra-royalist societies, such as the *Chevaliers de Henri IV* and the Companies of Jesus and the Sun, were still operating in 1815. These gentlemen had not been averse to murder in the past, and they certainly did seek to create trouble in 1815–16, but there was no mass violence in Lyons during the White Terror. In part this was due to the commanding presence of General Bubna and his Austrian troops. But the federation had been popular in Lyons and there were more than enough *fédérés* to make attacks a risky proposition; royalism had lost its popular base and even the *chasseurs de Henri IV* of the Rhône numbered no more than 300 men drawn mostly from other departments. For these reasons, *fédérés*, Protestants and owners of *biens nationaux* fleeing the south often took refuge in Lyons, where they were assured 'de la bienveillance de la population'.[36]

The *fédérés* had been armed and organised and, under the command of General Mouton-Duvernet, had played their part in a defence of Lyons which lasted until 11 July 1815. When news of the disaster of Waterloo was made public on 24 June, *fédérés* thronged the streets, leading torchlit processions behind a bust of the *roi de Rome* and calling 'Vive l'Empereur!' They reacted even more forcibly when, on 14 July, they learned of the capitulation of Lyons, in part negociated by their president Jars. Forty cannons in the Place Bellecour were seized in order to continue resistance. Singing the *Marseillaise* and the *Chant du départ* and crying 'Nous sommes trahis! Mort aux royalistes! Vive l'Empereur!', groups of *fédérés* marched to the *hôtel de ville*, where a collision with the National Guard was only avoided because of the timely intervention of Teste, whose hatred of the Bourbons could not be doubted. *Fédéré* leaders opened discussions with General Bubna, who granted that the tricolour and Imperial officials would be maintained. This helped restore calm until 17 July, when Bubna allowed the Bourbon prefect Chabrol to proclaim restoration of the government of Louis XVIII. *Fédérés* then responded by threatening royalists wishing to plant the Bourbon standard; one such monarchist had his head chopped off and a second was wounded. The entry of Austrian troops put an end to anarchy; however, as Chabrol noted, *fédérés* were disconcerted by the change in circumstances, but did not consider themselves beaten.[37]

Thereafter, relations between the *fédérés* and Austrian occupiers were remarkably cordial. Not only did Bubna firmly oppose royalist designs on

---

[36] AN, F⁷ 3786, bulletin of 4 August 1815; F⁷ 9695, Prefect to Minister of the Interior, 21 September 1815; G. Ribe, *L'Opinion publique*, p. 90.

[37] AN, AFIV 1937, Duke of Albufera to Minister of War, 13 June 1815, F⁷ 9695, Prefect to Minister of the Interior, 19 July 1815; Houssaye, *1815 – La Terreur Blanche*, pp. 440–3; Ribe, *L'Opinion publique*, pp. 41–4.

the properties of *fédéré* leaders, he also kept an open door to *fédéré* deputies. In numerous reports, the prefect of the Rhône complained that *fédérés* were stating they would rather see Lyons detached from France than live under Bourbon rule. De Corcelles, commander of the National Guard and a leading member of the central committee of the federation, told the prefect that such was his desire. According to the prefect, leading *fédérés* in Grenoble were expressing the same sentiments to military authorities from Piedmont. It is difficult to determine the reliability of such reports; after all, *fédérés* had expressed their desire to fight Allied soldiers often enough during the Hundred Days. It may well be, however, that certain *fédérés* hated the Bourbons more than the Allies. Whatever the case, it is certain that *fédéré* leaders had several amicable interviews with Bubna, and any suggestions to incorporate parts of the Rhône and Isère into Savoy must have interested him. Perhaps *fédéré* esteem of the Austrian general had something to do with the opinion of Napoleon himself: at the commencement of the *voi d'aigle* Bonaparte had written to Marie-Louise, and it was to Count Bubna, then at Turin, that these letters were dispatched. Be that as it may, when in August the royalist lieutenant of police decided to prohibit a theatrical performance because one of the leading actors was a notorious *fédéré*, Bubna overrode this proscription and the play was duly performed, with a large number of Austrian soldiers maintaining order.

Given this situation, Prefect Chabrol had to act cautiously. In late November 1815 he offered to purchase the guns distributed during the Hundred Days. This measure produced few results, so he turned to the Army for the necessary house searches. Only after most, but not all, *fédérés* had been disarmed did royalist agitations become a problem, and these were not popular in nature. Some twenty members of a *corps de cannoniers* took to dressing up as National Guardsmen in order to threaten reputed opponents of the regime with cries of 'les fédérés à la potence!' and sabre rattling. They might have gone further, but local citizens made clear their disapproval. The young soldiers then took to assaulting individuals. Gailly, the *fédéré* actor whom Bubna had protected, was their first victim. Later they attacked the Duke of Bassano's brother, causing a good deal of consternation. These were acts of intimidation, but no murders resulted from them and the authorities were more worried about the reaction of opponents of the regime than about the assailants themselves. They had reason to be; as late as 1818 royalists were still subject to attacks by a hostile populace.[38]

---

[38] AN, F⁷ 3785, bulletins of 8 and 17 August 1815, 30 March, 11 and 12 April 1816, F⁷ 3737, bulletins of 2 May and 28 June 1816; Ribe, *L'Opinion publique*, pp. 203, 221–3, 279; Champollion-Figeac, *Fourier et Napoléon: L'Egypte et Les Cent-Jours* (Paris, 1844), p. 225.

In essence, there were simply too many *fédérés*, and too many men who sympathised with them, for extreme royalists to attempt any mass reprisals in Lyons. However, in the west, *fédérés* were in a very different situation. Yet here too, they were not subjected to mob violence.

There were several reasons for this. Breton *fédérés* had conducted themselves in a disciplined manner in their expeditions during the Hundred Days; they had not murdered or plundered. R. Grand, in his history of *chouannerie* in 1815, has concluded that this was a civil war fought within certain bounds; massacre and atrocity were eschewed. A large measure of credit for this could be attributed to the examples set by generals such as Lamarque and Bigarré and the soldiers under their command. Lamarque's conduct seems all the more laudable when contrasted with that of Gilly in the south. Nor did *fédérés* go beyond maintaining order during the difficult period following Napoleon's second abdication. Although they may have threatened royalists, they did not resort to violence. Finally, when royalist officials returned to their posts after the second restoration of Louis XVIII, *fédéré* leaders wisely recognised the futility of attempting to maintain power. This was more than could be said of their compatriots at Avignon and Nîmes.[39]

In towns such as Vannes, where monarchists clearly had the upper hand, *fédérés* had to endure the abuse of royalist volunteer soldiers who occasionally made house searches a pretext for pillage. But even in the Vendée, where isolated individual *fédérés* might well be subjected to beatings, revenge did not go so far as murder. *Fédérés* were fortunate in not having set any precedents in this regard.[40]

Matters were somewhat different in *fédéré* strongholds such as Rennes, Brest, Saint-Brieuc and Dinan. When royalist officials returned to these places, they found *fédérés* still very much in control. We have seen that D'Allonville, on his arrival at Rennes, found royalist volunteer forces threatening to invade the city, and have noted the actions taken by the prefect to defuse this explosive situation. Royalist prefects took similar measures throughout the west. To establish order, officials had simultaneously to bring both *fédérés* and royalist volunteers under control. The measures employed by Pépin de Bellisle, prefect of the Côtes-

---

[39] See the example of Dinan as described in AN, F⁷ 9650, Sub-prefect of Dinan to Minister of the Interior, 29 July 1815, and unsigned letter to the Minister of the Interior, 14 July 1815. On Lamarque and civil war without dishonour, see R. Grand, *La Chouannerie de 1815* (Paris, 1942), p. 251.

[40] AN, F⁷ 9682, Prefect to Commander General of the Morbihan, 11 January 1816; F⁷ 3736, bulletin of January 1816; F⁷ 3735, bulletin of 6 October 1815; A. Bouton, *Le Maine, histoire économique et sociale au XIXᵉ siècle* (Le Mans, 1974), pp. 211–13; E. Gabory, *Les Bourbons et La Vendée* (Paris, 1947), p. 5.

du-Nord, provide a good case-study of how officials went about this task.[41]

In late July 1815, both Saint-Brieuc and Dinan remained in the control of *fédérés*. Indeed, the flag of the Bourbons was not restored to its former eminence at Dinan until 24 July. Matters were complicated by the fact that the presence of a volunteer army in a nearby commune made *fédérés* more combative and gained them the support of more moderate citizens. To defuse this and an equally volatile situation in Saint-Brieuc, Bellisle followed a policy that involved three basic steps. He organised the National Guard by removing opponents of the government. This enabled him to use the National Guard for the maintenance of public order so that he did not need to have recourse to royalist volunteers. He also had royalist volunteers either disbanded or incorporated into the regular army, where they were forced to conduct themselves with greater discipline. Finally, he had the *fédérés* disarmed.[42]

Bellisle succeeded in restoring Bourbon authority without violence because he took these three steps simultaneously. It would have been exceedingly difficult to have disarmed the *fédérés* without armed conflict if measures had not been taken to bring royalist volunteers under control. Bellisle, D'Allonville and other western prefects deserve a good deal of credit for ensuring that Bourbon government was restored in the west without violence.

By combining these examples, we can fully explain why mass violence was restricted to the south during the White Terror. In the east and northeast, where the federative movement was strongest, there were simply too many *fédérés* and *fédéré* sympathisers for extreme royalists to embark on pillage and slaughter. Moreover, Allied troops were a further check to any such inclinations. Where the *fédérés* were not in such a strong position, as in the west, they were saved by the fact that they had conducted themselves with circumspection during the Hundred Days and had not attempted to oppose the restoration of Bourbon government immediately afterwards. Even in potential trouble-spots, such as Rennes, Saint-Brieuc and Dinan, violence was averted by the sage measures of Bourbon officials who took care to establish control over both *fédérés* and royalist volunteers.

---

[41] AN, F⁷ 9656, *Situation politique du département du Finistère à l'époque du mois de juillet 1815, suivie de celle à l'époque du mois de novembre même année*, F⁷ 3735, bulletin of 16 November 1815, F⁷ 9650, Sub-prefect of Dinan to Minister of the Interior, 27 July 1815, F⁷ 3735, bulletin of 26 November 1815, F⁷ 3737, bulletin of 8 May 1816.

[42] *Ibid.*, F⁷ 9650, Sub-prefect of Dinan to Minister of the Interior, 27 and 29 July 1815, unsigned letter to Minister of the Interior, 14 July 1815, Prefect to Minister of the Interior, 7 and 10 August, 8 November 1815.

Although *fédérés* in the north, east, west and centre of France were not subjected to violent White Terror, they did suffer a good deal of persecution. In order to reduce the threat posed by *fédérés*, Bourbon officials throughout France took certain basic steps. To remove the possibility of rebellion, *fédérés* were disarmed. To reduce their influence, *fédéré* leaders were removed from positions of local authority and the more radical were exiled. To intimidate *fédérés* of lesser influence, full use was made of the sedition laws.

This process unfolded in typical fashion at Grenoble. After capitulation on 9 July, those who took part in the defence of the city, particularly *fédérés*, were subjected to house searches, arrests and incarceration by the Austrians. Not unnaturally, Grenoblois who had been appointed during the Hundred Days lost their offices. On his arrival in early August, the new prefect Montlivault set about organising disarmament of *fédérés*. De Barral, the seventy-four year old *premier président à la cour d'appel* and vice-president of the federation, was summoned to the prefecture to explain his past actions. By mid-September, the combination of Bourbon and Austrian harassment had given rise to a deluge of anti-Bourbon propaganda, and in October Montlivault decided that removal of disloyal elements from the judiciary, *gendarmerie* and tax administration was necessary to 'improve' public opinion. Due to the obvious opposition of students at the law and medical schools, he was particularly concerned about the danger of confiding academic positions to 'des individus qui au lieu d'instruire et de former les sujets fidèles au roi et à l'état, déshonorent leur noble profession en infectant la jeunesse de leurs opinions et de leurs regrets'. In consequence, the Commission of Public Instruction dismissed Berriat Saint-Prix, Champollion *le jeune* and Bilan on the specific ground that they had been *fédérés*. For the same reason, central committee members de Barral, Reboul, Boissonet and Chanrion lost their government appointments.[43]

Agitation continued in the capital of the Isère, and the prefect therefore set about netting leading opponents. Aided by a *fédéré* turned informant, Montlivault hauled in five *fédérés* in late December, but his reports to the Minister of the Interior made clear that these men were but small fry. He drew up a list of bigger catches, and among seven individuals cited as worthy of exile were four members of the federative central committee:

---

[43] H. Dumolard, 'Grenoble au début de la Restauration', *Annales de l'Université de Grenoble (Lettres)*, 3 (1926), pp. 134–8; A. Rochas, *Biographie de Grenoble* (Paris, 1856–60); AN, F⁷ 9667, Prefect to Minister of the Interior, 6 August, 9 October, 31 December 1815 and 10 January 1816.

Ovide-Lallemand, Boissonet, Champollion *le jeune* and Bilan. Significantly, Montlivault reported that all seven had informed him of their submission to the Bourbon government, but he also added: 'en dernier analyse ils en sont les ennemis irréconciliables et ne seront soumis qu'autant qu'ils trouveront en danger à ne pas l'être'. In the prefect's estimation, the greatest prize would be Ovide-Lallemand, 'un ardent Révolutionnaire', dangerous because of his wealth and position. The *fédérés* Perrin, conspirator and rumour-monger, and Chavas, who had carried Napoleon's proclamation from Grenoble to Lyons during the *vol d'aigle*, would also be worth keeping out of circulation. Seizing upon various pretexts, such as the posting of Bonapartist placards, by April 1816 Montlivault had managed to rid Grenoble of Proby, a notary, Ovide-Lallemand, Perrin, Chavas and Champollion *le jeune*. As a result, he thought he could vouch for the security of Grenoble in the future. We shall have more to say on the latter subject when we discuss the Didier conspiracy in the following chapter.[44]

Although disarmament took place throughout France, it was not conducted in a uniform manner. This probably reflected the fact that the government was often incapable of conducting such exercises during the early months of the Second Restoration. In certain places, such as Vannes and Caen, royalist volunteers acting on their own initiative disarmed *fédérés*. Prussian troops carried out house searches at Vitré. However, procedures had been regularised by late 1815. The prefect ordered a general disarmament of *fédérés* in the Morbihan in January 1816, and this was conducted by the National Guard. At Nevers, where the federation had had a popular character, the upper middle-class National Guard, staunchly royalist, conducted the exercise. *Fédérés* found in possession of guns at Foix were judged by a military tribunal. House searches were still carried out by National Guardsmen in Lyons in March 1816.

Disarmament appears to have been conducted most thoroughly in the Haute-Garonne. When Boyer-Fonfrède was arrested, police officers were able to seize the registers of the federation of the Midi. Thus, authorities were able to identify *fédérés* who had been provisioned with guns, and royalist volunteer armies could be used to conduct house searches in points as distant as Blagnac and Salies. Although searches seldom uncovered guns, they led to numerous arrests.[45]

[44] AN, F⁷ 9667, Prefect to Minister of the Interior, 13, 19, and 23 March 1816.
[45] *Ibid.*, F⁷ 9682, Prefect to Commander General of the Morbihan, 11 January 1816, F⁷ 3736, bulletins of 17 January and 30 March 1816, F⁷ 3786, bulletin of 3 August 1815; E. Duminy, 'Nevers pendant les Cent-Jours', *Bulletin de la Société nivernaise des lettres, sciences et arts*, 11 (1906), p. 345; Duc de Castries, *La Terreur Blanche* (Paris, 1981), pp. 153–4; AD H-G, 4M35, Sub-Prefect of Toulouse to Prefect, 18 August 1815, Mayor of Salies to Prefect, 4 August 1815, Boyer-Fonfrède to Prefect, 14 August 1815.

Dismissal of *fédérés* from government and civil institutions was probably the simplest part of the process of undermining their influence. *Fédérés*, who could hardly be relied on for the enforcement of Bourbon government, were weeded out of the National Guard. *Fédéré* police officers, such as Roupe and Fossard at Lyons, Plain and Marchand at Toulouse, and Armand de la Moinière at Nevers, lost their positions for similar reasons. To ensure royal justice, *fédéré* judges were subjected to close attention and those who proved too lenient in political trials lost their posts. Magistrates too obviously compromised by their actions during the Hundred Days, such as Clerc at Besançon, and Rambaud, Vouty-de-la-Tour and Puthod at Lyons, were dismissed immediately.[46]

Wholesale changes were conducted in government administration. By 2 August 1815 all *fédérés fonctionnaires* had been dismissed at Privas and, for good measure, Baraillon, *inspecteur des forêts*, had been banished from the department of the Ardèche. Dubois, *employé au cadastre*, was escorted out of Saintes and directed never to return. The purge affected men in influential posts such as Guinet and Monnot *fils*, tax administrators at Mâcon and Besançon, and individuals who held less exalted positions, such as the two *fédéré* post office employees who were dismissed at Ploermel. Le Gorrec at Saint-Brieuc and Duleu at Nantes lost positions at the prefecture; Poullier became an *ex-commis à pied du droits réunis* and Séré was no longer *controleur de l'enregistrement* at Salies-du-Salat (Haute-Garonne). The government could also remove the licences on which certain *fédérés* depended, as fifty-eight *débitants de tabac* in the Morbihan discovered in January 1816. Finally, official disapproval could make the positions of *fédérés* dependent on public favour exceedingly tenuous. Vicherat, an actor at the *théâtre des Célestins* at Lyons, had made the mistake of carrying a bust of Napoleon in a *fédéré* street march. As a result, he lost his position and was forced to seek employment at Paris where he could find no work due to his 'reputation'. Ultimately, he was able to gain employment at Senlis where the police took care to watch over his social activities and political opinions.[47]

Administrative purges could not be conducted too rapidly, or government would have ground to a halt. Given this situation, prefects went about

[46]	AN, F⁷ 3737, bulletin of 20 August 1816, F⁷ 3028, *extrait des arrestations*, 506, 152, 580, F⁷ 9698, Minister of the Interior to Prefect, 3 January 1816; C. Weiss, *Journal 1815–1822* (Paris, 1972), pp. 187, 199; Ribe, *L'Opinion publique*, pp. VI–VII; AD H-G, 13M57 *bis*, *Etat de Police en exercice le 20 Mars 1815*.

[47]	AN, F⁷ 3735, bulletins of 2 and 14 August, 26 November 1815, F⁷ 3737, bulletin of 8 May 1816, F⁷ 9698, Prefect to Minister of the Interior, 15 October 1815, F⁷ 9682, Prefect to Minister of Police, 27 November 1815, F⁷ 3736, Prefect to Minister of the Interior, 14 March 1816, F⁷ 3028, *extrait des arrestations*, 556, 392, 238, 851, F⁷ 6630, *notes de police*, 242; AD I-et-V, 1M96, *Procureur du roi* to Prefect, 6 January 1816.

the task of removing *fédérés* in a gradual manner. This probably allowed some of the less compromised *fédérés* to make their peace with the Bourbon government and to avoid losing their occupations. However, the more compromised were dismissed immediately after the return of Louis XVIII and changes continued to be made well into 1816. Bellisle, for instance, began by removing *fédéré* mayors, municipal councillors and tax administrators in the Côtes-du-Nord. He then proceeded to lesser officials and was still conducting his purge in June 1816, taking care to secure competent replacements before making changes.[48]

In assessing the administrative aspect of White Terror, we should be careful not to impute the motive of these purges to simple revenge. Prefects such as Bellisle were far from being extremists, but they believed they were fighting for the very existence of the Monarchy. Given the extent of the federative movement and the attitude of the *fédérés*, this was perhaps more readily comprehensible than historians have generally recognised. Nor were administrative purges simply a matter of safeguarding against a second return of the Eagle. The example of Barrusseau, a *fédéré* of Nancy, is instructive in this regard. Despite being condemned for taking part in a *fédéré* attack on a royalist National Guardsman in late June 1815, Barrusseau was soon released. He drew the obvious conclusion and took part in another assault on monarchists celebrating the *fête* of Saint-Louis in August 1815. This time he was found innocent and again released. In order to prevent men such as Barrusseau from acting in this manner, it was imperative that the Bourbon government assure that *fédérés* no longer enjoyed 'la protection des pouvoirs publics'.[49]

Dismissal from office was a clear warning to *fédérés* of the danger of opposing the government. So too were trials of leaders such as Hernoux and General Veaux (see chapter 7). However, some of the more incorrigible *fédéré* leaders continued to express their opposition to the Monarchy and therefore the government resorted to arrest, trial, imprisonment and exile. The prefect of the Haute-Loire had three of Le Puy's leading *fédérés* exiled; Gayard and Bernardin were forced to leave Chaumont and reside outside the Haute-Marne. One of the founders of the federation of Dunkirk was imprisoned at Lille, and Theuillé, a merchant, was banished from Lyons. Losne-Rochelle, a *fédéré* leader at Vitré, and Dubois, president of the federation of Chalon-sur-Saône, were imprisoned. Le Gorrec, founder of the federation at Saint-Brieuc, was arrested for allegedly possessing a seditious

---

[48] AN, F⁷ 9650, Prefect to Minister of the Interior, 23 and 25 August 1815 and 26 June 1816, F⁷ 3737, bulletin of 20 June 1816.

[49] G. Richard, 'L'Esprit public en Lorraine au début de la Restauration', *Annales de l'Est*, série 5, *année* 4, no. 2 (1953), pp. 204–6.

pamphlet. Jamet, ex-justice of the peace, and Goussin, ex-officer of the *garde*, were arrested in the Maine. In the autumn of 1815, *fédérés* were also exiled from Angoulême and Lyons.[50]

The government's treatment of Chauchard, a Brestois *fédéré* and wealthy merchant, gives us an instructive example of how Bourbon officials sought to reduce the influence of *fédéré* leaders. When the prefect of the Côtes-du-Nord decided to exile Chauchard, the chamber of commerce of Brest officially protested. The prefect agreed that Chauchard could remain in Brest, provided that he abjured his federative oath. Chauchard refused to do so and therefore was sent on his way to Bordeaux. Along the way, he had the pleasure of spending a night in a prison at Saintes. After Chauchard had travelled to Bordeaux, a Saintes *fédéré* turned informer entered the prison in order to chat with some of his old friends. While there, the spy learned that the *fédérés* of Brittany were planning an uprising in March 1816. The prefect of the Gironde therefore decided to put all the men whom Chauchard contacted under close surveillance.[51]

Fédéré leaders prudent enough to forego overt manifestations of hostility to the Monarchy also came under the watchful eye of the authorities. At least twelve *fédérés* were kept under surveillance at Lorient. In certain instances police officers were directed to make their spying activities blatantly obvious in the hope that this would discourage opposition leaders from showing their faces in public. The isolation of troublesome individuals was, of course, part of a policy of preventing *fédérés* from continuing to act collectively. Such measures were especially difficult to implement at Nantes where, in a typical incident, Deslandes picked a fight with a royalist and shortly thereafter enjoyed the company of some twenty fellow *fédérés*. As a result of such incidents, several cafés in Nantes were forced to close. A number of *fédérés* responded by drawing up plans for an assault on the Café Molière, a favourite resort of young noblemen. Authorities therefore placed guards around the café and had lists of the most notorious *fédérés*

[50] AN, F⁷ 3785, bulletins of 3 August, 10 September and 20 November 1815, F⁷ 3735, bulletins of 3 and 20 December 1815, F⁷ 3736, bulletins of 16 and 19 January and 27 February 1816, F⁷ 3737, bulletins of 16 April and 20 June 1816, F⁷ 9650, Prefect to Minister of the Interior, 23 and 24 August 1815 and 26 June 1816, Bouton, *Le Maine*, p. 215; P. Jacquot, *Opposition et Terreur Blanche en Haute-Marne sous la Restauration* (Saint-Dizier, 1981).

[51] *Ibid.*, F⁷ 3735, bulletins of 29 November and 13 December 1815, F⁷ 3737, bulletin of 20 December 1816; J. Mouchet, 'L'Esprit public dans le Morbihan sous la restauration', *Annales de Bretagne*, 45 (1938), pp. 89, 129–30; E. Gabory, 'La Terreur Blanche dans l'ouest', *Revue des études napoléoniennes*, 7ᵉ année, 3 (1918), pp. 314–20, and by the same author, *La Vendée*, p. 3.

drawn up. Several native *fédérés* were exiled and all those who were not permanent residents were forced to depart.[52]

Among the instruments of repression at the prefect's disposal were the sedition laws, but the massive application of these makes one wonder whether they did more harm than good. Ultimately they probably did serve to regain a certain superficial appearance of stability, but it is doubtful whether they increased veneration of the Monarchy. Perhaps more dangerously, they prevented people from venting their frustrations in a manner which generally held little real threat. They also taught a lesson concerning how to go about opposition in the future. Nevertheless, it took some time for many *fédérés* to grasp the obvious conclusion. Baron *fils* was banished from Autun for creating troubles at the theatre. *Fédérés* at Saint-Brieuc chanted 'Vive l'Empereur!', attempted to replace the Bourbon flag with the tricolour, and insulted royalist soldiers in the streets in October 1815. Nuguet, a clerk, could not resist insulting National Guardsmen at Fougères in January 1817 and was finally arrested for shouting 'Vive l'Empereur!' in August of the same year.[53]

Despite the fact that their leaders had been exiled from Bourges in August 1815, *fédérés* were still insulting members of the National Guard with cries of 'Vive l'Empereur!' in April 1816. Exile of *fédérés* remained necessary in Limoges at the same time. Nor does the forced departure from Le Puy of *fédéré* leaders appear to have altered public opinion. A *colporteur* was arrested in Le Puy on 4 March 1816 and found to be carrying portraits of Napoleon and his family, a package of imitation crosses of the Imperial Legion of Honour, and metal eagles with the letter 'N' on them. Apparently there remained a demand for such items. *Fédérés* continued to predict the imminent fall of the government at least until May 1816.[54]

In one instance, persistent *fédéré* agitation led a prefect to take one repressive step too many. Troubled by Bonapartist exploitation of economic misery in the Meurthe, Comte de Kersaint requested the service of a secret agent of the Minister of Police in July 1816. When Dechazeaux arrived at Nancy, he duly infiltrated a lodge of Freemasons and subsequently drew up a list of suspects which included the *fédérés* Duvey, a *colporteur*, and Voirin, an artisan. Although the following house searches

[52] The application of these laws has been made the basis of a study of Popular Bonapartism during the Second Restoration in B. Ménager, *Les Napoléon du peuple* (Paris, 1988), pp. 15–40, 61–9. On *fédéré* sedition, see AN, F⁷ 3535, bulletins of 24 October and 28 November 1815 and AD I-et-V, 1M97, dossier Nuguet.

[53] AN, F⁷ 3784, bulletins of 4 and 10 September 1815, F⁷ 3736, bulletins of 7 April, 13 March and 2 May 1816, F⁷ 3737, bulletin of 19 May 1816.

[54] G. Richard, 'Une conspiration policière à Nancy en 1816', *Annales de l'Est*, année 10, no. 3 (1959), pp. 173–88.

led to several arrests, in the subsequent trial it was revealed that Dechazeaux had attempted to provide his suspects with guns. The work of this *agent provocateur* became an embarrassment to the government, no imprisonments resulted and de Kersaint had to be removed from his post. There were limits as to how far government officials could go and these were more narrowly defined in the east than elsewhere.[55]

More effective were the measures taken against the most notorious *fédérés*. Old regicides who had rallied to Napoleon in 1815 were not included in the Amnesty Law of January 1816 and prefects therefore undertook to discover whether they had voted for the *Acte Additionnel* or accepted government office during the Hundred Days. As a result, men such as Monnot at Besançon were condemned to external exile. In February he departed for Switzerland, though not before being treated to insults by young royalist officers. Within two months Monnot had been caught trying to sneak back into France. Unfortunately for the aged regicide, the man whom his son had hired to care for him turned out to be a spy of the prefect. However, Monnot was to prove more fortunate than most regicides and in January 1819 was allowed to return to the *patrie*; he was much too decrepit to pose a problem any longer.[56]

Thus *fédérés* were earmarked for White Terror. We should not overstate the extent to which they were persecuted however; the vast majority of *fédérés* were not directly harmed, either in their persons or interests, by the return of Louis XVIII. Physical violence was largely confined to certain trouble-spots in Provence and Languedoc. In other parts of France rank-and-file *fédérés* were not made to suffer, provided they kept their opinions to themselves. On the other hand, *fédéré* leaders were dismissed from government posts all over France and were subjected to a great deal of harassment by prefects, police officers and military officials. In the latter regard, they shared the experience of less prominent *fédérés* who could not resist the temptation to voice their hostility to the Monarchy.

To a certain extent, the Monarchy was caught in a trap. It could not retain in office men who had publicly avowed their opposition, but the very necessity of assuring that administration was placed in safe hands led it, in far too many places, to fall back on the unquestionably loyal men who had previously prepared the way for Napoleon's *vol d'aigle* by their intransigence. The ultra-royalist answer to opposition proved to be White Terror. Repression had a certain short-term merit and even moderate monarchists

---

[55] G. Richard, 'Une Conspiration policière à Nancy en 1816', *Annales de l'Est, année* 10, no. 3 (1959), pp. 173–88.
[56] Weiss, *Journal*, pp. 95, 102, 235.

made extensive use of the laws of exception in their efforts to restore royal order. Definitions of sedition proved very broad indeed, and one could see in this the over-reaction of a fragile regime.

Extensive repression was possible because of the Allied power behind the throne; even the legal aspects of White Terror could not have been executed otherwise. But the threat of further Allied intervention could not negate resistance forever, nor was repression the means of gaining the popular support necessary to found a stable regime. Wishing to gain the affection of all his subjects, Louis XVIII dismissed the *Chambre Introuvable* in September 1816, and set a course of moderate government in the hope of creating a France united in loyalty to constitutional monarchy. What would be the response?

Chapter 11

Fédérés *and opposition to the Bourbon Monarchy during the Second Restoration*

That *fédérés* of Dijon and Rennes remained at the forefront of opposition during the Second Restoration emerges clearly from the preceding case-studies, but the question remains whether these men were typical. Did *fédérés* elsewhere also react to repression by participating in the three main lines of resistance: rebellion, conspiracy and, when these failed, 'constitutional' Liberal Opposition?

The central objective of the federative movement during the Hundred Days had been to prevent reinstallation of the Bourbon Monarchy. After the Provisional Government's capitulation in July 1815, this cause was lost and *fédérés* had little choice but to admit the fact. After all, they were hardly capable of opposing the Allied forces victorious over the French Army at Waterloo. The man around whom they had united had again gone into exile, and federative assemblies had to cease. *Fédérés* entered a period of disarray and the more compromised, such as Azaiis at Nancy, had to take flight or go into hiding, as did Boyer-Fonfrède at Toulouse.

It took some time for Bourbon officials to regrasp the reigns of control. Along with containing anarchy in parts of the south, avoiding civil war in the west, preventing rebellion in the east, and controlling the remnants of the Imperial Army stationed south of the Loire, government representatives had to deal with the demands of the Allies. In certain places Allied commanders were reluctant to grant Bourbon officials any authority whatsoever; in most places their requisitioning and outright plunder caused the government serious problems. In much of France during the period of July–August, it was not just the opposition that was in disarray.

As order was slowly restored and Bourbon government renewed, so opposition again manifested itself. *Fédérés* were at the centre of the latter development and the following report made by the prefect of the Haute-Loire was not untypical:

Ma position devient de jour en jour plus difficile . . . il existe en ce département une association qui s'était formée sous le nom des *fédérés*. Elle se composent des mau-

248

vaises sujets de tous les temps et de quelques hommes faibles et par conséquence facile à entraîner. Les gens faibles se sont rétirés mais les autres persérvèrent plus que jamais dans leurs projets du bouleversement de nos institutions.

Already in this early report we can see an important distinction being made between *fédérés* who remained adamant in their opposition and those who appeared to have given up the battle; subsequently this would evolve into an attempt to isolate *fédéré* leaders in order to reduce their influence on men who were 'weak'.[1]

Repression often produced the reverse of what was intended. In November 1815 *fédérés* at Caen, buttressed by discontented army officers, were reported to be stating 'hautement' that the political issue was not yet settled. The prefect of the Rhône reported that *fédérés* were becoming increasingly dangerous due to their exasperation with administrative purges and the sedition laws. Their hostility to the regime was fuelled by the tales of horror brought to them by refugees from Provence. To destabilise the government, they spread false rumours and distributed bulletins fictitiously attributed to Napoleon. The latter activities were part of an extensive anti-government propaganda campaign which touched virtually all parts of France.[2]

Oppression and obloquy produced a certain *fédéré* solidarity which occasionally manifested itself in public. *Fédérés* at Niort were so little ashamed of their past that they refused offers of re-entry into the National Guard because this necessitated abjuration of the federative oath. In this, they were following the same line as their counterparts at Rennes. As noted previously, when leading Dijonnais *fédérés* were put on trial, rank-and-file *fédérés* repeatedly demonstrated their support for the defendants. When the Rennais *fédéré* Gaudin was put on trial in Brest, local *fédérés* successfully intimidated prosecution witnesses. After the acquittal, they rubbed salt into the wounds of royalists by giving Gaudin a banquet in celebration. Tactics of this sort were thus by no means a novel device when the Liberal Opposition began to employ them.[3]

When the prefect of the Côtes-du-Nord decided to exile the *fédéré* Chauchard from Brest, the local chamber of commerce sought to intervene. This was probably a result of the fact that Guilhem, a founder of the federation at Brest who had contributed large sums of money to the association, was president of the chamber of commerce. When the government arrested

---

[1] AN, F⁷ 3785, bulletin of 10 September 1815; for a similar report, see the bulletin of 6 November 1815.
[2] *Ibid.*, F⁷ 3735, bulletins of 8 October, 6 and 11 November 1815, F⁷ 3736, bulletins of 14 January and 22 March 1816.
[3] *Ibid.*, F⁷ 3737, bulletin of 20 August 1816, F⁷ 3735, bulletin of 3 November 1815.

Dubois, president of the federation of Chalon-sur-Saône, the National Guard had to quell a minor uprising. Similarly, at the time of the trial of General Travot, in February 1816, an angry crowd began to march from Lorient to Rennes and had to be dispersed by troops. During resultant skirmishes a *fédéré* lawyer named Arnould was killed.[4]

There were numerous other signs that *fédérés* continued to enjoy their own company. In late January 1816, when royalists were commemorating the death of Louis XVI, three *fédérés* at Château-Chinon (in the Nièvre), two of whom had been stripped of their administrative positions, decided to put on a ball, despite a prefectoral proscription of all such disrespectful activities. Of course the three were arrested; the prefect appears to have been all the more wrathful because the ball had been staged in the old *fédéré* assembly hall. *Fédérés* at Périgueux also showed wayward inclinations. In March 1816 some forty *fédérés* met just outside the city to celebrate the anniversary of the *vol d'aigle*. This was their reply to an expiatory fête in honour of the Duke of Enghien ordered by the prefect of the Dordogne.[5]

Although they served to keep the fires of opposition burning, such public manifestations of discontent presented the authorities with little immediate threat; more troublesome were the frequent police reports that *fédérés* continued to meet in sizeable numbers. Officials assumed that *fédérés* would use their old contacts to form new associations with the intent of bringing about revolution. Knowing that the White Terror was creating an increasing number of desperate opponents, prefects reacted strongly when reports arrived of even a handful of *fédérés* continuing to meet. Opposition to Bourbon government was what had brought these men together originally, and the authorities had good reason to view subsequent meetings with suspicion.

Reported meetings appear to have varied in importance. The 'soupers à la violette' given by Mlle Pelleport in Lyons were attended by several leading *fédérés*. It is difficult to believe that any significant rebellions could have resulted from such genteel occasions, but the point is that *fédérés* continued to remain in contact, and the title of these dinners speaks well enough of the tie that bound them. Attempts by *fédérés* in Nantes and Niort to organise literary societies were probably designed to cover other sorts of discussion, but the membership of these societies soon brought them under suspicion and led to their rapid closure. At Saint-Médard, close to Périgueux, Dr

---

[4] *Ibid.*, F[7] 3735, bulletin of 10 December 1815, F[7] 3736, bulletin of 4 February 1816, F[7] 3737, bulletin of 16 April 1816; J. Mouchet, 'L'Esprit public dans le Morbihan sous la restauration', *Annales de Bretagne*, 55 (1938), pp. 130–2.

[5] AN, F[ic] III Nièvre 8, Prefect to Minister of the Interior, 31 January 1816, F[7] 3736, bulletin of 18 April 1816.

Dupuis continued to entertain *fédérés* at his house, where he and Laroche, a lawyer from Martignac, preached 'le républicanisme de 1793'. Opponents of the government continued to meet at Nevers throughout 1815. After one such unlawful assembly in mid-January 1816 led to a spate of placards predicting the imminent fall of the Monarchy, the prefect decided to crack down. Of twelve individuals subsequently arrested, two had been members of the federative central committee. While this did teach opponents in the Nièvre to be more discreet as to their identity, the flood of propaganda continued. Among numerous examples of lingering hatred of the regime, the following poem discovered at Clamecy is perhaps the most striking:

Eglise à vendre
Curé à pendre
Sous-préfet à étrangler
Maire à décapiter
Adjoints à étouffer
Vive l'Empereur!

Leading *fédérés* at Nevers continued to hold meetings well into 1816. Using rumours that these men had been in contact with the insurgents at Grenoble, and that they were collecting funds for some unknown reason, the prefect exiled several of them in May 1816.[6]

Not only were there signs that *fédérés* were maintaining their hostility, there were also indications that they were seeking to establish contact with other potentially dangerous groups. At Nevers in July 1815, *fédérés* sought to take advantage of the passage of the remnants of the Imperial Army to provoke rebellion. They ran through the streets crying 'Vive l'Empereur!', but soldiers refused to respond and the National Guard was able to put an end to the commotion. Shortly thereafter the mayor castigated *fédérés* for visiting encampments outside Nevers 'pour égarer l'opinion des braves . . . dans le dessein de les associer aux sinistres projets qu'ils brûlent d'exécuter contre tous les citoyens honnêtes de cette ville'. He issued the following warning:

Nous déclarons, en conséquence, que tout habitant de Nevers qui, sans une permission de l'autorité locale, chercherait à s'introduire dans le camp voisin de cette ville ou au milieu des postes qui y sont établis, sera arrêté et traduit devant les tribunaux compétents pour y être jugé suivant la rigueur des lois.

---

[6] *Ibid.*, F^7 3735, bulletins of 8 October, 25 and 31 December 1815, F^7 3787, bulletin of 22 February 1816, F^7 3636, bulletins of 18 January and 1 March 1816, F^7 3737, bulletins of 7 June and 23 October 1816.

Not deeming this sufficient, Chabrol de Chaméane also invited 'friends of order' to inform him of the identity of anyone seeking to foment discord.[7] Similar problems arose at Toulon, where in early August 1815 *fédérés, demi-soldes* and retired soldiers marched through the streets at the head of a crowd of 500 to 600 citizens shouting 'Vive Napoléon! Morte aux Bourbons!' Apparently Provence was not uniformly royalist. A major reason for the repressive measures taken at Nantes by Cardaillac, 'le Carrier blanc de la Restauration', was the habit *fédérés* and old *chasseurs de la Vendée* had of parading through the streets in full uniform and provoking fights with royalists. *Fédérés* and soldiers at Saint-Brieuc and Ploermel conducted similar exercises, leading to several arrests. *Fédérés* were also thought to have taken part in an uprising of demobilised soldiers at Périgueux. Fear of this sort of combination led authorities to view the participation of two officers in the celebration of the anniversary of the *vol d'aigle* with particular concern.

Linking of *fédérés* and military men became the woof and stuff of official correspondence. General Exelmans was suspected of nocturnal meetings with *fédérés* at Clermont-Ferrand, where there were rumours of a new association formed by *fédérés* and soldiers of the local military division. General Vabre continued his relations with *fédérés* at Brest; he was therefore transferred to Grenoble, but chose instead to retire at Brest. General Darricau, ex-commander of the *fédérés-tirailleurs* of Paris, was ordered to leave the Landes and was put under surveillance at Niort, suspected of instigating troubles amongst *demi-soldes*. Retired officers, *demi-soldes* and *fédérés* were said to have leagued together at Toulouse and Saint-Béat. *Fédérés* at Le Puy were also reported to be meeting with half-pay officers in the Spring of 1816.[8]

Fédérés continued their work of 'spreading enlightenment' after the Hundred Days; the difference being that such activities had become seditious. Mater, exiled from Bourges to Châteauroux, kept himself occupied by writing pamphlets predicting a third coming of Bonaparte. Morbihan *fédérés* in towns such as Vannes, Ploermel, Pontivy, Auray and Hennebout kept the authorities busy by disseminating Bonapartist tracts, especially amongst soldiers. *Fédérés* in Vannes were still hard at work in

---

[7] E. Duminy, 'Notes sur le passage des Alliés dans le département de la Nièvre', *Bulletin de la Société Nivernaise des lettres, sciences et arts*, 11 (1906), pp. 253–5.

[8] C. Alleaume, 'La Terreur Blanche dans le Var', *Bulletin de la Société d'études scientifiques et archéologiques de Draguignan*, 45 (1944–5), p. 11; H. de Berranger, 'La Cour Prévôtale de la Loire-Inférieure (1816–1818)', *Bulletin de la société archéologique et historique de Nantes et de la Loire-Atlantique*, 109–10 (1970–1), pp. 26–34; G. Rocal, *La Seconde Restauration en Périgord* (Angoulême, 1976), p. 17; AD H-G, 4M35, *Commissaire-Général de Police* to Prefect, 1 August 1815, and spy reports of 2 and 3 August 1815.

October 1817, distributing a newspaper report that Napoleon had landed in America. The prefect reported that *fédéré* propaganda efforts were making progress amongst the local peasantry.[9]

Rumour-mongering served the same destabilising end. Two *fédérés* of Grenoble, Lallemand and Perrin, were put under surveillance in February 1816 for spreading stories that they were about to take part in a major insurrection. In March, a pamphlet telling of uprisings led by soldiers in Strasbourg, Metz, Paris, Lyons and Besançon was being passed from hand to hand. One place-name was conspicuously absent; the uprising at Grenoble will be discussed shortly. A report on Lanpébie and Jouanet, whose house served as a meeting place for the *fédérés* of La Souterraine (Creuse), contained the following useful description of how the rumour trade worked:

Là se fabriquaient et se vendaient toutes les nouvelles infernales qui couraient ensuite la ville et les campagnes. On arrête le passant, on cause avec lui et demande les nouvelles, on lui fait part de celles qu'on a reçues ou qui l'on vient de fabriquer. Aussitôt, surtout les jours de foire et de marché, cela se répand avec rapidité, et l'on ne peut remonter à la source, parce que trop de gens les redisent.

This was a simple operation, difficult to prevent, and, in a department such as the Creuse where *le menu peuple* were hostile to the Bourbons, an effective means of restoring hope. Moreover, as Perrin and Lallemand explained to a former *fédéré* compatriot turned informant, false rumours served to frighten royalists and throw officials off the track of genuine conspiracies.[10]

Brief as it was in duration, the federative movement bequeathed an important legacy to the Second Restoration. By bringing the various opponents of the Bourbon Monarchy into a nationwide association, it created a network of personal contacts which could be mobilised to organise subsequent opposition. The nature of that opposition tended to vary in relation to the stability of the Monarchy and the repressiveness of its government.

By no means did all *fédérés* continue to participate in organised resistance. Indeed, some *fédéré* leaders such as Azaiis not only made peace with constitutional monarchy but actually emerged as champions of the moderate government of Decazes. The intervention of Baron Louis saved Pierre Giroud his position of receiver-general of the Isère. Giroud had used his influence to thwart measures proposed by more extreme *fédérés*, which

---

[9] AN, F⁷ 3785, bulletin of 4 September 1815, F⁷ 3736, bulletin of 7 April 1816, F⁷ 9682, Prefect to Minister of the Interior, 19 October 1817; J. Mouchet, 'L'Esprit public', pp. 129–32.
[10] AN, F⁷ 3736, bulletins of 10 February and 24 March 1816, F⁷ 9667, Prefect to Minister of Police, 19 January 1816; R. Boudard, 'L'Agitation politique dans le département de la Creuse au début de la Seconde Restauration', *Cahiers d'histoire*, 13 (1968), p. 304.

apparently mitigated his having been president of the association at Grenoble. Perhaps in consequence, Giroud did not take part in any Second Restoration opposition groups; neither did his son, who became receiver-general in 1819.[11]

Examples of rallying to the Monarchy are rare however; the overwhelming majority of *fédérés* who remained politically active took the opposite course. In doing so they formed a sort of vanguard which linked Second Restoration Opposition not only to the Hundred Days, but also to the Revolution itself. To the extent that these men remained influential, and to the extent that they were able to organise opposition, they posed a threat to the regime. Hence the efforts of the Bourbon government to silence and intimidate them. By themselves, *fédérés* did not pose a great danger to the throne, but their efforts to sustain and increase opposition could create serious problems, especially during periods of extensive Bourbon unpopularity. In a very real sense, *fédérés* were in open combat with government attempts to restore order and make the Monarchy popular. They were to prove remarkably durable and flexible in this *guerre à l'outrance*; along the way to 1830 they were to be joined by many other important, often younger, opponents of the regime, but it was the *fédérés* who gave the opposition continuity throughout the Restoration.

It is often argued that reactionary government under Charles X was the cause of the fall of the Bourbon Monarchy. There is a large measure of truth in this; repression certainly increased the unpopularity of the regime, making easier the task of those who wanted to topple it. But more than is generally recognised, this reaction itself was provoked by men who, although they may have donned the guise of constitutional monarchists in public, were no friends of the Crown. Throughout the period, a cat-and-mouse game was played by the government and men who wished to be rid of the Bourbons. In the aftermath of Waterloo, government repression provoked a series of rebellions which had little chance of success, but which revealed widespread hostility to the Monarchy. A period of moderate government then followed and the result was the extraordinarily rapid development of a Liberal Opposition which left royalists again fearing for the security of the throne in 1819. Given the role of *fédérés* in this opposition, one begins to comprehend the basis of such fears. Renewed reaction was the government response and this gave birth to another series of rebellions in the early 1820s. But unlike previously, after its initial success,

---

[11] For the decision of Azaiis to support a government he neither liked nor esteemed, see M. Baude, 'P. H. Azaiis, temoin de son temps d'après son journal inédit (1811–1844)', Ph.D. thesis (University of Strasbourg II, 1975), p. 147; on the Giroudés, see AN, F[7] 9667, Prefect to Minister of the Interior, 19 March 1816 and 20 April 1819.

reaction was then intensified. Considering the results of the previous experiment with moderate government, this was perhaps to be expected, but eventually it opened the floodgates to revolution in 1830. Paris gave the lead, but most provincial capitals responded with an alacrity suggesting that the groundwork had been well prepared.

The extent of *fédéré* contacts soon became apparent to government ministers via reports from the provinces. For example, when de Vaure was exiled from Paris, it was noted that he immediately took up the company of *fédérés* in Saintes. Local authorities were well aware that *fédérés* in Ploermel maintained correspondence with their compatriots at Rennes. Redon, a *fédéré* of Moissac placed under surveillance at Toulouse, was found in possession of criminal correspondence and a cipher for coded messages. He was therefore removed from Toulouse, where there were too many enemies of the regime to keep him company. Thus, when individual *fédérés* were linked with rebellion, official attentions became all the greater.[12]

As often as not, the names of *fédéré* central committee members had been published during the Hundred Days; moreover, because the associations had been public, it was never very difficult to identify *fédéré* leaders, although association registers could seldom be uncovered. It was relatively simple, therefore, to determine which *fédérés* were worthy of attention and to follow their movements. The significance of meetings at Laval between Goyet and Losne-Rochelle, a founder of the federation at Vitré, was not missed; Losne-Rochelle was acting as a liaison between the *fédérés* of Brittany and the Mayenne. Losne-Rochelle, *bête noire* of the prefect of the Mayenne because he was 'l'ennemi prononcé du roi', was interned in the Laval gaol. He then sent a haughty letter of protestation to the prefect and was transferred to La Force in Paris for his troubles. After his release, Losne-Rochelle returned to Vitré where he took up close relations with Aubrée, a leading *fédéré* of Saint-Brieuc recently dismissed from his official post. Significantly, Jamet, ex-justice of the peace, and Goussin, ex-officer, were subsequently arrested at Laval for predicting an uprising that was to be led by Breton *fédérés*. The names of Goyet, Aubrée and Losne-Rochelle are worth noting; they were to be at the centre of significant later developments.[13]

[12] AN, F⁷ 3875, bulletin of 4 September 1815, F⁷ 3736, bulletin of 7 April 1816, F⁷ 9682, Prefect to Minister of Police, 17 November 1815; AD H-G, 4M39, Prefect of the Tarn-et-Garonne to Prefect of the Haute-Garonne, 20 May 1816, Minister of Police to Prefect, 20 May and 10 June 1816.
[13] *Ibid.*, F⁷ 3735, bulletin of 18 November 1815, F⁷ 3736, bulletin of 14 February 1816; A. Bouton, *Le Maine, histoire économique et sociale au XIXᵉ siècle* (Le Mans, 1974), pp. 214–15; A. Bouton and M. Lepage, *Histoire de la Franc-Maçonnerie dans le Mayenne* (Le Mans, 1951), p. 151.

Rumours of rebellion led to numerous searches for hidden arms in the forest of La Guerche, close to Vitré. Apart from the antipathy of most of the citizens of the village of La Guerche, little was found, but officials remained wary. In January 1816 Rennais police officers discovered an unsigned letter posted from Nantes and addressed to the lawyer Rebillard, allegedly revealing plans for a general insurrection. Rebillard was, as we know from our study of Rennes, one of the prime movers of the Breton federation who certainly continued his opposition to the Bourbons after the return of Louis XVIII. Whether there really was a scheme for a general uprising we probably will never know, but Rebillard undoubtedly did have contacts in Nantes, Angers, Lorient and Châteaubriand. He also had a friend in Paris who, on 24 November 1815, had cautioned him and several other Rennais *fédérés* that they had been denounced by a government prosecutor. Despite this warning Rebillard continued to predict great things of the Breton federation in December 1815. Perhaps he thought himself safe in doing so in Saint-Brieuc, but his careless words led to arrest and banishment to Bordeaux in January 1816. The necessity of secrecy was thus taught to several key *fédéré* leaders.[14]

As Bourbon government grew more effective, opposition tactics evolved. Reports concerning a new revolutionary federation in Mâcon began in December 1815, when a merchant was arrested in possession of a 'cordon rouge liséré en noir'. Two months later, authorities informed the Minister of Police that this was the symbol of a society called the *Lion Dormant* and warned that there were many old soldiers of the Army of the Loire in this secret association. According to the latter report, members of the society took an oath to restore the Imperial dynasty to the government of France, and expected a general uprising in the Spring of 1816. By the end of March, similar reports had come in from the Seine-et-Marne, Yonne, Jura, Nièvre, Vienne, Haute-Loire, Aveyron and Dordogne. A report from Nevers specified that the *Lion Dormant* was composed of *fédérés* and retired officers; these men were also said to be hoping for a general uprising to celebrate the anniversary of Napoleon's *vol d'aigle*.[15]

Little of significance appears to have come of all this, perhaps because such men were placing their hopes on a return of the Emperor which never took place. By 4 August 1816, Decazes, Minister of Police, had decided that these reports were not sufficiently substantial to warrant particular police

[14] AN, F⁷ 3785, bulletin of 27 November 1815, F⁷ 3786, bulletin of 7 February 1816; AD, I-et-V, 1M97, dossier Rebillard and prefectoral order of 9 January 1816.
[15] AN, F⁷ 3735, bulletin of 19 December 1815, F⁷ 3736, bulletins of 5, 11 and 14 March 1816; G. Bourgin, 'L'Affaire du Lion Dormant', *La Révolution Française*, 51 (octobre 1906), p. 356.

measures. Nevertheless, Cugnet de Montarlot, an *ex-commissaire de guerre* reported to have 'fait passer dans son quartier une liste pour la fédération parisienne', was arrested in May 1816 for conspiring against the throne as part of the *Lion Dormant* of Paris. Cugnet certainly had been a member of the Parisian federation and had given 100 francs to the association's collection of *dons patriotiques*. He had even gone so far as to advertise that he had been removed from his office as *commissaire de guerre* by Louis XVIII, which helps to explain why the police were constantly on his trail. Parisian authorities had hoped to catch a certain Richard-Lenoir in this alleged conspiracy, reported by a police spy to involve some 30,000 *fédérés* and soldiers, but they could produce no evidence and had to let the matter rest.[16]

Not unnaturally, other societies whose activities were largely secret, if not seditious, were also subjected to close scrutiny. In the eyes of government officials, the membership of *fédéré* leaders tended to confirm suspicions. The lodge of Freemasons at Buxy (Saône-et-Loire) ceased operations after Dariot, a venerable, had been arrested; a similar fate awaited the venerable Dubois, president of the federation at Chalon.

At Toulouse, Mayor Villèle had the local masonic chapters closed because they were 'composée d'artisans presque tous fédérés', and presided over by men who had signed the federation registers. Such men were enemies of the royal government and should not be allowed to meet under any pretext whatsoever. Not surprisingly, the masonic lodge at Rodez was forced to close shortly after it made Fualdès a venerable, on 2 February 1816.[17]

Whether revolutionary societies were directly linked to the political rebellions of 1816–17 has never clearly been established, but it is at least possible to identify certain *fédérés* involved in revolt. In our case-study of Paris we noted that the Patriot conspiracy was largely an affair of deliriously misguided *fédérés*. In the Spring of 1816, attempts were made to provoke rebellion at Lyons. A member of the central committee of the federation of the Rhône, Dr Montain, was one of three men subsequently arrested. During his trial Montain was defended by the lawyer Lombard, who was soon to emerge as a leading liberal organiser. Lombard had also been a federation central committee member, a point on which at least one

---

[16] Bourgin, 'L'Affaire', pp. 353–5; 361; *Le Patriote de '89: journal de soir, politique et littéraire*, 3 June 1815.

[17] P. Lévêque, *Une Société provinciale: La Bourgogne sous la monarchie de juillet* (Paris, 1983), pp. 424, 481; J. J. Hémardinquer, 'Un Libéral: F.-B. Boyer-Fonfrède (1767–1845)', *Annales du Midi*, 73 (1961), p. 180; H. Enjalbert, *Histoire de Rodez* (Toulouse, 1981), p. 214; AD H-G, 4M46, Mayor of Toulouse to Prefect, 31 October, 4 and 6 November 1815.

witness saw fit to comment. Montain was sentenced to five years of imprisonment.[18]

One of the conspirators at Lyons who was not apprehended by the police was a lawyer named Paul Didier. In a report on the *fédérés* Perrin and Lallemand, the prefect of the Isère noted that Didier was thought to be in the vicinity of Grenoble. Shortly thereafter both Perrin and Lallemand were exiled for predicting a major rebellion. Were they in contact with Didier? It is difficult to say, but Didier certainly was in contact with the *fédéré* Berriat-Saint-Prix and Joseph Rey. The latter and Champollion *le jeune*, secretary of the Grenoble federation, had already founded a secret society known as the Union, which will be discussed in detail later.

On 4 May 1816 Didier tried to take Grenoble with a force which perhaps numbered between 1,000 and 2,000 men. However, the men in revolt were primarily recruited in small towns and villages surrounding the capital of the Isère and Didier found little support in Grenoble itself. It would appear, therefore, that the prefect's actions against *fédéré* leaders had given them sufficient cause to avoid risky involvement. Rey too remained uncompromised, which enabled him to defend rebels subsequently brought to trial. Didier's motivation remains shrouded in mystery, but the uprising certainly gave officials an excellent pretext for cracking down on *fédérés*, who were arrested at points as distant as Bourges and Belfort. In August 1816, the general prosecutor of Grenoble directed the commander of the *gendarmerie* of Valence to lead his men into the surrounding countryside in pursuit of 160 individuals identified as *fédérés*. As late as February 1817, authorities were still watching Didier's son and noting his meetings at Lyons with Grenoble *fédérés* such as Perrin. The ferocity of repression after the Didier Affair provided grist to the mill of Liberal Opposition and, as we shall see, it produced some extraordinary results at Grenoble.[19]

Thus, the vigilance of government authorities made participation in any sort of organisation a difficult and possibly dangerous proposition. Nevertheless, the more ardent *fédérés* were clearly trying to regroup in the midst of White Terror.

Despite an armed rebellion in Lyons in June 1817 which appears to have been at least partly instigated by police *agents provocateurs*, and numerous

---

[18] AN, F⁷ 3787, bulletin of 6 September 1816, F⁷ 3738, bulletin of 7 September 1816. See also R. Sanchez Mantero, *Las Conspiraciones libérals en Francia* (Seville, 1972), pp. 129–30.

[19] AN, F⁷ 9667, Prefect to Minister of Police, 29 January 1816, F⁷ 3736, bulletin of 23 May 1816, F⁷ 3737, bulletin of 7 June 1816, F⁷ 9667, Prefect to Minister of the Interior, 23 February 1817; P. Leuilliot, *L'Alsace au début du XIXᵉ siècle* (Paris, 1959), p. 165; H. Dumolard, *La Terreur Blanche dans l'Isère: Jean-Paul Didier et la conspiration de Grenoble* (Grenoble, 1928), p. 77; Lacouture, *Champollion* (Paris, 1988), pp. 197–8.

disturbances occasioned primarily by crop failures and high grain prices, France entered a period of relative political calm in late 1816 which lasted until 1819.[20] During this period the Liberal Opposition emerged as a significant political force.

Restoration politics was very much the preserve of a small plutocracy largely composed of landowners. At most, some 90,000 Frenchmen were entitled to vote for candidates to the Chamber of Deputies, and even this figure decreased significantly until the late 1820s. The latter decline can be attributed largely to the efforts of Restoration prefects who, especially during the ministry of Joseph Villèle, systematically sought to remove from electoral lists men who were likely to vote for the Opposition. Thus, elections were a poor indicator of public opinion; they reflected the wishes of a small, conservative élite.

Nevertheless, elections were important because the Chamber of Deputies had a vital legislative role in the constitution. Moreover, as the centre of what little political life there was, the Chamber was the main forum for the expression of political opinion. Its debates became the focus of newspaper commentary and its activities were followed by people otherwise removed from the political process. Restoration governments thus strove to secure election results which would produce a Chamber supportive of their policies; opponents strove for the reverse. Any government which failed to secure a friendly Chamber would be beset by difficulties, whether the opposition came from ultra-royalists or liberals. When the lower house was dominated by ultra-royalists, the Bourbon Monarchy at least was in no great danger, but should the Liberal Opposition gain control, the future of the throne would not be so clear. Theoretically, of course, it was quite possible to be a member of the opposition and still be completely loyal to the Monarchy, but an ominous number of liberals were old republicans or Bonapartists whose loyalty was at best a moot point. It was not possible to avow frank hostility to the throne and remain a part of the constitutional political process; at most one could ostentatiously place emphasis on the Charter rather than on the Monarchy, but this in itself raised the suspicions of loyal monarchists – doubts which were largely confirmed by the events of 1830. By the latter date the Liberal Opposition had gained control of the Chamber of Deputies, an achievement which, given the nature of the electorate, bore remarkable testimony of the unpopularity of the throne. The failure of the Crown was further evidenced by its rapid fall in Paris and the absence of significant support in the provinces.

---

[20] On the insurrection at Lyons, see S. Charléty, 'Une Conspiration à Lyon', *Revue de Paris*, 4 (15 July 1904), pp. 268–302; A. Spitzer, *Old Hatreds and Young Hopes* (Cambridge, Mass., 1971), pp. 28–31.

Second Restoration Liberal Opposition at grass-roots level awaits its historian. While a good deal is known about leading deputies, theorists and journalists, and something is known about the organising activities of groups such as the *Aide-toi, le Ciel t'aidera*, we must still rely largely on vague general descriptions of the men who voted liberal and, equally important, the people who could not vote but still worked for the Opposition. This is all the more unfortunate because it can lead to a simplistic view of why the Bourbon government acted as it did in the later years of the Restoration. Was the reaction that began in 1819 simply a matter of royal unwillingness to compromise with a loyal opposition, or was the character of this opposition such as to make compromise perilous for the Monarchy? Government ministers and, ultimately, kings at least had the reports of agents in the capital and provinces on which to base their policies. Until we have similar knowledge, we should be careful about the extent to which we attribute the Revolution of 1830 to ultra-royalist intransigence. Was there, or was there not, reciprocal intransigence in the Liberal Opposition?

One way of broaching this problem is to look at the role of *fédérés* within the Liberal Opposition. In so doing, we should bear in mind that *fédérés* had sworn an oath against the Bourbon Monarchy. Caricatures of the *girouette* (a man whose political allegiance followed the direction of prevailing winds) are, of course, legion in Restoration literature, but it was one thing to avow allegiance to successive regimes as a municipal councillor and quite another to join an association dedicated to opposing a second restoration and possibly take up arms for the purpose. Royalists clearly made this distinction by making *fédérés* the focus of repression, and the latter seldom showed any renunciation of their past actions or opinions. The increasing effectiveness of the government in punishing sedition meant that open avowals of opposition to the throne were at best foolhardy; those who wished to continue operating within the political theatre would have to settle for staunch devotion to the Charter. Even so, allegedly 'constitutional' *fédéré* liberals quickly resorted to revolutionary conspiracy in the early 1820s when the government took measures to put an end to liberal electoral progress. Their mistake lay in relying on an Army largely unwilling to rebel. Changes in voting eligibility, outright fraud and the reaction of a conservative electorate to the threat of revolution then produced a series of ultra-royalist electoral triumphs. Given such a situation, liberals, *fédérés* included, had little option but to return to the constitutional position. In short, they consistently pushed their opposition to the fullest practical extreme: as the Liberal Opposition recovered from 1827 onwards, the demands of the Opposition grew, ultimately provoking the ordinances which brought the fall of Charles X. This was not the behaviour of a collection of *girouettes*, though it did indicate a certain pragmatism.

As shown in our case-studies, certain federations had a sizeable middle-class contingent, and a significant number of *fédérés* were entitled to vote during the Second Restoration. This was not uniformly the case, however, and in a department such as the Nièvre, where the popular and lower middle-class nature of the association had brought it into conflict with the National Guard, *fédérés* were subsequently reported to have little influence because they lacked the necessary wealth and social standing. Thus, the chief electoral problem for the prefect was an ultra-royalist faction, despite the fact that most citizens possessed little 'chaleur de Royalisme' and were either Bonapartist or indifferent. Matters must have been different however in the Basses-Pyrénées, where the president of the electoral college, after describing the federation as an association of proletarians armed against landowners, found it necessary to warn electors at Pau against the influence of *fédérés*. This gained a poor response from the electors.[21]

Fédérés played a crucial role in the organisation of Liberal Opposition in the west. In regard to the Morbihan, J. Mouchet has stated: 'Réduits à l'impuissance lors de la Restauration, les libéraux se sont réorganisés sans bruit, souvent secrètement, dans les cadres des anciennes fédérations.' *Fédérés* remained 'les opposants les plus audacieux' of the Bourbon government.[22]

At Brest, in the Finistère, 'les chefs fédérés' became 'les maîtres à penser de l'opposition libérale et anticléricale jusqu'à 1830 et au delà'. The leading Brest liberal, J.-P. Guilhem, played a role similar to that of Hernoux in Dijon. Guilhem had helped to organise the federation in Brest and had been one of the town's delegates at the formation of the Breton federation in Rennes. He was elected to the Chamber of Deputies in October 1818, and this marked the beginning of an exceedingly tumultuous period. When the bishop of Quimper attempted to establish a Jesuit mission in Brest in October 1819, he was treated to a *charivari* of some 1,000 Brestois shouting 'A bas les prêtres! les calotins à la lanterne!' When the bishop renounced his plans, this was seen as a great victory for the *fédéré* leaders who had organised the demonstration. General Comte d'Hoffelize wished to arrest 'les chefs des *Fédérés* de 1815', but action proved impossible because local officials were sympathetic to the liberals. Bishop Dombideau reached similar conclusions about the role of *fédérés* in anti-clerical demonstrations at Châteaulin, Quimper and Landernau, but once again local police officers refused to make arrests. When Edouard Corbière was brought to

---

[21] AN, F^{ic} III Nièvre 8, 22 July 1816; P. Hourmat, 'Les élections des 14 et 22 août 1815 dans les Basses-Pyrénées', *Société des sciences, lettres et arts de Bayonne, nouvelle série*, no. 166 (1965), pp. 45–7.

[22] Mouchet, 'L'Esprit public', pp. 126, 129–32.

trial, he was found innocent by the jury and then treated to the usual celebratory banquet.

Anti-clericalism was of course nothing new to the west; it was part of a long-standing blue–white antagonism begun during the Revolution and renewed with the First Restoration. Nor was unwillingness to forget the past a one-sided affair: manifestations such as those at Brest were sparked by priests who refused burial sacraments to owners of *biens nationaux* and sought to force old blues to make large contributions to the mission as restitution for past sins. In subsequent years, two triumphal receptions of the deputy Guilhem would be turned into *charivaris* against the government prosecutors who had helped send Ney and Travot to their deaths. On one such occasion, Guilhem was given a banquet of 500 tables. In a city of 28,000 inhabitants this was a massive show of support; clearly, Guilhem's following included many who could not vote. Eventually the patience of the government was exhausted and the Villèle Ministry sent Swiss troops to enforce Bourbon order. However, the presence of foreign soldiers, purges in local administration and the National Guard, and resultant clerical ascendency, served only to strengthen the opposition of the liberal bourgeoisie in Brest.[23]

At Dinan, Beslay, a *négociant* who had founded the local federation, went on to become a leading member of the Liberal Opposition. The Beslay family had built its own dynasty over twenty years in Dinan by dominating government posts and administering sales of *biens nationaux*. The influence of Beslay was revealed in August 1815 when both he and Miel, former Imperial sub-prefect of Dinan, were elected to the Chamber of Deputies. Indeed, three royalist candidates received all of 36, 35, and 34 votes from the 100 electors in the *arrondissement* of Dinan. They were easily outpolled by the seven candidates whom the authorities considered 'révolutionnaires'. The Bourbon government had made a serious error in allowing Beslay to act as President of the electoral college. Beslay maintained his seat until 1824, during which time he opposed the laws of exception, supported a petition calling for exiles to be allowed to return to France, and sat with the left, although he was known for his independence.[24]

In the Sarthe, where White Terror had been directed against *fédérés* and

[23] Y. Le Gallo, ed., *Histoire de Brest* (Toulouse, 1976), pp. 208–14; Y. Le Gallo, 'Anticléricalisme et structures urbaines et militaires à Brest sous la monarchie constitutionnelle', *Actes du Quatre-Vingt-Onzième Congrès Nationale des Sociétés Savantes: Rennes* (1966), vol. III, pp. 102–34; AD, I-et-V, 1M96, address of the *jeunes gens* of Brest to their counterparts in Rennes.

[24] AN, F[7] 9650, Prefect to Minister of the Interior, 27 October 1815; J. Pascal, *Les Députés Bretons de 1789 à 1983* (Paris, 1983), pp. 130, 139, 147, 176; A. Robert, E. Bourloton and G. Cougny, *Dictionnaire des Parlementaires Français* (Paris, 1891).

anyone suspected of republicanism or Bonapartism by Jules Pasquier and the ultra-royalist *Chevaliers de la Foi*, Rigomer Bazin first took up the cause of opposition in 1816 by publishing small brochures of commentary on current affairs. The brochures proved popular in the countryside, but Bazin was provoked into a duel and slain by a royalist in January 1818. Charles Goyet, an old *fédéré*, then stepped into his friend Bazin's place by publishing the *Propagateur de la Sarthe*, which was funded by subscriptions from owners of *biens nationaux* and proved even more successful than Bazin's brochures. Goyet then set up a liberal electoral bureau and organised the opposition. According to A. Bouton:

Goyet a organisé par canton la distribution des bulletins de vote aux électeurs censitaires, leur à fait prendre des engagements précis, a veillé à leur réception au Mans, a retenus leur logement chez des hôteliers qui lui sont dévoués et les a entretenus pendant la durée du vote dans les dispositions qu'il leur avait suggérés.

Given the intimidating and occasionally violent actions of the *Chevaliers de la Foi*, such painstaking measures were necessary. The results of Goyet's work were astonishing: elections held in 1818 and 1819 produced four liberal deputies, including Constant and Lafayette, in what was thought to be a bastion of royalism. Goyet was then subjected to a great deal of official and unofficial harassment, which led him to take measures which will be discussed shortly.[25]

Goyet was a republican – something he shared with much of the Liberal Opposition in the west. With regard to the towns of the Côtes-du-Nord, the general prosecutor of Rennes wrote in 1820 that there was a 'tendance aux idées républicaines et un peu de bonapartisme' and the same was true of the Finistère. On liberalism in the Morbihan, he reported that 'la républicanisme est le fond de la pensée du parti, autant éloigné de regrets impériaux que d'attachement à la monarchie légitime'. Thus, descriptions of the Liberal Opposition echoed those of the Breton federation; little had changed since 1815.[26]

For the rest of France, there is also substantial evidence of significant *fédéré* participation in the Liberal Opposition, although matters are rendered somewhat difficult by the paucity of *fédéré* names in our possession. One *fédéré* who certainly did not join the Liberal Opposition was the Chevalier de la Roulière, an old *émigré* who had returned to France shortly after Bonaparte's *coup d'état*. Despite several denunciations for his

[25] A. Bouton, *Les Luttes ardentes des Francs-Maçons Manceaux pour l'établissement de la République, 1815–1914* (Le Mans, 1966), pp. 11–40; F. Dornic, ed., *Histoire du Mans et du pays manceau* (Toulouse, 1975), pp. 251–2.
[26] G. Weill, 'L'idée républicaine en France pendant la Restauration', *Revue d'histoire moderne*, 2 (1927), p. 329.

part in the federation, de la Roulière was maintained as mayor of Niort and sat with the centre as a deputy in the *Chambre Introuvable*. Under the Villèle government in the 1820s, he was a ministerial candidate. On the other hand, Claude-Denis Mater, a lawyer, led the Liberal Opposition at Bourges while remaining an ardent Bonapartist.[27]

Boyer-Fonfrède fought the good fight for liberalism in Toulouse throughout the Second Restoration. Freshly released from prison in 1816, he wrote a pamphlet defending his actions during the Hundred Days. He followed this with a petition to the Chamber of Deputies, 1,500 copies of which were distributed in Paris. In the petition he warned the King that he must attend to the needs of the 'people' if he wished to gain their loyalty. Worse still, he defended the actions of the *fédérés* during the Hundred Days! In the following year, Toulousain police seized 959 copies of a pamphlet in which Boyer-Fonfrède styled himself as the former president and colonel of the *fédérés* of the Midi. In 1818 he paid for a series of caricatures of Toulousain *ultras* that were sold by merchants in Toulouse. Later he wrote a pamphlet calling for a more democratic constitution. The lawyer Dominique-Louis Romiguières also went on to become a leading Toulousain liberal. Appointed lieutenant-general of the police during the Hundred Days, and described by Bourbon officials as a *fédéré* 'chef', Romiguières had to go into hiding during the White Terror. Police officers hunted for him in points as distant as Châteauroux and Paris, where he was arrested in the autumn of 1815. Nevertheless, he returned slightly over a year later to Toulouse, where he championed the cause of mutual schools and frequently defended liberals in court. Among those whom he defended was the Carbonaro Armand Carrel when the latter was brought to trial for his part in attempts to subvert French soldiers sent to Spain to restore the Spanish Bourbon Monarchy. In electoral terms, the Haute-Garonne was, of course, strictly royalist terrain, but a third Toulousain *fédéré*, Chaptive, did manage to finish second to Villèle in the *arrondissement* of Villefranche in October 1821.[28]

Our knowledge of *fédéré* leadership in the east is greater, and consequently we can present more substantial evidence of the *fédéré* role in the Liberal Opposition. In the north-eastern department of the Aisne, Baron

---

[27] AN, F⁷ 3735, bulletin of 25 November 1815; Robert *et al.*, *Dictionnaire des Parlementaires*.

[28] On Boyer-Fonfrède see Hémardinquer, 'Boyer-Fonfrède', pp. 183–4, and AD, H-G, 4M36, report of the *Commissaire de Police*, 19 April 1817; on Romiguières see AN, F⁷ 3735, bulletin of 8 November 1817, F⁷ 3028, *extrait des arrestations*, 361; D. Higgs, *Ultraroyalism in Toulouse* (Baltimore, 1973), pp. 67, 84, 160; Robert *et al.*, *Dictionnaire des Parlementaires*; on Chaptive, see AD H-G, 2M24, *Procès-verbaux* of the election conducted at Villefranche, 1 and 2 October 1821.

Méchin was first elected to the Chamber in 1819 and then sat continuously until 1831. As a member of the extreme left, he became known for his mordant criticism of the successive ministries; not only did he oppose the laws of exception and the law of the double vote, he was one of the few deputies who voted for the admission of the Abbé Grégoire to the Chamber![29]

Perhaps the area least touched by White Terror was Alsace, where there was little violence and administrative purges were not as sweeping as elsewhere. Jean de Briche was maintained as secretary-general of the prefecture at Colmar, and Jean-Daniel Ensfelder kept his post of *adjoint* at the *mairie* of Strasbourg. Due to the support of the prefect de Serre, Golbéry was able to return to the tribunal of Colmar, but subsequently angered royalists by his lenient judgements of Carbonari and his anti-clerical writings. Cunier, who appears to have initiated the federative movement in Alsace, was shown no such grace however and was still considered an 'ennemi déclaré du gouvernement' by the prefect in 1823. Jacques-Frédéric Brackenhoffer managed to resign as mayor of Strasbourg before he was sacked; despite being described in a government report as a nonentity who had been made 'le chef des Fédérés d'Alsace', he was elected to the Chamber of Deputies in 1815 and again in 1819. During his tenure, he sat with the left and opposed the laws of exception, and became known as a charter member of the 'parti ... turbulente' of Strasbourg.[30]

At Besançon, old central committee members Clerc, Gaiffe, Viguier, Violand and Proudhon represented the various shades of Second Restoration opposition. Gaiffe, 'connus par ses opinions anarchiques', was arrested and imprisoned in June 1817 for having spread alarming rumours, but was released shortly thereafter. Viguier wrote articles for the *Constitutionnel*. Proudhon, supported by Violand, stood as a candidate for the Chamber of Deputies in 1819; Charles Weiss's description of Proudhon's candidacy could not have been better: 'C'est un grand bonapartiste, et c'est à ce titre sans doute qu'il mérite les suffrages de quelques prétendus libéraux.' Clerc, another liberal candidate, does appear to have rallied sincerely to the Monarchy, but that was not enough to gain him election, nor did it free him of the enmity of local ultra-royalists.[31]

Three members of the central committee at Chalon-sur-Saône went on to become key opposition figures. Moyne, son-in-law of J.-B. Petiot, and Coste helped to organise the victories of General Thiard. In time, Moyne

[29] Robert *et al.*, *Dictionnaire des Parlementaires*.
[30] Leuilliot, *L'Alsace au début*, pp. 87–8, 97–8, 113, 225, 232, 323, 342; AN, F⁷ 9693, Prefect to Minister of Interior, 24 September 1820.
[31] C. Weiss, *Journal 1815–1822* (Paris, 1972), pp. 172, 254, 256–8, 303.

himself was to become a deputy. Although forced to flee the department at the time of the White Terror, Emiland Menand returned to work for republicanism, gaining a surprising number of votes at Autun, though not election. Perhaps the most famous of the departmental *fédérés* was the lawyer Maughin, who was gaining repute in Paris for his defence of the opponents of the regime (such as Pleignier, who was involved in the Patriot Affair).[32]

Further to the south, Lyons remained sullenly hostile to the Monarchy. Perhaps nowhere else was the vicious cycle of repression, rebellion and renewed repression more evident than in this bastion of revolutionary Bonapartism. From August to December 1815, some 210 individuals were arrested for political 'crimes'. The result was the Rosset conspiracy of January 1816, which led to a further round of arrests. In June 1817, rebellion led to seventy-nine more condemnations. *Fédérés* remained intransigent in their hostility. In 1818, one claimed the honour of having been the fourth *fédéré* on the registers and added 'que les royalistes n'étaient que des brigands qui avaient payé les étrangers pour les faire venir en France, que depuis vingt-cinq ans les Bourbons avaient été mendié chez les puissances étrangères pour se faire remplacer sur le trône, et qu'en conséquence, ils étaient tous les lâches'. In 1819, a second bragged of being 'un bon et franc républicain fédéré'. In 1820 a third called 'ceux qui soutiennent le Roi, de canailles, bandits, banqueroutiers'. Throughout this period *fédérés* continued to agitate, mixing calls of 'Vive la Charte!' at the theatre with renditions of the *Marseillaise* in the streets. Was it surprising that royalists viewed advocates of the Charter with suspicion?[33]

As in other places where the middle and lower classes had joined in revolutionary Bonapartism, the liberal bourgeoisie enjoyed the support of the populace. This gave liberalism in Lyons a double edge: while some members preferred legal means, others were willing to resort to violence and were in contact with men willing to undertake rebellion. As a consequence, liberals of both stripes were feared by royalists. As early as 1816, old *fédérés* such as Lombard-Quincieux, Martin Gras and Jars began to organise a local liberal party. Until 1819 Jars, president of the federation, remained 'le chéri du parti opposé au Gouvernement', but thereafter the influence of de Corcelles *père* became ascendent. Banished during the White Terror, de Corcelles had spent the intervening period travelling abroad; when he returned, Liberal Opposition became more radical. In 1819 de Corcelles was elected to the Chamber of Deputies. He had been ably supported by Lombard, who also wrote a pamphlet attacking restric-

[32] Lévêque, *Une Société*, pp. 481, 494.
[33] G. Ribe, *L'Opinion publique et la vie politique à Lyon lors des premières années de la Seconde Restauration* (Paris, 1957), pp. 207, 227–8, 247, 288, 305.

tions on the press. Among those who gathered at the Café Cornet, a liberal centre, the presence of individuals 'connus pour avoir figuré dans la Fédération Lyonnaise' was marked by police officers. When Lyonnais liberals drew up a petition opposing changes in the electoral laws in December 1819, the *fédéré* Billet was involved in collecting signatures.

In 1820 the General Prosecutor made the following comments about liberalism in Lyons:

Le Comité et tout le parti dont il est l'organe sont tombés sous la dépendance d'un seul homme: de M. de Corcelles qui est le correspondant des chefs de Paris. Telle est la confiance aveugle qu'il lui accorde que, si cette député eût donné, il y a quelques mois, le signal d'un mouvement politique, ce mouvement eût été tenté.

Although a republican, de Corcelles took pains to cultivate old Bonapartists, thus fostering the continuation of revolutionary Bonapartism. Supported by their deputy, Lyonnais liberals petitioned the Chamber to abolish the hated Swiss Guard. Soon noted for his radicalism in the Lower House, de Corcelles naturally attacked the law of the double vote. Although passage of this law helped secure ultra-royalist victories elsewhere, in 1822 the weakness of the ultra party in Lyons was demonstrated by the election of a second *fédéré* liberal named Couderc. During the campaign de Corcelles and Couderc had jointly issued the following address to the electorate:

L'opposition veut dans l'intérêt de tous la Charte, toutes les libertés qui en dérivent, la responsabilité des ministres . . . Vous n'avez donc point à balancer dans le choix de vos députés. Prenez-les dans les rangs des libéraux, ceux qui vous sont offerts ne sacrifieront point leur conscience aux promesses et aux menaces des ministres.

Having failed to secure the desired result, the prefect then doctored electoral lists, a ploy which brought temporary success in the mid 1820s. However, we should not interpret this simply as a sign of ultra-royalist intransigence. Despite the constitutional trappings of the above address, de Corcelles had long since taken the path of revolution as a member of the Carbonari. In short, both sides were waging a war which went well beyond the confines of the Charter.

Although Lombard-Quincieux was unsuccessful in a bid for election in 1824, his published letter to the electors of the *arrondissement* of Vienne caught the eye of the authorities. The prefect of the Isère wondered whether passages such as the following were seditious:

Quant à mes opinions politiques, elles sont inviolablement fondées sur l'amour de mon pays, de la gloire, et surtout de la liberté; dans toutes les phases de la Révolution, et dans toutes les circonstances de ma vie, j'ai conservé ce sentiment.
C'est assez vous dire que je me ferai un devoir et une gloire de m'asseoir au Coté

Gauche, irai-je démentir trente années de sentiments élevés et généreux, faire rougir mes amis et moi-même, en devenant l'esclave d'un Ministère aristocratique et fauteur des privilèges . . . ?

Such statements were not quite sufficient to bring Lombard-Quincieux to trial, but they did show that the nature of his opposition had not changed since 1815.[34]

Matters were much the same at Grenoble, where Liberal Opposition was organised by Joseph Rey. Having shrewdly avoided participation in the Didier revolt, Rey went on to defend many of the accused. Due to the hostility which severe government reaction to the Affair provoked, Rey's influence increased. However, Rey himself was already involved in conspiratorial activities: in February 1816 he and Champollion le jeune had founded the Union, a republican secret society which tended to recruit avowed Bonapartists. Slowly Rey established branches elsewhere: a Lyonnais fédéré named Duplan organised the Union at Lyons and de Corcelles helped in Paris. Another fédéré affiliate was Teste who, however, remained exiled from France.

In September 1817, the Decazes Ministry put an end to repression in Grenoble by appointing Choppin d'Arnouville prefect of the Isère. Choppin believed that members of the 'revolutionary party' could be reconciled to Bourbon rule if they were assured of their possession of biens nationaux and allowed to return to their old administrative positions. He sought to gain the support of moderate liberals and entered into cordial relations with old opponents of the Monarchy such as Champollion le jeune, recently returned from exile at Figeac. Champollion was allowed to return to his teaching position at the collège royale, enjoyed the support of the prefect in founding a mutual school, and even conducted archival research for the government in a matter pertaining to claims on French lands made by the King of Sardinia and Piedmont.

However, this period of apparent reconciliation proved short in duration. In July 1818 local liberals and jeunes gens decided to hold a banquet to commemorate the defence of Grenoble from the Allies in 1815. While the prefect interpreted this as mostly a celebration of the 'courage que les Bourgeois montreront en défendant leurs foyers', he feared that its significance would be misconstrued. Opponents of the regime would note 'que les Libéraux ont solennisé leur résistance aux alliés du Roi, et donné

---

[34] Ibid., pp. 101, 107–9, 194, 306–9, 341–57; M. Gergnaud, 'Agitation politique et crises de subsistances à Lyon de septembre 1816 à juin 1817', Cahiers d'histoire, 2 (1957), pp. 165–75; A. Kleinclausz, Histoire de Lyon (Lyons, 1952), III, pp. 37, 46–8; AN, F⁷ 6741, dossier Rhône, Lieutenant of Police to Minister of the Interior, 8 December 1819, dossier Isère, Prefect to Minister of the Interior, 27 February 1824.

par là la preuve qu'ils étoient loin de désirer Son retour'. Wishing to avoid the heavy-handed tactics of his predecessor Montlivault, Choppin allowed the banquet to take place, but personally asked leading liberals not to attend. It would appear that this produced a split in the liberal camp, with constitutional monarchists deferring to the prefect's wishes, while more determined opponents attended a banquet of some 140 individuals.

By 1819, relations between Bourbon authorities and Grenoble liberals had seriously worsened. Using information supplied in part by the *fédéré* Perrin, Rey had published several pamphlets attacking Montlivault and General Donnadieu for their actions at the time of the Didier Affair. Perrin had helped launch a radical opposition journal, the *Echo des Alpes*, and a second *fédéré*, Michaud, had drawn up a petition against proposed changes in the electoral laws. The strength of the local Opposition was indicated by the fact that the petition gained 817 signatures in Grenoble alone. A second banquet celebrating the defence of Grenoble took place and this time a sizeable number of electors attended. Worse still, Joseph Rey and the Union were campaigning for the election to the Chamber of Deputies of the Abbé Grégoire – republican, *conventionnel* and 'regicide by intention'! This was a poor reward for Choppin's moderate policies.

Although local ultra-royalists connived in it, Grégoire's election sent shock waves throughout royalist France. The election was annulled by the Chamber of Deputies, but the death-knell of Decazes' moderate government began tolling. Choppin was one of the first victims, but his removal from the prefecture in late 1819 did not improve matters. In May 1820, the Duke of Angoulême was given a hostile reception which included street fights between royalist soldiers and *jeunes gens* crying 'Vive l'Empereur!' A third commemoration of the defence of Grenoble led to more tumult in July. The *Journal libre de l'Isère* published several articles attacking the decision to exclude Grégoire from the Chamber and advising voters to re-elect him. And when the editor of the *Journal libre* and several *jeunes gens* were brought to trial in December 1820, Michaud, in his capacity as president of the court of assizes, used his influence to assure that the prosecution failed to gain guilty verdicts. Indeed, in an address to the jurors, Michaud went so far as to declare that the election of Grégoire was the product of 'un élan du Patriotisme le plus pur du département de l'Isère'. Such incidents led the new prefect, Baron D'Haussez, to begin yet another administrative purge in 1821. As we shall see shortly, this produced only further rebellion.[35]

[35] G. Weill, 'Les Mémoires de Joseph Rey', *Revue Historique*, 157 (mars–avril 1928), pp. 296–301; H. Dumolard, 'Joseph Rey de Grenoble (1779–1855)', *Annales de l'Université de Grenoble (Section Lettres-Droit)*, 4 (1927), pp. 77–99; Lacouture, *Champollion*,

In the early 1820s, a concerted attempt by various opposition groups was made to topple the Monarchy. Whether the decision to resort to revolution was actually made during passage of the law of the double vote or after the annulment of Grégoire's election has been a major debating point amongst contemporaries and historians because it appears to mark a transition from legal to illegal opposition. What is clear, however, is that the revolt took place in response to the government's attempts to halt the progress of the Liberal Opposition. Liberals were subsequently inclined to argue that they had resorted to unconstitutional means only after the government had broken the rules of political competition by changing electoral procedures. The extensive presence of republicans and Bonapartists within this revolutionary movement, however, causes one to view this with a good deal of scepticism; at best, the Liberal Opposition was showing very little patience when its progress was halted.

The groups that linked arms in conspiracy during the early 1820s have generally been given the appellation 'Carbonari'; for the sake of convenience we shall maintain this term, but it should be understood that the Carbonari was an amalgam of conspiratorial societies, several of which were formed well in advance of 1820. That *fédérés* were natural recruits to the Carbonari has occasionally been noted, but the extent of the *fédéré* contribution has yet to be recognised. The latter point is important, because it lifts the Carbonari revolt out of the immediate context of the 1820s and places it in the broader context of continuous Second Restoration opposition to the Monarchy. To establish the connection between the federative movement of 1815 and the conspiratorial groups, the most significant components of the Carbonari will be discussed in turn.[36]

As mentioned previously, *fédérés* were involved in Joseph Rey's secret society from its inception and helped to extend it. The Union developed primarily in the east and, in this regard, *fédéré* involvement in the Carbonari described in our case-study of Dijon should be noted. As was to be expected, the Union was especially strong at Grenoble, where it appears to have been led by Champollion *le jeune* and his friend Renauldon. Both these men were influential amongst the *jeunes gens* of Grenoble, and the latter group provided the shock troops in a minor revolt on 20 March 1821. Perhaps misled by a rumour that Louis XVIII had abdicated in favour of the

pp. 213, 218, 222–3, 227, 235–8; AN, F⁷ 9667, Prefect to Minister of the Interior, 11 September 1817, 1 and 7 July 1818, 11 May, 7 and 22 July 1819, 5 July 1820, Prefect to Minister of Police, 3 December 1820, F⁷ 6740, dossier Isère, Prefect to Minister of the Interior, 1 and 3 March 1819.

[36] There appear to be almost as many works on the Carbonari as there were members; the best synthesis is Spitzer's *Old Hatreds*.

Duke of Orleans, Renauldon and a band of law students invaded the prefecture and demanded that the tricolour be raised. Meanwhile, Champollion had led a charge on the citadel, which initially surprised the guards and enabled him to hoist the tricolour for all to see. But little more than this act of defiance was achieved, as the authorities rapidly regained control and placed the city in a state of siege. In the aftermath of the rebellion, Champollion was stripped of his post as professor of history; he only escaped trial by precipitously moving to Paris. Thereafter he wisely turned to exclusive study of the inscriptions on the famous Rosetta stone, although he remained a republican at heart.

The law students were less fortunate in that their school was subsequently suspended. This measure, specifically designed to prevent liberal-led rebellion, appears to have been effective. Despite the intrigues of Chavas and Genevois, *fédérés* reputed to have organised secret society meetings, and countless rumours of revolt, Grenoble remained relatively tranquil in 1822. Nevertheless, D'Haussez continued to counsel against reopening the law school, and conducted another selective purge of government administrators notorious for their opposition. He did not flatter himself that he had gained the 'conversion' of other *fonctionnaires* 'trop prononcées dans leurs opinions libérales pour adopter les opinions royalistes', but was certain that they would no longer contradict official policies or preach pernicious doctrines. In sum, then, Grenoble liberals remained sullenly hostile to the Bourbon Monarchy, although rebellion was no longer likely.

The Parisian branch of the Union attracted a host of liberal luminaries: among them were de Corcelles *père* and Maughin (old *fédérés*), the journalist Dunoyer, and Mérihlou, another lawyer specialising in defence of opponents of the regime. The presence of the latter two is especially interesting in that, as noted in our study of Rennes, they had both seen fit to pay visits to Losne-Rochelle and Pierre Aubrée at the time of Dunoyer's trial at Rennes in 1818. It will perhaps be recalled that these distinguished liberals had enjoyed the company of a guard of *jeunes gens* during their visits to Aubrée and Vitré.

Aubrée was in fact a leader of the Breton federation – still in existence, though now clandestine. A retired Army veteran wounded at the battle of Saragossa, Aubrée had hosted the banquet at Saint-Brieuc when Blin and the *commissaires* from Rennes had come to found the local federative chapter in 1815. Aubrée was probably a republican; his toast at the banquet conspicuously made no reference to the Emperor and his co-authorship of a pamphlet denouncing Constant's *Acte Additionnel* also suggested reservations concerning Napoleon. Having lost his administrative post at Saint-Brieuc during the White Terror, Aubrée had retired to

Vitré, where he maintained close ties with the family of Beaugéard – an exiled regicide. Through Losne-Rochelle, Aubrée was also in contact with Charles Goyet, the organiser of liberal victories in the Sarthe.[37]

Goyet's success had perhaps put his life in danger; certainly he had been subjected to constant threats from ardent royalists. Wishing to have a force capable of combatting the *Chevaliers de la Foi*, Goyet arranged a clandestine rendezvous with Aubrée at Laval. The result of these discussions was the formation, in October 1820, of the *Chevaliers de la Liberté*, timed to coincide with a visit of the liberal deputies Constant and Lafayette. The *Chevaliers de la Liberté* developed rapidly, extending from Orléans to Nantes and most points in Brittany. According to A. Bouton:

> Elle recrute beaucoup parmi les anciens membres des pactes fédératif bretons, angevins et manceau, les étudiants de Rennes et de Nantes lesquels comme fédérés viennent de lutter, en 1815, les armes à la main contre les chouans. Ce sont là les éléments tout trouvés qui expliquent l'extraordinaire développement de la jeune société secrète.

Thus, not only was the *Chevaliers de la Liberté* formed by old *fédéré* leaders, it was comprised largely of rank-and-file *fédérés*. Indeed, a list of suspected conspirators in the Mayenne in 1820 was composed solely of some of the more notorious *fédérés* of 1815. White Terror had failed to break the old association and it was no coincidence that the two Rennais convicted for their part in the *Chevaliers* uprisings at Thouars and Saumur were both old *fédérés*.[38]

One of the smaller Carbonari tributaries was Cugnet de Montarlot's *Chevaliers du Soleil*, a group which appears to have conducted most of its operations in the east. As noted in our study of Paris, Cugnet had attracted the attention of the police by his actions as a *fédéré*, leading to several arrests during the White Terror. Thereafter Cugnet had taken to publishing the *Nouvel homme gris*, a satiric anti-royalist tract which found its readership in opposition centres such as Grenoble. By May 1820 Cugnet was involved in several conspiracies in the east, timed to coincide with a visit made by the Duke of Angoulême. One of the relay points and action centres of the conspirators happened to be the Chapeau Rouge hotel in Dijon – a locale well known to *fédérés* and liberals. While the Duke travelled in the Jura, Cugnet turned up at Champlitte, where he distributed seditious songs

[37]   AN, F[7] 9667, Proclamation of the Lieutenant-General of the Seventh Military Division, 20 March 1821, Prefect to Minister of the Interior, 28 January 1822, 15 January 1823, F[7] 6769, dossier Isère, Prefect to Minister of the Interior, 18 February and 21 March 1822; Lacouture, *Champollion*, pp. 239–46.

[38]   On Aubrée see R. Durand, *Le Département des Côtes-du-Nord* (Paris, 1925), II, pp. 437–47; Bouton, *Les Luttes*, pp. 41, 53; H. Imbert, *Histoire de Thouars* (Niort, 1871), p. 371; AN, F[7] 6684, Prefect to Minister of Police, 9 January 1820.

and, apparently, engravings of his own portrait. Although thought to be acting as a liaison between a *comité directeur* in Paris (supposedly run by Lafayette) and activists in the east, and although arrested both in Besançon and back in Paris, no evidence of sedition could be found and Cugnet had to be released.

It is difficult to determine whether Cugnet was involved in the subsequent attempt to raise rebellion in the east of August 1820, but shortly thereafter he had to take flight for Spain, where he continued to ply the revolutionary trade, repeatedly slipping in and out of police nets. After an attempt to incite rebellion at Saragossa ran aground in 1821, Cugnet published a proclamation to the French people, calling on liberals to support their Spanish brethren. Interestingly, Cugnet was in contact with Boyer-Fonfrède, suspected of acting as a liaison between Spanish and French revolutionaries. Boyer-Fonfrède made several trips to Spain before Cugnet was finally captured and executed in 1824. Despite the collaboration of Spanish police, however, Toulousain authorities were never able to prove that the old federation president had been aiding Spanish rebels. Nor were they able to establish that Boyer-Fonfrède was involved in a minor uprising of Toulouse law students in March 1825.[39]

More central to the Carbonari were the *Amis de la Vérité* and the *Amis de l'Armorique*, composed of *jeunes gens* (students and otherwise) who, under the cover of Freemasonry, spent a good deal of time discussing their dislike of the regime. Such opposition was, of course, nothing new in Paris. The original suggestion of forming a Parisian federation in 1815 had come from four *jeunes gens* who had cautiously requested Imperial permission to recruit in the schools and public administrations of Paris. Students of the *école de medecine* joined the Parisian federation and formed a battalion of *cannoniers* which ultimately became part of the *fédérés-tirailleurs*. There were some 195 law and medical students in the eleventh battalion of the *fédérés-tirailleurs*.[40]

By the summer of 1820, the young men of the *Amis de la Vérité* and the *Amis de l'Armorique* had joined forces with Joseph Rey's Union and a significant number of army officers in an attempt to provoke rebellion in Paris and the east. The attempted *putsch* in Paris proved a fiasco and in its wake two of the *jeunes gens*, Nicolas Joubert and Pierre Dugied, departed for Naples, where they learned the organisational methods of the Italian Carbonari. When they returned, they and several of their compatriots set about establishing a new revolutionary society based on Italian lines. The

[39] G. Richard, 'La Conspiration de l'Est, mai 1820', *Annales de l'Est*, 9 (1958), pp. 23–59; Weiss, *Journal*, pp. 292, 302, 304, 315, 344; Hémardinquer, 'Boyer-Fonfrède', pp. 191–2.
[40] APP, A A/300, 46; AN, F⁷ 662, Colonel Hugo to General Darricau, 1 June 1815.

result was the Carbonari: a hierarchical network of affiliated associations founded precisely in the areas where the federative movement had been strongest.[41]

There is a good deal of evidence to support Adolphe Crémieux's contention that Carbonari recruits in the provinces 'ne soient autre chose que les cadres de l'organisation des Cent-Jours'. The Carbonari in the west were in essence simply the *Chevaliers de la Liberté*; as we have seen, the *Chevaliers* were *fédérés* under a new name. Of course, rank-and-file membership would not have been entirely the same; new recruits, especially from the law and medical schools, would have been added and some would have fallen away. But local leadership remained remarkably constant – alongside Aubrée, Losne-Rochelle and Goyet, we find Chaussard and Guilhem at Brest, Le Gorrec at Saint-Brieuc and Busseau at Niort. In the east, matters appear to have been similar, although here the connecting link between *fédérés* and Carbonari was Joseph Rey's Union. De Corcelles *père* was in charge of the Carbonari at Lyons, Champollion at Grenoble, Maughin at Beaune, Lerouge (with help from Cabet) at Dijon and Menand at Chalon-sur-Saône.[42]

There was also a good deal of continuity apparent at Paris. Among the younger Carbonari were Beslay *fils*, a *fédéré commissaire* at Dinan in 1815; Paul Dubois, who had fought at Guérande as a *fédéré*; Pierre Leroux, a *fédéré* at Rennes; and de Corcelles *fils*, like his father, a *fédéré* at Lyons. Among the older luminaries involved, De Corcelles *père*, Maughin, Félix Barthe and Cabet had all entered the federative movement. All of these men had contacts with the various opposition groups in the provinces and it was this that gave the Carbonari an extensive national dimension.

Despite numerous attempts to provoke rebellion, the Carbonari failed miserably in their attempts to topple the regime. The Army resisted attempts at subversion and this proved crucial. Co-ordinating actions amongst the various groups proved difficult and amidst growing recriminations the movement gradually fell apart. By 1824 most members had moved on to shrewder forms of opposition. However, the Carbonari was important in two regards. First of all, it demonstrated what many liberals really thought of the Bourbon Monarchy, despite constant championing of the Charter. Secondly, by confirming the suspicions of true royalists, the Carbonari encouraged the government to sustain a period of reaction which ultimately proved to be its downfall.

---

[41] Spitzer, *Old Hatreds*, pp. 230–46.
[42] A. Crémieux, *La Censure en 1820 et 1821* (Paris, 1912), pp. 86–104; A. Calmette, 'Les Carbonari en France sous la Restauration', *La Révolution de 1848*, 9 (1912–13), pp. 17–38, 120; Spitzer, *Old Hatreds*, pp. 245–6.

The cumulative effect of the law of the double vote (giving the wealthier quarter of the electorate two votes), increased prefectoral doctoring of voter lists, and the fear produced by the resort to revolutionary means led to a precipitous decline in liberal electoral fortunes. Among those who fell between 1820 and 1824 were *fédérés* de Corcelles *père*, Couderc (defeated in 1823 but successful in 1824), Guilhem, Beslay, Hernoux and Brackenhoffer. With ultra-royalism clearly in the ascendent, liberals were placed squarely on the defensive. In a Chamber shorn of the more radical liberal element, a change in the nature of opposition became apparent as liberals fell back on the tactic of portraying themselves as loyal to the Monarchy, but determined to defend the Revolutionary heritage sanctified by the Charter. At least in terms of electoral strategy this was always their strongest suit, for while the electorate wanted no part of a revolution which might bring the masses back into the political picture, neither did it want a return to the *ancien régime*.[43]

As the Villèle Ministry replaced that of Richelieu, and Charles X replaced Louis XVIII, the argument that the Charter was under attack from *ancien régime* privileged groups gained credibility. Under Villèle, the tenure of elected deputies was extended to seven years, thus assuring maximum results from current high conservative electoral fortunes. Liberal Opposition was further attacked by repressive press legislation and for good measure trial procedures were changed to make convictions more likely. As a direct result, political battles tended to be waged in court – giving *fédéré* lawyers such as Barthe, Maughin, Cabet and Romiguières ample opportunity to castigate the government.

Politics continued to reflect the deep divisions of the Revolution. The Villèle government passed a bill indemnifying those who had lost their lands through confiscation during the Revolution. In doing so Villèle had hoped to put an end to a long-standing source of acrimony, but the reaction of liberal journalists such as Carion in Dijon assured that the indemnity was seen only as the first step in a process which would ultimately lead to repossession of all *biens nationaux* by their former owners. Such fears were exacerbated by the close association of Charles X with the Catholic Church. Anti-clericalism was nothing new to the Liberal Opposition, but the actions of Charles X and his government, as exampled by the coronation ceremony at Reims and the sacrilege law, played into the hands of liberal journalists eager to exploit a powerful issue.[44]

Historians occasionally speak of the rise of a younger generation of

[43] See P. Thureau-Dangin, *Le Parti Libéral sous la restauration* (Paris, 1888), pp. 265–306.
[44] See G. de Bertier de Sauvigny, *The Bourbon Restoration* (Phildelphia, 1966), pp. 365–93.

opponents who, in the mid to late 1820s, emerged as leaders of the opposition and elevated political discourse to a higher plane. There is clearly something in this; one cannot doubt that the arrival of men such as Thiers, Mignet, de Rémusat and Carrel added fresh force to the opposition. But whether the arrival of the 'generation of 1820' had much impact on the nature of opposition prior to 1830 is questionable. Thiers, for instance, reflected the opinions of his mentors accurately enough. While two young Breton *fédérés*, Paul Dubois and Pierre Leroux, went on to found the high-toned *Globe*, their *fédéré* compatriots, Beslay *fils* and Guilhem *fils*, were not averse to the traditional practices – both were involved in anti-clerical riots at Brest and Dinan in 1826–7. More importantly, even the more sanctimonious members of the generation of 1820 were quite willing to join hands with those 'sullied' by the past when it came to opposing the government.[45]

Due to a host of problems which were to appear trivial in the light of what was to follow, Villèle decided to call a general election in 1827. Liberals entered the battle with a flood of propaganda, but more importantly they also set about organising potential support in a manner similar to that of Goyet in the Sarthe in 1818–19. Under the leadership of François Guizot, the *Aide-toi, le Ciel t'aidera* society was established in Paris and branches were set up in most of the departments. The chief work of the society was to combat prefectoral doctoring of voter lists. Liberal literature informed the public of voter qualifications and how to assure that they were on registration lists if so entitled. Equally important, liberals at the local level aided in the registration of potential supporters and then assured that they exercised their rights. One result of these activities was a remarkable increase in the number of votes cast; another was a dramatic shift to the left in the Chamber, although precise numbers are difficult to establish.[46]

Because little is known of the organisation of the *Aide-toi* at the local level, it is difficult to assess the role of *fédérés* in it. We can, however, note the presence of Dubois, Cabet and Barthe in the Parisian committee, and add that de Corcelles, Beslay *fils*, Rivier (at Grenoble), Maughin, Hernoux and Bernard of Rennes were at the head of local chapters. The turn in electoral fortunes brought an increasing number of *fédérés* into the Chamber. Guilhem, Maughin, Coste and Jars joined the ever-present Méchin in 1827; Michaud (of Grenoble) would have entered but died before taking his seat.

[45] On the younger generation, see Thureau-Dangin, *Le Patri*, chapter 3 and especially pp. 202–16; A. B. Spitzer, *The French Generation of 1820* (Princeton, 1987), especially chapter 4. On Dubois see P. Janet, 'Le Globe de la Restauration', *Revue des deux mondes*, 34 (1 August 1879), pp. 481–512. On Beslay see C. Beslay, *Mes Souvenirs* (Paris, 1873), pp. 83–4. On Guilhem *fils*, see Le Gallo, 'Anticléricalism', p. 120.

[46] The book to read is S. Kent, *The Election of 1827* (Cambridge, Mass., 1975).

In 1828 Couderc again returned and was joined by de Corcelles (elected this time in Paris) and General Lamarque, who finally succeeded in the Landes. Hernoux regained a seat in 1829. All of these men voted for the famous address of the 221 and were returned in 1830.[47]

One *fédéré* who had not managed to regain his seat by 1829 was the republican Beslay *père*. Nevertheless, he remained involved and in the autumn of 1829, in response to the King's summoning of the Polignac Ministry, drew up a document calling on taxpayers to form associations which would be based on refusal to pay taxes should the King 'violate' the Charter. That representatives of the Breton association were supposed to assemble at Pontivy indicated that Beslay had the old federative principle in mind. The manifesto of the Breton Association was sent to the editor Bert at Paris, who published it in the *Journal de Commerce* accompanied by a report that the associations had already been established. The latter was false, however, and the editors of the *Journal* and a host of other Parisian and provincial newspapers were taken to court by the government for exciting 'hatred and contempt for the King's government'. Beslay's initiative was then taken up by the *Aide-toi*; the associations gained substantial support and 'proved a useful and legal means of uniting liberals in opposition to Polignac' before Parliament met in 1830. The prefect of the Charente described the local association as a 'séditieuse entreprise, qui n'est qu'un renouvellement de la fédération des cent-jours', and his counterpart in the Finistère initially referred to the association of his department simply as the 'fédération'. Among liberal deputies who headed local associations were the old *fédérés* Maughin, Hernoux, Delaborde, Guilhem, and de Corcelles. When Charles X called for new elections in July 1830, Beslay reaped his reward as both he and Bernard (who had organised the Breton Association at Rennes) gained election.[48]

At the national as well as the local level, the Revolution of 1830 gave more than ideological satisfaction to old *fédérés*. Seven *fédéré* regicides were at last able to return to France (Beaugéard, Choudieu, de Bry, Dumont,

[47] Robert *et al.*, *Dictionnaire des Parlementaires*; AN, F[7] 6776, Prefect to Minister of the Interior, 19 January 1830.
[48] On Beslay and the Breton Association, see C.-H. Pouthas, *Guizot pendant la Restauration* (Paris, 1923), pp. 425–30, and D. L. Rader, 'The Breton Association and the Press: Propaganda for "legal resistance" before the July Monarchy', *French Historical Studies*, 2 (1961), pp. 64–72. The above authors appear to have underestimated the extent and impact of the associations; see P. Pilbeam, 'The Growth of Liberalism and the Crisis of the Bourbon Restoration, 1827–1830', *Historical Journal*, 25, 2 (1981), pp. 363–4. The original manifesto is printed in Beslay, *Souvenirs*, pp. 85–6. See also AN, F[7] 6768, dossier Charente, Prefect to Minister of the Interior, 31 October 1829, F[7] 6776, dossier *Association Bretonne*, Prefect to Minister of the Interior, 21 October and 20 November 1829.

Lefiot, Levasseur and Thibaudeau), four of whom were granted state pensions for past services (Choudieu, de Bry, Lefiot and Thibaudeau). Three men closely involved in the Breton federation were nicely rewarded: Baron Méchin regained a prefecture (this time in the Nord); Leroy, who had been made a Chevalier of the Legion of Honour for his part in founding the movement in 1815, became prefect of the Ille-et-Vilaine; General Bigarré was returned to active service and given command of the 13th Military Division. Prior to the Revolution it would not have been possible for Romiguières to have become general prosecutor at Toulouse, for Mater to have become first president of the *cour royale* at Bourges, nor for Menand to have become a member of the *parquet* at Chalon-sur-Saône. At a less exalted level, Plain of Toulouse was reinstated as *commissaire de police*, a position which he had lost by order of the Duke of Angoulême in August 1815. Perhaps the *fédérés* who profited most by the change in regimes were Barthe and Teste, who entered several July Monarchy governments.[49]

Not surprisingly, *fédérés* viewed favourably a revolution which was to their profit. Maughin, for example, was one of the first liberal deputies to call for active resistance to the July ordinances of Charles X. As members of the municipal committee of Paris, Maughin and Barthe helped to assure that no compromise was made with the King. But as the Orleanist government took on an increasingly conservative complexion, *fédérés* began to take on divergent paths. The litmus test of political orthodoxy proved to be the Ministry of Périer, which forced Frenchmen to choose between the parties of *mouvement* and *résistance* (roughly, whether they thought the revolutionary settlement constituted significant political progress). One of the first tasks undertaken by Périer was an onslaught on the National Associations that had been organised to resist possible foreign intervention in the aftermath of the Revolution, but that also had marked democratic tendencies. Among *fédéré* deputies actively involved in the National Associations were Hernoux, Maughin, Bernard of Rennes, Dubois, Couderc, de Corcelles and the Generals Delaborde and Lamarque. By April 1831, Périer had forced the dissolution of the National Associations, but this in turn fostered the growth of republican societies which were to pose severe problems for the consolidation of the Orleanist regime.[50]

---

[49] E. Newman, 'Lost Illusions: The Regicides in France during the Bourbon Restoration', *Nineteenth-Century French Studies* (Fall-Winter 1981–2), pp. 72–4; C.-H. Pouthas, 'La Réorganisation du ministère de l'intérieur et la réconstitution de l'administration préfectorale par Guizot en 1830', *Revue d'histoire moderne et contemporaine*, 9 (1962), pp. 259–62; R. Grand, *La Chouannerie de 1815* (Paris, 1942), p. 45; Robert *et al.*, *Dictionnaire des Parlementaires*; AD H-G, 13M57 *bis*, *Etat de Police*, 5 October 1830.

[50] P. Pilbeam, 'The Emergence of Opposition to the Orleanist Monarchy, 1830–31', *English Historical Review*, 85, 334 (January 1970), pp. 12–28.

The way in which the July Monarchy brought to light differences among old *fédérés* became apparent in their parliamentary careers. Twelve emerged as conservative Orleanists: Mater, Romiguières, Méchin, Barthe, Teste, Lerouge, Dubois, Gaillard de Kerbertin, Jars, Jollivet, Bernard de Rennes and Moyne. Ten could be identified with the left, generally voting in opposition to the government but not necessarily opposed to the Monarchy: Maughin, Lamarque, Golbéry, Couderc, Hernoux, de Corcelles *père*, de Corcelles *fils*, Beslay *père*, Beslay *fils* and Cabet. This parting of ways was, of course, to be expected of men who shared only their opposition to the Bourbon Monarchy.[51]

Thus *fédérés* contributed directly to all the major manifestations of political opposition to the Bourbon Monarchy. White Terror had served to confirm their hostility, while failing to break their influence or isolate them. Repression did teach them not to manifest the full extent of their hostility in public, but it did not prevent them from continuing their resistance to the Second Restoration.

The role of *fédérés* appears clear. Their experience and personal contacts, gained during either the Revolution or the Hundred Days, enabled them to provide rapid organisation on a national level. Hence their contribution to the formation of the Liberal Opposition, the Carbonari, the *Aidetoi* and Beslay's Associations. Moreover, *fédérés* gave the Opposition a certain continuity with the Revolution and Empire, and a perseverence and pugnacity which troubled royalist officials. They formed the part of the Opposition least likely to compromise, and most likely to drive the government to repression. Men who had sworn an oath against the Bourbon dynasty were unlikely to form a loyal opposition; their actions and participation within the furthest extremes of opposition confirmed that *fédérés* remained enemies of the Bourbon Monarchy. If the political story of the Restoration was failure to compromise, then the role of *fédérés* was integral to the period.

[51] Robert *et al.*, *Dictionnaire des Parlementaires*.

Conclusion

As formal organisations, the federations of 1815 were short in duration, existing for little more than two months in most places and a good deal less in many. Federative assemblies were seldom held more than twice a week, though central committee members doubtless met on a more frequent basis. The associations did not act as social centres; they did not provide reading rooms or subscribe to journals, nor did *fédérés* concern themselves with economic problems such as provisioning the poor and the unemployed. Federations could not, therefore, have been indoctrination centres comparable to the Jacobin and popular societies of the Revolution. The fiery speeches to which *fédérés* listened were designed to bolster courage and enthusiasm, but the speakers were addressing audiences already convinced of the rightness of their cause. *Fédérés* were, of course, actively involved in spreading 'enlightenment' (propaganda), but the essence of the movement was to unite men with a common interest, not to educate them as to the nature of their interests. When a man signed a federation register, he publicly avowed his choice between the two leading alternatives for French government. Moreover, he was stating his willingness to confront the opposition (foreign or domestic) with force. To become a *fédéré* required significant commitment.

Fédérés united for a specific purpose – to prevent the Allied Powers and French royalists from reimposing Bourbon government. They had a host of reasons for supporting this cause: patriotism because the King was the choice of the invading enemy, hatred of social and fiscal privilege because the King appeared to favour *ancien régime* élite groups, anti-clericalism and concern over possession of *biens nationaux* because the King was closely linked to the Catholic Church, career considerations because Bourbon government appeared to view those who had risen during the Revolution with disfavour, or simple preference for (or idolisation of) Napoleon Bonaparte as leader. Because there were so many motives for becoming a

280

fédéré, the movement tended to be heterogeneous in both political and social character.

As demonstrated in our case-studies, the social character of the associations varied from region to region. Typical of the west, the association of Rennes was decidedly middle-class; typical of the east, at Dijon the federation contained substantial numbers drawn from both the lower and middle classes. Paris was the great exception in that it produced two separate associations, one of which was popular and the other middle-class. Because they varied substantially in social composition, attempts at generalisation on a national basis are hazardous and writers who have interpreted the federative movement in Paris as exemplary have been especially prone to error. To explain the social nature of an individual federation one must know a great deal about local experience of both the Revolution and the Empire, and no monocausal explanation will suffice. The federative movement did to a certain extent reflect the Revolution, and the associations at Rennes and Dijon did largely align with their Revolutionary (Jacobin and popular) predecessors. But before we jump to the conclusion that the Revolution was the decisive epoch, we should reflect on the fact that Lyons produced a powerful federation, whereas Marseilles contributed not a jot. The latter two examples appear to indicate the primacy of economic factors – Lyons had largely prospered under the Empire, while Marseilles had continued to experience a decline begun during the Revolution. However, while economic factors clearly are part of the equation, they do not fully explain the strength of the association at Rennes (any more than the conflict between blues and whites can be explained in simple economic terms), and are not much help in explaining why large parts of Normandy proved unresponsive to the federative appeal. In short, then, the social composition of federations varied as a result of a complex web of causes to be located in local history and any attempts at generalisation at the national level are apt to obscure more than they clarify.

More precise conclusions can be drawn concerning the nature of *fédéré* leadership. With a few interesting exceptions (such as de Corcelles at Lyons), the men of the central committees were drawn from the Imperial nobility and the middle classes. Given the nature of nineteenth-century society, this was perhaps to be expected, but it should be noted that the number of government officials and *fonctionnaires*, judges, lawyers, notaries, doctors, professors and college students actively involved in the associations raises serious questions concerning arguments that the middle classes betrayed Napoleon in 1815. Perhaps something of this interpretation can be salvaged if we make it more precise. Instances of *fédérés* clashing with National Guardsmen in the provinces were numerous; moreover, our case-studies indicate that the *grands notables* were generally not attracted to the movement. It would appear, therefore, that the wealthier, non-noble elements of society were less receptive than their social 'inferiors', but this generalisation should not be extended to include the whole of the middle class.

On the political level, previous characterisations of the movement as either predominantly Bonapartist or Jacobin have largely missed the point. One can identify significant numbers of Bonapartists and Jacobins (either Girondin or Montagnard) in virtually every federation; one can also point to a large number of young men free of such appellations, who in the future would be known as liberals. Moreover, if *fédéré* literature points to any one thing, it is the common ground that all of these men found in seeking to rebuild the unity of 1789. The regicide Jean de Bry was correct in predicting that the federative movement would have great impact in 'renouvellant des relations et établissant une confraternité capables de doubler nos forces morales'.[1] The fusion which we have termed 'revolutionary Bonapartism' was certainly fostered by the rhetoric of Bonaparte's *vol d'aigle*, but Napoleon was only exploiting a resurgent *élan* born of previous invasion, defeat and First Restoration government. Bonaparte's approval of the federative movement brought his traditional followers into co-operation with old republicans and young liberals, but the willingness of the latter groups to support Imperial government can only be ascribed to the extent to which Bourbon government had alienated them. Napoleon's return did not divide France; he returned to find a nation already divided. On one side were those who, above all else, opposed the Bourbon Monarchy; the federative movement was the most significant manifestation of this phenomenon.

Accurate numbers are hard to come by, but membership clearly numbered in the hundreds of thousands. The movement continued to expand at least until Waterloo, and extended into the vast majority of departments. The few indicators that we do possess suggest that recruitment in the older federative centres continued to increase as the prospect of war grew more certain. Given that there is no evidence that men were forced to join, and that active soldiers did not play a large role in the associations, one can readily understand why re-establishing Bourbon authority proved so difficult in the period following the Hundred Days.

Perhaps because he was preoccupied by the apparent paradox of Bonapartists and old revolutionaries collaborating, the historian Le Gallo made several errors concerning the federative movement which have often been repeated in general histories. Convinced that the associations were largely revolutionary and popular, Le Gallo assumed that Napoleon's hesitation

---

[1] AN, F⁷ 9693, Prefect to Minister of the Interior, 30 May 1815.

over arming the *fédérés-tirailleurs* of Paris was typical of his attitude to the movement and that his government purposely sought to restrict and emasculate the federations. Whether or not the volatile *fédérés-tirailleurs* should be armed was an exceptionally thorny problem however; elsewhere, the central government consistently fostered the associations of the provinces. Providing arms was often difficult because they were in short supply, but when guns for civilians could be procured, it was the *fédérés* who got them, occasionally to the exclusion of National Guardsmen.

That the movement developed so rapidly was due partly to the assistance given to local patriots by Imperial authorities. The organisational experience and personal contacts which some patriots had gained by their past activities as Jacobins and members of popular societies also facilitated matters. Taken in combination, these two elements go a long way towards explaining why the movement developed, and did not develop, where it did. Acting on directions from Napoleon, Imperial officials sought to establish a federation at Marseilles, but local patriots in this royalist bastion were too few in number to respond. In parts of Normandy the reverse situation occurred when local citizens called for a federation, but prefects failed to give the necessary encouragement. However, when individual prefects took this position, they were not following central government policy, and several were reprimanded by government ministers in consequence. This is not to say that relations between the government and *fédérés* were completely free of strain; at times it was necessary to oppose or ignore the more extreme *fédéré* initiatives, but this was a matter of directing the movement, not of curtailing it.

In arguing that the movement had been emasculated and therefore had been prevented from saving France from a second foreign intervention, Le Gallo took insufficient notice of what the *fédérés* actually accomplished. In their pacts, *fédérés* committed themselves to helping maintain Imperial order within France, while the Army and mobile National Guard fought the enemy abroad. They cast themselves in a supporting role, although they also undertook to help defend France in the event of invasion. The mere size of certain associations sufficed to reduce royalist manifestations to a minimum in many parts of the country. Elsewhere, when rebellion arose, *fédérés* fulfilled their pledges and proved themselves more than willing to engage the enemy, generally to the applause of resident officials. Even in the west, revolt was largely quelled when news of Waterloo arrived to resuscitate flagging *chouan* forces. It is worth stressing that the Bourbon Monarchy was restored because of the defeat of the Army at Waterloo and subsequent government capitulation; the *fédérés'* cause was lost at the frontier, not in the interior.

Orthodox historical interpretation, apparent in Le Gallo's work and that of many others, has long held that Napoleon, after exploiting the revolutionary current during the *vol d'aigle*, soon turned his back on his new-found supporters by wooing liberals and allowing Constant to put forward an *Acte Additionnel* in which the franchise was not especially liberal, and hereditary peerage was maintained. He thus forfeited the support of old Jacobins, who expected better. There is a certain logic to this interpretation, but study of the federations suggests that it requires revision. Put simply, the federative movement developed after publication of the *Acte* in the *Moniteur*, and the federations were evidence of sustained revolutionary support for the Imperial government despite Constant's constitution. There was no real paradox in this however; even disillusioned *fédérés* were quite capable of simultaneously rejecting the *Acte* and supporting the government. The essential reason for this was that the paramount concern of *fédérés* was to oppose the restoration of the Bourbon Monarchy; other matters were secondary.

After Louis XVIII had returned to Paris, royalists paid testimony to the significance of the federative movement by making *fédérés* leading targets of repression. After all, *fédérés* had sworn an oath of opposition to the Bourbon Monarchy, and it was not unnatural for monarchists to take them at their word. In parts of the south, White Terror took the form of bloody reprisal, but even where *fédérés* were not subjected to mob violence, official reports make clear that they were viewed with fear and mistrust and often treated to a good deal of harassment. *Fédéré* leaders were systematically removed from positions of authority and influence and often banished from their departments as a means of giving warning to others. Rank-and-file *fédérés* repeatedly ran foul of the sedition laws; the slowness with which they learned not to express their political opinions in public demonstrated the strength of their animosity towards the regime. The sedition laws were only part of a gamut of repressive measures provided by the ultra-royalist *Chambre Introuvable* and enforced by even the most moderate of royalist officials. It would be naive to see this as ultra-royalist revenge pure and simple; the answer of moderate and immoderate royalists alike to widespread opposition to the Monarchy was repression. In the short term, this tactic proved successful: conspiracies and attempts at rebellion were easily defeated, and Bourbon authority was restored. But repression also re-enforced an enmity which was to prove enduring; the punishment meted out to *fédérés*, either Jacobin or Bonapartist, gave them further common cause.

Fédéré participation in the various strands of opposition to the Second Restoration government was considerable, and recognition of this sheds much light on both the nature of that opposition and the government's reaction to it. Despite the pleas of Madame De Staël, many friends of liberty continued to work in common opposition with Bonapartists – this was fruit born of the Hundred Days, and at the core of this was the federative movement. Federations had brought old revolutionaries, Bonapartists and young liberals into a single organisation and taught them that they could work together. The tie that bound these men was not simply opposition to the government of the day; it was opposition to the Bourbon Monarchy itself. The prominent role of *fédérés* in the Liberal Opposition tended to confirm the suspicions of royalists concerning the loyalty of all liberals; when Liberal Opposition grew dramatically under the moderate government of Decazes, resort was again had to the politics of reaction. Liberals substantially confirmed such doubts by their rapid recourse to revolutionary conspiracy in the early 1820s, and *fédérés* played a major part in this. Attempts to provoke rebellion having proved counterproductive, liberals then fell back on 'constitutional' opposition but, as the mayor of Rennes noted, there was something exceedingly dubious about the loyalty of young liberals and old *fédérés* who demanded cries of 'Vive la Charte!', but refused to shout 'Vive le Roi!' Between certain elements of the Liberal Opposition and the Bourbon Monarchy there could be no true accord. From 1827 onwards, the progression towards final confrontation was rapid; neither side showed much patience with, or confidence in, the other. Though at this stage a small part of an expanding opposition, *fédérés* contributed significantly to the improved organisation that brought liberal electoral triumphs. When revolution did occur in Paris in 1830 it was not the work of liberals, who did not play much of a role in the business of street fighting. But liberals did reveal their true colours by jettisoning Charles X on first opportunity and, at least at Dijon and Rennes, *fédérés* led the overthrow of Bourbon authority in provincial France. As was to be expected, *fédérés* were not last among liberals in rushing for the spoils of revolution.

Neither the Liberal Opposition nor the Carbonari were simple reexpressions of the federative movement, though all three were combinations of republicans, Bonapartists and liberals, who shared common opposition but little else. The federative movement had a popular element which the largely middle-class Carbonari lacked, and was much greater in numbers. On the other hand, the Liberal Opposition ultimately came to include men such as François Guizot who, while *fédérés* had been swearing their oaths and clamouring for guns, had joined Louis XVIII at Ghent. But *fédérés* gave continuity to all forms of Second Restoration opposition; they represented the hard core – basically intransigent and always a cause for royalist alarm. Many of them had begun their opposition to the Bourbons during the Revolution; the vast majority of those who remained politically active continued their resistance throughout the Second Restoration, until success in July 1830 finally broke the tie that had bound them in 1815.

Bibliography

MANUSCRIPT SOURCES

ARCHIVES NATIONALES

AFIV 1935–48 *Bulletins de l'Intérieur (Cent-Jours)*
BB³ 35¹ *Poursuites en matières politiques, 1815–17*
BB³ 40 *Mise sous la disposition de la haute police, 1816–27*
BB³ 151–61 *Délits politiques, 1815–16*
BB³ 171–2 *Rapports des parquets sur la situation politique, 1802–21*
BB¹⁸ 943–1035 *Correspondance générale de la division criminelle*
Fⁱᵇ II Côte-d'Or 5 *Esprit public (Cent-Jours)*
Fⁱᶜ 1–3 *Rapports de l'esprit public, 1815*
F⁷ 3028–30 *Arrestations politiques et surveillances, 1815–18*
F⁷ 3646 *Dépêches télégraphiques concernant les événements de mai–juillet 1815*
F⁷ 3733–40 *Minutes des bulletins de police, 1815–17*
F⁷ 3900 *Bulletins de la gendarmerie. Mai–juillet 1815*
F⁷ 6625–35 *Affaires politiques (Police politique 1814–17)*
F⁷ 6684–9 *Sociétés secrètes*
F⁷ 6740–1 *Elections et esprit public*
F⁷ 6767–72 *Situation politique: Rapports des préfets*
F⁷ 6776 *Associations contre le paiement de l'impôt*
F⁷ 9627–712 *Police générale: situation des départements, 1815–30*
F⁷ 9876–87 *Individus surveillés (loi du 29 octobre 1815)*
F⁷ 9938–76 *Individus condamnés mis à la disposition du gouvernement ou placés
    en surveillance à l'expiration de leur peine, 1814–58*
F⁷ 9993–7 *Etat des individus condamnés*
F⁹ 476–7 *Garde Nationale: Côte-d'Or*
F⁹ 530 *Garde Nationale: Côtes-du-Nord*
F⁹ 661–2 *Garde Nationale: Paris*

ARCHIVES DE LA GUERRE

1K1 46–8 *Papiers Davout (1815)*

ARCHIVES DE LA PREFECTURE DE POLICE DE PARIS

A A/330–1 *Fédérés-tirailleurs: dossiers, pièces diverses*

ARCHIVES DEPARTEMENTALES DE LA COTE-D'OR

K 2 4–6 *Arrêtés du Préfet, 1815–17*
K 6 5 *Correspondance ministériale, 1815–17*
K 8 8 *Journal du Côte-d'Or, 1815–17*
K 8 9 *Mémorial administrative de la Côte-d'Or, 1815–16*
1M 1–15 *Personnel administratif du département, 1800–31*
2M 18–23 *Listes électorales, 1814–31*
3M 29–42 *Listes des électeurs, 1814–31*
3M 28 *Affaires politiques: Assemblée du Champ de Mai, 1815*
4M 1–2 *Personnel du Conseil Général*
4M 3 *Personnel des Conseils d'arrondissements*
6M 1–2 *Affaires générales, an VIII–1831*
8M 23–4 *Commissaires de Police: rapports diverses, an IX–1820*
1N 1 *Sessions du Conseil Général: instructions, correspondance, an VIII–1853*
Q 1159–60 *Sommaires des comptes ouvertes avec les acquéreurs de biens nationaux*
Q 1161–2 *Journal d'enregistrement (biens nationaux)*
12 R 2 *Surveillance des officiers en demi-solde*
UIII Ca-4 *Cour d'Appel de Dijon: liste des condamnés, 1812–37*
UIII Ca-6 *Répertoire des arrêts sur appel correctionnel, 1815–16*
UIII Cb-2 *Registre des arrêts de 1815–16*
UV A3–4 *Cour d'Assises: registres d'arrêts de 1815–18*
UV B63–90 *Dossiers de procédures*
UIX Cd-15–16 *Tribunal de I^e instance de Dijon: jugements correctionnels, 1815–16*

ARCHIVES DEPARTEMENTALES DE LA HAUTE-GARONNE

1M 60–6, 73–5 *Personnel administratif du département, 1800–31*
2M 20–4 *Listes électorales, 1814–31*
4M 34–47 *Police: rapports périodiques, 1815–30*
13M 57 bis *Etat de Police*

ARCHIVES DEPARTMENTALES D'ILLE-ET-VILAINE

IH *Indicateur historique: contribution des Archives à l'histoire du département d'Ille-et-Vilaine de 1789–1980*
6KA 5–6 *Arrêtés du Préfet, 1815–17*
L 1557 *Société des Amis de la Constitution*
1M 88–100 *Situation politique du département, 1815–17*

2M 1–83 *Personnel administratif du département, 1800–31*
3M 31–7 *Collèges Electoraux, 1815–20*
4M 31–3 *Police: rapports périodiques, 1815–33*
4M 90–1 *Port d'armes, an VIII–1820*
4M 93 *Versement d'armes à Rennes, 1813–25*
1Na 1 *Conseil Général: délibérations, 1815–17*
1Nb 1 *Rapports du Préfet au Conseil Général, 1815–17*
3Nd 1 *Conseil d'Arrondissement de Rennes: délibérations, 1815–17*
7 Rb 14 *Contrôle nominatif des officiers de la Garde Nationale, 1814–37*
1U *Cour d'Appel: registre des condamnés, 1811–62*
1U 200 *Décisions criminelles, 1816–17*
2U 5 *Cour prévôtale*
2U 202 *Cour d'Assises: arrêtés, 1815–17*
2U 527–47 *Cour d'Assises: dossiers, 1815–17*
3U 314–42 *Tribunal de Rennes: jugements civils*
9U 1 *Conseil de la Préfecture: délibérations, 1815–17*
9U 3 *Conseil de la Préfecture: arrêtés, 1815–17*

ARCHIVES MUNICIPALES DE DIJON

1D1 21–2 *Conseil Municipale: registre des délibérations, 1815–20*
2D1 *Conseil Municipale: arrêtés et correspondance, 1815–30*
3H *Garde Nationale de Dijon, 1815–27*
2I *Liste des individus mis en surveillance (affaires politiques), 1790–1831*

ARCHIVES MUNICIPALES DE RENNES

1D1/22 *Conseil Municipale: registre des délibérations, 1812–16*
2D1/6 *Registre des arrêtés et correspondance de la mairie de Rennes, 1814–16*
2D1/7 *Registre des arrêtés de la mairie, 1815–26*
2D2/4 *Registre de correspondance de la mairie, 1816–18*

PRINTED SOURCES

BIBLIOTHEQUE NATIONALE

Lb[46] 86 *Les Fédérés de tous les temps, traités comme ils le méritent*
Lb[46] 287 *Addresse aux habitants du faubourg Saint-Antoine*
Lb[46] 303 *Fédération parisienne. Addresse et pacte des fédérés parisiens*
Lb[46] 319 *Fédération du Rhône*
Lb[46] 362 *Les crimes des fédérés, moyen d'anéantir cette secte d'anarchistes et de
    cimenter le trône des Bourbons*
Lb[46] 396 *Mairie de Strasbourg. Fédération alsacienne. Relation des journées des 5
    et 6 juin 1815*
Lb[46] 454 *Fédération parisienne*

Lb⁴⁶ 571 *Fédération. Les Lyonnais à toutes concitoyens*
Lb⁴⁶ 579 *Fédération des faubourgs Saint-Antoine et Saint-Marceau*
Lb⁴⁶ 580 *Préfecture de Police. Ordonnance concernant les mesures d'ordre à
    observer*
Lb⁴⁶ 598 *Procès des auteurs et fauteurs de la conspiration de 1816*
Lb⁴⁶ 650 *Fédération Bretonne*

BIBLIOTHEQUE MUNICIPALE DE DIJON

Ms. 1697 *Mémoire justificatif fait à Paris pour M. Carion en 1816*
Fonds Delmasse, no. 2218 *Fédération bourguignonne*

NEWSPAPERS

L'Indépendant: chronique nationale, politique et littéraire, May 1815–July 1815
Journal des débats, March 1816–July 1816
Journal de l'Empire, May 1815–July 1815
Journal de Paris, May 1815–July 1815
Le Moniteur Universel, April 1815–June 1816
Le Patriote de '89: journal de soir, politique et littéraire, May 1815–July 1815
Petites Affiches de Dijon, April 1815–July 1815

OFFICIAL CORRESPONDENCE

Correspondance de Napoléon I, publiée par ordre de l'Empereur Napoléon III,
    vols. XXI, XXVII (Paris, 1859).
Bingham, D. A., ed., *A Selection from the Letters and Despatches of the First
    Napoleon*, vol. III (London, 1884).
Chuquet, Arthur, ed., *Inédits Napoléoniens*, vol. I (Paris, 1913).

MEMOIRS AND CONTEMPORARY WRITINGS

Audin, Jean Marie, *Tableau historique des événements qui se sont passés à Lyon
    depuis le retour de Bonaparte jusqu'au rétablissement de Louis XVIII* (Lyons,
    1815).
Barante, Amable de, *Souvenirs*, vol. II (Paris, 1892).
Barère, B., *Mémoires*, vol. III (Paris, 1843).
Barrucand, Victor, ed., *Mémoires et notes de Choudieu* (Paris, 1897).
Bernis, René de, *Précis de ce qui s'est passé en 1815 dans les départements du Gard
    et de la Lozère* (Paris, 1818).
Beslay, Charles, *Mes Souvenirs* (Paris, 1873).
Bonaparte, Lucien, *La Vérité sur les Cent Jours* (Paris, 1835).
Carnot, Hippolyte, *Mémoires sur Lazare Carnot*, vol. II (Paris, 1861–3).
Carnot, Lazare, *Exposé de la conduite politique de M. le Lieutenant-général* (Paris,
    1815).

Champollion-Figeac, Jacques-Joseph, *Fourier et Napoléon: L'Egypte et les Cent-Jours* (Paris, 1844).

Constant, Benjamin, *Mémoires sur les Cent-Jours*, second edition (Paris, 1829).

Fauvelet de Bourrienne, Louis Antoine, *Mémoirs of Napoléon Bonaparte* (London, 1885).

Fleury de Chaboulon, Pierre Alexandre, *Memoirs of Napoleon in 1815* (London, 1820).

Fouché, Joseph, *Les Mémoires de Fouché*, ed. L. Madelin (Paris, 1947).

Frénilly, M. de, *Considérations sur une année de l'histoire de France* (Paris, 1815).

Guizot, François, *Memoirs to illustrate the History of My Time*, vol. I, translated by G. J. W. Cole (London, 1858).

Hobhouse, Thomas Camden, *Last Reign of Napoleon*, 2 vols. (London, 1816).

Lasserre, Bertrand, *Les Cent-Jours en Vendée d'après les papiers inédits du Général Lamarque* (Paris, 1906).

Lavallette, Antoine Marie, *Memoirs*, vol. II (London, 1831).

Lemaire, M. Cauchois, ed., *Lettres sur les Cent-Jours* (Paris, 1882).

Noailles, Marquis de, ed., *The Life and Memoirs of Count Molé, 1781–1855*, vol. I (London, 1923).

Pasquier, Etienne-Denis, *Mémoires du Chancellier Pasquier*, vols. IV, VI (Paris, 1894).

The Memoirs of Chancellor Pasquier 1767–1815, translated by Douglas Garman (London, 1967).

Pozzo Di Borgo, Charles, *Correspondance Diplomatique, 1814–1818*, vol. I (Paris, 1890).

Regnault de Warin, J. B., *Cinq mois d'histoire de France* (Paris, 1815).

Rémusat, Charles de, *Mémoires de ma vie*, vol. I (Paris, 1958).

Roserat, Alphonse, ed., *Mémoires de Madame de Chastenay*, vol. II (Paris, 1896).

Thibaudeau, Antoine-C., *Mémoires, 1799–1815* (Paris, 1913).

Thomas, Jean-Pierre, *Précis historique des événements arrivés à Montpellier pendant les Cent-Jours de l'Interrègne*, ed. Gaston Vidal (Montpellier, 1976).

Weiss, Charles, *Journal 1815–22*, ed. Suzanne Lepin (Paris, 1972).

PRINTED WORKS

BOOKS

Baratier, E., ed., *Histoire de La Provence* (Toulouse, 1969).

Barral, Pierre, *Les Périers dans l'Isère au XIXe Siècle* (Paris, 1964).

Benaerts, Louis, *Le Régime Consulaire en Bretagne* (Paris, 1914).

Bergeron, Louis, *L'Episode Napoléonien: aspects intérieurs* (Paris, 1972).

Biget, J. L., ed., *Histoire d'Albi* (Toulouse, 1983).

Blordier-Langlois, *Angers et le Département de Maine-et-Loire*, vol. II (Angers, 1837).

Bluche, Frédéric, *Le Bonapartisme* (Paris, 1980).

Le Plébiscite des Cent-Jours (Geneva, 1974).

Bouton, André, *Le Maine, histoire économique et sociale au XIXe siècle* (Le Mans, 1974).

Les *Francs-Maçons Manceaux et la Révolution Française (1741–1815)* (Le Mans, 1958).

Les *Luttes Ardentes des Francs-Maçons Manceaux pour l'établissement de la Républic, 1815–1914* (Le Mans, 1966).

Bouton, André, and M. Lepage, *Histoire de la Franc-Maçonnerie dans le Mayenne* (Le Mans, 1951).

Brelot, Jean, *La Vie politique en Côte-d'Or sous le Directoire* (Dijon, 1932).

Bricaud, Jean, *L'Administration du département d'Ille-et-Vilaine au début de la Révolution, 1790–1791* (Rennes, 1965).

Bury, J. P. T., *France 1814–1940* (London, 1985).

Capefigue, M., *Les Cent-Jours*, vol. I (Paris, 1841).

Castries, René de la Croix, duc de, *La Terreur Blanche: l'épuration de 1815* (Paris, 1981).

Chabot, Georges, *La Bourgogne* (Paris, 1941).

Charléty, Sébastien, *La Restauration, histoire de France contemporaine*, vol. IV (Paris, 1921).

Cobb, Richard, *Les Armées Révolutionnaires* (Paris, 1963).

The *Police and the People* (Oxford, 1970).

Cochin, Augustin, *Les Sociétés de pensée et la Révolution en Bretagne, 1788–1789*, 2 vols. (Paris, 1925).

Contamine, Henry, *Metz et la Moselle de 1814 à 1870*, I (Nancy, 1932).

Corne, Eugene, *Pontivy et son district pendant la Révolution* (Rennes, 1938).

Cornillon, Jean, *Le Bourbonnais pendant les Cent-Jours* (Moulins, 1925).

Crémieux, Albert, *La Censure en 1820 et 1821* (Paris, 1912).

Daudet, Ernest, *La Terreur Blanche* (Paris, 1878).

Dornic, F., ed., *Histoire du Mans et du pays manceau* (Toulouse, 1975).

Drouot, Henri, *La Côte-d'Or* (Paris, 1925).

Duchatellier, A., *Histoire de la Révolution Française dans les départements de l'Ancienne Bretagne*, II (Paris, 1836).

Dumolard, Henry, *La Terreur Blanche dans l'Isère: Jean-Paul Didier et la conspiration de Grenoble* (Grenoble, 1928).

Dupuy, Roger, *La Garde Nationale et les débuts de la Révolution en Ille-et-Vilaine, 1789–mars 1793* (Rennes, 1972).

Durand, R., *Le Département des Côtes-du-Nord* (Paris, 1925).

Ellis, Geoffrey, *Napoleon's Continental Blockade: the Case of Alsace* (Oxford, 1981).

Enjalbert, Henri, ed., *Histoire de Rodez* (Toulouse, 1981).

Fitzpatrick, Brian, *Catholic Royalism in the Department of the Gard, 1814–1852* (Cambridge, 1983).

Fizaine, Simone, *La Vie politique dans la Côte-d'Or sous Louis XVIII* (Paris, 1931).

Gabory, E., *Les Bourbons et La Vendée* (Paris, 1947).

Gaffarel, Paul, *Dijon en 1814 et en 1815* (Dijon, 1897).

Giboury, J. P., Dictionnaire des Régicides (Paris, 1989).

Gildea, R., Education in Provincial France (Oxford, 1983).

Girard, Louis, La Garde Nationale, 1814–1871 (Paris, 1964).

Gonnet, Paul, La Correspondance d'Achille Chaper, 1831–1840 (Dijon, 1970).

Grand, Roger, Les Cent-Jours dans l'Ouest. La Chouannerie de 1815 (Paris, 1942).

Gras, Albin, Grenoble en 1814 et 1815 (Grenoble, 1854).

Guerrini, Maurice, Napoléon et Paris (Paris, 1967).

Guillau, A., ed., Biens Nationaux: Index Alphabétique des acquéreurs et des soumissionaires (Rennes, 1910).

Guillau, A., and Armand Rébillon, Documents relatifs à la vente des biens nationaux (Rennes, 1911).

Heguenay, Louis, Les Clubs dijonnais sous la Révolution (Dijon, 1905).

Higgs, David, Ultraroyalism in Toulouse (Baltimore, 1973).

Houssaye, Henry, 1815, 3 vols. (Paris, 1889–1909).

Huard, R., ed., Histoire de Nîmes (Aix-en-Provence, 1982).

Imbert, Hughes, Histoire de Thouars (Niort, 1871).

Jacquot, Pierre G., Opposition et Terreur Blanche en Haute-Marne sous la Restauration (Saint-Dizier, 1981).

Jardin, André, and André-Jean Tudesq, La France des notables: l'évolution générale, 1815–1848 (Paris, 1973).

Johnson, Christopher, Utopian Communism in France: Cabet and the Icarians, 1839–1851 (Ithaca, New York, 1974).

Jones, P. M., Politics and Rural Society: The Southern Massif Central c. 1750–1880 (Cambridge, 1985).

Kennedy, Michael, The Jacobin Clubs in the French Revolution, the First Years (Princeton, 1982).

Kent, Sherman, The Election of 1827 in France (Cambridge, Mass., 1975).

Kerviler, René, La Bretagne pendant la Révolution (Rennes, 1912).

Répertoire général de bio-bibliographie bretonne (Rennes, 1888).

Kleinclausz, Arthur, Histoire de Bourgogne, second edition (Marseilles, 1976).

Histoire de Lyon, 3 vols. (Lyons, 1952).

Lacouture, Jean, Champollion: Une vie de lumières (Paris, 1988).

Lacretelle, Charles, Histoire de France depuis la Restauration, vol. I (Paris, 1829).

Lagrée, Michel, Mentalités, religion et histoire en Haute-Bretagne au XIXᵉ siècle: le diocèse de Rennes, 1815–1848 (Paris, 1977).

Lamartine, Alphonse de, Histoire de la Restauration, vol. IV (Paris, 1851).

Langlois, C., Un Diocèse breton au début du XIXᵉ siècle: le diocèse de Vannes, 1800–30 (Paris, 1974).

Laurent, Charles-M., Histoire de la Bretagne (Paris, 1875).

Lebrun, François, ed., Histoire d'Angers (Toulouse, 1975).

L'Ille-et-Vilaine: des origines à nos jours (Saint-Jean d'Angély, 1984).

Lefebvre, Georges, Napoléon (Paris, 1969).

Le Gallo, Emile, Les Cent-Jours (Paris, 1923).

Le Gallo, Yves, ed., Histoire de Brest (Toulouse, 1976).

L'Homer, Jean, *Les Cent-Jours et la Terreur Blanche en Dordogne* (Paris, 1904).

Lemaire, Louis, *Histoire de Dunkerque* (Dunkirk, 1927).

Leuilliot, Paul, *L'Alsace au début du XIXe siècle* (Paris, 1959).

La Première Restauration et les Cent-Jours en Alsace (Paris, 1958).

Lévêque, Pierre, *Une Société provinciale: La Bourgogne sous la monarchie de juillet* (Paris, 1983).

Lewis, Gwynne, *The Second Vendée* (Oxford, 1978).

Lubis, F. P., *Histoire de la Restauration*, 6 vols. (Paris, 1848).

Lucas-Dubreton, J., *Le Culte de Napoléon. La Légende de l'Aigle dans l'opinion publique depuis Waterloo jusqu'à l'aurore du Second Empire* (Paris, 1960).

Louis-Philippe et la Machine Infernale (1830–35) (Paris, 1951).

Madelin, Louis, *Les Cent-Jours, Waterloo* (Paris, 1954).

Fouché, vol. II (Paris, 1901).

Maillet, Dominique, *Histoire de Rennes* (Rennes, 1845).

Mansel, Philip, *Louis XVIII* (London, 1981).

Mantero, Rafael Sánchez, *Las Conspiraciones liberals en Francia* (Seville, 1972).

Markham, Felix, *Napoleon* (London, 1964).

Maulion, A., *Le Tribunal d'appel et la Cour de Rennes* (Rennes, 1904).

Ménager, Bernard, *Les Napoléon du peuple* (Paris, 1988).

Meyer, Jean, ed., *Histoire de Rennes* (Toulouse, 1972).

Millot, H., *Le Comité permanent de Dijon* (Dijon, 1925).

Monnier, Raymonde, *Le Faubourg Saint-Antoine, 1789–1815* (Paris, 1981).

Moulard, Jacques, *Le Comte Camille de Tournan* (Paris, 1914).

Palau, Pierre, *Histoire du département de la Côte-d'Or* (Dijon, 1978).

Parisse, Michel, ed., *Histoire de la Lorraine* (Toulouse, 1978).

Pascal, Jean, *Les Députés bretons de 1789 à 1983* (Paris, 1983).

Penaud, Guy, *Histoire de Périgueux* (Périgueux, 1983).

Perrenet, Pierre, *La Terreur à Dijon* (Dijon, 1907).

Perrin, René, *L'Esprit public dans le Meurthe de 1814 à 1816* (Nancy, 1913).

Pingaud, L., *Jean de Bry* (Paris, 1909).

Pinkney, David H., *The French Revolution of 1830* (Princeton, 1972).

Ponteil, Felix, *La Monarchie parlementaire, 1815–1848* (Paris, 1949).

Pouthas, C.-H., *Guizot pendant la Restauration* (Paris, 1923).

Ramet, Henri, *Histoire de Toulouse* (Toulouse, 1935).

Rébillon, Armand, *Histoire de Bretagne* (Paris, 1957).

Rémond, René, *La Vie politique en France* (Paris, 1965).

Resnick, Daniel, *The White Terror and Political Reaction after Waterloo* (Cambridge, Mass., 1966).

Ribe, Georges, *L'Opinion publique et la vie politique à Lyon lors des premières années de la Seconde Restauration* (Paris, 1957).

Richard, Jean, ed., *Histoire de la Bourgogne* (Toulouse, 1978).

Richard, Jules, *Histoire du département des Deux-Sèvres sous le Consulat, l'Empire, la Première Restauration et les Cent-Jours, 1800–1815* (Saint-Maixent, 1848).

Robert, A., E. Bourloton and G. Cougny, *Dictionnaire des Parlementaires Français* (Paris, 1891).

Roberts, J. M., *The Mythology of Secret Societies* (London, 1972).

Rocal, Georges, *De Brumaire à Waterloo en Périgord* (Paris, 1942).

La Seconde Restauration en Périgord (Angoulême, 1976).

Rochas, Adolphe, *Biographie du Dauphiné* (Paris, 1856–60).

Sauvigny, Guillaume de Bertier de, *The Bourbon Restoration* (Philadelphia, 1966).

Seillac, Victor de, *Histoire politique de la Corrèze sous le Directoire, le Consulat, l'Empire et la Restauration* (Tulle, 1888).

Sieburg, F., *Napoléon, les Cent-Jours* (Paris, 1957).

Soboul, Albert, *The Sans-Culottes* (Princeton, 1980).

Les Sans-Culottes parisiens en l'an II (Paris, 1962).

Spitzer, Alan, *Old Hatreds and Young Hopes* (Cambridge, Mass., 1971).

The French Generation of 1820 (Princeton, N.J., 1987).

Staël, Madame G. De, *Considérations sur la Révolution Française*, ed. Jacques Godeschot (Paris, 1983).

Stenger, Gilbert, *Le Retour de l'Empereur* (Paris, 1910).

Sutherland, Donald, *The Chouans: the Social Origins of Popular Counter-revolution in Upper Brittany, 1770–1796* (Oxford, 1982).

France, 1789–1815: Revolution and Counter-revolution (London, 1985).

Taveneaux, René, ed., *Histoire de Nancy* (Toulouse, 1978).

Thibaudeau, Antoine-C., *Le Consulat et l'Empire*, vol. VIII (Paris, 1835).

Thiers, M. A., *Histoire du Consulat et de l'Empire*, vols. XIX, XX (Paris, 1861).

Thiry, Jean, *Les Cent-Jours* (Paris, 1943).

Thureau-Dangin, Paul, *Le Parti Libéral sous la Restauration* (Paris, 1888).

Tönnesson, K. D., *La Défaite des Sans-Culottes* (Paris, 1959).

Tudesq, André-Jean, *Les Grands Notables en France*, 2 vols. (Paris, 1964)

Tulard, Jean, *Les Révolutions* (Paris, 1985).

Napoleon (London, 1984).

Napoléon et la noblesse d'Empire (Paris, 1979).

Nouvelle histoire de Paris: Le Consulat et l'Empire (Paris, 1970)

Vaulabelle, Achille de, *Histoire des deux Restaurations*, 6 vols. (Paris, 1845).

Viard, Paul, *L'Administration préfectorale dans le département de la Côte-d'Or sous le Consulat et le Premier Empire* (Paris, 1914).

Vidalenc, Jean, *Aspects de la Seine-Inférieure sous la Restauration 1814–1830* (Rouen, 1981).

Le Département de l'Eure sous la monarchie constitutionnelle, 1814–1848 (Paris, 1952)

Les Demi-Soldes (Paris, 1955).

Weill, Georges, *Histoire du parti républicain en France, 1814–1870* (Paris, 1928).

Wolff, P., ed., *Histoire de Toulouse* (Toulouse, 1988).

Woloch, Isser, *Jacobin Legacy: the democratic movement under the Directory* (Princeton, 1970).

ARTICLES

Adher, Louis, 'Les Membres de la Chambre des Représentants (de mai 1815)', *Politique*, nos. 21–4 (1963), pp. 33–95.

Alexander, R. S., 'The *fédérés* of Dijon in 1815', *The Historical Journal*, 30, 2 (1987), pp. 367–90.

Alleaume, Charles, 'La Terreur Blanche dans le Var', *Bulletin de la Société d'études scientifiques et archéologiques de Draguignan*, 45 (1944–5), pp. 5–17.

Baumont, Georges, 'Saint-Dié en 1815', *Le Pays Lorrain*, 16 (1924), pp. 225–34, 288–98.

Baumont, H., 'Stanislas de Girardin', *La Révolution Française*, 55 (1908), pp. 193–235.

Berranger, H. de, 'La Cour Prévôtale de la Loire-Inférieure (1816–1818)', *Bulletin de la Société archéologique et historique de la Loire-Atlantique*, 109–10 (1970–1), pp. 26–34.

Bluche, Frédéric, 'Un aspect de la vie politique à Paris: le plébiscite des Cent-Jours', *Bulletin de la Société de l'histoire de Paris et de l'Ile de France*, 92 (1971), pp. 207–19.

'Les Cent-Jours: aspects du pouvoir', *Revue historique du droit français et étranger*, 51 (Oct.–Dec. 1973), pp. 627–34.

Boudard, René, 'L'agitation politique dans le département de la Creuse au début de la Seconde Restauration', *Cahiers d'histoire*, 13 (1968), pp. 303–26.

Bourgin, Georges, 'L'Affaire du Lion Dormant', *La Révolution Française*, 51 (Oct. 1906), pp. 350–66.

Bouton, André, 'Luttes dans l'ouest entre les chevaliers de la foi et les chevaliers de la liberté', *Revue des travaux de l'académie des sciences morales et politiques*, 115 (1962), pp. 1–13.

Bruchet, Max, 'L'invasion et l'occupation du département du Nord par les Alliés, 1814–18', *Revue du Nord*, 6 (1920), pp. 261–99.

Brucker, Raymonde, 'Le Champ de Mai', *Paris Révolutionnaire*, 4 (1838), pp. 159–87.

Calmette, A., 'Les Carbonari en France sous la Restauration', *La Révolution de 1848*, 9 (1912–13), pp. 401–17, 10 (1913–14), pp. 52–73, 117–38, 214–30.

Cappodocia, E., 'The liberals and Madame de Staël in 1819', in R. Herr and H. T. Parker, eds., *Ideas in History; Essays Presented to Louis Gottschalk* (Durham, N.C., 1965).

Cardot, Charles-Antoine, 'Les débuts de la presse libérale à Rennes (mars–octobre 1819)', *Actes du Quatre-Vingt-Onzième Congrès National des Sociétés Savantes: Rennes*, 3 (1966), pp. 23–49.

Cauvin, C., 'Le Retour de l'Ile d'Elbe et les Cent-Jours dans les Basses-Alpes', *Bulletin de la Société scientifique et littéraire des Basses-Alpes*, 21 (1926–7), pp. 122–41, 22 (1928), pp. 36–76.

Cavaignac, Jean, 'Les Cent-Jours à Bordeaux', *Revue historique de Bordeaux et du département de la Gironde*, 15 (1966), pp. 65–72.

Cézard, Pierre, 'Les Cent-Jours dans le département de la Creuse à travers les rapports des préfets', *Mélanges d'archéologie et d'histoire offerts à H. Hemmer* (1979), pp. 67–72.

Chandelier, Marcel, 'Les difficultés d'une ville de province sous l'occupation des Alliés (Meaux, 1814–15)', *Actes du Soixante-Dix-Septième Congrès des Sociétés Savantes: Grenoble* (1952), pp. 435–53.

Charléty, Sébastien, 'Une Conspiration à Lyon', *Revue de Paris*, 4 (15 July 1904), pp. 268–302.

Cobb, Richard, 'Quelques aspects de la mentalité révolutionnaire (avril 1793–Thermidor An II)', *Revue d'histoire moderne et contemporaine*, 6 (1959), pp. 81–120.

Connac, E., 'La Réaction royaliste à Toulouse (1815–1816): trois lettres inédits de Picot de Lapeyrouse à l'avocat Romiguières', *Revue des Pyrénées*, 10 (1898), pp. 431–51.

Corciulo, Maria Sofia, 'Les élections à la Chambre Introuvable en août 1815', *Parliaments, Estates and Representation*, 3, 3 (Dec. 1983), pp. 123–34.

Crouzet, François, 'Les Conséquences économiques de la Révolution. A propos d'un inédit de Sir François d'Ivernois', *Annales historiques de la Révolution Française*, 34 (1962), pp. 182–217.

'Wars, Blockade and Economic Change in Europe', *Journal of Economic History*, 24 (1964), pp. 567–88.

Curie-Seimbres, Lucienne, 'Joseph-Léonard Decazes et les derniers bonapartistes tarnais (1815–1819)', *Revue du Tarn, troisième série*, no. 81 (Spring 1976), pp. 71–84.

Dautry, J., 'La police impériale et les révolutionnaires', *Annales historiques de la Révolution Française*, no. 194 (Oct.–Dec. 1968), pp. 557–8.

Denis, Michel, 'Rennes au XIXᵉ siècle: ville parasitaire?', *Annales de Bretagne*, 80 (1973), pp. 403–39.

Drouot, Henri, 'Côte-d'Or et Côte-d'Oriens sous le Consulat et l'Empire', *La Revue de Bourgogne*, 10 (1920), pp. 262–84.

Duminy, Edmond, 'Notes sur le passage des Alliées dans le département de la Nièvre', and 'Nevers pendant les Cent-Jours', *Bulletin de la Société nivernaise des lettres, sciences et arts*, 2 (1906), pp. 249–89, 328–45.

Dumolard, Henry, 'Grenoble au début de la Restauration', *Annales de l'Université de Grenoble (Lettres)*, 3 (1926), pp. 131–71.

'Joseph Rey de Grenoble (1799–1855)', *Annales de l'Université de Grenoble (Section Lettres-Droit)*, 4 (1927), pp. 71–111.

Dupuy, R., 'Aux origines de "fédéralisme" breton: le cas de Rennes (1789–mai 1793)', *Annales de Bretagne*, 82 (1975), pp. 338–60.

Durand, R., 'La Révolution de 1830 en Côte-d'Or', *Revue d'histoire contemporaine* (1931), pp. 161–75.

'Le Département de la Côte-d'Or en L'An XII', *Annales de Bourgogne*, 5 (1933), pp. 170–3.

Ellis, Geoffrey, 'Rhine and Loire: Napoleonic Elites and Social Order', in Lewis,

Gwynne and Colin Lucas, eds., *Beyond the Terror, essays in French regional and social history, 1794–1815* (Cambridge, 1983), pp. 232–67.

Forgues, Eugène, 'Le Dossier secret de Fouché', *Revue historique*, 90 (March–April 1906), pp. 269–306.

Gabory, Emile, 'La Terreur Blanche dans l'Ouest', *Revue des études Napoléoniennes, septième année*, 3 (1918), pp. 313–36.

'La Révolte des Cent-Jours en Loire-Inférieure', *Annales de Bretagne: mélanges offerts à M. J. Loth* (Paris, 1927), pp. 204–10.

Gaffarel, Paul, 'Les Cent-Jours à Marseille', *Annales des facultés de droit et des lettres d'Aix-en-Provence*, 2 (1906), pp. 153–219.

'Un épisode de la Terreur Blanche. Les massacres de Marseille en juin 1815', *La Révolution Française*, 49 (1905), pp. 316–50.

'La Terreur Blanche à Marseille', *Revue historique*, 122 (1916), pp. 240–87.

Gonnet, Pierre, 'Les Cent-Jours à Lyon', *Revue d'histoire de Lyon, études, documents, bibliographie*, 7 (1908), pp. 50–67, 111–23, 186–210, 286–303.

Guillaumot, Paul, 'Chalon pendant les Cent-Jours: souvenirs de la fédération bourguignonne', *La Bourgogne*, 2 (1869), pp. 165–80.

Hauteclocque, G. de, 'Les Cent-Jours dans le Pas-de-Calais', *Mémoires de l'Académie des sciences, lettres et arts d'Arras*, 2ᵉ série, 36 (1905), pp. 29–185.

Hémardinquer, J. J., 'Un Libéral: F.-B. Boyer-Fonfrède (1767–1845)', *Annales du Midi*, 73 (1961), pp. 165–218.

Hourmat, P., 'Les élections des 14 et 22 août 1815 dans les Basses-Pyrénées', *Société des sciences, lettres et arts de Bayonne*, no. 166 (1965), pp. 41–60.

Janet, Paul, 'Le Globe de la Restauration', *Revue des deux mondes*, 34 (1 Aug. 1879), pp. 481–512.

Laurent, Jacques, 'Mélanges: Un Témoinage sur la Révolution de Juillet à Dijon', *Annales de Bourgogne*, 2 (1930), pp. 369–79.

Lavalley, Gaston, 'Le Duc d'Aumont et les Cent-Jours en Normandie', *Mémoires de l'Académie des sciences, belles lettres, et arts de Caen* (1898), pp. 171–339.

Lefebvre, Georges, 'Foules révolutionnaires', *Annales historiques de la Révolution Française*, 11 (1934), pp. 1–26.

Le Gallo, Emile, 'Carnot et Napoléon pendant les Cent-Jours', *Revue des études Napoléoniennes*, 38 (1934), pp. 65–83.

'Les Deux Missions de Thibaudeau, commissaire extraordinaire dans le 18ᵉ division militaire pendant les Cent-Jours', *Annales de Bourgogne*, 16 (1944), pp. 81–96.

Le Gallo, Yves, 'Anticléricalisme et structures urbaines et militaires à Brest sous la monarchie constitutionnelle', *Actes du Quatre-Vingt-Onzième Congrès National des Sociétés Savantes: Rennes*, 3 (1966), pp. 75–139.

Leuilliot, Paul, 'L'Alsace en 1815', *Revue d'Alsace*, 75 (1928), pp. 65–76, 130–46, 242–59, 356–74, 479–87, 549–53.

Loubet, Jean, 'Le Gouvernement toulousain du duc d'Angoulême après les Cent-Jours', *La Révolution Française*, 64 (1913), pp. 149–65, 337–66.

Lucas-Dubreton, J., 'Une Conspiration sous Louis XVIII', *La Revue des deux mondes*, 18 (1 Nov. 1933), pp. 118–52.

'Le Complot de Canuel à Lyon', *Revue des deux mondes*, 17 (1959), pp. 443–9.

Lyons, Martin, 'The Jacobin élite of Toulouse', *European Studies Review*, 7, 3 (July 1977), pp. 259–84.

Mansel, Philip, 'How Forgotten were the Bourbons in France between 1812 and 1814?', *European Studies Review*, 13 (1983), pp. 13–37.

Maughin, G., 'La Confédération Picarde', *Revue des études Napoléoniennes*, 24 (1935), pp. 33–4.

Maurel, Blandine, 'Vente de biens nationaux et popularité de l'Empereur', *Revue d'histoire économique et sociale*, 53 (1975), pp. 248–55.

Michel, Denis, 'Les "alliés" en Haute-Loire, l'occupation et ses problèmes (1814–1815)', *Cahiers de la Haute-Loire* (1968), pp. 37–64.

Missinne, Léo-E., 'Un Pédagogue bourguignon: Joseph Jacotot (1770–1840)', *Annales de Bourgogne*, 36 (1964), pp. 5–43.

Monnier, Raymonde, 'De L'An III à L'An IX, les derniers sans-culottes', *Annales historiques de la Révolution française*, no. 257 (July–Sept. 1984), pp. 386–406.

Mouchet, Jean, 'L'Esprit public dans le Morbihan sous la Restauration', *Annales de Bretagne*, 45 (1938), pp. 89–182.

Newman, Edgar, 'The Blouse and the Frock Coat', *The Journal of Modern History*, 46 (1974), pp. 26–59.

'Lost Illusions: The Regicides in France during the Bourbon Restoration', *Nineteenth-Century French Studies*, 10 (1981), pp. 45–74.

Paillet, André, 'Les Cours prévôtales (1816–18)', *Revue des deux mondes*, 4 (1911), pp. 123–49.

Picaud, René, 'L'Esprit public à Rennes et le "fédéralisme" dans l'Ille-et-Vilaine, août 1792–septembre 1793', *Annales de Bretagne*, 25 (1909–10), pp. 287–94.

Pidancet, Jean, 'L'Indemnité aux émigrés en Côte-d'Or', *Annales de Bourgogne*, 23 (1951), pp. 157–71.

Pilbeam, Pamela, 'The Emergence of Opposition to the Orleanist Monarchy, August 1830–April 1831', *English Historical Review*, 85, 334 (Jan. 1970), pp. 12–28.

'The Growth of Liberalism and the Crisis of the Bourbon Restoration, 1827–30', *Historical Journal*, 25, 2 (1982), pp. 351–66.

'The "Three Glorious Days": the Revolution of 1830 in Provincial France', *Historical Journal*, 26, 4 (1983), pp. 831–44.

Pouthas, C.-H., 'La Réorganisation du ministère de l'intérieur et la reconstitution de l'administration préfectorale par Guizot en 1830', *Revue d'histoire moderne et contemporaine*, 9 (1962), pp. 241–63.

Quenson de la Hennerie, A., 'Les Propos séditieux sous la Restauration dans le département du Nord, 1815–30', *Revue du Nord*, 11 (1925), pp. 36–53, 114–25.

Rader, D. L., 'The Breton Association and the Press: Propaganda for "legal resistance" before the July Revolution', *French Historical Studies*, 2 (1961), pp. 64–82.

Radiguet, Léon, 'L'Acte Additionnel de 1815', *Revue des études Napoléoniennes*, 1 (1912), pp. 204–39.

Richard, Gabriel, 'La Conspiration de l'Est, mai 1820', *Annales de l'Est, 6ᵉ série*, 9 (1958), pp. 23–59.

'Les Cent-Jours à Nancy', *Pays Lorrain*, 38 (1957), pp. 81–96.

'L'Esprit public en Lorraine au début de la Restauration', *Annales de l'Est, année* 4, 2 (1953), pp. 183–208.

'Une Conspiration policière à Nancy en 1816', *Annales de l'Est, année* 10, 3 (1959), pp. 173–88.

Rude, F., 'Le Réveil du patriotisme révolutionnaire dans la région Rhône-Alpes en 1814', *Cahiers d'histoire*, 16 (1971), pp. 433–55.

Sadesky, Colette, 'La Crise et le relèvement des collèges en Côte-d'Or sous la restauration', *Annales de Bourgogne*, 32 (1960), pp. 35–59.

Saint-Jacob, P. de, 'La Municipalité de Dijon sous le Consulat et l'Empire', *Annales de Bourgogne*, 4 (1932), pp. 205–21.

Schnerb, Robert, 'La Mission en Bourgogne du conventionnel Bernard de Saintes', *La Revue de Bourgogne* (1921), pp. 372–8.

Sée, Henri, 'L'Etat économique de la Haute-Bretagne sous le Consulat', *Annales de Bretagne*, 36 (1925), pp. 151–63.

'Le Rôle de la bourgeoisie bretonne à la veille de la Révolution', *Annales de Bretagne*, 34 (1919–21), pp. 405–33.

Seillac, Victor de, 'La Corrèze au Cent-Jours', *Bulletin de la société de la Corrèze*, 8 (1886), pp. 462–87.

Sicotière, L. de la, 'L'Association des étudiants en droit de Rennes avant 1799', in *Mélanges historiques, littéraires, bibliographiques* (Geneva, 1972), vol. II, pp. 3–74.

Spitzer, Alan B., 'Restoration Political Theory and the Debate over the Law of the Double Vote', *Journal of Modern History*, 55 (March 1983), pp. 54–70.

Stone, Daniel, 'La Révolte fédéraliste à Rennes', *Annales historiques de la Révolution Française*, 43 (1971), pp. 367–87.

Tavernier, Félix-L., 'Les Cent-Jours à Marseille', *Provence historique*, 37 (1959), pp. 150–81.

Thuillier, Guy, 'Le Corps Préfectoral en Nivernais de 1814 à 1830', *Actes du 96ᵉ Congrès National des Sociétés Savantes: Toulouse*, 1 (1971), pp. 365–95.

Tonneau, André, 'Un Promoteur des idées libérales en Bretagne: Charles-Bonaventure-Marie Toullier (1752–1835)', *Actes du Quatre-Vingt-Onzième Congrès National des Sociétés Savantes: Rennes*, 2 (1969), pp. 329–42.

Tönnesson, K. D., 'Les Fédérés de Paris pendant les Cent-Jours', *Annales historiques de la Révolution Française*, 54 (1982), pp. 393–415.

Trélat, Ulysse, 'La Charbonnerie', *Paris Révolutionnaire*, 2 (1838), pp. 275–341.

Vanel, Jean, 'Le Mouvement fédératif de 1815 dans le département du Tarn', *Gaillac et le pays tarnais, 31ᵉ congrès d'études de la fédération des sociétés académiques et savantes de Languedoc-Pyrénées-Gascogne* (Gaillac, 1977), pp. 387–95.

Vergnaud, M., 'Agitation politique et crise de subsistances à Lyon de septembre 1816 à juin 1817', *Cahiers d'Histoire*, 2 (1957), pp. 163–77.

Viard, Paul, 'Une Enquête politique dans l'arrondissement de Dijon en 1816', *Annales Révolutionnaires*, 14 (1922), pp. 387–412.

'Les Fédérés de la Côte-d'Or en 1815', *Revue de Bourgogne*, 16 (1926), pp. 23–39.

'Les Levées militaires en Côte-d'Or pendant les Cent-Jours', *Revue de Bourgogne*, 3 (1913), pp. 65–74.

Vidal, Michel, 'La Cour Prévôtale du département de l'Hérault', *Annales du Midi*, 87, 123 (July–Sept. 1975), pp. 289–311.

Vidalenc, Jean, 'La Cour Prévôtale de la Seine-Inférieure (1816–1818)', *Revue d'histoire moderne et contemporaine*, 19 (Oct.–Dec. 1972), pp. 533–56.

'L'Emigration royaliste de 1815', *Revue d'histoire économique et sociale*, 53 (1975), pp. 304–28.

'L'Opinion publique dans le département de la Seine-Inférieure à la fin du Premier Empire', *Revue des sociétés savantes de Haute-Normandie (Rouen)*, no. 15 (1959), pp. 69–82.

'L'Opposition sous le Consulat et l'Empire', *Annales historiques de la Révolution Française*, no. 194 (Oct.–Dec. 1968), pp. 472–88.

Vieuxville, George de la, 'La Loge de Rennes en 1815', *Revue des études historiques*, 90 (1924), pp. 189–96.

Vitté, Marcel, 'L'Opinion publique mâconnaise à la fin du Premier Empire', *Annales de l'Académie de Mâcon*, 43 (1956–7), pp. 12–21.

Weill, Georges, 'Les Mémoires de Joseph Rey', *Revue historique*, *53ᵉ année*, 157 (March–April 1928), pp. 291–307.

'L'Idée républicaine en France pendant la Restauration', *Revue d'histoire moderne*, 2 (1927), pp. 321–48.

DISSERTATIONS

Baude, Michel, 'P. H. Azaiis, témoin de son temps d'après son journal inédit (1811–44)' (University of Strasbourg 2, 1975).

Eisenstein, E., 'The Evolution of the Jacobin Tradition in France: the survival and revival of the ethos of 1793 under the Bourbon and Orleanist Regimes' (Radcliffe College, 1952).

Gonnet, Paul, 'La Société Dijonnaise au XIXᵉ Siècle' (Paris, 1974).

Newman, Edgar, 'Republicanism during the Bourbon Restoration in France, 1814–1830' (Chicago, 1969).

Pruitt, William, 'Opposition to the Bourbon Restoration in Rouen and the Seine-Inférieure, 1815–1830' (University of Virginia, 1981).

Sibalis, Michael David, 'The Workers of Napoleonic Paris' (Concordia, 1979).

Index